Lit. Oeuvre Expérience.

It is experiment, approach, that excites the artist — going beyond an interesting point. But it is annoying for the non-artist to be inundated with what is essentially a collection of raw material — witnesses shreds of a false realism. What can we tell of this approach to a region beyond ordinary civilization. Why do we have this authorless writing which would like to pass for books? And isn't it strange that at a moment when books are becoming unimportant literature has become an important activity.

∴ literature becomes not just a set of forms or an activity — but rather

LIFE WRITING SERIES

In the **Life Writing Series**, Wilfrid Laurier University Press publishes life-writing criticism in order to promote autobiographical accounts, diaries, letters and testimonials written and/or told by women and men whose political, literary or philosophical purposes are central to their lives. **Life Writing** features the accounts of ordinary people, written in English, or translated into English from French or the language of the First Nations or from any of the languages of immigration to Canada. **Life Writing** will also publish original theoretical investigations about life writing, as long as they are not limited to one author or text.

Priority is given to manuscripts that provide access to those voices that have not traditionally had access to the publication process.

Manuscripts of social, cultural and historical interest that are considered for the series, but are not published, are maintained in the **Life Writing Archive** of Wilfrid Laurier University Library.

Series Editor
Marlene Kadar
Humanities Division, York University

LIFE WRITING SERIES

MARIAN ENGEL'S NOTEBOOKS

"Ah, mon cahier, écoute..."

Edited by Christl Verduyn

Wilfrid Laurier University Press

This book has been published with the help of a grant from the Humanities and Social Sciences Federation of Canada, using funds provided by the Social Sciences and Humanities Research Council of Canada. We acknowledge the support of the Canada Council for the Arts for our publishing program. We acknowledge the financial support of the Government of Canada through the Book Publishing Industry Development Program for our publishing activities.

Canada

CANADIAN CATALOGUING IN PUBLICATION DATA

Engel, Marian, 1933-1985
Marian Engel's notebooks: "Ah, mon cahier, écoute..."

(Life writing; 8)
Includes bibliographical references.
ISBN 0-88920-333-4

1. Engel, Marian, 1933-1985 – Notebooks, sketchbooks, etc.
I. Verduyn, Christl, 1953- . II. Title. III. Series.

PS8559.N5Z53 1999 C813'.54 C99-931026-7
PR9199.3.E5Z47 1999

Cover design: Leslie Macredie
Cover illustration: an excerpt from *Cahier* VII of Marian Engel's notebooks
All photographs appear courtesy of Charlotte Engel.

Printed in Canada

WILFRID LAURIER UNIVERSITY PRESS
Waterloo, Ontario, Canada N2L 3C5

CONTENTS

ACKNOWLEDGEMENTS

I would like to acknowledge and thank several individuals, groups and institutions for their support of this project.

First and foremost, I wish to thank Charlotte Engel and William Engel, without whose cooperation this book would not have been possible. I am deeply grateful for their permission to publish material from the Marian Engel Archive and for their patience and providence. It has been my great pleasure to have made their acquaintance.

The Research and Archives Division of McMaster University Library comprises a tremendously helpful staff who provided cheerful assistance throughout my work with the Marian Engel Archive. I would like to extend my thanks to all the members of the staff, and in particular to Dr Kathy Garay, who catalogued Engel's papers and whose remarkable knowledge of the archive led to hours and hours of conversation about the material. I thank her for sharing my enthusiasms and interests with such generosity and intelligence and for the friendship that has grown out of our discussions.

The presentation of Engel's *cahiers* in this book generated a number of technical challenges qualitatively different from those of other texts. These challenges could not have been met without the assistance provided by Jennifer Gillard della Casa in the early stages and by Joëlle Favreau throughout, and the research and technological expertise of Kerry Cannon and Joanne Ward in the crucial final stages. I am extremely fortunate to have had the help of these talented women, and I thank them for their energy and interest, and for many lively conversations about the notebooks.

Numerous other conversations with colleagues and students contributed to my thinking during the course of this project. I would like to acknowledge these exchanges that helped clarify my ideas and confirm the importance of my research pursuits. Early on, a workshop on women's archives was highly motivating. Stimulating presentations by Gwendolyn Davies, Carole Gerson, Mary Rubio, and the workshop co-organizers, Helen Buss and Marlene Kadar, spurred me on in my own research. Invitations from Trent colleagues to speak about my work in their classes or on occasions such as International Women's Day helped me focus on research in the midst of administrative responsibilities and demands. A conference on *Women and Texts* at the University of Leeds in July 1997 was a rewarding opportunity to present visual aspects of the *cahiers.* These and other more casual occasions for discussion and exchange with students and colleagues helped maintain the momentum of this project.

This book has benefited enormously from the efforts made by Wilfrid Laurier University Press to explore life writing. Press director Sandra Woolfrey and Series editor Marlene Kadar demonstrated interest in and commitment to the project from an early stage, for which I am grateful.

I would like to acknowledge the ongoing support of the Social Sciences and Humanities Research Council. I have been very fortunate to have received a series of grants from the Council over the past decade. This had been instrumental in sustaining my research on women's writing in general and on Marian Engel in particular. I wish to take this occasion to thank the Council for its continued support and to urge governments and foundations in Canada to maintain and increase their support of research in the humanities.

Final thanks belong to Robert Campbell and our four growing children for their ongoing understanding and support as I juggle administrative, teaching, research and family lives and responsibilities. Thanks to them, life and writing continue to be interesting, and I remain *à leur écoute.*

Ah, mon cahier, écoute...[1]

Away from genres, rubrics, prose, poetry, novel, eye-witness account, refusing to be categorised. As if it were the "essence" of literature.... Art is always becoming.
[...]
Every book looks passionately for a non-book. Every book decides for itself what literature is.[2]

What I wrote was intended at least for one other eye ... but my dreams were all my own.[3]

1 Marian Engel, *Cahier* VII [28].

2 Marian Engel's notes on Maurice Blanchot, *Le Livre à venir* (Paris: Gallimard, 1959) *Cahier* XXVI [18].

3 Mary Shelley, "Introduction," *Frankenstein* (London: H. Colburn and R. Bentley, 1831).

INTRODUCTION

"As a writer..."

"As a writer who has sold her papers," Marian Engel remarked only weeks before she died, "I hope to be found uninteresting until I've been dead as long as Boswell. I'd rather people read my fiction."[4]

Marian Engel's published fiction[5] comprises seven novels, two collections of short stories, two children's books and numerous short stories published individually in magazines such as *Chatelaine.* These accomplishments earned her the Governor General's Award for Fiction in 1976, for *Bear*; the 1978 Canadian Authors Association Silver Medal for Fiction, for *The Glassy Sea*; the 1979 McClelland & Stewart Award for fiction writing in a Canadian magazine, for the short story "Father Instinct";[6] and the 1981 City of Toronto Book Award, for *Lunatic Villas.*[7] Given these achievements, and the author's admonition against "turning the knobs on writers' closets," why a volume presenting Marian Engel's notebooks?

A half-dozen interests and enthusiasms animated this project, beginning with Engel's fiction. In keeping with the author's wishes, albeit inadvertently at the time, I first read Marian Engel's novels and short stories, and became interested in a study of her work. In *Lifelines: Marian Engel's Writings,*[8] I explored the author's fiction, alongside her non-fiction, essays and articles, personal papers and notebooks, located in the Marian Engel Archive[9] at McMaster University. I found that Engel's unpublished writings shed useful light on her published work, and are a valuable complement to her fiction. This was especially the case of the author's notebooks—or *cahiers* as she often referred to them.

There are more than forty *cahiers* in the Marian Engel Archive, dating from the late 1940s until the author's death, 16 February 1985. Engel had a "Gallic

---

4 "A plea to stop turning the knobs on writers' closets," *The Globe & Mail,* 17 November 1984: "Books," Literary Supplement 1.

5 Her unpublished fiction includes five novels and dozens of short stories, in various stages of polish and completion. Her non-fiction includes a book on the islands of Canada and many articles and columns in magazines and newspapers.

6 Marian Engel, "Father Instinct," *Chatelaine* (August 1979): 32 ff.

7 Engel shared this award with Claude Bissell, author of *The Young Vincent Massey.*

8 Christl Verduyn, *Lifelines: Marian Engel's Writings* (Kingston and Montreal: McGill-Queen's University Press, 1995).

9 Catalogued by Dr Kathleen Garay, The Marian Engel Archive (MEA) is also the subtitle of a publication of the Archives and Research Collections, McMaster University,

passion" for the *cahier* and acquired the habit early of recording "ideas, notes on books read, drafts of letters never sent, plot outlines and many other things."[10] When she decided at the age of ten to be a writer, Engel bought a notebook and declared her intentions.[11] The *cahiers* were inexpensive and unpretentious—simple school exercise booklets for the most part. But they played an important role in the author's life and work. Themes explored in the notebooks recur in the novels.[12] Marian Engel was interested in female identity and creativity, and the constraints on their development, including social conventions and family expectations, economic and emotional insecurity, and lack of recognition of the efforts of women committed to living on their own terms—as artists.

Marian Engel formulated the project for an artistic life early on. In a 1949 notebook, the then sixteen year old wrote that one must "live creatively": "I mean live so that the pattern you make of your life is a work of art in itself."[13] For Engel, this meant life *as a writer*. In her last *cahier*, the author commented that life had brought her "a very great deal," even if hers had been "a very strange life when you consider how many identities I have had & how my work has been a struggle for identity."[14] Identity and creativity were inextricably linked for Marian Engel—fundamental ingredients in a defining drive in her life—to be a writer. This drive was the force behind her novels and notebooks alike, and the two forms of writing are related. The *cahiers*' interest as complement to Engel's fiction could in itself justify their publication. But at least four additional reasons reinforce the undertaking.

To the ten-year-old aspiring writer, the notebook may have been first and foremost an outlet for her ideas, jottings and draft texts, a function the *cahiers* would fulfil for Engel throughout her life. To a reader today, the notebooks may be seen as a unique form of life writing. Life writing as a genre and critical practice is changing the way we think about literature and what constitutes literary genre and text. This volume is inspired by a sense of excitement about life writing's capacity for an evolving notion of the literary text, and Engel's *cahiers* as a significant life writing practice contributing to this evolution.

Library Research News 8.2 (Fall 1984), compiled with the assistance of Norma Smith, preface by Dr L.A. Braswell. Dr Garay also prepared the finding guide to the second accession of Engel's papers (*The Marian Engel Archive, Second Accession, Finding Guide*, 1994). The first accession corresponds to Boxes 1 through 30, the second accession to Boxes 31 through 34. With her permission, this book uses some of the brief descriptions with which Dr Garay identified Engel's papers, otherwise organized under box and file numbers.

10 Garay 34. "Gallic passion" is Garay's excellent phrase.

11 "I decided to be a writer when I was 10. I bought a notebook and said, 'I'm going to be a writer, Mother.' And she said, 'That's very hard.' I said, 'I don't care.'" "Beginnings," *Today Magazine* 2 May 1981: 3.

12 For a more in-depth discussion of this, see Verduyn, *Lifelines*, chapters 1 and 2.

13 *Cahier* I [2].

14 *Cahier* XVI [70].

Marian Engel's notebooks also offer one woman's record of an important era in Canadian literary history. This was the post-war period when Canadian literature and several of its prominent practitioners came into their own. Engel's *cahiers* were written throughout a time of significant cultural and social change as experienced by a woman determined to live as an artist in Canada. The author's notebooks provide excellent insight into what this could mean for a woman of her time and place.

In addition, the *cahiers* are a fascinating blueprint of the creative process, demonstrating clearly how a book emerges and evolves. Drafts of novels and short stories, numerous reflections on art and literature, together with musings about life and people, combine to make Engel's notebooks compelling reading. The sum effect of these features is that Marian Engel's *cahiers* are not only valuable but interesting—despite her public wish to the contrary.

Engel's *cahiers* are in themselves important and worthy of publication. They stand on their own, displaying the characteristics, craft and content that qualify them as the distinct literary achievement Elizabeth Podnieks has discerned in the diaries of novelists Anaïs Nin, Elizabeth Smart and Antonia White.[15] These writers' diaries, Podnieks argues, are separate and significant accomplishments within literary modernism. A similar case may be made for Marian Engel's *cahiers*. Maintained throughout her life, Engel's notebooks were a major writing project, for which recent research on life writing, and renewed interest in diaries, provide a productive theoretical context.

Life writing

In *Essays on Life Writing: From Genre to Critical Practice* (1992), editor Marlene Kadar describes life writing as a "genre of documents or fragments of documents written out of a life, or unabashedly out of a personal experience of the writer."[16] Life writing encompasses many kinds of text, all linked by a common thematic concern with the life of a self. Distinguished by a blend of traditional and marginal forms of writing, fiction and non-fiction, these texts range from more familiar generic expressions such as autobiography and biography, letters and diaries, memoirs and confessions, to what Helen Buss calls "auto/biographical acts involved in the collection and editing of oral histories and archival accounts" (11). Buss offers the useful understanding of life writing

15 Podnieks, "(Life-) writing a Modernist Text: The Literary Diaries of Elizabeth Smart, Antonia White and Anaïs Nin," PhD thesis, University of Toronto, 1995. Podnieks is one of several contemporary researchers who make a compelling case for reading diaries as literary works. See also Bunkers and Huff, *Inscribing the Daily* (1996).

16 This particular quotation is from an essay that Kadar contributed to a preliminary collection of working papers on life writing, *Essays in Life Writing* (Toronto: Robarts Centre for Canadian Studies, York University, 1989). The essay cited is "Whose Life Is It Anyway: Preliminary Notes on Life Writing," 5.

as process, one "that borrows from every other mode of writing to make new vehicles for self expression" (11). The best life writing, Buss suggests, breaks down "artificial binary oppositions between intellect and feeling, private and public life, high and low art" (14). Within the agreeably elastic boundaries of life writing, Marian Engel's *cahiers* find their niche.

Renewed interest in diaries, one of the more familiar forms of life writing, provides further context for presenting Marian Engel's *cahiers*. A growing body of literature on diaries, enhanced in recent years by feminist literary criticism,[17] has drawn attention to women's practices of the genre. In their introduction to *Inscribing the Daily: Critical Essays on Women's Diaries* (1996), editors Suzanne L. Bunkers and Cynthia A. Huff review the many challenges and questions posed by women's diaries, notably concepts of self and truth and text. A key focus for many contemporary theorists—of varying critical perspectives—is how we understand identity, in particular with respect to language, by which it may be expressed and mediated. Feminist and postmodern critics have interrogated models of identity that posit a coherent, rational, centred, autonomous self. New concepts of identity are proposed, which take into account factors of gender, race and class, among others, and which allow for the possibility of selves that are multiple or fragmented, de-centred or marginal. As the essays in *Inscribing the Daily* show, diaries serve women as a "testing ground for constructions of identity and narrativity" (17). Marian Engel's notebooks served in such a capacity for their author, who declared all her work to have been a struggle for identity.[18] In these constructions, gaps and exclusions are as significant as inclusions.

"This is not a diary, it is an inner record." [19]

While Engel's *cahiers* exhibit traits of various forms of life writing, mostly diary, biography and autobiography, they do not exemplify these forms as traditionally conceived.[20] Several notebooks do contain lengthy sections in which Engel

---

17 Much of this literature considers autobiography along with the diary. See Shari Benstock (1988), Harriet Blodgett (1988), Margo Culley (1985, 1992), Robert Fothergill (1974), Gail Godwin (1988), Elizabeth Hamsten (1982), Carolyn Heilbrun (1988), Estelle Jelinek (1980, 1986), Philippe Lejeune (1989), Judy Nolte Lensink (1987), Nancy Miller (1991), Shirley Neuman (1991), James Olney (1988), Elizabeth Podnieks (1995), Lawrence Rosenwald (1988), Judy Simons (1990), Sidonie Smith (1987), among others.

18 *Cahier* XVI [70].

19 *Cahier* XXX [54].

20 Diaries as conceived in theory do not necessarily exist in practice, Elizabeth Podnieks has shown (11). The diary is a much more multifarious form of writing than is suggested by the popular view of it as the private record of a person's life, synonymous with spontaneity and secrecy. This view is relatively recent and limited. Close examination of the origins and history of the diary (mostly men's) reveals that it evolved through several stages and forms. Podnieks provides an in-depth review and analysis of this critical literature.

dates and describes her daily experiences in diary-like fashion. This is often the case during trips, notably excursions to islands (one of Engel's passions) or to cities (in particular, Paris, France). But for the most part, the *cahiers* are neither dated nor chronological. "Scrambled" was Engel's word for them,[21] a not inaccurate term for the effect rendered by the author's frequent return to, and reuse of, earlier notebooks containing blank pages. With their disregard for chronology and dates, Engel's scrambled *cahiers* are not traditional diary, biography or autobiography. They do tell readers about Engel's life—but not all of it, as might be expected of biography. For Engel such expectation was ill founded. In "A plea to stop turning the knobs on writers' closets," she insisted more than pleaded that "a biographer can't tell the whole story." It simply was not possible to know everything about another human being. "Psychoanalytical criticism and psychobiography in good hands are fascinating," she acknowledged. Moreover, "as biography becomes ever more intimate, it becomes more enjoyable." But only fictional characters can satisfy our desire for perfect consistency, Engel argued, making a case for fiction even as she admitted the appeal of biographical and psychological approaches to literature. If Engel did not rule out psychological criticism or biography, neither did she advocate them, particularly with regard to her own work.

This volume of edited notebooks meets Engel's biographical line in the sand. It is about Engel, especially Engel *as a writer*, but it is not biography or autobiography in the familiar sense. It does not tell the whole story, nor does it aspire to. It ascribes value to a writing activity that occupied a major part of Engel's life, one which she pursued from the time she was a girl until her death. Within the context of life writing, Engel's *cahiers* capture the "scrambled" life of a busy woman determined to be a writer in addition to being a daughter, wife, mother, homemaker, friend. The fragmented nature of the notebooks is arguably the illustration par excellence of the incompleteness that Engel felt characterized our knowledge of one another, and possibly of ourselves.[22] Engel's notebooks, and their edited presentation here, claim neither the completeness of biography or autobiography, nor the chronological detail of the diary, as these genres traditionally are understood. For this and further reasons, not all the contents of the notebooks are reproduced here.

---

21 "Scrambled journals indeed." *Cahier* IX [23].

22 Many researchers argue that fragmentation and incompletion are highly typical of women's self-(re)presentation, suggesting links with women's multiple, fragmented selves. Irregularity and discontinuity, Estelle Jelinek maintains, episodic, anecdotal, non-chronological and disjunctive style, are all familiar in women's autobiographical tradition (Jelinek 1980; 1986. These adjectives appear in Bunkers and Huff 7). Not all researchers agree. Some see such traits as different principles of organization. Rebecca Hogan, for instance, theorizes that women's diary texts are organized through operations of association and accumulation, a process she terms parataxis (Hogan 1991). Still others, such as Margo Culley, suggest that fragmentation is linked to the nineteenth-century development of the split between public and private life (Culley 1985; see also B. Welter 1966).

In "Telling Secrets," an essay written in response to controversy surrounding her biography of Anne Sexton, Diane Wood Middlebrook argues that the privacy of the living ought not be invaded. While it may be the case, Middlebrook reasons, that "once a person's lifework is terminated by death, the circumstances surrounding the life and the work can be asked every kind of question," it is also the case that "what is ethical is not the same as what is legal" (128). Nancy Mairs expresses a similar view in *Remembering the Bone House* (1989): "It is one thing to expose one's own life, taking responsibility for the shock and ridicule such an act may excite, and quite another to submit the people one loves to the same dangers" (xi). Although Middlebrook's comments are directed to biography, and Mairs's to autobiography, they may apply here. As Engel's article in *The Globe and Mail* suggested, she was not keen about "such telling" based on anecdote and written document. "You, too," she wrote persuasively, "have silly secrets, cravings you have fortunately left unexpressed, obsessions, letters you ought not to have written. You, too, have gone through a batty period after a death or a divorce, made erratic judgements, changed your mind, been unkind." *Cahier* entries about individuals in Engel's life—family, friends, colleagues—in some instances have been left out. This does not mean that they are unavailable or that Engel did not wish them to be read. The notebooks in their entirety are open to public readership at McMaster's Marian Engel Archive. This is as Engel intended. Not only did she leave her notebooks to public archives, she requested that only one of them (*Cahier* XXX) be embargoed, and then only for five years. Moreover, numerous notations within the *cahiers* indicate that Engel reread them and was quite aware of their contents.[23]

Traces of self-reflexivity or self-consciousness, Elizabeth Podnieks notes, convey an expectation or intention of readership,[24] or at least an awareness of potential readership. The traces in question may be as simple as the occasional comment on or correction to entries. They may be as blatant as an address to readers. Or they may be detected in a subtle shift in tone or length of entries, as in Engel's *cahiers* during the second half of the 1970s. After her Governor General's Award in 1976, and divorce the following year, the author's

---

23 Two entries in *Cahier* XXXI might serve as examples:

"Splendid agonies represented here. But they all turned out to be phony—no, not phony, unnecessary in the end. No, probably necessary"

"They don't seem that in retrospect
When I read this in JR's office"

The phrases "they all turned out" and "in retrospect" indicate a rereading and awareness of the content of this notebook, and others. See also *Cahier* IX [11] ("on rereading my own work") and *Cahier* IX [26], where Engel adds an insert.

24 Podnieks (17) offers an excellent discussion of issues concerning intentionality and privacy, upon which I draw in this and the following paragraphs.

notebook entries often displayed deeply reflective, (self-) explanatory or self-conscious dimensions, and concomitant lengths. Handwriting, especially varied styles by the same author, can be another index of self-consciousness or awareness of self-representation.[25] In her *cahiers*, Engel's handwriting is not only highly variable, but she is highly conscious of this fact and how it may be linked to a sense of self. "Why this funny handwriting?" the author asked in a 1975 *cahier*, noting "inconsistency & lousy handwriting."[26] A few pages later, the question is posed again: "Why has my handwriting changed?"[27] Cynthia Huff writes of correlations between diaries' textual construction and markings and diarists' emotional and physical states (127); such correlations might be discerned between Engel's feelings and experiences and the force and varied styles of her handwriting. Entries in notebooks from the mid-1970s are a case in point, as are notebooks written towards the end of Engel's life, in which the following entry appears: "Handwriting is changing again, damn it. Who am I?"[28]

Indices of self-reflexivity and self-consciousness reinforce the view that "by their choice of mode as written documents all diaries imply readership, even if the reader and writer are one and the same" (Simons 10). From its inception, Podnieks points out, the diary comprised its own self-conscious tradition.[29] Indeed, it may be possible to argue that "there has never been a time when all diarists truly wrote unselfconsciously, unaware of the implications embedded in the act of writing itself."[30] It is the *act of writing* that is so consequential. To write, and in particular to preserve what one writes, is to invite, indeed to intend, readership.[31]

---

25 Attention to handwriting was part of Philippe Lejeune's study of diaries kept by girls in late nineteenth- and early twentieth-century France, too. See *Le Moi des Demoiselles: Enquête sur le Journal de Jeune Fille* (Paris: Editions du Seuil, 1993).

26 *Cahier* XXVIII [5].

27 *Cahier* XXVIII [14]. Other examples include: *Cahier* III [42], regarding the diary of murder victim Barbara in "Death Comes for the Ya Ya": "The cramped neurotic handwriting told a story"; *Cahier* IX [5]: "To be noted: Sensations of handwriting"; *Cahier* XXXV [87]: "Goodness, my handwriting is someone else's."

28 *Cahier* XXXVIII [15].

29 This may be traced across the four types of journals identified by Robert Fothergill in *Private Chronicles*. These include the early travel diary, clearly intended to be read by individuals at home, and by the traveller her/himself; the diary as "public" journal, also written for an audience; the journal of conscience, which could serve to prove one's moral obedience and devotion to fathers and spouses, potential readers; and finally, the journal of personal memoranda, the "record of things done and seen and heard" (Fothergill 19). Out of such a tradition and informed by the same intention of readership, Podnieks demonstrates, came the personal diary (Podnieks 17).

30 Podnieks 17.

31 What of the diarist who dies before being able to destroy her/his writings? To guarantee secrecy, Rosenwald contends, one must not write and preserve. Gail Godwin concurs; diarists write for "some form of posterity" ("A Diarist on Diarists" 14). The extreme proof

The agency implied here is explicit in Lawrence Rosenwald's statement that the diary is "a commodity within its author's power" (12). This is particularly true of the professional writer, who is never "off-duty," Lynn Bloom asserts; "The writer's mind is invariably alert to the concerns of an audience and shapes the text, even letters and diaries, to accommodate these" (24-25). For a professional writer there are no private writings, Bloom insists. Authors' agency and power extend to the private/public nature of the text. In order for a text to be truly private, unread by any other, it must be destroyed. Allowed to exist, it is susceptible to readership.

That Engel too intended her notebooks to be read does not mean their entire contents ought to be reproduced here. Selections have been guided in part by the argument of privacy for individuals associated with the subject and by a vivid interest in the notebooks as an illustration of life writing. They have also been informed by a view of the *cahiers* as social and historical document.

"My own history is the history of hundreds of people I know."[32]

Engel was part of a generation of writers that emerged from the renaissance of Canadian literature during the 1950s and 1960s. These decades mark a period of social and political change fuelled by economic growth, the burgeoning women's movement and a swelling of nationalism that crested in Expo '67. The latter sentiment contributed to the fostering of Canadian culture, assisted by economic resources; feminism sought changes in women's roles and status in society. While the stereotype of women's fulfilment in marriage and motherhood, teaching or nursing did not disappear, the possibility nevertheless emerged that women might respectably pursue alternative life paths, including those leading to a career in the arts. This could mean a rough ride along a road strewn with marital wreckage and economic potholes. At the same time, there could be cause for celebration, particularly for those interested in Canadian culture, where several welcome developments occurred after the Second World War.

Setting the stage was the 1951 Massey Commission report on national development in the arts, letters and sciences. In 1952, plans were made for a permanent structure for the National Library. In 1956, the National Film Board (founded in 1939) took up headquarters in Montreal. The same year, the National Gallery opened on Elgin Street in Ottawa. In 1957 the Canada Council was created. Towards the end of the decade, numerous literary magazines and small presses appeared. *Tamarack Review* was founded in 1957 (replacing

---

of intended readership is the publication and circulation of diaries, mainly men's, a tradition generally thought to have begun with the 1818 publication of John Evelyn's (1620-1706) journal. In 1825, portions of Samuel Pepys's diary were published, followed by Byron's journals (in Thomas Moore's *Memoirs*) 1830. Fanny Burney's diaries were next, in 1842-46 and 1889.

32 MEA, Box 6 File 25, "The Greening of Toronto: A Footnote to Mordecai Richler."

Northern Review), and *Canadian Literature* in 1959. The momentum for growth and expansion continued through the 1960s. By the early 1970s the foundations were being laid for the Writers' Union of Canada, with early meetings held at Engel's home, on Brunswick Avenue, in Toronto.[33]

Such positive developments notwithstanding, these were not easy times for Canadian writers. Most struggled to make a living from their work. A less tangible but difficult problem was the lack of role models for Canadian writers. Margaret Atwood articulated this lacuna when recalling "what it was like in 1957 ... we did not study any Canadian poets; we studied dead English people.... You have to realize that it was a complete blank" (qtd. in Abley 28).

The absence of role models, and by extension of community, had differing impacts for women and for men. This is clear from two accounts of the period, one by Louis Dudek, the second from Phyllis Webb. Both authors describe late 1950s Montreal, a time and place considered crucial in the development of literature in Canada. Dudek recalls:

> In 1951, I came to teach at McGill. I came with the perfect confidence that I was coming where I had to be to do my important work. It was not just for myself that I was going to do this work, but for this city and this country. I was ready for it, and I knew it was going to be important. We were going to change our world, so to speak. Somehow that involve[d] the many things I had learned in New York. I had studied modern poetry there. I had studied under Lionel Trilling, Jacques Marzun, and Emery Neff. I was full of the sense of what the modern is, and the transformation that modernism must bring to poetry and life. So I came back and a friendship was soon renewed with Irving Layton, and we began to publish together. The first book was *Cerberus*—three poets together, Layton, Dudek, and Souster, with prefaces by each.... Leonard Cohen turned up at McGill and he wanted to bring out a book, so actually I proposed that the McGill Poetry series start with his book.[34]

In contrast to this is Phyllis Webb's recollection of the same scene:

> I suppose one of the marked differences between then and now is that I didn't think of myself as "a woman writer," and there weren't many things that reminded me that I was a woman trying to write. I was very young at the time and there were hardly any women writers in this group. Miriam Waddington turned up occasionally, but

33 As Jennifer Gillard della Casa (1996) has shown in her thesis on the Union's early days, Marian Engel played a key role in the Union's development. She was first chair and prime mover for Public Lending Rights.

34 "An Interview with Louis Dudek," Hutchman 64.

> there wasn't much resonance between the two of us at that time. Aileen Collins was there—she was very quiet—and Betty Layton, and there were a few other women coming and going with the men, usually. Leonard Cohen always brought a new, young, beautiful woman, it seemed to us. But, as I remember it, which may be purely egocentric, I was the only young woman writer in the group, which included people like Irving Layton, Louis Dudek, Frank Scott, and Eli Mandel. Occasionally Al Purdy turned up, and Leonard Cohen, and others, like Robert Currie and Avi Boxer, so it was heavily, heavily male-dominated.... John Sutherland was another in that Montreal group ... when I try to visualize the scene in Layton's living-room, I don't see many women writers, so I was sharing all my problems of writing and excitements and so on with these gentlemen.[35]

The 1950s, which in Canada, Margaret Atwood suggests, extended well into the 1960s,[36] were not an easy time for any Canadian artist or writer. "In 1960, to publish 200 copies of a book was considered good," Atwood recalled. "There were only five literary magazines in English Canada, and it was almost impossible to publish novels. But there were a lot of people around my age who were coming into it, who had begun to write. There were people on the West Coast, and people here in the coffee-shop movement; there was that kind of public reading going on. And Irving Layton had come into view, and so had Leonard Cohen" (qtd. in Abley 28).

There with Cohen and Layton, equally determined to be a writer, but less visible, was Marian Engel. Engel arrived in Montreal in the fall of 1955 to pursue her MA at McGill. There she completed what is arguably the first Canadian graduate thesis on Canadian literature.[37] Her thesis director, Hugh MacLennan, was a model and mentor for her as for other young writers around McGill and Montreal in those years, including Robert Kroetsch and Leonard Cohen. But, as MacLennan himself acknowledged in later years, circumstances and conditions for women wanting to become writers in Canada at the time differed from those of men. "When I knew you in the old days I was a good judge of ability," MacLennan wrote in a letter to Engel dated 16 May 1981. "I knew Mordecai had it, and I got him the Canada Council that enabled him to write DUDDY KRAVITZ. I knew you had it, and did nothing for you except to give you encouragement and an electric blanket."[38]

---

35 "Read the poems, read the poems. All right?" Williamson 322.

36 "The sixties did not become the sixties, anyway, until 1967 or 68—it was the fifties until then." Abley 29.

37 "A Study of the English-Canadian Novel Since 1939," MA thesis, McGill University, 1957.

38 Christl Verduyn, ed., *Dear Marian, Dear Hugh: The MacLennan-Engel Correspondence* (Ottawa: University of Ottawa Press, 1995) 117.

Engel's *cahiers* uncover the many practical and moral or spiritual challenges facing women aspiring to be artists or writers in Canada at mid-century. These ranged from concerns about money and income to a need for role models with which to counteract societal expectations of marriage and motherhood. "We all chose to be writers and therefore NOT traditional women," Engel summed it up.[39] Engel's *cahiers* capture many of the twists and turns women like her encountered and navigated on the road to becoming writers. While accounts in kind are not available from peers such as Wiseman, Atwood and Munro,[40] there is little reason to think their experiences differed greatly.[41] In this way Engel's *cahiers* may be considered to have social and historical value. Beyond illuminating one person's life and art, the notebooks are fascinating for their reflection on, and of, a wider social spectrum and historical era. They can deepen understanding not only of Engel and her work, but of other women of her time and place.

> ***" A pee cahier***
> ***A sex cahier***
> ***A food cahier***
> ***A drink cahier***
> ***A cat cahier***
> ***A family cahier***
> ***A time cahier***
>
> ***Oh hell, just a notebook."*** [42]

Narrative unity is no more a concern than chronology in Engel's notebooks. Topics are varied and wide-ranging. Sophisticated reflections on contemporary cultural theory sit alongside grocery lists, and elegant passages of draft prose appear next to personal introspection. The subjects explored in Engel's *cahiers* are manifold and multifaceted; examples include literary theory and literary form, the nature of reality, the existence of truth, social stereotypes and conventions and their constraints for women, the tension between reason and emotion, spirituality, faith, finances, friends and family. The role of the family is key throughout the *cahiers*, where Engel considered her own unique family experience.

Marian Engel was born, the second of twin girls, on 24 May 1933, in Toronto. Given the economic difficulties of the Depression and disapproving

---

39 *Cahier* XVI [9].

40 That is to say they do not have notebooks, diaries, journals, etc., that are (yet) available to the public. James King's biography of Margaret Laurence (1997) reveals that the author began writing a journal in the late stages of her life.

41 Commonalities of race and gender may have been inflected by some difference in the realm of class. Engel was highly conscious of her family's working-class status.

42 MEA, Box 6 File 25 [18].

social mores, it was next to impossible for the twins' mother, eighteen and unmarried, to keep her daughters. So the sisters—then named Eleanor and Ruth[43]—spent the first years of their lives in foster care. They were separated around age three when Engel was adopted by Frederick and Mary Elizabeth Passmore. The Passmores were a hardworking family who valued church and school. An auto-mechanics teacher confronted with the depressed employment market of the 1930s, Frederick Passmore moved his family throughout southern and western Ontario[44] to what jobs were available. Mary Passmore worked as a secretary before her marriage, and thereafter as a homemaker with a strong sense of moral responsibility and social respectability, as well as a practical, self-disciplined approach to life. As Engel recalled in a letter to Margaret Laurence, 10 April 1979, her mother "was the lady with the typewriter who taught me Longfellow as I dried dishes."[45] The Passmores had an older daughter named Helen, and called their new daughter Marian.

The facts of Engel's birth and early life are not in the fore of her fiction, though they underlie it. They surface in the *cahiers*[46] amongst the many different foci, interests and elements of the author's life. In this way the *cahiers* compose the backdrop against which Engel's work unfolded and reveal the complexities of the context in which she, like other women writers, produced texts. Indeed, the links, overlaps, incursions of life into fiction and fiction into life, are among the most beguiling—and bedevilling—aspects of the *cahiers*. Time and again a passage that begins as if it were a slice of "real life" reveals itself, several pages later, to be fiction. The reverse also is true.

In this respect it is fascinating to note the genesis of creative work. This is another function fulfilled by the *cahiers*. The studious comparison of various versions and drafts of published works is a recognized scholarly pursuit, usually applied to "great" writers such as Marcel Proust and Virginia Woolf, for example. Closer to home, Engel's *cahiers* provide an equally compelling and instructive illustration of the creative process. A novel or short story might begin with a notation, an idea, a prose passage, a character or a question. The notebooks trace how these change shape and expression. Thus for instance, an

43 Ruth remained Engel's middle name. The author used both names—Ruth and Eleanor—in her fiction, the "Ruth stories" being a case in point (see *Lifelines* 188-89.) The names turn up in the author's *cahiers* as well, notably in the later ones (XXXV, XXXVII, XXXVIII, and XLI) when Engel is looking back over her life. In these, Eleanor appears at times in the shortened form "Nor" (e.g., *Cahier* XXXVII [33]).

44 Including Brantford, Galt (now Cambridge), Hamilton, Sarnia and Port Arthur (now Thunder Bay). For practical and economic reasons, the family lived in a trailer for part of these years, which afforded Engel several lyrical summers, when the trailer was stationed near a beach.

45 Margaret Laurence Papers, York University.

46 See Verduyn, *Lifelines* 17.

early version of Engel's powerful first novel *Sarah Bastard's Notebook*[47] features a character named Stel, subject of a long draft section that fills the first third of *Cahier* II. This early version includes Antonio, the protagonist's child by her brother-in-law. In the eventually published version, "Antonio" is never born; Sarah has an abortion. In like fashion, Engel's third novel *Monodromos* emerged from extensive, complicated and intriguing recastings, which the *cahiers* document in detail.

What all the drafts and early versions of subsequently published texts demonstrate clearly is that writing is work. This is the case even for a writer like Engel who could produce pages and pages of polished prose in a single sitting. Work often meant research, especially in the early stages of a book, and Engel's *cahiers* are full of notes. Research in turn triggered in-depth reflection on the nature of art and literature, and transformed the notebooks into sites of intense intellectual life. The latter is exceptional in Engel's case, because of her wide-ranging reading and research interests. She was well read in French- and German-language literatures as well as English-language literature, and she was as interested in Ontario social history as in French literary theory. The use of French throughout the notebooks is itself noteworthy, beginning with Engel's designation of her notebooks as *cahiers*. There are obvious reasons why French would appear in the author's notebooks: she did her undergraduate degree in French and German,[48] lived in Montreal from 1955-60,[49] and spent 1960-61 in France, in Aix-en-Provence.[50] But there are potentially symbolic dimensions to the author's penchant for the French language,[51] as for other languages that make their appearance in the *cahiers*, including German and Greek. Like varying styles of handwriting, the use of different languages may be linked to explorations of differing identities or selves—Engel's declared

47 This is the title under which the novel was released in the United States. In Canada, the novel was known as *No Clouds of Glory*. As noted in *Lifelines*, Engel informed her agent, Diarmuid Russell, that, with the Canadian publisher Longmans, the "title will not have Bastard in it—it will ruin library sales, apparently" (MEA, Box 3 File 20, letter from Engel to Russell, December 1966). When the novel was reissued in Canada by Paper Jacks (Don Mills, ON) in 1974, it bore the title that more accurately reflects its character and intentions: *Sarah Bastard's Notebook*.

48 See *Cahier* II, footnote 1.

49 With the exception of the academic year 1957-58, when she taught at the University of Montana.

50 On a Rotary Foundation Fellowship, for which she was encouraged to apply by MacLennan, whose advice it was that writers should strive for as much lived experience as possible. See Verduyn, ed., *Dear Marian, Dear Hugh* 80.

51 Engel had her own theories. On 25 December 1984[?], she wrote: "It comes to me now that most of my French romanticism comes from mother—a sort of Enchanted April world of class & prettiness was in all things French for her [...] Add to that my intellectual romanticism—the effect is powerful. Intellectual NEATNESS—that's the French thing." *Cahier* XXXIV [1].

main concern in her work. Like so many brief departures from one's learned language to a tongue tried by personal choice, the French, Greek and German phrases scattered throughout Engel's notebooks convey her keen sense of cultural difference, in particular how Anglo-Saxon language and cultural traditions are not the only ones. By reading, a person might explore different world views. The breadth and depth of Engel's explorations can be traced in the numerous lists of books throughout the *cahiers*.

The intellectual dimension of Engel's notebooks is striking for its challenge to the popular notion that personal writing is typically emotional writing. Not that emotion is missing from the *cahiers*! Rather, it goes hand in hand with the author's intellectual life. For Engel, feeling could be a form of thinking. Emotion and instinct were not illogical or unconnected to intellect and rationality. They were productive forms of expression. Writing was a process of "feeling through the emotions while making the fiction."[52] Emotion and instinct were key ingredients of Engel's intellectual life, and her *cahiers* were a crucial forum for its expression.

Selections and presentation

The preceding discussion outlines the framework in which selections for this volume were made. Material was retained which best illustrated the *cahiers* as life writing, social and historical document, philosophical and personal reflection, template of the creative process and Marian Engel's full life as a writer. To this end, readers will find various drafts of books, copious research notes for manuscripts in the works, considerations of literary theory, reflections on life, the occasional recipe, the odd back-of-the-envelope budget and, everywhere, lists: lists of books read and to be read, letters to write, groceries to buy; lists of names of people, places, colours, birds, flowers (annuals, biennials and perennials); lists of *words*. When these selections edged towards excessive length or repetition, I shortened or eliminated them. In all, approximately 30 percent of the original *cahier* material has been excised.[53] Beyond lengthy or repetitive passages, eliminated text falls into two categories. The first is material governed by the argument, outlined earlier, for the privacy of individuals associated with the subject. In this, I was guided by the author's children. Some entries about them, their father and a handful of other family members and friends, have not been included here. These entries represent less than 10 percent of the original *cahier* text. The second area of excised material

52 Marian Engel, *The Honeyman Festival* (1970; rpt. ed. Toronto: Penguin, 1986) 7.

53 Percentages are approximate and calculated using the total number of typescript pages before the editing process began. As passages and pages were eliminated, they were kept in separate files. An approximate 30 percent of the original typescript was set aside as follows: lengthy or repetitive passages, around 10 percent; material personal to members or friends of the Engel family, around 9 percent; dream recording, around 10.5 percent.

comprises entries that were very fragmented or difficult to follow. This is the case of most of Engel's dream recordings, and the decision was made to set these aside. But by far the greatest percentage—over two thirds—of the original *cahier* material is included in the pages that follow.

The presentation of all this material also was informed by a number of decisions. The *cahiers* are numbered I through XLI. This is an imposed ordering. There were two accessions of Engel papers, the first in 1982, the second a decade later in 1992. Archivist Kathy Garay, to whose cataloguing skills I am indebted, organized notebooks in the first accession into Box 6, Files 1 to 28. *Cahiers* in the second accession were catalogued in Box 34, Files 1 through 19. In presenting the *cahiers* here, I blended archive boxes 6 and 34 to create an ordering that maintains the effort towards chronology but does not guarantee it, since Engel moved back and forth between *cahiers*, some of them spanning several years. Archive box and file references are included in Appendix I.

Each *cahier* is accompanied by a short introduction highlighting a few of its features, and a brief notation indicating the temporal span and physical appearance of the notebook. Diary scholar Lawrence Rosenwald has argued that the physical aspect of the chosen writing format is very important, beginning with "the sort of book a diarist buys or makes to write in, and what it costs."[54] As mentioned earlier, Engel's *cahiers* were inexpensive, scribbler-style affairs available at all-purpose stores.[55] Rosenwald's lengthy list of physical traits to consider[56] is interesting, and a measure of the distance between the traditional diary and Engel's *cahiers*, with their sporadic dating, hit-and-miss punctuation, entries of varying length and subject matter, and informal beginnings and endings. Together these traits underscore the uniqueness of Engel's *cahiers*, even within the innovative field of life writing.

Within *cahier* texts, I have tried to reproduce in typeface the written layout on the notebook page. This accounts for the unusual line and page breaks as

---

54 Rosenwald 18.

55 If the quality of a notebook did not seem to matter to Engel, *who* gave it to her (in those instances when she did not buy it herself) did. She liked the *cahiers* given to her by Vera Frenkel, for example, but had some difficulties writing in one she received from the Brysons. *Cahier* XLI (MEA, Box 34 File 15 and Box 34 File 16).

56 "How a volume of the diary is presented *qua* volume, what span of time it characteristically includes, whether it is given a formal beginning or ending; whether the text is immaculate or scribbled over with revisions; whether the page is exploited as a unit of organization; where dates are placed relative to the entries they govern; what non-verbal marks accompany the words ... how long the average entry is, and how frequently and regularly entries are made; which subjects are treated at length, which in passing, which not at all; how entries are organized, whether by order of association or order of occurrence or order of exposition; what use is made of first- and second-person pronouns; what areas of the entry are habitual and which free...; how sentences are punctuated and words capitalized." (Rosenwald 18-20)

well as the widespread use of shortforms ("&" for "and").[57] Spelling oddities are marked [*sic*], except where they are the result of obvious typed slips (e.g., "shcool" instead of "school"), in which case they are silently corrected. As explained further in the introduction to *Cahier* XXXII, beginning in 1976 typed reflections began to form part of Engel's *cahier* production, though handwritten entries remained dominant. Obvious slips in punctuation also have been corrected, as when, for example, Engel forgot to close quotation marks or put a period at the end of a sentence. There has, however, been no attempt—or intent—to copyedit the *cahiers*. As much as possible, the *cahier* content appears *tel quel*.

Square brackets around ellipses indicate edited text. Where a word or words have defied deciphering, I have used [illegible]; a question mark between square brackets [?] indicates probable word(s) or spelling. Square brackets also serve to distinguish *cahier* page numbers from the page numbers of this book. Again, Engel herself did not number the pages of her *cahiers*. It proved useful to introduce the practice[58] in order to locate different parts of individual notebooks. Numbers between square brackets, then, refer to *cahier* pages. Finally, square brackets indicate the addition of explanatory information, a function fulfilled by the use of footnotes as well. The possibilities for the latter bordered on inexhaustible, given the substantive wealth and temporal span of Engel's notebooks. An approach adopted by Bruce Whiteman in editing the letters of John Sutherland[59] presented a helpful model. It seeks to balance what Whiteman calls the schools of exasperation (too few notes for some readers) and insult (too many for others) and thereby to satisfy general, informed and scholarly readers alike. A full range of readers is interested in texts of life writing, and the annotations provided in the pages ahead may at times reflect my personal curiosities, and thus neglect those of other readers. But as outlined below, the open-ended nature of Engel's *cahiers* invites readers' individual involvement and research.

These various efforts of selection and presentation have resulted in a text that seeks and responds to the "involved reader," identified by both Marlene Kadar and Helen Buss as the radical feature of life writing. Life writing fosters readers' own self-consciousness, Kadar suggests, humanizing and making the "self-in-the-writing" less abstract (Kadar 1992, 12). "At its most radical, the critical practice of life writing enhances reading as a means of emancipating an overdetermined 'subject,' or various subject locations," Kadar explains. "In the end, life writing problematizes the notion of *L*iterature. Without wanting to deny

57 Here is a list of the most common short forms appearing in the *cahiers*: abt: about; c: with; cf: compare; esp: especially; exp: experience; gt: great; k: knowledge; pt: point; q: question; thro': through; v or V: very; w: with; wk: work; wld: would.

58 I did not number blank *cahier* pages.

59 Bruce Whiteman, ed., *The Letters of John Sutherland, 1942-1956* (Toronto: ECW Press, 1992).

Literature, life writing allows us to see it, too, as only one possible category of special writing" (Kadar 1992, 12). Helen Buss discusses the "empowered reader" of life writing (14). Where fiction invites readers into the life of the text, life writing, Buss proposes, invites us to bring the text into our lives. It provides room to exercise active readership whereby we make our own meaningful stories, or make meaning of our own stories as we read (Buss 14). Many other researchers concur. "The story of one woman's life provides a script the reader enters, resignifies and in some collaborative sense makes her own," Jeanne Braham suggests.[60] Jane Marcus proposes that such collaboration is a reproduction of women's culture as conversation, in which the reader is expected to take an active role.[61] Reading is "a two-way street," Françoise Lionnet asserts in *Autobiographical Voices* (1989); "by implicating myself in my reading, I am in turn transformed by that activity ... my perspectives are also shaped, at least in part, by those present in the texts I discuss" (28). Speaking of diaries, Bunkers and Huff note that the perceived fragmented nature of the form makes readers assess "the social, political, and personal repercussions of segmenting our lives, our texts, our culture, our academic disciplines" (2).

This volume of Marian Engel's *cahiers* lends itself to Buss's vision of creative readers (15). Space and openings exist in which readers may engage in thoughts and reflections of their own. Different notebooks or periods in Engel's notebook writing may elicit differing responses from readers. Thus for example, some may be more drawn to the *cahiers* of the mid-1970s on, the post-*Bear* period when Engel's entries frequently exhibit the reflective quality of the more traditional forms of life writing, such as the diary or journal. Others may prefer the intellectual, theoretical musings of the late 1960s and early 1970s. Readers hopefully will find the complex evolution of the novel *Monodromos* throughout this period is a fascinating study in itself. Still other readers may be compelled by the youthful aspirations and expression of notebooks dating from the early 1960s, while at the other end of the scale, *cahiers* kept during the later stages of Engel's life and work have another urgency and effect. Readers will hopefully find all the notebooks interesting, as I have since first encountering them. It is the collection of *cahiers* as a whole that best conveys the countless nuances and complexities of Marian Engel's work and experiences as a woman and *as a writer*, as a woman writer pursuing her work in Canada in the second half of the twentieth century.

---

60 "A Lens of Empathy," Bunkers and Huff 57.

61 Jane Marcus "Invincible Mediocrity" 137, qtd. in Braham 57.

CHRONOLOGY

1933	Born 24 May, second of twin girls, Eleanor and Ruth, in Toronto
1936-46	Joins the Passmore family, as Marian; family lives in various Ontario towns including Port Arthur, Brantford, Galt (now Cambridge), Hamilton and Sarnia
1946-52	Sarnia Collegiate Institute and Technical School
1952-55	McMaster University BA (French and German)
1955-57	McGill University MA "A Study of the English-Canadian Novel Since 1939" (Thesis director Hugh MacLennan)
1957-58	University of Montana "The Pink Sphinx" (unpublished novel)
1958-60	The Study, Montreal Engel taught and worked on plays
1960-61	Aix-en-Provence, France Rotary Fellowship for year at Université d'Aix-Marseille
1961-62	London, England "Women Travelling Alone" (unpublished novel)
1962	27 January, marriage to Howard Engel
1962-64	Cyprus; taught at St John's School, Nicosia "Death Comes for the Yaya" (unpublished novel)
1964	Toronto—home base for next twenty years "Lost Heir and Happy Families" (unpublished novel) and early "Sarah Bastard," "Minn" and "Monodromos"
1965	30 April, twins William and Charlotte born
1968	*Sarah Bastard's Notebook/No Clouds of Glory* (novel)
1970	*The Honeyman Festival* (novel)
1971	March, return trip to Cyprus
1973	*Monodromos* (novel)
1973	Chair, Writers' Union of Canada

1974	*Adventure at Moon Bay Towers* (children's book) Major William Kingdom Rains research
1975	*Inside the Easter Egg* (short stories) *Joanne: The Last Days of a Modern Marriage* (novel) Toronto Public Library Board trustee (until 1978)
1976	*Bear* (novel) Governor General's Award June, Prince Edward Island, "Bear Summer"
1977	*My Name Is Not Odessa Yarker* (children's book) Divorce
1978	*The Glassy Sea* (novel) Canadian Authors Association Silver Medal for Fiction
1978-79	Writer-in-residence, University of Alberta, Edmonton
1979	Diagnosed with cancer
1979-80	Edmonton, University of Alberta, taught creative writing McClelland & Stewart Award for fiction writing in a Canadian magazine
1980	March, trip to Australia as Canadian representative at biennial Adelaide Festival Summer travels for research on "Islands of Canada" book
1980-81	Writer-in-residence, University of Toronto
1981	*The Islands of Canada* (non-fiction) *Lunatic Villas* (novel) City of Toronto Book Award (presented February 1982) October, trip to Germany as representative of Writers' Union of Canada. Side-trip to Sweden
1981-82	Columnist, *The Toronto Star*, "Being Here"
1982	24 May, Mary Elizabeth Passmore deceased Engel appointed Officer of the Order of Canada
1983	June/July, "Women & Words" Conference, Vancouver
1984	Metro Toronto YWCA Woman of Distinction in Arts and Letters "Elizabeth and the Golden City" and "The Vanishing Lakes" (unpublished novels)
1984	Paris, Christmas/New Year
1985	16 February, deceased

Cahier I[1]

March 8, 1949

Here I begin my "travels with a Unicorn" [51].

You yourself have to live creatively ... so that the pattern you make of your life is a work of art in itself [2].

Marian Engel's first *cahier* dates from her adolescent years (1946-52), when she was still Marian Passmore—nicknamed "Pass"—and spent summers working as a camp counsellor. Signatures and notations by friends and camp co-workers sprinkled throughout the *cahier* indicate that Engel had a healthy social life not untypical of other teenagers of her time and place. But the future writer might be glimpsed in the recopied poems, draft short stories and the lists of names of people and colours, like so much grist for a literary mill. There is even an editor's address[2] [22] as if Engel were planning to submit some work. Inventories of favourite movies, plays, actors, musicians and authors outline the contours of an identity in formation—or perhaps more accurately, an identity being formed in quite a conscious way. The lists in this *cahier* go beyond teenage jottings towards what the aspiring writer might have considered the necessary ingredients of an artistic life—classical music, "good" books [54], stimulating movies. Most striking is Engel's early sense of a major obstacle to life as an artist for a girl or young woman of her milieu and place: gender stereotypes. This is rendered graphically in the *cahier* through the use of cutouts, cleverly overlaid with comments by the young author.

The cutouts feature the "ideal" 1950s woman, full-skirted, narrow-waisted, gloved and girdled. To these, Engel has added tongue-in-cheek commentary. One tightly coiffed, arch-eyebrowed model, white-gloved finger pointing rather curiously to the ground, is accompanied by the exclamatory "Well!" Another, slope-shouldered and plunging-necklined, is ascribed the suggestive "I couldn't, but I'd love to!" Accompanying the models is an eclectic assortment of additional cutouts: a set of flatware ("My stainless"), a couple of flasks, two slippers

1 1949-52, black/brown leather covered spiral notebook; 72 pages used.

2 As You Wrote It. Editor
52 Vanderbilt Ave
New York 17 N.Y.

(one each of two different pairs), a mounted deer head, a hand and a striking collection of coats-of-arms. Offsetting these are two more intriguing selections, complete with commentary. The first features a mug full of pencils and the handwritten statement: "I've always wanted lots of pencils." The second is a paperweight in the shape of a seal, accompanied by the exclamation "It's a paperweight!"

Without reading too much into Engel's adolescent collage, it is possible to perceive difference and tension between the "writerly" wish for a good solid supply of pencils, and the young woman's awareness of the 1950s model of femininity. A real threat to the project of a creative life for young women in the 1950s was the stereotypical expectation that they would, indeed should, aspire to marriage and homemaking, motherhood and caretaking.

Cahier I documents an emerging writer processing her milieu and its messages about what paths girls and young women like her should follow—and how they should look *en route*! Countering societal imperatives, however, were personal passions. Already a voracious reader, Engel wanted to write. Even the early prose and poetry fragments of this *cahier* hint at themes she would develop. Thus, for example, a poem beginning "with careful strokes" [61], presents both the image of the young woman as artist and the theme of the twin other. The sense of being different or being an outsider is central to "The Immortals," written at Easter 1949 when, the author herself noted, she was just sixteen [62]. Another beginning of a short story, "Après le dîner," 25 August [1949], introduces the first of a host of Engel protagonists who love beaches—and islands, with their beaches all around [57]. The desire to live creatively—to be an artist or a writer—is clearly expressed in this first *cahier*. So too are the consequences of this unconventional preference, even during adolescent years as suggested by an entry dated April 19 [1949]: "I had to come upstairs where I could let my stomach out and be mad.... They haven't read any good books.... I hate idle chatter & sitting around ... why doesn't anybody understand?" [54].

[p.1]

Kitchikewana Camp Hymn[3]

Oh Beausoleil where'ere my footsteps wander
Ever to thee my heart I'll turn again
Ever to thee in love of truth and beauty
Until my love becomes akin to pain.
Where God is seen in every plant and flower
Where every soul responsive to his call
Obeys his will and to his footstool creepeth
The seat of Him who loves us one and all.
We love the land where Beausoleil was founded,
The camp we love and long will cherish well.
The bright calm days, the long still nights will linger.
The sunset colours ne'er shall fade away.
Oh Beausoleil! We pledge ourselves forever
To be the best that we can ever be.
We pledge ourselves to always serve our Maker
To come to him in prayer upon each bended knee.

God who touchest earth with beauty
    Make me lovely too.
With thy spirit recreate me,
    Make my heart anew.

Like Thy springs and running waters
    Make me crystal pure,
Like thy rocks of towering grandeur
    Make me strong and sure.
Like thy dancing waves in sunlight
    Make me glad and free,
Like the straightness of the pine trees
    Let me upright be.

---

3 Camp Kitchikewana, or Camp Kitchy for short, is located on Beausoleil Island in Georgian Bay Islands National Park, north of Toronto, Canada. A YMCA/YWCA-style camp, it has been offering traditional residential camp activities to children between the ages of seven and sixteen for over seventy-five years. This camp "hymn" or song is inserted into the front cover of *Cahier* I, and is accompanied by a handwritten musical score.

Like the arching of the heavens
Lift my thoughts above
Turn my dreams to noble action
Ministries of love.

God who touchest earth with beauty
Make me lovely too.
Keep me ever by thy spirit
Pure and strong and true.

[Handwritten musical score]

[p.2]

— The only thing that counts, isn't it?
PURSUIT in words
The immortality of beauty ^ in sounds, in shapes?
— That's part of it.

If people read these things, or listened to Bach, or looked at the Sistine Chapel, they couldn't destroy one another the way they do, could they?

— It isn't enough to read or listen or look. You yourself have to live creatively.

— What do you mean, live creatively?

— I mean live so that the pattern you make of your life is a work of art in itself. You don't have to write or paint or compose to do that.

[p.3]

Poetry—Anthology[4]

In A Tram

Stop staring at me like that, young man!
Don't you know that it's impolite?
(I polished my shoes, so it can't be that
And I'm certain my gloves are right).

4 This "anthology" comprises a variety of poems or fragments of poems by well-known authors such as Rupert Brooke, by less familiar authors such as Martha Thomas Banning and authors Engel did not identify. Where research efforts turned up the author's name, it is identified in a footnote. In some instances it appears that Engel herself wrote the poem.

Look over at somebody else, young man!
What kind of a necktie is that!
(I've powdered my nose and my hair is neat
Could it possibly be my hat?)
Why don't you get off and walk, young man?
(He's handsome enough, it's true.)
But I wish you'd stop staring me up and down
When I'm trying to stare at you!

Straight is the line of Duty
Curved is the line of Beauty
Follow the straight and thou shalt see
The curved line ever following thee.[5]

And shall Trelawney die
Here's twenty thousand Cornishmen
Shall know the reason why[6]

[p.4]

I was lithe & had dreams;
Now I am fat & have children.
Dreams are efflorescent
Dreams fade
Children do not
But then you do not have to
Wipe the noses of your dreams.

We are heaven's chosen few
The rest of you be damned
There's no room in heaven for you
We can't have heaven crammed[7]
—Haddow

---

5 Wording found on Royal Doulton china, c.1895.

6 This is the chorus of the unofficial Cornish "National Anthem," entitled "The Song of the Western Men." It was written by Rev Robert Stephen Hawker (1803-75) and published in T.B. Macaulay, *Macaulay's History of England: From the Accession of James II* (London: Longmans, Green, Reader & Dyer, 1849).

7 A verse by Jonathan Swift.

The rain it raineth every day
Upon the just & unjust fellow
But more upon the just because
The unjust hath the just's umbrella[8]

So what the hell!
My love is a redhot rivet
And I got scorched
Laugh, you damn fool
That goddamn rivet is on its way

[p.5]

The Soldier[9]

A[10] If I should die, think only this of me:
B That there's some corner of a foreign field
A That is for ever England. There shall be
B In that rich earth a richer dust concealed;
C A dust whom England bore, shaped, made aware,
D Gave, once, her flowers to love, her ways to roam,
C A body of England's, breathing English air,
D Washed by the rivers, blest by the suns of home.

A And think, this heart, all evil shed away,
B A pulse in the eternal mind, no less
C Gives somewhere back the thoughts by England given;
A Her sights and sounds; dreams happy as her day;
B And laughter, learnt of friends; and gentleness,
C In hearts at peace, under an English heaven.

Rupert Brooke—1914

---

8 Charles Synge Christopher Bowen (Lord Bowen), "Untitled," *Humorous Verse: An Anthology*, ed. E.V. Knox (London: Chatto & Windus, 1931) 50.

9 Poem by Rupert Brooke (1887-1915), a "war poet" who inspired patriotism in the early months of the First World War. [Brooke, *1914 & Other Poems* (London: Sidgwick & Jackson, 1915)]. A slightly older Engel had the following view of the poet whose work she collected as an adolescent: "When you want things all simple & squashy like Rupert Brooke you are being sentimental..." (*Cahier* II [13]).

10 Engel marked the rhyme sequence of the poem.

... "Then from the sad west, turning wearily,
I saw the pines against the white north sky
Very beautiful and still and bending over
Their sharp black heads against a quiet sky.
And there was peace in them....[11]

[p.6]

The Hill[12]

Breathless, we flung us on the windy hill,
Laughed in the sun, and kissed the lovely grass.
You said, "Through glory and ecstasy we pass;
Wind, sun, and earth remain, the birds sing still,
When we are old, are old ..." "And when we die
All's over that is ours; and life burns on
Through other lovers, other lips," said I,
"Heart of my heart, our heaven is now, is won!"

"We are Earth's best that learnt her lesson here.
Life is our cry. We have kept the faith!" We said;
"We shall go down with unreluctant tread
Rose-crowned into the darkness!"... Proud we were,
And laughed that had such brave true things to say.
—And then you suddenly cried, and turned away.
Rupert Brooke

[p.7]

The Voice[13]

Safe in the magic of my woods
I lay, and watched the dying light.
Faint in the pale high solitudes.
And washed with rain and veiled by night.

Silver and blue and green were showing,
And the dark woods grey....

———

11 This is the third stanza of Rupert Brooke's "Pine-Trees and the Sky: Evening," *Poems* (London: Sidgwick & Jackson, 1911) 78.

12 Brooke, *Poems* 27.

13 Brooke, *Poems* 51. The first six lines of the poem are recorded here.

Man is his own star; and the soul that can
Render an honest, and perfect man
Commands all light, all influence,
all fate;
Nothing to him falls early or too late.
Our acts our angels are, or good or ill
Our fatal shadows that walk by us still.
John Fletcher[14]

[p.8]

[Picture of a child, accompanied by the printed text below]

SIX YEARS OLD

When I was young and lived nearer the ground,
On account of not being tall—
I saw more sights, and I heard more sound,
And I seemed to go farther and get around,
And I never tired at all!

I waded through daisies and Queen Anne's lace,
Up to my shoulders and close to my face,
A foam of flowers, a surge of white
Tumbling around me ... my fist crushed tight
On a handful of strawberries, warm and sweet,
Dripping from fingers and staining my feet;
I touched more grasses, I heard more birds,
And I hadn't the need of answering words
To tell or be told, what my life would be,
I held the knowledge inside of me!

When I was young and lived close to the earth,
On account of being so small,
I was clutched by wonder, I knew the worth
Of delicious laughter and buoyant mirth—
And I never grew tired at all!
Martha Banning Thomas[15]

---

14 See "Epilogue," *An Honest Man's Fortune, The Works of Beaumont & Fletcher*, John Fletcher and Francis Beaumont 11 vols. (London: Edward Moxon, 1843) vol. 3: 453-56.

15 Martha Banning Thomas published *Poems for People* (1925) and *Stormalong Gert* (1936). Her poetry appeared in *Poetry, House Beautiful, New York Evening Post* and the *Saturday Evening Post* among other popular magazines from the early 1920s to the 1950s.

[p.9]

Names

Avril

A Annette, Aylean, Arden, Anne, Alicia, Angela, Amy, Ainsley,
Arden, Alan, Alec, Anthony

B Barbara, Bethea, Bernadette, Blanche,
Bruce, Barry, Brian, Bernard

C Cecelia, Cynthia, Carol, Clara, Claudia, Claire,
Christopher, Carl, Cob, Craig

D Donna, Donalda, Darlene, Dylys, Drusilla, Denise,
David, Dick, Derik, Denis, Duncan, Dale

E Edyth, Emily, Elizabeth, Elspeth, Eleanor, Elaine, Elvira,
Ernest, Eden, Eric

F Fanny Rose, Frances, Felicity
Frank, Francis

G Gillian,
Gregory, Gabriel, Gordon, Garth, Grant, Guy

H Helen, Hepatria, Hilary, Holly
Hugh, Hilary, Humphrey

I Isabelle, Ivy
Ian

J Joanna, Joan, Jeana, Jennifer, Jane, Janet, Jocelyn, Joy
Jeffery, John, Joel, Jocelyn

K Kathryn, Kitty, Kathleen, Kezia
Kit, Keith, Kenneth, Kim

L Louise, Lydia, Leslie, Laura, Lorna, Lucy
Laurence, Lecke, Leif Monica

M Marianne, Marjorie, Margot, Margaret, Madeline, Melissa
Miles, Mark, Malcolm, Mungo

N Nadine, Norma, Nancy, Norah,
Norman, Nigel, Neil

O Olivia,
Oliver

P Pauline, Phillipa, Petrova, Pat, Phyllis, Pegeen, Phoebe
Paul, Philip, Pierce, Patrick, Phineos

Q Queen

[p.10]

R Roberta, Robin, Rhea, Rhiema, Ruth, Rachel
Ralph, Roger, Robin, Rusty, Rennie, Russell, Rupert

S Solveig, Stephanie, Serena, Sylvia, Susan, Saskia, Sybyl, Sorel
Sandy Alec, Steve, Stanley, Searle, Scotty, Shane, Seth

T Theresa, Tanya
Terence, Trevor, Timothy
U Ursula

V Vera, Valerie, Verity, Veronica
Varian
W Wilena, Winnifred, Wanda
Wilbur (?), Ward, Warren, Wayne

Terence O'Mally	Ralph Randall
Hugh Armitarge	Gillian High
France Forbeau	David Cameron

	Surnames	Jennifer	John
Fortescue	Everett	Kathleen	David
Lawson	Uyvyan	Elizabeth	Shane
Armitage			Michael
Havelock			
Whittaker			
King			
High			
Weir			
Wright			

Roger Collison	Sorel Weston
Anthony Asherton	Molly Donalbain
Cyndy Sparks	Birdie MacThroy
Susan Hunter	Claire Murphy
Sir Varian Hughes	David Garfield
Saskia Astra	

[pp.11-16]

["Good-bye, good luck" dedications from camp co-workers]

[p.17]

Record of Records

150			Rem
	Beethoven -	Symphony #5 C-	
415			
	Moonlight	Symphony #7 A+	Col.
	Minuet in G		
300		Trio in B^6+	
100			
	Mozart—	Raus Concerto in F+	
AllaTurka		Excerpts from Haffner Serenade	CHS
	Dvorak—	Symphony #5 E-	RCA
	Tschaikovsky [*sic*]—	Romeo & Juliet Overture	Rem
330		Fantasy — Stolz	Con
300	Debussy	6 preludes	MGM
	Gershwin	An American in Paris	MGM
300	Strauss—	8 Waltzes	Merc
	Franck—	Symphony #1 D-	Capitol
	Brahms	Symphony C-	RCA
800			
	Beethoven	Symphony #9	RCA
	Mendelsshon [*sic*]—	A Midsummer Nights Dream	RCA
600	Debussy—	La Mer	
300	Bach	Welltempered Klavier	RCA
		— 8 — 16 Book I	
5.95	Bartok	Concerto in Orchestra	London

[pp.18-26]

[Addresses of camp co-workers]

[p.27]

[Drawings: sailboat, sun, pine tree with "Bill Married" written beside it, canoe with the inscription "red canoe." Beside the sun is the caption "Vaughan Rd '53."]

[pp.28-32]

[More addresses]

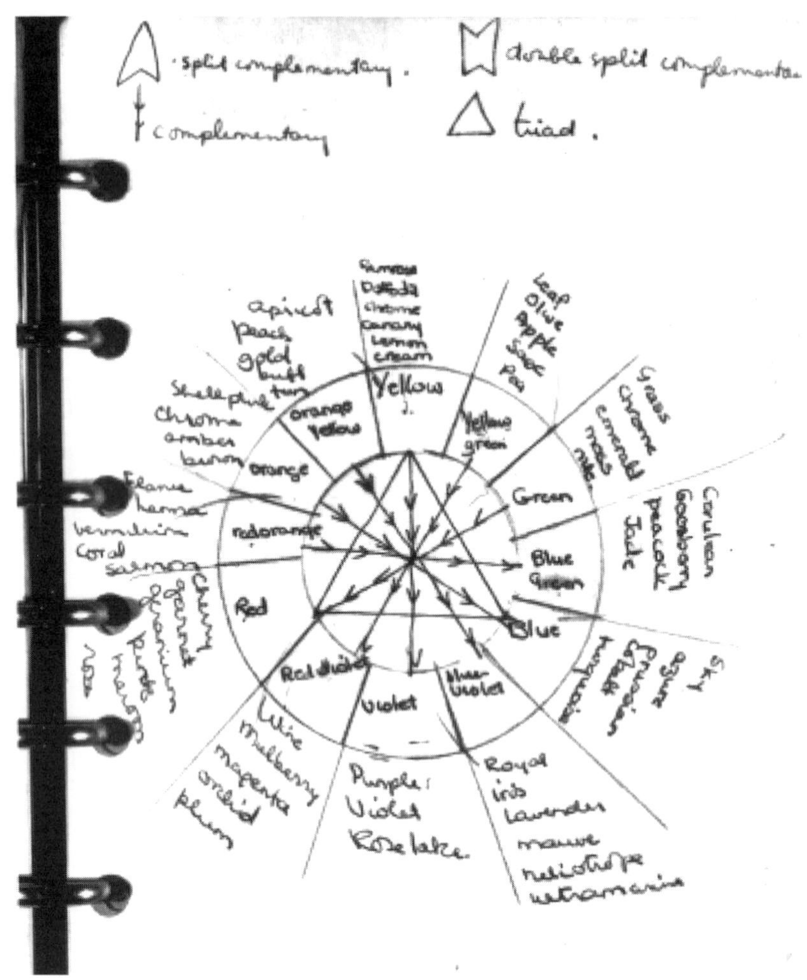

Colour chart, page 33

[p.33]

[Colour chart]

[pp.34-37]

[Addresses]

[pp.38-39]

[Collages: pencils in a mug—caption: "I've always wanted lots of pencils"; a hand; a coat of arms with caption: "winter coat!"; mounted deer head; slippers]

Pages 38-39

Pages 40-41

[p.40]

[Pictures: women from magazines. One caption says, "Washable Dacron," another "Pink!". Under the photograph of a slim woman wearing a sleeveless black dress, "I couldn't but I'd love to!"; picture of cutlery with the caption "my stainless," and under the photograph of pieces of paper weighed down by the sculpture of a seal, "It's a paper weight!"]

[p.41]

In the cake and ice cream after glow of Petty Harbour, six of the members of Sr. 3, enjoyed themselves, while the other four dreamed happily of the scenes which once passed before them. The parts of Holly, Kitty, Clara, Mary and the chorus were filled in admirable filled [*sic*] by members of the cabin. Bill's prop-painters & copy writers were also supplied from our cabin.

[Picture of a crusader ready to throw an arrow; picture of a mediaeval boat]

[p.42]

[Picture of coats of arms. The centre of the page is filled with names.
Afterwards, pictures of various coats of arms have been glued onto the page]
[...]

[p.43]

Books read

The Scent of Water	John Buchan[16]	
The Gulls Fly Inland	Thompson	285
Gypsy Gypsy	Godden	289
Summer Half	Thirkell	318
Wild Strawberries	"	316
The Crock of Gold	Stephens	312
Now Voyager	Prouty	240
My Chinese Wife	Eskelund	247
Peace Breaks Out	Thirkell	287
Greenmask	Farjeon	240
Three's a Crew	Pinkerton	316
My Danish Father	Eskelund	
Parnassus on Wheels	Morley	390
Seven League Boots	Halliburton	
Jamaica Inn	du Maurier	309
Hard Facts	Howard Spring	290
The Crowthers of Bankdam	Armstrong	618

16 The author of *The Scent of Water* is Susan Buchan, not John Buchan.

The Royal Road To Romance	Halliburton	399	
Dunkerley's	Spring	247	
Thunderbolt House	Pease		
The Treasure Seekers	Nesbit		
The Angelic Avengers	Andrézel		
As a Watered Garden	Keith		
Mr. Skeffington	Russell	330	Sept. 7-9
The Glorious Adventure	Halliburton	354	Sept. 2.
The Labyrinth	Cecil Roberts	278	Sept.10-11
In a Shaft of Sunlight			

[p.44]

Fortitude
The Citadel
In Search of Ireland
Argentina
Dear Brutus
Chaco Chapters

[p.45]

Books

[19]49-50

Shirley	C. Brontë	649	F[iction]
Pangoan Diary	Harkness	295	Travel
New Worlds to Conquer	Halliburton	368	Travel
The Prophet	Gibran		Poetry
The Little White Horse	Goudge		F.
The Loving Spirit	du Maurier	365	F.
Les trois mousquetaires	Dumas	217	F.
Birthday Party	A A Milne	240	F.
The Emperor's Snuff Box	Carn	219	F.
Van Loon's Lives			B.
Mr Poppers' Penguins	Atwater	139	F.
Masters of the Keyboard	Apel	365	Technical
Dear Brutus	J.M. Barrie		Drama
The Citadel	Cronin		F
Towers in the Mist	Gridge		F
Lost Boundaries	White		Biog
Boarding School	Woody		F
The Canoe	Pinkerton		Tech.
Elizabeth and the Archdeacon	Bermuston		F.
Barretts of Wimpole St	Besier	164	D.

Colour Scheme	Ngaio Marsh	346	F.
Fortitude	Walpole	495	F.
Death Be Not Proud	Gunther	260	Biog.
A Certain Rich Man	Sheean	378	F.
In Search of Ireland	Morton	300?	Trav.
The Incomplete Anglers	Robins	229	Travel
Mistress Masham's Repose	White	265	F
Message from a Stranger	Mannes	246	F

[p.46]

Musical Honours—	Kitty Barre	199	F.
The House on the Hill	Kyle	232	F.
Coming My Way?	Haynes	99 p.	Poetry
The History of Mr Polly -	Wells	234	F.
Liffey Lane	- Laverty	232	F.
Fortune My Foe	R. Davies	99	Drama
Chaco Chapters			
The Moon & Mine	Goortz	304	F
Thou Shall not Want	Collins	542	F
Gentian Hill	Goudge	400?	F
The Table talk of Samuel Marchbanks -		Davies	F
Your Voice and Speech			

1950-51

Fine Rider	Hopgard	320	F
And Then You Came	Ann Bridge	- 319	F
This Man from Lebanon	Barbara Young	188	B
Northland Post	- Alice Marwick		Hist.
As You like it -	WS		Dr.
There Shall be no night	Sherwood		Dr.
Golden Arrow - Webb - F			
Shadow on the Rock	- F -	Cather	
Byron	Maurois	B.	
The White Monkey	Galsworthy	F.	
Wuthering Heights	Brontë	F	
The Silver Spoon	Galsworthy	F.	
* The Razors Edge	Maugham		
* Poems	Edna St Vincent Millay		
* Kon Tiki	Torstein	Travel	
* I found no Peace	Miller	Biog.	

[p.47]

51-52

* At my Hearts Core —	Davies	—	Drama
* French Without Tears —	Rottigan	—	Drama
* My Name is Aram –	Saroyan	—	Fiction
* A Table Near the Band - - -	A.A. Milne F		
Murder in the Cathedral —	T.S. Eliot		Dr.
* Juno and The Paycock —	Sean O'Casey	—	Drama
Great novels & Their Authors -	Maugham	—	N
O Absalom!	Spring	—	F
* Our Town	Wilder	—	D
The Lodger	Belloc-Loundes	—	F
The Moon and Sixpence	Maugham	—	F
* Huntsman What Quarry	Millay	—	P
Opus 21	Wylie		N
The Cocktail Party	Eliot		D
* Wind Without Rain	Dewdrey		F
* Music in the life of Albert Schweitzer — Joy			- N
Liza of Lambeth —	Maugham		- F
Cakes and Ale —	"		- F
* Arrowsmith —	— Lewis		- F
* The Indigo Bunting —	Sheean		B
* The Death of a Salesman—	Miller		D.
Albert Schweitzer Life & Message — Ratter			N
* The Lady's not for Burning	Fry		D.
* Prophet in the Wilderness—	Hapedorn		B
* Blaze of Noon	Beattie		F
Two Solitudes—	McLennan [*sic*]		F
Tempest Tost—	Davies		F
Yesterday's Fortune—	IARWylie		F
Harem Scarem—	Taylor		F
The Long Walk Home—	Medd		B
The Bulwark—	Dreiser		
The Rains Came—	Bromfield		

[illegible]

[p.48]

The Mayor of Casterbridge— Hardy
Gone to Earth
The Christopher Fry Album
Vengeance is Mine
Thor With Angels

The Playboy of the Western World JM Synge
The Green Bay Tree — Bromfield
Leave Her to Heaven— Ben Ames Williams
The Gown of Glory
Tess of the d'Urbervilles– Hardy
The Ballad & The Source— Lehmann
The Ministry of Fear –
- David, Trial of A City, Straits of Anian Madame Bovary
Beyond the River & into the Trees
Ministry of Fear– Graham Greene
Madame Bovary— Flaubert
What Maisie Knew– James

[p.49]

Fiction

So Dear to My Heart—1946-49

46-47 a Tangled Webb; none But The Brave; The Golden Road Children of the New Forest, Count of Monte Cristo, The Robe, The Blue Castle, The Loon Feather, Party Frock, Great Expectations, Dear Enemy, Other Peoples Homes, Parnassus on Wheels, In the Same Boat, Kilmany of the Orchard, Emily Vine, Anne of Windy Poplars, Wind of the Vikings, Shuttered Windows, The Stolen Oracle, The Tree That Sat Down, On the Edge of the Fiord, Where the high wind blows, Cue For Treason, The Tenant of Wildfell Hall, Green Mansions, Jam To-morrow, Sir Percy Leads the Band, Alice in Wonderland, Magnificent Obsession, The Silver Pencil, The Silver Strain, The Tangled Skein, In Lightning on in Rain, Disputed Passage, The Ghost & Mrs Muir, Martin Eden

47-48-49 Great Northern: Return to Jalna, Brideshead Revisited, So Well Remembered, Crowns, Green Dolphin Street, Frenchman's Creek, Gift of the Desert, Down Wind , Pavilion of Women, Back to Victoria, The Crock of Gold, My Chinese Wife, Wilderness Wife, Jamaica Inn, Hard Facts, Royal Road to Romance, Dunkerleys' Glorious Adventure, The Other Room, Return to Elysium, How Green was my Valley, Flying Carpet, London Belongs to Me

[p.50]

Wuthering Heights, Precious Bane, The Big Fisherman, MacBeth, Made in China, Finian's Rainbow, Pilgrim's Inn, Ladies of Literature, Charade, Northern Summer, Storevik, The Rich Man, The Wall Between,

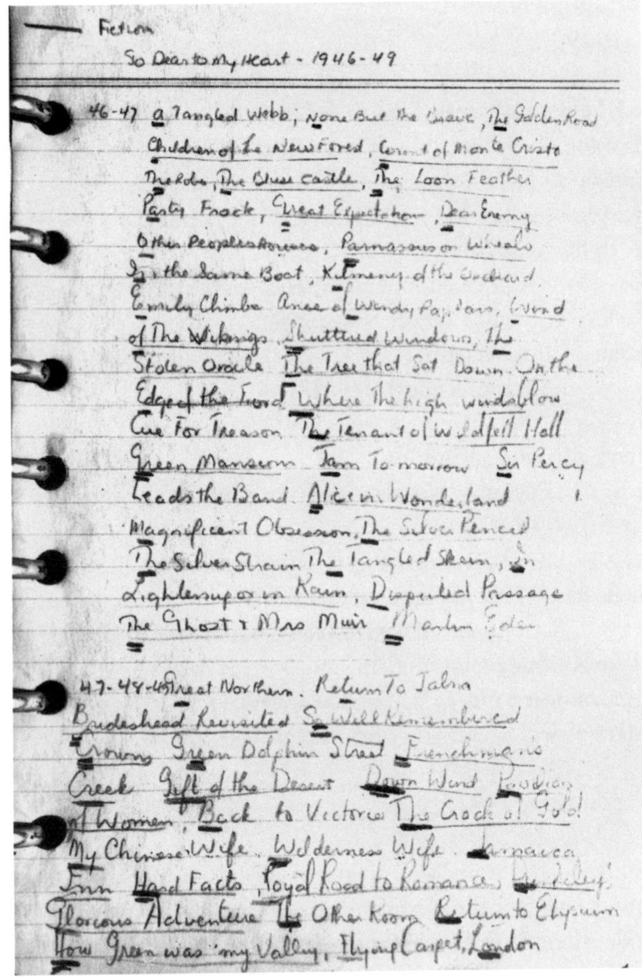

— Fiction

So Dear to My Heart - 1946-49

46-47 a Tangled Webb; None But the Brave, The Golden Road
Children of the New Forest, Count of Monte Cristo
The Robe, The Blue Castle, The Loon Feather
Party Frock, Great Expectations, Dear Enemy
Other Peoples Houses, Parnassus on Wheels
In the Same Boat, [illegible] of the Orchard,
Emily Climbs Anne of Windy Poplars, Wind
of The Vikings, Shuttered Windows, The
Stolen Oracle The Tree that Sat Down. On the
Edge of the Fiord Where the high winds blow
Cue For Treason The Tenant of Wildfell Hall
Green Mansions Jam To-morrow Sir Percy
Leads the Band. Alice in Wonderland
Magnificent Obsession, The Silver Pencil
The Silver Skein The Tangled Skein, In
[illegible], Disputed Passage
The Ghost & Mrs Muir Martin Eden

47-48-49 Great Northern. Return To Jalna
Brideshead Revisited So Well Remembered
[illegible] Green Dolphin Street Frenchman's
Creek Gift of the Desert Down Wind [illegible]
of Women, Back to Victoria The Crock of Gold
My Chinese Wife. Wilderness Wife. Jamaica
Inn Hard Facts, Royal Road to Romance, [illegible]
Glorious Adventure The Other Room Return to Elysium
How Green was my Valley, Flying Carpet, London

Page 49

P<u>an</u>goan Diary; <u>The</u> little white horse..., Th<u>e</u> Citadel - <u>L</u>ost Boundaries; <u>The</u> Canoe; F<u>or</u>titude; D<u>e</u>ath Be not Proud. <u>Message from a stranger</u>. The History of Mr. Polly. <u>For</u>tune my Foe, The Moon is Mine, Thou Shalt not want Gentian Hill, <u>The</u> Diary of Samuel Marchbanks - <u>The</u> Tabletalk of SM, She, And Then You Came, As You Like It - T<u>here</u> Shall be No night - This man from Lebanon - Golden Arrow. The Razor's Edge. Poems (Millay), Kon Tiki, I found no peace At My Heart's Core French Without Tears My Name is Aram Juno and the Paycock. Our Town Huntsman, What Quarry? Wind Without Rain Arrowsmith The Indigo Bunting The Death of a Salesman Prophet in the Wilderness, The Lady's Not for Burning Blaze of Noon.

[p.51]

March 8, 1949

Here I begin my "travels with a Unicorn"—not a lengthy account because I want to get at "the Blue Hills"—Goudge is at present my favorite author so far: So dear to my heart.

Movie: One night with you HAMLET of course
Play: Night must fall
Author—F—Goudge Stephens [→ *How could you Pass?* Aug '50][17]
BF Jack of course or Dave! & George
Musician—Nino Martini
Actors: Jean Simmons and John Mills
Radio—Stage 49
Teachers—Ritchie, Kitching
Friends: Liz Foster & Kit also others natch!

The travels have been dull to-day. Tuesday nicht wahr? I was in to see Miss Brown about Lessie's timetable. To-day feels as if something had happened but it hasn't [ink stain] wish Jack would come home. I forgot [ink stain] eyebrows - but he has a girlfriend! [→ *you bet he has* ('51)].[18]

The phone just rang & I hoped it wasn't Gibson. It wasn't! Back to bachelor days again. So far so good—future—bad.

[p.52]

Mar. 9. Wednesday [1949]

The journey has gone well to-day. I swam 15 lengths all at once—played volley ball at official's meeting, discussed dorm party. We read "The Sire de Malétroit's Door" in English—by RLS. I must really be better in French.

In Science Weaver explained about dew point to me. Now I understand. I like him. He has beautiful hands. He is rather beautiful in a way. He would die if he thought of it that way, I suppose, but in being beautiful, he has completely escaped being effeminate.

Mr Bond was horrid - "Lah me pooh I can't abide the horrid thing."

J E Metcalfe is super, nicht wahr? and I think that Miss Heasman could be human. I would like to know her.

---

17 Editorial comment by Engel added one year later.
18 Editorial comment by Engel added two years later.

[p.53]

April 7 1949

A bumpy road to-day.
— wrote the Tower Room - it is no good.
— read over Last Time I Saw Paris and others.
— en train de lisant [*sic*] "Shanghai lawyer," "A Tale of Two Cities," "Chinatown Family"
— Favourite movies: Red Shoes—Hamlet—One night, With You.
— BF - Jack, Eyebrows, George
— Teacher—Ritchie, Kitching—Sawers.

The travels are happy—a little bit dissolutioning [*sic*]—so romantic. Weaver isn't so handsome after all.

Lovely bachelor days.

April 8 1950

Sur la route à Toronto!! Brigadoon in a little while.
How little my tastes have changed.
writing Mouse[19]
reading Jungle Wife
Saw Adam & Evelyne
Taste in men in reversed order
Geo, Jack, Eyebrows. Only not the latter

[p.54]

19 April [1950]

I had to come upstairs where I could let my stomach out and be mad. I would have liked a spoon or a fountain pen. I wish I wasn't so in between. All the others are at ease. I look forward to it all so much, and then I hate it terribly. I can't chatter about University or exams because it isn't cute. They haven't read any <u>good</u> books. I'm brainy and I'm a child. I feel younger than George, but nobody "dear girls" me. I'm cuter than Joan but I haven't a boy friend. I hate idle chatter & sitting around. I can understand how mother feels so ill at ease—with Windy, Dolly and Whiny & Wheezy—Uncle Lloyd's pictures will get more applause than Daddy's.

---

19 A short story about a timid (mousy) young woman who aspires to be an artist. For further details, see Verduyn, *Lifelines* 49-50.

My teeth don't stick out, but I don't look as nice as Joan. Joan has Hugh to talk about. George can dance. George thinks I'm queer & dowdy. Why doesn't anybody understand?

[p.55]

Marian Passmore

July 11 [1950]

After a night cap of tomato juice, bread & grape jam, and marshmallows I decide to go to bed because Mother & Dad's lengthy discussion of the Buyer's Market prevents me from concentrating on Van Loon's Lives.

The dimly lighted room lends a sinister glow to the Chinese table top. The pagoda is clearly shadowed on the wall. The old [illegible] hunched over his pottery.

The floor is littered with pins and thread, innumerable pairs of shoes, and papers of all shapes and sizes. Overhead, the high ceiling, supported by four peach-coloured walls is blissfully bare.

Shining dimly The Head of Christ watches over all.

[p.56]

1949

1951

DATA:
BOOKS— PANGOAN DIARY
VAN LOON'S LIVES
HARD FACTS
MOVIES— SLEEPING CAR TO TRIESTE
TALES OF HOFFMANN
LA [*sic*] SPECTRE DE LA ROSE
ONE NIGHT WITH YOU
HAMLET
AUTHOR — ROBERTSON DAVIES EDNA ST VINCENT MILLAY
PLAY– OVER THE BOILER ROOM FORTUNE MY FOE
SUMMER THEATRES & BALLET
PAINTER— DÉGAS. —LA DANSEUSE
~~RICHARD HALLIBURTON~~ JOHN
GEORGE ~~NAPOLEON BONAPARTE~~
MR WATSON ALBERT SCHWEITZER
LOUIS ST LAURENT
Sam Marchbanks
CHILL NOVEMBER - THOMPSON

à demain

bon soir

mon cherie [*sic*]

[p.57]

[Doodle]

Aug. 25 après le dîner

I must wean myself from this diet of poetry, which, however pleasant it may be, is weakening to a prose-writer.

Arden lay in the sand, the hot sun beating down upon her head, and watched the morning.

Across the calm lake, the line of white cottages amongst green trees showed no signs of awakening. A breeze stirred the birch trees. Sniffing it, Arden revelled in the joy of summer as she watched two fishermen sitting still in their boat, expectantly watching the water. They seemed like a small island, their clothes of a dun gray colour at that distance appearing to blend with their boat.

The blue sky, blue water, green trees and grey rock formed an even monotone. An occasional gull flapped across the sky, and once the fishermen got a fish. Then all was still again.

A fat lady in a cerise coloured bathing suit came down to wash at the shore; forming at last, a

[p.58]

contrast to the greens and blues. Then she went away....

Arden lay in the sun, the hot sand scorching her body, the heat of the morning dissolving her mind until her thoughts became grey shapeless images of some other world far from akin to herself.

There was a grey man who played a violin, and wore a cerise coloured carnation in his button hole. Beside him stood a vivacious black and white girl, who danced to the man's music, with a cerise carnation in her teeth. Two gaunt grey fishermen rose out of mist behind the man and the girl. Throwing their arms about each other, they sang a dirge of the sea. From afar, a church bell clanged its message. The fishermen sank once more into the mist, leaving behind them only a small spotted fish that lay still on the ground.

[p.59]

The man struck up a polka on his violin. The black & white girl tossed her head and began to dance. The sun shone fitfully through the clouds, here casting a ray of light upon the ground. A green leaf fell and came to rest on the patch of light.

A swirl of music fell upon the ears of the watchers, and out of the mist, a pair of glowing green eyes appeared. While the girl watched with open mouth, and the grey man played as if his life depended upon it, the green eyes, and the green leaf rose in the sunlight in the form of a leaf green girl. She too danced to the grey man's music. On her toes, with her arms in the air, her eyes flashing & her long gold hair hanging over her green body she danced in the sunlight. She laughed a little wickedly and with a sweep of her hand, picked up the carnation that lay at the feet of the black & white girl. Then with a twirl on her toes, she too faded into the mists as the

[p.60]

fishermen. The grey man lapsed into a mournful song, and the black and white girl lay in a heap on the edge of the sunlight.

The sound of water lapping on the shore woke Arden. She rose, and shook herself. The lonely cry of a mourning dove overhead warning her that it was past midday. She turned away from the water, and headed through the birch trees.

[Drawing of a half profile—a large eye and a nose]

[p.61]

With careful strokes, and eager fingers,
she sketched jade Warriors of the Tong
against the oaken floors, between high walls.
The empty sound of footsteps rang.
Unhesitating in her art with gaze intent,
her pencil scribing beauty where it went,
the student heeded not the passing crowds
But laboured on, with head immersed in clouds.

~~Not far there sat another like herself~~
~~Whose fingers, not so young as Alison's~~
~~Sketched the same warriors with a firmer bond~~
~~That told of labours long, and battles won~~

His judging game [illegible]

✔/✔/✔/✔/✔/
✔/✔/✔/✔/✔/

[p.62]

Written at Easter 1949

age 16

The Immortals

My uncle Kees was an outsider, like myself, but only more so. Whereas I was a direct member of the family, he was only an in-law. But we were both born to dislike the hustle and confusion of my mother's family.

I was seven when Kees married my aunt Katine. I can remember only Kees, who stood straight, like a soldier, and looked very solemn. All the other memories have faded like yesterday's roses.

Now I am ~~nineteen~~ 17, and Kees, because he was twenty-two when he married Katine, must be thirty-four.

→ After Kees came home from the war, we had many parties. I often eyed this young uncle of mine, who was so very handsome. He was so much older than myself, but so much younger than all the other fat uncles. Katine wandered

[p.63]

absently around the house, smoking squat Turkish cigarettes, and Kees spent many hours in our little garden. I spent my time between the two people, making my observances on life and people in general—mostly Kees.

I fell in love with him.

Kees and Katine did not get along so well after the war.

They shared the chamber next mine, and I heard them quarrelling long into the night. When Katine bore Kees a dead son, they blamed each other, and things grew worse and worse.

Grandmother gave memorable parties, all in honour of Kees, for he was the only one of her sons-in-law who had returned from the war. There was always much wine and singing with fat "groszmutti" and fatter grandfather in the lead. I hated the parties for their sordid wine fibbing. I

[p.64]

did not love this family with all their vulgar celebrations.

The last party was given three years after Kees' homecoming. It was rowdy, as were the others, and the air was foul with vulgar mirth and false merriment. No one seemed to notice that Kees, the guest of honour was missing. Katine was in full circulation, fulfilling admirably her role as daughter of the hostess, and wife of the honoured guest. She clicked around in her thonged sandals and greeted the guests in a dry but cordial voice. She did not miss Kees either—only I missed him.

When the smoke grew too dense, the curses too frequent, I ascended the stairs to my room. At the top of the stairs I found Kees, with blood on his face. I gasped, but seeing he was alive, and apparently in pain, gently shook his shoulder.

[p.65]

"Kees—Kees, my uncle, what has befallen you, Kees?"

He was a small time coming to full consciousness. Then, in a low voice he urged me to help him to his and Katine's room.

I slid off my sandals, and with silent footsteps, supported him a little as he limped down the hall.

He lay on his bed while I bathed his face. There was a deep gash on his forehead. Groaning a little when I washed it with hot water, he seemed in some pain. He told me that Katine had attacked him with a knife. I was little surprised. Katine was a vicious animal, sly and deceptive.

"Ah Santia," he said, "You little know how Katine has changed, from the simple virgin I married to the witch I live with to day—She

[p.66]

was like you Santia, before."

My heart skipped a beat. "It was ever so in that family—" I said, "—Furry tiger cubs at first and then vicious beasts. That is why we stay on the outside Kees," I said.

His returning gaze was long. "It is ordained so by the Immortals, Santia—God save us from being on the inside." He would have said more but I heard Katine's panther-like tread in the hall and slid behind a screen. Kees shot me a funny sidelong glance, which I returned for some silly reason, with a blown kiss.

Katine saw my bare feet beneath the screen and I left the room as discreetly as I could to go walking on the terrace.

I dared go nowhere else. The moon was high, the party at its height — the garden filled with carousing guests.

[p.67]

The front terrace was empty and I stood alone in the shimmering silver moonlight.

There, I imagined Kees coming beside me. "I had to come Santia," he said, and I, in dreams, could envision his kissing me again and again. Katine would be helpless against our love so strong. In a few minutes my dream had us eloping to Cairo and soon his voice shattered my vision.

"It's cold on the terrace, child," he said, "go in—and by the way my dear, you've been very kind but don't blow kisses to married men—it isn't safe." His coldly impersonal voice froze my feeling. In the moonlight he looked paunchy for his thirty-odd years. My first feeling was one of

[p.68]

dissolutionment [*sic*], the second of contempt. I laughed because he seemed so old, so vague, and then I turned away.

The immortals had been unkind to me—he was so painful in the moonlight.

1950 summer Tent 14[20]

I almost killed
And I didn't want to kill.
I threw a bug
Into a candle flame
A little long red bug
Who popped & almost burst
But didn't ... so I rescued him.

The fascinating flame
Leaps & dies

Like life's enthusiasm
It quickly flies

A gust of wind
May carry it away

[p.69]

Song for "Swan Lake"

Glide o my swan	a
Dance to the music	b
Soar with crescendo	c
Die ... diminuendo	c
But ever dance on	a

Dance on white wings
Leap to sky's ceiling
Bow in the moonlight
Soar in the sunlight
As violin sings.

---

20 Efforts did not turn up a bibliographic source for the writer of "1950 summer Tent 14" and "Song for 'Swan Lake.'" It seems reasonable to conclude they are Engel's own.

Dance on forever
I'll not forget thee
Time may destroy me
But never touch beauty
Dance on forever

[p.70]

May 4th, 1951:

"For you all know security
Is mortal's chiefest enemy."[21]

August 2nd 1951

By this time I have grown up enough to realise that that is almost true.

August 6th

Love comic books are disgusting.... They mock the beauty of an emotion which I have begun to understand.

August 21st 51

Getting addresses. Sentiment[?] has departed with the advent of the Yiddish accent.

Green Pastures!

[p.71]

August 28th

Teen Age Camp—everything is all fixed up now. Rather lonely since George didn't come. Still it is his in that it is no one else's.

November 27th 51

Three months later, it is all fixed up still, only who likes it that way? Life is filled with dental appointments, Xmas plans, exam papers, manuscripts, all salted with BIG HOPES

---

21 *Macbeth*, Act III, Scene V.

April 28th 52

BIG HOPES partially filled—small hopes still weeping. How I could love if there were only someone. Other peoples' beauty is dazzling. Help Thou mine ugliness.

[p.72]

ESVM[22]

Indigo bunting, sing for me.
My voice is weak; I have not thy song
Indigo bunting, fly for me
My wings are flaccid. I do not fly long.
I am a ground bird, chirping high and shrill
Would be a sky bird – but I lack will.
Indigo bunting sing and fly for me!
I have need, I have need!

Souls shine like stars through physical
    impairments
of raiment and worldliness.
I saw thy soul.
Its light was too bright—mine eyes are
    out to other souls
I love thee so.

---

22 ESVM are the initials of Edna St. Vincent Millay (1892-1950) an accomplished poet, playwright and speaker and winner of the Pulitzer Prize for her book, *The Harp-Weaver and Other Poems* (1923). A biography of Millay, entitled *Indigo Bunting* (New York: Harper and Brothers, 1951) and written by Vincent Sheean, reflected on Millay's use of bird imagery in her poetry.

Cahier II[1]

We are led to believe we are determined by a series of dichotomies black—white, pro, contra—while all the time the shades are neglected [18].

While Marian Engel's first *cahier* dates from the early 1950s, the collection as a whole acquired its momentum in the early 1960s when the author was living in Cyprus. In the intervening years, an entire life had begun to take shape.

After graduating from Sarnia Collegiate Institute and Technical School in 1952, Engel entered McMaster University, where she completed a BA in French and German.[2] While at McMaster, Engel worked on the university's two student publications, the *Silhouette* and the *Muse*. She was vice-president of the Students' Council in her first year, a member of the Debating Club in her second (winning the debating trophy), and the club's vice-president in her third year. She was involved in theatre and in the fall of 1954 performed in *The Heiress*. She also joined the Philosophy Club and the Writers' Workshop. Her many extracurricular activities did not interfere with Engel's academic achievement. By the time she left McMaster, she had been awarded a number of scholarly distinctions.[3]

In 1955, Engel proceeded from McMaster to McGill, where she completed an MA in 1957, with a thesis on the English-Canadian novel, directed by Hugh MacLennan. Her experiences working with MacLennan and living in Montreal had lifelong significance for Engel. As she recalled in her essay for a conference in MacLennan's honour at the University in Toronto in 1982,[4] the

1 1962-63, beige notebook (Science Exercise Book), the cover of which reads "Engel I"; 35 pages used.

2 Doing her degree in French and German, Engel explained in an interview with Carroll Klein, allowed her to take all the English courses she wished without having to study Latin (Klein 6). In "The Office on the Landing," Engel wrote that "if you took Pass French and German, you could take all the English courses but two." See Verduyn, ed., *Dear Marian, Dear Hugh* 125.

3 These awards included an OHA scholarship, a Legion bursary, an MSB book prize and an Isobel Walton Memorial Prize. Joan Schuler, "Spotlight," *Silhouette*, McMaster University (26 November 1954): 3.

4 See Elspeth Cameron, *Hugh MacLennan: 1982: Proceedings of the MacLennan Conference at University College* (Toronto: Canadian Studies Programme, University of Toronto, 1982). See also "The Office on the Landing," Verduyn, ed., *Dear Marian, Dear Hugh* 125-29.

elder writer "turned the Montreal world of which I was very afraid into a real one.... I've never since worked with anyone or even talked to anyone who had such a sense of history.... He was teaching me an awful lot about *being*."[5]

Although MacLennan thought Engel's MA thesis had the potential for becoming a doctoral dissertation,[6] she decided not to pursue formal studies. She wanted to write. Meanwhile, a living had to be earned, and Engel accepted a position as a lecturer in English at the University of Montana in 1957-58. There she met Leslie Armour, a young faculty appointment in Philosophy, who became a lifelong friend and a one-time collaborator. With Armour, Engel completed her first full-length manuscript, "The Pink Sphinx." Full of lively characters and plot developments, "The Pink Sphinx" was never published. But its smooth writing convinced Diarmuid Russell, a New York literary agent with whom MacLennan put Engel in touch, that its author had talent. Engel joined the prestigious list of writers on whose behalf Russell acted, and worked with him until his death in December 1973. The author and her agent enjoyed a pleasant working relationship, which Engel recalled poignantly in "Into the Celtic Twilight."[7]

Engel made up her mind to return to Montreal and to continue writing. To support herself, she taught geography at The Study (1958-60), a private girls' school in the city's Westmount neighbourhood. Encouraged by MacLennan, she worked on plays. This resulted in two unpublished manuscripts, "The Deception of the Thrush" and "Beat Up the Rain," both about struggling artists, each a young woman not unlike Engel herself.[8]

A Rotary Foundation Fellowship enabled Engel to travel to Europe for a year's study at the Université d'Aix-Marseille in Aix-en-Provence in 1960-61.

---

5 "The Office on the Landing," Verduyn, ed., *Dear Marian, Dear Hugh* 128-29.

6 In a letter dated 23 January 1957, MacLennan wrote: "This thesis of yours—correct me if I'm wrong—could presumably be expanded into a Ph.D. if you need one. Actually I would have thought it about good enough for a Ph.D. in English, for it certainly fulfilled the requirements so far as I can tell." See Verduyn ed., *Dear Marian, Dear Hugh* 38.

7 "I came into contact with Russell when I needed the peculiar support he could give me; I needed not a personal friend but a friend for my work, and he was perfect. His uncluttered mind cut through my confusion and he was honest and straightforward. I never felt I could send him a bad sentence. He came, after all, out of the Irish tradition that produced very great writers. Still, when I write to the old firm I feel as if I'm dealing with the heirs of the Celtic Twilight..." MEA, Box 33 File 103. See excerpt published in Christl Verduyn, "Marian Engel's Cahiers," *Prairie Fire* 16.3 (Autumn 1995): 127-34.

8 Engel's titles were inspired by her readings. "The Deception of the Thrush" is from T.S. Eliot's *Burnt Norton*, part one of his work *The Four Quartets* (1941).

The author described that experience as follows:

> [I] attended lectures here and there, attended cooking school and had tea with marvellous old women. I picked up a really good French accent in a snobbish boarding house—which I would have written more about if I hadn't opened up the *New Yorker* one day and seen a sentence that went (*in a French accent*), *Madame Duport opened up the window and, beating a fork on her tin pan, called "Minou, Minou."* I thought, my God. I looked at the end of the story and sure enough, it was written by M.F.K. Fisher.[9] She'd had the room that I was in the year before me, and she had done everything up in print and there it was in the *New Yorker*. I had to cut out a whole section of my first novel.[10]

At the end of the year, rather than return to Canada, Engel found work in London, England, translating foreign credit reports. During this time, she worked on "Women Travelling Alone," her second unpublished novel. She also was married, on 27 January 1962, to Howard Engel, who was freelancing for CBC in London. In late October 1962, the couple left London for Cyprus, where Howard continued his freelance work, and Engel taught at St John's RAF School in Nicosia.

These events can be traced through Engel's correspondence with family and friends.[11] Although Engel wrote devotedly throughout the period, her efforts found their outlet in the unpublished plays and novels as opposed to *cahiers*. A 1962 date book offers glimpses of life in London.[12] Like two other date books (for 1969 and 1977) found amongst Engel's papers, the 1962 one makes it eminently clear that the traditional dated diary format fulfilled only part of Engel's purposes in keeping *cahiers*. While they present some of the same factual, daily-life information—appointments, meetings, tasks, reminders, etc.—that is integral to the *cahiers*, they offer none of the philosophical reflection or fiction writing that

9 Mary Frances Kennedy Fisher (1908-1992) was an essayist, short story writer and a prose writer, best known for her writings on food and travel e.g. *Serve it Forth* (1937), *How To Cook a Wolf*, (1942) and *The Gastronomical Me* (1943). But she should also be noted for her memoirs (*Stay Me, Oh Comfort Me: Journals and Stories 1933-1941* and *Last House Reflections, Dreams, and Observations 1943-1991* among others). In France, she lived in Dijon, Aix-en-Provence and Marseilles.

10 Cathy Matyas and Jennifer Joiner, "Interpretation, Inspiration and the Irrelevant Question: Interview with Marian Engel," *University of Toronto Review* 5 (Spring 1981): 5.

11 See MEA, Boxes 1, 2, 3, 31 and 32.

12 It appears to have been used jointly by Howard Engel and Marian Engel.

distinguishes the *cahiers*. Thus, for example, *Cahier* II comprises almost entirely draft fiction. Its contents demonstrate how—and in some cases how long!—manuscripts evolve to their final form. This *cahier* from the early 1960s presents characters and settings from both *Sarah Bastard's Notebook* and *Monodromos*, published five and ten years later. As *Cahier* II shows, the two novels started out in the same pages. The narrative voice in this *cahier* resembles Sarah's in *Sarah Bastard's Notebook*—rough and tough, self-denigrating but intelligent.[13] The setting, however, is that of *Monodromos*—a Greek island, here specifically identified as Cyprus.

In the evolution of the material in *Cahier* II towards the novels *Sarah Bastard's Notebook* and *Monodromos*, the charming character Antonio, the narrator's young son (by her brother-in-law), is lost. This is of some regret, as the little boy is introduced to good effect in the pages of this *cahier*. At the same time, other characters, themes and concepts introduced here became recurring features in the author's work. They include "the old struggle between reason and emotion" [18]; the tyranny of dualistic thinking;[14] the idea that truth is always "somewhere in between" [18]; the difference between men and women;[15] the difficulty but the importance of living in the present;[16] and the struggle for self-acceptance.[17]

Finally, *Cahier* II contains two idiosyncratic items: the discussion of cannibalism [4];[18] and a piece of mirror writing [27], which reads: "Mirror writing is fantastically easy when one is drunk but not now."

---

13 "How was this useless self-condemnation bred in me?" the narrator asks rhetorically. "If it were Christian & constructive it might be born, but proceeding on the assumption that one is shit, unredeemable shit, not even fertilizer, is surely unhelpful," is her spicy reply [5].

14 "We are led to believe that we are determined by a series of dichotomies..." [18].

15 "I'm not really wrong, I'm just different from you," the narrator informs the male character Stel. "I believe that time is continuous, enveloping, circular and you want it to be periodic" [3].

16 "You've never accepted a day as a day—the present as something to be lived for itself," Stel criticizes the narrator [2]; "the pressure of a moment," she reflects in turn. "You have to be very strong" [3].

17 "Here I've been trying all my life to accept myself—becoming a bore—and Stel now says it's <u>things</u> one has to accept," the narrator exclaims [1].

18 This resurfaces in *Cahier* II [4, 8], *Cahier* III [inserted page], *Cahier* IV [13], *Cahier* IX [18] and *Cahier* XVIII [18].

[p.1]

My Antonio

I don't know how they made me do it, but they did. I drove a hard enough bargain, it makes me toss at night, but I had to and here we are.

Not Scott [*sic*] free, not by any means, with Antonio peeing in the streets and flushed with his own pathetic horrors by the evening. But I don't think we're trapped any more. Not doubled [*sic*] trapped, not trapped by others, just by our own constricting selves—even Antonio, at three, doubled up under the weight of his own personality—and I, nearing thirty, doubled up, bent, knuckled under, too. Though I still do not know who I am.

So Stel says.

I think I know quite well, but I don't feel myself.

It's a case of knowing that you know. Accepting things. Stel says. Here I've being trying all my life to accept myself—becoming a bore—and Stel now says it's <u>things</u> one has to accept.

I don't know what Joe says. He's in Israel breaking his heart.

[p.2]

Stel says—I am much under his influence now my eyes follow him like puppies—and I can't keep secrets, I can't even stop quoting though I say that on one level he doesn't touch me at all—the rim I hang onto to keep me from falling in—into Stel falling would be sensational but it's not allowed because submerging—I've tried it before. You wake up eventually, disintegrated.

Stel says—he says a lot. Sometimes I even get tired of his saying, which is not the same as talking. It's making pronouncements. "You've never accepted a day as a day—the present as something to be lived for itself." He makes these pronouncements & they shock me out of mental response, leave wounds of feeling, which I lick (how masochistically) for three days and then when my weak mind has plucked the idea at last from the wound it's too late to say "I'm not really wrong, I'm just different from you—I believe that time is continuous, enveloping, circular and you want it to be periodic." And how long can you study a moment, a sensation, without opening another of those great wounds.

Unless of course you're intact.

[p.3]

I like the moment when it is isolated and intense, too—oh I like particularly in these flirtatious hours, to hold a sigh—but the pressure of a moment: You have to be very strong.

[p.4]

A sonnet is a moment's monument.

Stel has me living in sonnets. I'm living as undiluted sonnetry with no time to swallow either. Please, I want to say, give me time to take them in.

Stel is a stranger. But so then is everyone else. Why do we want this intimacy, this destructive nearness? Both of us are cannibals, we will destroy the wholeness, thus the object, yet we eat, eat, destroy. He has big teeth—not long teeth: shining white square, aggressive pegs.

Aroint thee, witch, the rump-fed Runyon [*sic*] cried.[19]

Wright Morris wrote a better book about it and when I told Archie I wanted to make a study of cannibal women, he promised a big advance. But of course I'm in no position to criticise.

Once when my aunt was staying with us—my aunt who was all soft and cool, and, Mother said, selfish, but warm-eyed & unworried—once I went into the bathroom—aged five—and crammed my toothbrush into the case with hers. A beautiful, smooth pearly composition (no plastic then) pink case. They had to cut it to

[p.5]

get them out. The bristles were locked together.

The only surprise about Antonio was that he came so late.

I'm careful not to eat him—oh, very. I've kept my teeth off Joe as well, nobility requiring some corresponding virtue. My eating field is restricted to people who'll eat back. No use involving myself with good souls...

Look, here, back to mosaics, I've done it again—turned a grumble about myself into a grumble about other people—I am not good. Stel loves me, ergo, he cannot be good. How was this useless self condemnation bred in me? If it were Christian & constructive it might be born, but proceeding on the assumption that one is shit, unredeemable shit, not even fertilizer, is surely unhelpful. Stupid word.

But about Antonio I feel good. It is something to have made him and not to have ruined him yet. He's tough & physical and without illusions, already he lives hard and his chances of growing up a mess are no greater than those of rest of the kids his age. Not on to-day.

---

19 *Macbeth*, Act I, Scene III.

[p.6]

Stel has been away for three days and already he is fading, which is why I refuse to consider him inedible. But the memory of his name, the sight of his car in the alley behind his office—and I have to pass the alley to get to the market, with a drunken lurch at the eroticism of a mere license place [*sic*] I have to pass—and the old shabbiness, the I haven't had a cigarette for six hours feeling returns...

I thought this year would be a resolution. Going off to find myself, I was, and a lot of rubbish in that concept too. I knew already I was a literary dictionary well defined romantic, case book reveller in the remote and strange, the more introverted the moment, the farther I reach towards that great extroverted mesomorph, who pretends to think with his belly and his balls, and then he comes out in sonnets.

Categories are treacherous; education teaches us to make neat divisions, the rest of our lives to hammer at their partition walls. Even male-female isn't firm, and I keep saying that the ability even to conceive of wavy walls is a sign of maturity, but how the tired mind wants generalisations, simplification. I wish I were Antonio, sleeping, rosy now, sucking and breathing like the queer undersea boy he is.

[p.7]

In a secure world the categories are well defined and you know where you are: Mummy, Daddy, sister, brother, friend, foe—(the understandable enemy is always male—the snake at the root female.) Will Antonio be ahead or behind after fifteen years of this equivocal chaos?

I let him cling to his routine, though I despise it—so dark is bed & light is play, noon is hunger, rising, peeing. Not that he should become dependent on this routine, only have a few stable gestures in his travelled life. Anna teaches him that he is male & to be indulged, something I should never dare concede to, and this, too, is a pole for him. He has Anna & me and his rude friend Pambos across the street—and Aristides the lottery ticket vendor, he knows where he is, if not who or why. So maybe he is as secure as he needs to be?

[p.8]

Stel says...

I really must before I fall into it wrestle with the concept of this man.

The R.A.F. puts out a magazine called Out & About.

The best black figs are at the Turkish market.

The best Turkish delight comes wrapped in squares of waxed paper with pink labels.

The Cambridge University Press is English agent for the University Presses of California & Duke.

Antonio's left foot is bigger than his right.

[p.9]

To-day Stel was cold and commanding. After Joe's diffidence his sureness is usually a pleasure, but its pervasiveness is in the long run even more annoying—do this, do that; when he tells me I'm a fool it is one thing—when he orders Antonio about it's another. I want to flutter about like a mother whippoorwill, but Antonio has sense and an instinctive recognition of Authority—so we both spent an afternoon under Stel's regime.

If he were Joe, I should remember that he is tired, trying to master a situation to prevent its fatiguing him further. But Stel is only in business. The teacher in me rejects the possibility that business can be important and fatiguing—particularly for a man who works for himself, has no superior to rely on when he is weary & fumbling.

Not that he would. I have seen him weary & fumbling—all the bigness of him splayed—one of these big Christlike bearded Greeks. You think it's the world's weariness on him. I keep having to remind myself it's only a hangover and a failed contract & my will is worth as much as his.

So one puts him on a wall, a sad eyed Byzantine Saint with this three dimensional aggressive vitality. There aren't many like him, though.

[p.10]

The dead rain falls in strings; thunder belches; the house across the street, half-demolished (brick by tile) has gleaming ochre walls, streaked in the wet, with the chocolate mud of disintegrating bricks.

Not the sort of day on which one can be bothered with love.

They built the houses here for centuries of this gracious, malleable adobe brick, plastered against the rain and stained indigo, ochre, white. The Turkish villages leave their mud brick alone: huddles of khaki walls on the plain. The rain shapes & smooths them, slides over the triangular vents, past the unpainted dovecotes.

On the road to polis there is a dovecote in a cliff—just holes in the cliff and doves ranged, ranked, in their white plumpness, smooth-eyed. A surprise, coming out of a clump of stunted banana trees, to drive past this.

Cyprus in the rain—though it's rare enough to frighten the Greeks.

They hate wetness. We who are more used to it are advised to cover heads, feet, take taxis, forebear. The same with the sun—it is, in fact, to be feared at noon in the summer. It is the enemy of Cyprus, and its benefactor. You can see here why it was worshipped....

Were there any Nordic sungods?

It dominates life here as never in England.

[p.11]

The rain stopped: I put Antonio, rosy and wicked, to bed with sticky kisses, and had not been long lingering over the commencement of an air letter to Joe when the inevitable bell clanged for Stel and, to-night, Leda and the Buttricks—all gay they dined out on the way and purported to be coming to my rescue.

I was quite happy alone. Was I rescuing them?

I do not think these people ever face each other alone. Habit has dulled their taste for exhibiting & reciprocating feelings. In front of me they exchange their day's trivia, erupt into veiled quarrels. At least Joe & I communicate superficially.

Stel and Leda agree only on negatives. But it was not a night for sonnetts and eternities. They got into the brandy while I changed into the dress Stel suggested (why & why?) and they had reached the second stage of intoxication when my hair was combed: Stel singing to himself, methodical music, Leda transfixed by some interior dream, the Buttricks staring at each other like cats unable to decide whether to fight or mate—off to a long rowdy evening of knee-pressings and contretemps desire rising like a tide of apple-cores in us.

[p.12]

The feeling with Stel dies down when Leda is there: one can't hurt her. But I am a kind of excitement-addict

— as the bulge of emotion subsides, I have to have a raised eyebrow, a look, t[o] sustain this adolescent beating in the breast.

INCANTATION POEM.

[p.13]

And so we come to Joe, who creates excitement, does he? No—but if sentimentality is overpaying with emotion, and I am sentimental, he is not, and the excitement is living and learning with Joe—who cannot make Stel fade by his presence, which is what I first asked him to do. He simply exists like a better poem. When you want things all simple & squashy like Rupert Brooke you are being sentimental anyhow....[20]

---

20 See poems, and footnote 9, in *Cahier* I.

Stuck in permanent self-indulgent adolescence, living rudderless on excitement, bound to fall in love once a week, prattle, drink, be a bore. Gauche approaches. Still socially unsure, therefore bullish. Still, in fact, myself.

The thing is, we had a party last night, because I'm thirty—

It began badly. I had been bossy & said I'd do the food—then of course Joe says you haven't, you're letting all these new friends down ... so we quarrel and I cook until too late, look stringy, answer the door crooked and leggy....

Joe feels it. Stel feels it. Leda is sympathetically assured, listens as I babble, so carefully that I am sure I have bad breath.

[p.14]

Ag. Omologitas comes in—the singing tailor who loves us—we love him but he's wrong and why does Joe mix him in with us when records are more appropriate than chatista?

All the wrong people Joe brought—but were they so wrong when the usual people, the Burtons, the de la Hayes, Savva—were behaving badly —you surely must not at a party sit sad in corners—and Stel is unsure & exhibitionist, trying to show he owns the house ... all there was enough of was drink and I drank too much.

But I was having the anxieties. This was the last birthday I'm to celebrate ... I shall keep, after this, my disintegrated personality in a can.

[p.15]

Sergeant can I have 2 more notebooks?

[p.16]

There are some poems I want in Richard's rooms in London, and three books at home, and I left Antonio's boomerang with Patrick and Solange in Paris—hope for the traveller...

Joe travels towards me, Stel travels towards me, three lines intersect in space and it is not really a tribute. I feel I have to fill the house with people, Joe must sulk and Stel go wild—turn himself into a big-footed Zorba, fine on the seacoast but the landlord asks no stomping joy. I resign, sorry in a corner, myself to the brandy bottle, wave goodbye to the guests sprawled across the blue chair, and me in orange canvas. Stel exits by the drainpipe, Leda not screaming after him, but calmly descending the stairs.

The police come, and the English couple are frightened but Stel's raucous Greek explains, points, slaps at them. His penguin's walk & Leda's tripping make swaying shadows & the street is quiet. I look around for Joe, who is stumped in a corner reading Wyndham Lewis. If I had the energy, I'd hit him.

[p.17]

And the hangover: but with a hangover I am always clear & quiet, breakfasting calmly with Antonio before Mrs Anna comes to clear him away. Joe is cautiously asleep, under the sheets....

What is she like, this Aviva, I ask him?

Like Leda, only a cannibal, like your Stel.

[p.18]

Flux

Every day our relationships change and uncertainties creep in—it takes all one's time to recognise and realise. All morning to analyse last evening's unrest.

After the visiting ballet: we are getting too sophisticated—away from the soil of Cyprus.

After coffee in a village—despair—no hope of making contact—but, God, to live in the mud of an adobe compound rather than souse oneself in brandy sours on Famagusta beach.

Crie [*sic*] de coeur.

Temptation with Stel to move into a dream world of glossy magazine sophistication which which which....

Is a trap for the tasteless.

Broken trains of thought.

The ideas I struggle with are not complex, but require sorting, sit uncomfortably side by side. The old struggle between reason and emotion. Roundhead and cavalier — a bore to outline, think through again—chiefly because we are led to believe that we are determined by a series of dichotomies—black-white, pro, contra—while all the time the shades are neglected and we count ourselves unlucky to be able to forget that there are shades and stripes. It is a bore that the truth should always be somewhere in between, that I should half-love Stel, that I should half-love Joe. But one always does, if one is sane, half-love, I mean

[p.19]

how can you love the wens of a colicky intellectual's personality, or the sensitive squashiness of the mesomorph.

Stel and I are squashy, all right, squashy about the navel, where we try to think—where we create these dichotomies, as labour-saving devices. So you think you are living intensely and ____?

Intense inschmens inschmen.

Wake up with a hangover—quietly bundle Antonio off (Anna's free day again: they roll around) go back to bed with Joe and The Naked Lunch,[21] cup of coffee, no piece of pie....

Halfway through first half of The Naked Lunch when the drug shootings, orgies and fantasms [*sic*] are beginning to crawl up me like those spiny worms, Joe wakes up, is sick again and instead of being disgusted I am, like last night, again physically hurt, as if he were Antonio my own flesh ... then he confesses that Ronnie Buttrick, on the night of Anne's confinement, has taken him off to a club after the bar closed. Big fat Spanish girls in leopard leotards, and Joe, good sport, says no, I'm too poor, but Ronnie grabs the fattest ugliest one (mouth like an old carp) and says be a sport old man, it'll be cheaper two of us to one room, I just asked. Anne in labour. Joe

[p.20]

sensitive about these things, comes home to be sick.

I spent the evening with Leda. We got into the wine when we talked of Anne—no communication, mind you—only gossip. Until we ran out of cigarettes. Stel pounced on us at the end (proto-Spanish club girls too?) He fed us nicotine, said "Cass, you're dissolving again" and drove me home—erect & reproving. Leda giggled us away & he went back grim to have her.

So this thing with Stel is a protracted fiction. Joe is in pain again & here I belong.

[p.21]

Yet we continue these weekend parties and, conscious of Joe's grief, I with a thousand excuses, continue to dissolve. I explain the pressures: Stel practically sneers & returns with relief to Leda. Joe whines in the night and wraps unwillingly his arms about me. I diffidently devote myself to Antonio but afraid of overmothering, find myself leaving him to other mothers. Joe is full of charity. His eyes scream Christlike devotion, what

---

21 William S. Burroughs, *The Naked Lunch* (New York: Grove Press, 1959).

he has learned through this Israel affair. I am as irritable throughout as Anne Buttrick, avoiding, however, venting my feelings on Antonio, who exists quite separate as usual, like some egg yolk in a saucer, pour a little oil on him and he'll keep a week.

A passive child, though his private world is more violent than mine.

On the beach: lying in this sun is toil, watching the biddies careen....

[p.22]

ODOS [?]OYS

Emotion has to burst like a boil. Men fight, I weep, groan, shout, cry. Why? Because on the beach I sit with the women and the men cavort like seals, doing men's things and barking. Even Antonio barks. The little girls fuss & fiddle. I play with my hateful nail polish, bulge my belly under the bikini—at the end of the day scream & dissolve. Some kind of prison.

So emotion seems to burst, and then builds again—Stel and Leda reject us in the most knowing way—by which I mean you know there are contretemps and their please do, though cordial, has you feel another meaning beyond their power: as a couple you must realise that of course they have other obligations (this introverted handwriting) as a couple—and isn't it nice to see them together again as a couple?—so they take off after having more or less invited you to the beach—and you are bereft & foolish, like hymns only no God shines.

So you boil home with the Buttricks, half-hearted for lunch and inarticulately altercating between yourselves, separate. There's Anne Buttrick half-hearted in the kitchen—suddenly saying...

[p.23]

Cats Trot

So many Cypriots want
to [illegible] your soul
& the Anglo Saxons here)

[p.24]

Saying—half-telling the story.

Never mind what the story says—it proves that the instincts are right.

Leda is not super—but proto-human, whence her serenity.

Stel has needs. Needs to put his trademark on anything he loves, takes, desires, admires (oh, possessive about Joe already)—and Antonio is like this—one must remember...

Stel needs to make things, and women.
I used to be admired.
Pussy's whispers

[p.25]

Anne & Phil Buttrick
Cyprus & Montana equated

[p.26]

And so—Joe hears Anne's story, says he's a monkey if it's true—back on the merrygoround [*sic*]. Anne says Leda is like A; Anne looks to us as if she is A—I mean has all those characteristics she grouped under A when she accused Leda.

Mind you I still don't trust serenity.

I also know that Anne has longed for Stel...
It makes you want to sew or pot or count marbles, doesn't it?

[p.27]

Mirror writing is fantastically easy
when one is drunk but not now [22]

Basic truths in a bouzoukhia nightclub over ouzo & mezé, drowning out exaggerated amplifiers.

Life gets simpler as we sail & swim, but sitting on the beach is as usual destructive. The men get bored and wander off to their boats and masks or cylinders, the women resent having to watch the children, gossip maliciously.

Malice, I think, sets in chiefly with idleness, this enforced idleness in which we are captives of heat, children, husbands and distance. If only the sun were not too bright for reading, the book not miles away, the children not irritable and scorched, Joe not off on a boat ... I lie grumbling to Anne—who exercises her malice, and it is as if she were scraping a broken fingernail on my sunburnt thigh. Joe has forgotten to shave & to-night will be much the same. Ian has taken the cold drinks to the boat. Stel is unwilling to amuse us (how he hates lying on the beach!)—why do we inflict these outings on ourselves.

Antonio & I shall find a cave to live by the sea, wearing only bits of cloth around our sensitive parts;

22 In the original text, these words are written backwards.

[p.28]

we shall live on lemons and vine leaves and sheep, dive for Byzantine coins.

Grace Sturgeon blocks out the sun before us. "Have you all been deserted again—come to us!" She is an American, big in spirit and thigh, outcast with her beachcombing Englishman, a specialist at the rescue, bringing us to the shade. We have wet ourselves again and trail off carrying baskets, extra bikinis and babies, flipping our flip flops to the shade of her orange grove. Nigel has strung up fragments of Byzantine glass in the breeze. The tinkle is solid and fugues with the ice.

After the weekend we vow to spend a fortnight on our own by the sea. Joe and Antonio both want that care: we shall fill it with books and leave it only to swim naked at the extremities of the day. We shall be pastoral, parochial, idyllic ... only there is my report, Joe's thesis.... "Come to Israel." "No, you stay here." Hell, it's too hot...

So we go to the mountains...

[p.29]

Economy

[p.30]

Suddenly very tired of Cyprus. Nothing seems genuine, it's all midway between the primitive and the hypercivilised with shepherds toting plastic waterbottles (reed-embossed). Profoundly inartistic. Oh, I'm grumbling, but now in the heat one never stops to glory in the crowds of carob trees. The fields are lumpy and harsh—you can't count on the outside world anymore, and never have I found personal relations so unsatisfactory.

Now that his sore has a tidy scab, Joe is clinging. Now that he has patched his quarrel with Leda, Stel is capriciously inattentive, and as he becomes more friendly with Joe, hang dog when he attends—as if I wanted him.

Oh but I do, but with an abstract hunger. He has become a splendid representation and any—oh I'm a trickster and a pig, the way I lead his glint.

He's too big a person to be accused.

The Buttricks have become a quarrelsome bore. I begin to understand about weather. About dissolving in the tropics.

Antonio grows thin & feverish & whiny. I want to slap him: it's like being slapped myself. Continuity vanishes. Somehow life takes place in the livingroom & the bar. No one has anything to say. We try to cure this by reading but have not the energy to discuss.

[p.31]

Great lakes on a map
like a bow knot

Easier to be holed up in an office not communicating

[p.32]

So we think there is no possibility of continuing and fly away to the sea. Three on a motor scooter (rented) bathing....

___ · ___ · ___ · ___ · ___

We have to push off sooner or later the old bat redwigged said....

Reading D.H. Lawrence. He is terribly right but one must remember that the social structure has changed. He seemed perfectly appropriate to the Canada I grew up in, which had its colliers, working class structure imposed early on. And he is still frighteningly appropriate to my own feelings, but surely not true to the way other people think, viz Antonio.

[p.33]

A Reading List

The novel: English
c 18
Jane Austen
Evelina
The Vicar of Wakefield
Moll Flanders
Jonathon Wilde   Journal of the Plague Year
c 19
Dickens: GE DCBR BH
Scott: Bride of Lammermoor cf Dicken's Women
Thackeray: Vanity Fair, Esmond.
Butler: TW of All Flesh, Erewhon
Alice
c 20: Hardy: The Return of the Native
S. Maugham: The Moon & Sixpence; Cakes & Ale.
The Forsythe Saga.
Arnold Bennett: Anna of The Five Towns. etc
V. Woolf: To the Lighthouse
EM Forster: Where Angels Fear to Tread.
Americans:

Fitzgerald – Great Gatsby
Hemingway – A Farewell to Arms
Short Stories
Schulberg: The Disenchanted (About Fitzgerald)
Salinger: The Catcher in the Rye
For Esme with Love & Squalor
Franny & Zooey.
Cather: Shadows on the Rock
A.B. Guthrie: These Thousands Hills
Stegner: The Big Rock Candy Mountain

[p.34]

Van der Post Venture to the Interior
The Dark Eye in Africa
The Lost World of Kalahari

Paton: Cry, The Beloved Country.

Moorehead The White Nile
The Blue Nile
Slocum: Sailing Alone Around the World.

[p.35]

Clean rooms
plan the dinner
shop for Barbara
take shoes in
cinema

EUVRARD[23] 113 rue du cherche-midi
Paris 6me

Mezé Lounza
Salad-stuffed tomatoes
Chip & yoghourt dip in new dish
Fried Halloumi
Devilled Eggs
Orange Sections
Bread sticks
Peanuts

Call Willis
Pay Papadopoulos
Reno

23 Michel Euvrard, a friend of Engel. See *Cahier* IX, footnote 2 for further reference.

Olives	Dinner
Figs	Money
Chop a lot of onions:	4
	2
Lettuce	4
Tomatoes	2
Yoghourt	Bennetts?
1 doz. eggs	Lolis & Lella

Cahier III[1]

She saw things no one else saw & put them in a personal mosaic: but baroque [1].

This *cahier* comprises two draft narratives that converge on passages of personal introspection. The first narrative [1-4] presents characters from *Sarah Bastard's Notebook* and showcases Engel's talent for dialogue. The second and longer draft narrative starts on the last page of the *cahier* and reads "backwards" to page seven.[2] It is part of the murder mystery that Engel wrote while in Cyprus (1962-64). Howard Engel had suggested that she try her hand at writing a thriller. The resulting "Death Comes for the Yaya" was never published, though Engel incorporated it in ingenious ways into her third novel *Monodromos*. Murder mysteries, Marian Engel concluded in a later journal,[3] were not her *forte*. They were to be Howard Engel's, who created the successful Benny Cooperman series, beginning with *The Suicide Murders* (1980).

An interesting feature of the draft material for "Death Comes for the Yaya" is the role played by a diary. The latter belongs to the murder victim, Barbara. Seen by most as little more than a beautiful blonde, Barbara is revealed in the pages of her diary as a complex and talented person. "The journals told not a story of Barbara's infidelities but a story of life's infidelities to a spirit and a talent which had been originally very pure and special" [42].

Inserted amongst the pages of *Cahier* III is a newspaper clipping featuring a photograph of two actors on a motor scooter in Paris—Philippe Forquet and Jean Seberg, star of the film *Joan of Arc*. Engel might have saved this clipping as much for the look of carefree independence evoked by the photograph as for reasons related to her writing.

---

1 1962-63, khaki-covered Cyprus notebook on which Engel has written "III," "Novel," "Death Comes for the Yaya" and "Monodromos"; 64 pages used.

2 For purposes of clarity here, the narrative has been reproduced "as it reads"—that is from the back to the front of the *cahier*. Hence, *cahier* page numbers are not in normal sequential order.

3 *Cahier* IX [15].

[p.1]

"I can tell you about his wife—she's a rather fat and desperate woman."

"Babs Rutherford—Bounne's sister."

But I did not think I wanted to hear the story from those mouths—one a carp's mouth with coffee-stains, the other niggling[?]. What did they know? Lucy Carpenter could tell a year's story but it would not be about his wife. I had heard her weave spells before—a fine story-teller, but not a true one: she saw things no one else saw & put them in a personal mosaic: but baroque. I had heard what she said about me. Carp Carpenter, kids called her, knowing she valued them for scandal.

Marge Rush was all family: born intertwined with other hands, clutching tendrils of nieces and branches of suppurating male

[p.2]

cousins, sucking the family tree, screaming but no tits.

"Actually I think I'd rather leave it for another day."

The two heraldic harpies drank each other's [*sic*] eyes. They ought to have been tristesses [?]. "The coffee pot's not empty. Have some more."

It is obvious that I'm greedy. What did she say about me "A man-eater in the vampire sense? A sponge." What she means is that I'm a bit dry for love. But she won't get me.

"I knew her," Lucy began against my diffident eyes, "I knew her when she was a graduate student at McGill."

"Ronnie," Marge put in, "was the sort the Americans call 4F."

[p.3]

"She's fattened him up."

"If anyone could."

"I knew Babs better—the sister—y'know she only re-married about four years ago."

"Son's about twelve now."

"Then how old is she?"

"Babs? About forty-two?"

"Not Babs—Margaret."

"Must be thirty-seven."

"Looks older."

"She stayed quite young until a year or so ago—caved in."

Warning looks are exchanged.

"Margaret's a character."

"But she keeps a dirty house. So unlike the others. I remember the other two—Babs and Leda—such a

[p.4]

name!"—(Indignation: WE don't give Canadians fancy names).

You can't fade away from a staff room & a coffee pot & two old trout, if they knew it.

"God ____ the dentist!" I screamed.

And ran.

Sometimes I love my old bods. As the only genuine original foot-sitter, I collect them. Only they see too much & know too many people.

The only thing that you can do with a name like Ronald Parker is put a sir on the front of it—or a Dr. For Ph.D.

They needn't think I can't.

[p.5]

I don't think H. has any feeling of obligation towards the world.
N. would like to be this way.
But N. is not as nice...
I am too prejudiced to comment.
He has no real quality.
I feel like a bull
[just call me Europa][4]

We are free to give our best to each other
This is the tragedy of marriage
(But we don't)
Howard is the only man I have ever liked more in presence than in imagination. I am away to restore his freshness.)

[p.6]

[...]

[p.43][5]

VIII

Barbara

If you have ever observed children in an unsentimental way, as I was forced to do when I was teaching, you will have noticed that even the most carefully raised are horrifyingly uncivilised. People are not naturally nice.

---

4 Engel repeats this (and the comments that follow about Howard Engel), in *Cahier* IX [10]. Europa was a Phoenician princess who was adored by Zeus. In an attempt to win her over, Zeus took the form of a beautiful white bull and tricked Europa to climb onto his back. He then kidnapped her and swam off with her across the sea to Crete. Square brackets appear in the original text.

5 This is beginning of the second draft narrative that starts on the last page of the *cahier* [43] and reads "backwards" to page [7].

When I was reading Barbara's endless diaries on the submarine rocks this feeling I had when I was watching children in my classroom, of seeing humanity with its teeth bared, returned so strongly that I would plunge distractedly into the water to see through my mask the comforting flat-sided fish, the grey coral, the black urchins ... a cleaner world than ours.

[p.42]

Yet, strangely, the impression of nastiness I got had no reference to Barbara herself. The cramped, neurotic handwriting told a story I had to wash off myself, as the white cranes dangled by, and the white lilies forced themselves out of the sand to bloom.

The journals told not a story of Barbara's infidelities—but a story of life's infidelities to a spirit and a talent which had been originally very pure and special. They were skilfully written—and day after day as I sat reading on the rocks or in my white hotel room, with my watchdog police man a discreet distance away, day after day I wanted to scream and weep for her distorted life.

[p.41]

The diaries were, in a way, chronological, beginning about five years ago, when Tony was posted to Malta. The first one was a regular account of her early life and included a marvellous description of hunting with the horsey set in Bucks. A totally ordinary upper-middle class childhood had been forced on the bland child like an iron maiden. She had done a secretarial course after school, made her debut, and quickly married Tony, an eligible deb's delight just beginning in the foreign service. All this was told as if it were totally unreal—seen through a goldfish bowl. You could feel the thin glance of her vague blue eyes as she told it all—playing her rôle of

[p.40]

delicious blond with super Mummy & Daddy, nice, nice, Tony, influential grand-dad—and all the time wanting more, more, more.

Wanting to know, wanting to communicate. Wanting to show someone that the gorgeous husk—which was in no way altered by the birth of two sons—hid a—no, not a mind, and I hate to talk about spirit because it's such a YMCA-misused term—shall we say, a life?—which was quite, quite different from that which anyone had seen.

I read those diaries praying for some kind of coup de foudre—some breakthrough with Tony or more likely with someone else, which would release

[p.39]

the real Barbara into someone's perceptions.

Yet it never happened. The tone in the journals grew increasingly self-centred and embittered. Finally, they were posted to Cyprus.

By this time she was a different woman. The Cyprus diaries—which Tony must have attempted to read—were a simple chronicle of bitter and straightforward infidelities. The men began with A and at the end—one of the last entries must have been written the day I interrupted her at Af's studio—she was at H (Harry?—or was she merely being maddeningly alphabetical.)

What emerged, after I had spent three days reading the

[p.38]

pile of green Philip & Tracey "Leander" exercise books—was particularly the hypocrisy of women like Nora and me: the determinedly faithful demons of domesticity (Not that I wanted to be—but O Barbara, I was conditioned—you broke away).

She might, even in Cyprus, have met a man—who could really love her—give something to her & appreciate the quality of her feeling for experience. A man to whom she could talk. But she was by this time so cynical that no one could take her very seriously. "A" could say to her: "You're basically wild as a fish" and "C"—"You'll do anything with me as long as you don't get Tony into hot water—What if

[p.37]

you get me into hot water?" What if someone had said to her "You're basically as intelligent & as perceptive as you are beautiful?" Would she have had to blur her blue eyes at the Brigadier?

Bill came one day & found me crying at the diaries. "Why did you just use her?" I cried. "Why did you all just play the foul male?"

"I was afraid," he said simply. "Afraid to fall in love with her. Tony would never have let her go—nor Nora me. When I felt her pulling at me, I ran away." He threw me a hangdog look I chose not to understand.

"And Harry?"

"Harry has been loving you for too long to take her seriously—

[p.36]

once a man has loved an intelligent woman—zut—alors—he is a prisoner. He cannot bear the thought of her mockery."

So—mockery—that was me.

"You are quite wrapped up in these diaries. May I read them?" He fingered one tentatively.

"No—they are not for the eyes of a man."

"All right. But what are you going to do with them?"

"Return them to Tony, perhaps?"

"Are you going to use them to find out who murdered her? It should be easy."

[p.35]

Bill's comment returned me to pedestrian reality. It was up to me to decipher the names of her lovers. To run down this alphabet (was 8 a lot of lovers for two years? It made 3 months for each—too long for her sporadic descriptions).

"All right," I said to Bill, "I'll go over the list with you. But tell me —what have you found out?"

"There were no strangers in the village that week—except for you and me, your friend Mrs Wender, and the English family. They were based at Akrotiri & there is no evidence that Barbara knew the man."

"Go on."

"No English people have come on the bus since the 18th

[p.34]

of August."

"Go on."

"The shepherd who dips his sheep off the rocks where you swim thinks you have a pretty figure—but you should wear the top of your bathing suit all the time."

"Thanks."

He was sitting on the spare bed in my little cubicle room. Against its whiteness he looked very dark and droll, and through the window those jagged, rustic mountains & their Lusignan-turrets loomed at him. He had tried to put lightness into the conversation & failed. There was something he was holding back.

"Liz, come for a walk."

So we trod the thorny fields, not down to the abandoned

[p.33]

sulphur springs, but up to the green, propped carob trees, where we lay down in pretended relaxation. Suddenly he took my arm. "Look."

Down in the bay the treacherous taut fisherman had thrown a charge of dynamite. "They are making the new Cyprus, the bastards," he commented.

We sat silent for a while in comforting closeness. Sharing an as yet unnamed misery. Finally:

"Liz, we are in trouble."

"Why?"

"Both Harry & Nora have been here last week"

Somehow it was no surprise to me.

"Let's go back to the hotel & talk over beer."

[p.32]

The working out: The First A and several of the others had only been passing fancies. Their actions had been somewhat cynically and clinically described, but they were never referred to again after the original entries. B. and C. however, appeared to have been "chronic lovers"—their intrigues had lasted from a period shortly after the Beatrice's arrival up to a month before her death. At first everything had been scrupulously arranged—later, it appeared, she had felt free to keep in open contact with them. This indicated that at least one was an habitué of the Brigadier, and that they had both been here longer than Harry & me. If Bill had been speaking honestly, the dates were wrong for him, too … which left Af, Adrian, Colin Sandhurst (whose three-year posting was just about finished),

[p.31]

Firos—and all the people I didn't know.

A.B.C. D. might well have been Bill. I rather gloated over that (who was high-handed, athletic and quickly annoyed). You could see that he was a dear, but not her medicine.

E? An American airforceman passing through. I refused to think about whether F or G or H was Harry—they were all brief seductions of men brassed off by nesty [?] wives. So be it. It happens to everyone. There but for the Grace of God.…

But with the coming of the summer the material of the diaries had changed from heavily literal accounts of love affairs to worried speculations about Tony. How much did he care? How

[p.30]

much would her admittedly contemptible conduct affect his career? There was talk of a promotion of some sort—and certainly of late he had been doing a lot of confidential work. But the diplomatic was so personal. Would they consider her a suitable wife? She had talked this over with Af during the portrait-painting sessions—though they had been friends before, and she had apparently used his studio for assignations (did he peer through the skylights?) and he had apparently been encouraging. It was he who had pointed out to her that both abortions & murders could be arranged for £15 in Cyprus—so she was safe. Anyone who interfered with Tony's career—exo. He had even offered (covetous, impecunious Af!) to keep a £15 deposit.

[p.29]

In between discussions with Af she amused herself lunching & swimming with the ever faithful B and C. She seemed, indeed, to derive a perverse pleasure from decorating the same spot of turf on Wednesday with C that she had adorned on Tuesday with B. Where in the parched hostile summer landscape of Cyprus she found to hide herself was the mystery. (Harry and I had given up the search for places for bucolic love-making.

There were always shepherds or carob pickers), but when B was ingenious, C profited next day, and fair was fair in a queer sort of way.

Therefore—B and C both had cars. Af, Adrian and The White Russians twins (fancy that!) were out. They had

[p.28]

ACROPOLIS, Hammersmith King Street

long lunch hours—Paul Duncan was out—he lunched with Sandra always. One of them had the afternoon off in summers—so it had to be Colin Sandhurst, with his big, white, tax-free car, and unemployed afternoons, and angry wife. The other? Firos, perhaps, if he had the staying power, but I rather suspected he preferred to take poules to horror films during siesta.

———— . ————

Goes back to Nicosia via Cyprus. Bill who takes her to Nora, who is in a state—I would have liked to kill her—but she asked me there & never showed up herself. She said it was terribly important & if it came out, it would affect me and Bill & you and a lot of other people.

[p.27]

Lunch there—then a swim—Bill suggests she was blackmailing someone in return.

[...]

Colin Sandhurst an improbable suspect. Everybody knew about all her affairs. Unlikely that more damage could be done. Therefore she had let out a secret which would affect them all? Or perhaps it was first a story to raise money to protect Tony.

Passing by Sandhurst to Tony's—quarrel.

[p.26]

Stops to ask Tony what would hurt his career most....

"Communistic implications"—but no one could make them—he was clear—always had been.

Then—I suppose a really public scandal about my wife—like this last trumped-up rape case, or a charge of buggery, or something....

I kept putting off going back to the empty house—whether it was a widow's feeling I had, or a naughty child's, I kept turning my car down the wrong streets.

Bar scene:
Paul: Do you know who that is, smoking on the corner over there—it's the local Don Juan, Dr Stavros Onisiforou. He's in a fine state. This morning your Mrs Wender accused him of having bereft her of her maidenhead when she was 18.
Me: He's the gynaecologist down the street.

[p.25]

P: and a pretty dapper fellow at that.
Sandra: Looking a bit lost without Barbara.
P: That's gossip, Sandra, you'd better watch out.
Sandra: Well, Paul, everybody knows they've been driving past our place every Thursday at 12:15 for years & years.

B, B, beautiful B!

Paul: Your Mrs Wender is the only woman I've ever seen put him at a loss. He looked as if a phantom from the dim past had bitten his_hand. I was in here at 10 when she did her recognition scene & I can tell you, it was pretty powerful stuff. She accused him of

[p.24]

despoiling her youth, putting a knot in her marriage—
Sandra: I bet he was efficient even then…
Liz: And later she became a local authority on ancient Greeks!
Paul: She probably got that from her father. Still—I haven't seen old Stavros look so shaken since they told him he'd have to pay all his back income tax. Still—how are you getting on with the detective work?
Liz: Who told you?
P: Mrs Wender, who else. She said you were nosing about Davlos with Barbara's journals under your arm?
Sandra: Gorging on beautiful fish, more likely.
Liz: And chips—and KOUPES—and olives, grapes & watermelon—halloumi, tomatoes, haricot beans—everything.

[p.23] [6]

He had been waiting half an hour to put this question in the right way. I thought I had better waste an equal amount of time fishing for the right answer.

6 The following sentence, appearing at the top of [23], reads like the author's instruction to herself "—P [Pass, Engel's nickname]—Find a sacrificial victim yet so we can all have our catharsis!"

"Who needs money here?" I asked.

"I do," Firos interrupted. "I hope Af comes in to-day; he owes me a lot of money."

"You'll never get if from Af," Paul said. "Not unless you get the American lady to buy one of his pictures." He said this very loud & I saw Dr Onisiforou shift uncomfortably on the end stool. He was getting a bit owlish … I would tackle him later.

"Af should be making a bit these days." Paul was getting tight enough to distribute more of his tid-bits of information. "I hear he's been making keys again."

[p.22]

Adrian growled. "I wouldn't mind one to Barclay's Bank."

"He does marvellous phoney Byzantine cows, too," Sandra giggled. The summer had hit us all pretty hard.

"Let's get him to make an ignition key to a helicopter & get off this island."

"I'll never forgive you for Mrs Wender, Liz," Adrian mumbled—"the grilling she gave me!"

"She must know a lot about all of us by now." This from Firos.

"Dr Onisiforou," I called down the bar—"How did you like Davlos?"

His manicured fingernails moved to his mouth; he rolled his debonair eyes. "Davlos? I have no patients in Davlos."

"I thought you'd been there for a cure."

"Oh," sigh of relief, "I went one day

[p.21]

last spring—when we were at Kantara for Easter. Yes—it's—very nice."

No change there. Everything suddenly blurred and dreary. "It's not fair," I burst out.

"What's not fair"—Paul

"They give me this job to do & nobody's any help. How am I supposed to know if Barbara went to the yiayia?"

"Ask Dr Stavros—he works on the same street."

The gynaecologist turned cowed, weary eyes on us—the boy who'd been at the cookie jar. "Yes—she went—and was refused."

"But why did she go?" I breathed. "Who was after her for money?"

"Only the old lady knew. She wouldn't tell me."

"When did she go?"

"The day before the old one was sent

[p.20]

[Small sketch of a woman's head]

[...]The day before she was killed. Now you know why Barbara was frightened." He spoke with such pallor of spirit that I suddenly liked him. If he had been B—he might even have loved her. His neat little bird-like wife was after all absorbed with her social position, her mother, her children. "Dr Stavros," I began, but was interrupted by the quarrelsome explosion into our circle of the Sandhursts. "But Colin, you are a pig—we can't afford it, you know how Af charges. And Tony will want it..."

"Stop shouting at me, you brindled bitch—do you know what this French apple tart did to me today?"—addressed to anyone who would listen—"she picked a murderous fight at the top of her lungs when the wing-commander

[p.19]

next door was giving a luncheon—everybody heard her. I'm finished in the R.A.F."

"And I, for one, am glad," Guinèvre snapped. "Give me a brandy sour, Firos."

Their public quarrels were always unpleasant: this one was an insult to its audience. Adrian mumbled about moving off to his "office" (a room in a warehouse where he wrote commercials to read over the C.B.C. English service) Sandra muttered about the baby-sitter. Dr Stavros Onisiforou said loudly "If Mrs ___ will allow me—I will accompany her to her house on my way to my office. I have something to say." Paul gave me a deeply visual OK. We were the first to leave, without a good-bye to Colin & Guinèvre.

[p.18]

"One doesn't often see you there," I began.

"It is not my bar—are you taking your car?"

"Let's walk."

"No—to-day, I wanted to see the scene of the crime."

"But that was Davlos."

"Is it not obvious one of her English friends has killed her? No Cypriot would go to all that trouble—carrying her up a hillside to a carob store. We are a lazy people, Mrs Liz."

"Perhaps."

"You are not convinced? I will tell you. You know I was her lover?"

"Of course."

"I was very—fond of her—you say? Yes. She was impossible, but very nice. Good, neat—and—I have a bad reputation with women, but I

[p.17]

restrain myself when I must. This Barbara—it is not often you find a woman who allows you perfect sexual freedom."

I wondered if he knew she'd been passing it on. But could anyone see old Stavros lugging a wet body up those rocks? "When did you learn she was in trouble?"

"Only a few days before she died. She told me she had been to the Yiayia—and asked me for money. But as you know, I am something of a miser. And if you start lending money to your mistress, where will it end? When I advised her to go to her husband, she told me it was to save him that she wanted the money."

"Did you give her anything?"

"Finally—£100."

"Did she ask you to go to Davlos?"

[p.16]

<u>Reunion in Paradise</u>

"Never—after the first time—at Easter. I slipped away from my wife."

"Did she like it there?"

"Very much. She thought it was some kind of paradise."

So that was that. Automatically she picked it as a refuge.

Passing Nikos' house, we saw that it was still draped in black. Maro was taking it hard. "Are the police interested in Nikos?"

"They are playing with him, although since Barbara has died—panagia mou—they take him less seriously."

Since I had begun to like him, since the old panama-hatted seducer knew something, I asked him in for a drink.

"Harry," I called, "Harry." No Harry.

Quiet courtyard, abandoned

[p.15]

looking. Dead. House as I had left it—one empty glass on the coffee table. I went to the fridge, & returning heard Dr Stavros behind me—"Panagia mou—pan—a-gi—a mou!"

I wheeled—and saw Bea Wender, so much like an old dead crow, suspended from one mespil tree.

XI

It was the only time in my life I have ever fainted and I regret it severely. Instead of going thro' her handbag I apparently lay in my own courtyard moaning for Harry. Instead of inspecting the house, I had to be resuscitated by

[p.14]

smelling salts. Woke to find Bea Wender, poor dried bird, laid on the tiles too near me, and Dr Stavros flitting worried between us, muttering "Béatrix, Béatrix –"

"Listen," I remember saying, "all I want is that Harry."

The police seemed a bit suspicious, and I don't wonder. Why should I mess up their precincts with so many murders? Nikos was brought in & looked at me balefully—obviously all this was holding up the probate of the Yiayia's will. Yes, Mrs Wender—if that was her real name—had been to see him—asking too many questions—what right had she. Of course Barbara had tried to borrow money from the Yiayia, but she never lent to English people, since interest had been set by

[p.13]

the English before the Troubles at 19½%—she charged 15—sometimes 20—it was bad business to lend to the English—they might tell.

No, he had not heard their conversation. The Yiayia always sent them downstairs—and made sure they went.

Dr Stavros, tragically embarrassed, admitted having known Barbara "rather too well", but denied his old affair with Bea. "She was a crazy woman -- very bad luck" he kept repeating. I thought he was not many generations away from his village [illegible]....

Paul turned up suddenly & packed me in his minute Fiat. "I've told Bill to get hold of Harry," he said, "You need him, now."

[Loose page, tucked into notebook with clipping]

March 30.

There doesn't seem to be anywhere to go in this house & we are depressed: the last two days without a sense of direction—one longs for even a suicidal decision. First my hysteria. Then Howard's depression.
I wear old cloth & wonder have I lost a baby. Possible. But not worth exploring to-day, except that one longs to find a reason for pain & cruelty.
No mood for the children of Israel & the Chanteclair. No mood for much. But we have books—a worthy Patrick White kick.
Mine seems to have dropped dead. Want a good visual beginning.
Howard wants a good something. Does he brood as darkly as Me? I eat his guts, not wanting to, but, part carnivore by nature, I tear at him until breeding cries out. Guilt. Scuffling sulks. Then up again, each time higher, until we make music.
He used to eat me too ... but he is too kind.
"Didn't say anything" means "of importance."

Davlos, Lily Bay, page 12

[Loose page, opposite side]

Knockout Af & Kays
business...

[Insert, captioned photograph of a couple on a scooter][7]

[p.12]

[Drawing of Davlos, Lily Bay]

[p.11]

Party

The Duncans did the sensible thing and threw a sort of wake that night and everybody but Tony came—even the gynaecologist who was just about as dazed as I was. Firos closed the bar early, Bill and Nora came up from Famagusta. The Sandhursts looked especially smart—a sign of further discord in the bungalow; Af & Adrian turned up with the white Russian twins—a quartet of saltimbanques. In the still centre, Paul & Sandra, composed & ironic as ever, pouring from flagons of village wine, helping. I decided to get a little drunk—try to annihilate the pressure in my breast—try to elucidate the riddle of our lives: things are always clearer when you're a few sheets to the wind. Sandra put on some dance records—music belonging to our own pie

[p.10]

twist era. For a while, like a patient just out of a mental hospital, I just sat & watched—thinking about the people—thinking how little, on this island of

7 The caption reads: "SIGHTSEEING IN THE FRENCH STYLE—Actress Jean Seberg hitches ride behind French actor Philippe Forquet as they scoot through streets of Paris. She played the title role in Joan of Arc."

comings & goings, we knew about each other. We had spent a lot of time together—a lot of good drinking time—exchanged a lot of confidences, but Bill and Nora were the only ones of whose inner miseries & dreams I had any apprehension at all. I knew, for instance, that Adrian had held several responsible positions in England before coming here—but what was driving him to this daily anaesthesia? (We were all good topers[?], but with the rest of us it was a summer thing.) He could barely support himself here & lived in terror of his creditors banding together & having him deported home. And Af?

[p.9]

An odd, merry soul, who poached his rent money in goods & services, guiding tourists, painting portraits, designing rings. Firos a simple soul—but what Levantine deviousness behind his lazy, hooded eyes? The white Russian twins were permanent war refugees—they took turns wearing a doorman's uniform at the Hungarian embassy and lived together in a crab-like gloom. The Sandhursts—they must have been quite nice people before they decided to sand-paper each others' nerves. Oh the hell with them, I thought, and accepted Bill's invitation to dance.

"I'm going to pretend to be much dumber than I am, I whispered.

"You won't have to try too hard."

"How's Nora?"

"Smooth as cream. She was away

[p.8]

only that one day."

I drifted off with Paul. Guinèvre will have my neck if you get any closer—I shouldn't have minded if she'd been strung up instead of your Mrs Wender."

"Why my Mrs Wender?"

"One tends to put Americans & Canadians in the same box. Liz, you know I couldn't have done this one: I've been safe with my bloody wife all day."

"When were you last at Davlos?"

"Just—after Easter. With Barbara. They killed us a chicken at the hotel; you can ask."

Paul: "We're counting on you, Liz."

[p.7][8]

The ending—suddenly realising it's a "no girls in the Mounties" situation & she is being kept away from Nicosia. Adrian is involved with

8 See pp. 63-65 for the first six pages of this cahier. Pagination resumes at [44].

1) The Murderer
2) Harry
or
3) His own red herring

She turns up country, saying she has no petrol. Offers to let Adrian out: pretends she knows the road & that she is afraid of him.
Arrives in Nicosia—what happens?

[pp.44-56]

[More narrative involving Liz, Harry, Nora, "Cyprus Bill, etc.]

[p.57]

<u>ΠΑΡΑΔΙΣΟΣ</u>

Why is Bea so bloody interested?

She takes the diaries to Cyprus Bill and reads them in <u>Davlos</u>?
"Nora, I have to borrow your husband."
Confides her worries to Bill—
about Harry.
"You had better go home, then, &
see what he says when he
turns up." What does Bill
know?
Why does Nikos look embarrassed?
It seems from the diaries
to be Tony or Adrian.
Bea picks Adrian.

Two murders—are they
connected—Bea thinks so.
What is the connection between the victims? Has Barbara
borrowed money?
Finally asks Maro—yes.

ΜΑΓΔΑ
ΜΑΡȢ
ΡΕΝȢ
ΣΤΆVΡΟ
ΚΛΟΔΙΝ
ΜΑΡΚΟΣ
ΧΡΙΣΤΗΆΝ
ΧȢȢΥΑΡΝΤ
ΜΆΡΙΑΝ
ΠΑΣ
ΕΔΟΥΑΡΝΤ
ΕΝΓΕΛ
ΈΓΓΕΛ
ΜΠΙΚ

[p.56]

TICK: 2 beer &
mezé
1 <u>beer alone</u>
1 wine (mikró)

Everything in Cyprus is
so public? How were
the two murders private? **<u>Must</u>** have been done by a
foreigner. TONY? best motive—yet he is OPEN and heart-broken. Weak. But somehow innocent—not crooked—weak—not without a sense of obligation—it was this that drove Barbara mad.

———— . ———— . ———— . ————.

Well—who could have done it? Any man with a car.
Donkey-hiring. Did anyone?
Foreigners? At the hotel. A tall dark man who spoke Greek. Who saw Barbara?

If Barbara went to Yiayia & both were murdered—it might have been money, not love, the motive.

[pp.58-64]

[More notes and plot outlines for the murder mystery]

Cahier IV[1]

Order and Chaos.
How to remember all that was said and felt and done [1].

The opening pages of *Cahier* IV offer personal reflections on a wide range of topics including marriage, children, femininity, social standards, Engel's belief that "the truth lies in between" and the need to belong.[2] These reflections are followed by draft material related to *Sarah Bastard's Notebook*. In an entry linking personal thoughts on family and femininity with outlines for what would become *Sarah Bastard's Notebook*, Engel asked: "What are the rules? What are the values?" and found for her answer: family solidarity, feminine modesty, chastity and obedience [23]. For Engel's modern-day protagonists (Sarah and her three sisters in *Sarah Bastard's Notebook*), as for the author, societal standards posed a problem when they left little or no room for female desire for adventure, power, self-expression and recognition.

The remainder of *Cahier* IV is committed to notes on Henry Miller and Lawrence Durrell.[3] The research on Miller is vintage Engel. It comprises lengthy lists of books—by and about Miller. "We must look at his w[or]k thro[ugh] the man & pin him down," Engel recorded [38]. Miller's forte was an art that Engel admired—the art of living—a goal she had formulated in her first *cahier*.

Engel's notes on Miller include a chronology comparing his achievements to those of another author who was a major literary influence for her:[4]

---

1 1962-63, khaki green Cyprus notebook, with a cover featuring a caricature of a woman's face, and the words "Tome IV" and "Pass"; 53 pages used.

2 Names of individuals Engel knew in Cyprus and two brief observations on her marriage, are not included in the reflections reproduced here.

3 Henry Miller (1891-1980) was a New York novelist and essayist whose autobiographical novel *Tropic of Cancer* (1934) was banned for decades in Britain and the United States. He was eventually hailed as a major figure in struggles for literary and personal freedom.

Lawrence Durrell was born in India in 1912, spent his late teens in England, lived in Paris in the 1930s and thereafter in the eastern Mediterranean. He is best known for *The Alexandria Quartet* (1969) and his travel books, including the three "island books": *Prospero's Cell* 1945 (Corfu), *Reflections on a Marine Venus* 1953 (Rhodes) and *Bitter Lemons* 1957 (Cyprus).

4 "Long talk about book-influences—Durrell is becoming a shameful confession!" *Cahier* XVI [19].

Lawrence Durrell. Engel had read Durrell's *Alexandria Quartet* and *Bitter Lemons*. The latter concerned Cyprus, the setting of her murder mystery, "Death Comes for the Yaya," and her third novel *Monodromos*. Excerpts of Engel's notes on Miller are reproduced here for the portrait they provide of Engel as a diligent and thorough researcher.

[p.1]

Order and Chaos

How to remember all that was said and felt and done. For instance S's talent (destructive) for reducing people to a power framework. At the moment this is what he tries most to believe in [...]. His lack of power over me (?) interests him. But the negro girl's complete abasement made him happy without interesting or satisfying him. Is this playing with people Levantine? Hooked nose and half-closed eyelids—you think he is just half-dreaming and later know that the experience has been planned & timed: distressing — but it takes away the need to be anything but oneself.

[p.2]

Strength: The strong are obliged to accept the fact that they must lead the weak. That they are getting something from the weaker which must be paid for in a well reasoned concept of responsibility. The strengths of the apparently weak must not be minimised—one has to remember why one originally felt tied. One has drunk from the well & acquired knowledge (finesse) but cannot just go away.

[p.3]

Marriage: Monogamy is unsatisfactory esp. for those who married for need rather than romantic love, without being able to say "This person will satisfy me completely for the rest of my life"—Thus unless one is very clever, one is forced to choose between destruction & frustration. This is where for a man an old fashioned slave-wife arranged marriage can be satisfying. But it is a cynical choice.

Indubitably marrying out of one's social context is more difficult: & the accompanying liveliness can degenerate into tired quarrelling.

[p.4]

Sex: Relying on sex only drives one into frantic self-disgust. Denial, on the other hand, eventually distorts one's whole life. Feeling absolutely <u>free</u> in all departments is the best relationship but one doubts if it can survive cohabitation.

[p.5]

———————.

[...] Last night—the feeling of the kids who weren't invited to the birthday party. Then—the relief. Then—the feeling of having each other.

———————.

Howard's grace & pain & tact. He is in love with us both.

————————.

[p.6]

Hospital day: Still this terrible urge to protect—or inability to break away from—our more lasting relationship. We keep telling ourselves we couldn't have left it at Dovks[?] for the sake of future flights of fancy. More truly—it has to be repeated—habit, knowledge, etc. And frustration builds—after D we are driven, not driving. In a way he has lost all but physical reality for me. Still they made him out of the black bull & the eagle.

Pub-talk: The Levantine—is—the Canadian mind, the former not being afraid to admit its schemes—therefore commits itself to them & carries them out.
Rather ill-at-ease & preoccupied.

[p.7]

Party coming up & I like a birthday child. I made a not too unsuccessful skirt, press it badly. Jas is coming for lunch—I unwilling.

Remember the New Yorker heading—These Precious Days?

Driving to St Hilarion at night with Sasher—memories of trees. How this is going to haunt me!

PLAN AHEAD.

[p.8]

The Party in the Pines.

[...]

[p.9]

[...] I didn't really plan enough ahead. We should have camped in the clearing.

Our equivocal position.
Diffidence.

[p.10]

<u>**A Monday**</u>

Noon: telephone—can you come to Kyrenia for lunch?
In the car: stiff
(At Theos Stiphado)
S. talks over party—I was the only one who wasn't having a good time. I get more & more resentful & lay it on thick.
At Theo's: Conversation:
1) S. thinks Max is going on the 10th.—is Max a traitor? I go paranoid.

[p.11]

[Get Excerpt of Cypria for H.][5]

A Tuesday
1) Revise your ideas on marriage & femininity.
2) Always remember that to be a woman you must be desirable.
3) Be honest with people—don't go around doing the proper thing.

This has not worked here.[6]

> Once you decide to run your life by your mind rather than by your emotions, you give up a lot of joy, but you gain power over your life & that is worth everything.

[p.12]

[...]

The woman who ate her husband backwards by forcing him into a weak position & talking about it.

Take 1 good man with an ordinary streak of bum
1 spoiled woman who likes to be top
1 island of friends & brandy
1 constant & cannibalistic friend
2 sets of weaknesses.

[p.13]

So I tried to explain & he almost got me on his side again—but the truth does lie in between—actually in my dishonesty and in our sensitivity.

---

5 Square brackets appear in the original text.
6 This comment was added in the margin.

In my love of crying on other people's shoulders, WHICH MUST STOP. Surely I can make myself happy enough to be useful by exerting a very little pressure. [...]

[p.14]

But look, don't roll over as if it were a nightmare. Pass—what he said is true, true ... and don't be ashamed to be desirable. Lately you haven't even be[en] clean. You can't be & drink so much.

A Paris Book Meanwhile?

[p.15]

Use all this:[7] its effect on a Rhone-character
its unexpected effect on me.

[p.16]

Unhappiness in Canada.

Days of misery—Why?
Similar feelings: SARNIA MONTANA

The not-receiving-an-invitation-I didn't-want-anyway complex.

Desire to have a <u>real</u> platform from which to look down ON—people!

1) I drink more & more
2) I am less & less logical
3) I am less & less sure of my rightness—& of which level things come from: hysteria

[p.17]

WHY:
ME: I feel guilty for too many things.

I am egoistic to an extreme degree & <u>know</u> it.

I am not sure of the standards of the people who criticise me (since we've had chances i.e. everybody knows about the same amount) one has to judge the quality of another person's mind & this is anti-democratic. In Europe, I am more willing to respect, having been not so often disillusioned.

I am on the defensive about being a woman.

I am on the defensive about my own illogical (i.e. emotional) attitudes. Am therefore alternately tearful & aggressive & defeat my own prideful purposes.

---

7 Engel the novelist at work, instructing herself on writing.

[p.18]

THIS COUNTRY:

The NORM is too narrow to make life comfortable—for any but suburbanites & natural rebels. I am not naturally a rebel. I want desperately to belong when there is something around to belong to. Oh God, to be a happy compromising anarchist.
[...]

[p.19]

MARRIAGE:

I do not want to write the hell that I feel I am making Howard's life down. There is an emptiness between us—I made it. He has had to fall back on thinking of me as a foolish female.

. —— . —— .

You can be either good or bad but not both. Some people don't get away with anything. I want to be tough—but when you play with the boys you get hurt. [...]

[p.20]

CHILDREN.

2) The world is overpopulated.
   ∴ having children is self-indulgent.
3) The responsibility of giving a child a world-view is overwhelming.
4) With birth control there are no mistakes. It <u>must</u> be by decision.
5) Since there is no logical reason (i.e. continuation of race) to have a child, the decision to have one must be a decision in favour of self-indulgence. But is it a pleasure to have a child?

[p.21]

NO FURNITURE — The Apotheosis of Polyana

BASICS FOR ANGUS

I live on an island.	I have a house.
I have a child.	I have a wife
I have a mother.	I have a business.
Why ruin it?	

BASICS FOR SARAH

I live no where.	I have nothing (I cannot claim [I] mind)
I am a teacher.	I have no job. I am
no one.	Why go on?

BASICS FOR LEDA

I live on an island.	I have a house.
I have a child.	I have beauty.
I have a husband.	These things are
in a story.	I have no one.

[p.22]

NOTES: THE DECEPTION OF THE THRUSH II

A RECOLLECTION OF DAYS: THE APOTHEOSIS OF POLYANA: NO FURNITURE

1) The Long Day — Despair
2) The Elopement — The Workings of The System.
3) The day of The Chateau: 2 phases.
   (Oliver in Ollioulles—Angus at Night)
   —Europe is an escape/improvement.
4) The Day of The Play & Interview
   The System turns The Screw
5) At the Beach—Impossibility of Adjustment
   Defiance of Subject.
6) The Long Day—How to surrender
   without being taken i.e. appear to submit but then
   violate ALL rules to get freedom.

[p.23]

What are the rules?

	Family	solidarity
What are the values?	Feminine	modesty
	"	chastity
	"	obedience

—— . —— . ——

Play Day— St Ardath's pamphlet
Mr Bastard
The Notebook—The knowing that you will not be understood because you are not big enough to say what you want.

—— . —— . ——

Monologue: Angus
Who we are: background
Where " " —islands, microcosms
What " " vs. others—simple
conniving & landscape
—political (deception)
What we are doing:
Why —empathy vs "values"
—defiance/need/hatred & love of Leda.

How it succeeds
Conseq[uences]—destruction, change, flight

[p.24]

Angus: I have pinned you to an act & its consequences. You accuse me of being Machiavellian. I submit that without admitting it you are also—that is the difference between us. If you were truly teachable....

[p.25]

About HM[8]

1943	HM	Nicholas Moore—England
1946	Happy Rock—SF (Bern Porter, Berkeley	
1945	HM—Chron. & Bib. " " "	
1956	My Friend HM—A Perlès . 9 21 M	
1959	Reunion in Big Sur—A. Perlès.	
1959	Art & Outrage—AP & LD 9 21 M	

[pp.26-34]

[Notes on Miller including a Miller-Durrell chronology]

[p.35]

ART & OUTRAGE [9]

I D to P.

[Idea a longtime—began—Paris: Pix of Miller
(bring back French world.

[Henry on disc now–works not allowed in own country–A-S [Anglo-Saxon] irony. G[rea]ter than Columbus. desc. America of the soul–but had to outrage people. Recognized but still banned.

8 As the list below suggests, Engel consulted the following books: Nicholas Moore, *Henry Miller* (Wigginton: The Opus Press, 1943); Bern Porter, *The Happy Rock: A Book About Henry Miller* (Berkeley: Packard Press, 1945); Alfred Perlès, *My Friend Henry Miller* (London: N. Spearman, 1955); and Perlès, *Art and Outrage: A Correspondence About Henry Miller Between Lawrence Durrell and Alfred Perlès* (New York: Dutton, 1959).

9 Engel used (unclosed) square brackets throughout these notes.

[Can we put works in perspective since only essays, travel books circulate? Unknown, really—genius vs Faulk[ner], H[eming]way–journeymen.
[Can I tempt you? We know him.
[Your portrait—concentrates on the man but leaves mystery. Can we get to it?
[Not anecdotes, use theme: Is art always an outrage?
[HM wanted truth about himself.
[Did he get there?

[p.36]

II AP—LD

[Yes. We could do it best—witnesses to unfolding.
[How? Lists? Synchronise memories—a party with Miller.
[Memories—when you came in, cat was out of bag. Impact—miracle of reality, knowing him.
[But I owe him too much—traumatic, creative shocks—a disciple.
[My gospel dint quite come off. Man OK, work not—tho. intertwined. Must disentangle him from porno. legend. Innocent genius.
[Did that make for his unevenness?
Geniuses often write badly—gems & ash of volcano.

[p.37]

III LD—AP

[Intention of his work often unclear to reader.
Portrait of himself often not real—he says he leaves out good side.
[We must situate his intention & descr[ibe] his masks. Must do this as disciples for posterity.
[No haste. Carbons to HM
[<u>WORKS</u> Cf. other SOLIPSISTS—Casanova, Rousseau, de Sade—but HM religious. Rank's "personality development"—influence?
HM intends to dismantle, reform morality.
Exfoliates—Rabelais-like?
[Intention—spiritual search—shreds body but transcends it—inverted <u>moralist of the soul</u>. Rapport with rhythms of nature.
[Puritan backlash....

[pp.38-46]

[Ongoing Notes from Art and Outrage, Chapters IV-VII]

[p.47]

[No famous philosopher — just himself — nothing new said — just a creator — can make the old new — miracles of freshness.
[Digestion of shark → new interpretations.
[Writing careless but incandescent — what do bad patches matter? <u>Is</u> a writer.

[But an amateur — with no ability to write down.
[Art of living ultimately his forte.
[But T[hank] G[od] none of us are there.
[& TG no plans adhered to by H.
[Loves suffering & laughter—displays his welts—belly laughs too.
[En resumé—there's nothing wrong with Henry

[pp.48-53]

[Notes, mini-budget, library call numbers]

Cahier V[1]

Having men help one onto donkeys in a prurient way.
Am I a puritan? Yes, by God & proud of it! [7]

In *Monodromos*, set on a Greek island, protagonist Audrey Moore hires a donkey to travel to a mountain monastery. She is unaware that the donkey is accustomed to travelling down, not up, the mountain. As a result, Audrey's journey to the monastery is very trying for her, though very funny for the reader.

Entries in *Cahier* V depict a similar real-life journey Engel made during her time in Cyprus.[2] It is not clear if the entries were written during the trip or after, from memory. They are fairly sketchy and many Greek words that Engel jotted are difficult to decipher. The text is nevertheless reproduced in part here for its glimpses of Cyprus as seen through Engel' s eyes. From these quick strokes, Engel was able to create memorable scenes in *Monodromos*.

[p.1]

64651 – Reno

[p.2]

Lithrodonda—Nicosia

Left Nicosia about 8—Mark started me off. Katerina starts at once to head home. Hard to get on her. So we walk through Strovolos. We walk to Tseri. The sun blazes. I meet Costas. He and George help me to get to the village. There are intimate ways of helping a woman onto a donkey. Businesslike ways too! Katerina will not go.

1 1963, red Cyprus notebook, with Greek lettering and the words "Travels with a donkey" on the cover; 30 pages used.

2 Engel made the trip again 1 April—April Fools Day—1971. The author travelled to Cyprus in March 1971 for research purposes—both for an article commissioned by *Maclean's* (payment for which helped fund the trip) and for her novel *Monodromos*.

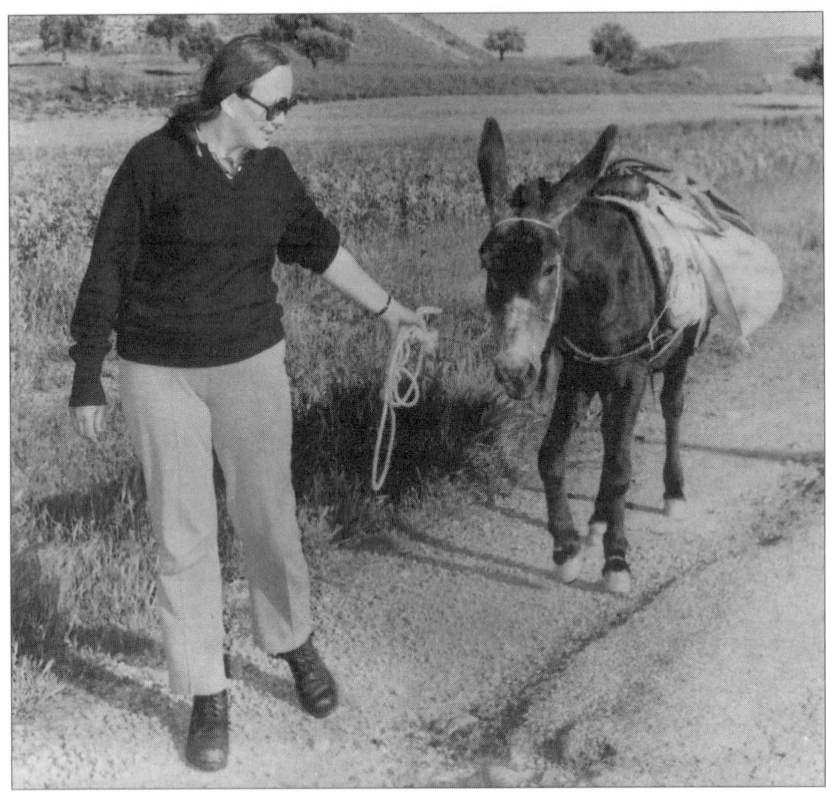

Cyprus 1971

Tseri: Café—Costas & George buy me coca-cola—halloumi olives (old) bread. Prop. has been in Australia. Costas is in the P.O. at Nicosia. George was a sailor.

[p.3]

Smouldering eyes. Costas "a kiss." "No." Why not? One husband is enough.

Tseri—Allionda—hoping to meet S. Nothing. Death in the desert—almost. v. sunburnt.
Allionda—meet Leondias the drover who hitches K[aterina] to his 2 donkeys, thank God. Good man. A cousin of R. Wideson.
Lythrodonda—boiled wheat Fri night—old women offer it. Soldiers & young bucks in restaurant—Kymacon family—they take me home ∵ room full of people.

[p.4]

Innkeeper—Katerina—Leondias says she must have oats—she goes well on oats.

Cold to-day.
Not only cold. It started to piss with rain at the forest station. By the time I reached St Onophoron church—hoping to God it was Maecheras—it was too bad to go on. I was trying to cook nescafe over a devotional candle, feeling, well, what can happen, when a car pulled up—are you going to Maecheras—2 priests. You can' t keep the donkey in the church doorway, etc. Went back in & spilled the nescafe & spent $^1/_2$ hr wiping the church floor, tried

[p.5]

again—saddling again etc. Old donkey, old saddle, wet ropes, blinding rain. Rockslides started. Pulled Katerina. Donkey stopped. We turned around. Just got back to St Onophoron—car pulled up—big bloody mercedes. Unloaded Priest, Panaye the butcher—a small neat Mr Engel, & a man who speaks English. "We are here to take you to Maecheras." So we put poncho & oilskin on Panayi & me in the car—pronto. To kitchen, to fire—coffee heat—then "The abbot will see you."

The abbot has big melting eyes, seems v. intelligent & is called Dionysios.[3] Obviously finds me interesting. He offers red Zuania—it is very good. Coffee. Glibis of almonds on a spoon. Served by a nervous acolyte ... when you are a man of the world—my boy.

[p.6]

The man who speaks English refers constantly to the blighty donkey & says I am too fat for it.

Service—very beautiful in a way, v. tired at others. Everyone kissing the abbot' s hand. Censers. Ikons. Byzantine music. Quavering old voices, bits of conversation. Guests singing the Gospel. Not a new church, but hadn't 4 pillars.

One monk is 102!

M. is an independent monastery.
D. studied here & in Athens.

Saw the dog-headed St X[Christ]opher![4]

---

3 Engel spelled this name in various ways throughout the notebooks. She constructed a similarly named character in *Monodromos*.

4 In *Monodromos*, Audrey's lover, an English poet named Max Magill, has an interest in this saint, and asks her to research it for him during her stay on the island.

[p.7]

The point is does one want to be a tart or not? Does one simply want to get & not to give? God knows how Hand travels but having men help one onto donkeys in a prurient way. Am I a puritan? Yes, by God, & proud of it.

Not to forget: the kindness of the Coracan family. Leondias the drover. The glibis. The long dinner table. 4 monks, the abbot, 3 guests.

[p.8]

Sunday: a lesson in reality
The shaking attentions of Dyonysios, Abbot of Maecheras,
threw everything out of perspective & I was left miserable. Blue-purple dignity & beautiful voice—without him, service is nothing.
HWAT IS YUOR HOPPY? MY HOPPY IS BYZANTINE MUSIC.
No hobby this. "I am a monk, but I am a man etc." Creeps.

The dog-headed Christopher. The old monk 102 "who has loved many women."
Panayi, the butcher who rode Katerina through the storm.

Politics. The mason—there will be trouble with the Turks. Baldish, 45, religious, works for monasteries.
Reads in church.

[p.9]

STON KALON!
The Christening—people from Limassol & Lahatannia—enfant Marius drinking beer instead of brandy—less attractive but more practical.

Monastery wine—light & sweet. Red Zuania: Tharma.

Michaelis from Dali: the realist—"You are the laughing stock of Lithrodonda." But also, about Enosis—"There are drugs all over the world, now."

Leondias—£4 per week.

The Archimandate—a sharp X sava face, a clever man. Leaves no doubt that he knows what is going on.

[p.10]

Crazy weekend—didn't know what was going on last night. Sat & shook. Then the enormous gale—wires & trees down. Couldn't sleep. Dreamt of

S handing me a hotel bill in salt. Mr Michaelis.

That donkey will not go up hill. He's bloody well right.

"You & your blinking donkey."

1. Car comes. Panayi takes the donkey.
2. Get to monastery. I am shown where to pee, given coffee in kitchen.
3. "The abbot will see you now."

Who is who?

Abbot + 2 Staff—servers in service

Archimandate

2 elderly chaps, one 102

[p.11]

tall thin, next chap, long face

curly hair

4 giggly boys—1 the abbot's nephew, one a cherub who is beautiful & can sing

4 away in Athens

= 15, as he said

Asked to take pictures for Christening. Then lunch—taramasalata, bean-soup—good.

The wind roars here & howls Winter!

Drinking troughs for animals—broken bottoms of huge terra-cotta pots.

Birds—partridge—buff & blue swallows, magpies, crows.

[p.12]

Kerosene in an olive oil bottle for the fire.

Don' t forget at least £ for the church.

Old 102 man & his Gk pictures. "They are old" in that scornful voice. Has a sign outside his door. The old man? The Saint? "He liked women very much."

A.M. No one is pacing in front of my door![5] "If you did not have the donkey, you could come to Nicosia with me."

Coming down the mountain—grouse, hare, warblers. Pine like Ponderosa w. big scabby bark.

Katerina v. good until the turn for Lithrodonda.

---

5 In *Monodromos*, Audrey hears someone—her host?—pacing outside her door.

[p.13]

Ayios Heraclectos[?]
    15 nuns
    sewing
    making Glihismata[?]
    shellwork
    ikons
painted white for Easter.
black habits—skirts, tops,
cardigans, shawls.
2 speak French, 1 English.
Maria, etc.
swallows, old capitals, mosaics,
    marvellous ikons.
In the morning 3 did their sewing.
The youngest fed the goats &
did the flowers. Some washed.
Some attached a big motor to
a mixmaster for Glibiswata[?].
Some laid boiled barley out
on blankets for Easter stuff.
Very charming, very French.

[p.14]

A swarm of schoolchildren arrived—bees buzzing.

(Caramondanis plastic yoghurt pot in Lythrodonda)

On the way back—no Denise in Pera. Lots of waves & laughs. At Psomolophou a woman (Maria) asked me into her house for new halloumi, yaourte, coca-cola, bread. Coffee in the café afterwards. A man had a 200-year-old house. The older houses are very good in this village.

Rest-stop by the Pedios—where we did before, just after Deftera.

[p.15]

Everyone waved & made remarks. At Labatamia the grocer offered coffee & oranges. The village idiot photographs. The daughter invites me to her house—we telephone. Poor old Katerina begins to limp.

Coming back—into Strovolos. People are less friendly. (Shaking the Abbots hand instead of kissing it).

Dasoupolis—what a stupid way to go!

But how I have depended on people!
Hilchie's[?] pale Canadian box lunch.

[p.16]

Things to do

1. Call Hilchie
2. Get hotel room Kennedy's Excelsior
3. Get suit
4. Move!

Story: see — Padre
Mens Quarters
New officers

Start with swimming meet at Ledra Palace pool.

See Pananyi Sergio
Sotiri

[p.17]

The top of the flour mill in the heat.
women
saunas
Canadian food

Politics: the mason at Maecheras—There will be trouble in 6 months.

Young marriages with problems. Little privates—one go at the night club & comes home in tears. The wives feel they have volunteered. By himself keep them identifying with each other.
Older guys—separations bring people together.

[p.18][6]

"Little things drop away"
[...]

[pp.19-20]

[...]

[p.21]

Helliers also think there will be trouble soon.

---

6 The balance of [18] and [19-20], regarding some military officers serving on the island, are not included here.

Nicosia Palace—Arabs & English—pleasanter than Ledia.

Get:	worry beads presents all round Hana–Mum–Dad

Hutchison[7] says his is a very young group. Col. Marsau got 112 wives over. Hardest for privates—their wives are very young & they are not free to travel—or accustomed to.

[p.22]

The English are the real travellers.

Xeros—Tent w Maple Leaf flag on painted floor. 4 beds, cane-roofed verandah, padded benches.
Electricians tent—well supplied.

One room passementerie of playboy pictures. Decoupage, rather painted walls, efforts to humanize old factories, gov[ernmen]t buildings. Public Works Dept—fireplaces, unusable because of damaged chimneys.

Are Canadians the dullest people in the world? Yes!

[p.23]

[...]
The Canadians are as pale as their bread.
It is the Irish who get[8]

[p.24]

on with the villagers.
The Nescafe breakfast
this morning—nescafe,
oranges, bad cookies, scone.
But they loved the generosity of the
man who gave them a pail of oranges.
[...]

[p.25]

Canconcyp Bricon
Dancoucyp Swedcon
Unciupol Ircon

7 One of the military men mentioned on preceding page (not included).
8 This line is actually on page [22] of the cahier.

names like names of diseases
lady beggar
but not so many as before
[...]

[p.26]

[...]
300 year old shops on all sides owned by the Turks—once a place for monks of some kind.
Before that?

[p.27]

Things not to forget: smells.
fried halloumi
mines
fennel

[p.28]

If you have £ left
get Georgeakis[?] book.
[...][9]

9 Page [29], which reads only UNFICYP, and [30], which contains an address and what seems to be a dinner guest list, are not included here.

Cahier VI[1]

Sea-kissed Cyprus.
Consecrated to remind me of my country [24].

This is a *cahier* of drawings and lists of Greek vocabulary related to Engel's translation of the poem "Helen" from *George Seferis: Collected Poems, 1924-1955.*[2] The nine pages of drawings feature sketches of cats, clothing, faces, a chair and a woman in a bath.[3] This cahier contains one of Engel's recurring speculations about handwriting. On a page of varying script slants and pressures she asks: "How do I write normally?" [6]. Several pages of the *cahier*, comprising lists of vocabulary or sketches, are not reproduced here.

[p.1]

Ibiza[?] contrast

Cyprus Programme

1. Grimey
2. Bing
3. Root
4. Newcombe
5. Mike
6. Fat George

1. Narrator
2. Eliot Paul
3. Durrell
4. Tourist agent

Sounds — clocks — (studio)
— music
— night to morning sounds
— vendors
— market

1 1963, orange Cyprus notebook, stamped with Greek writing and "32 Ballantine" scribbled diagonally across the cover; 26 pages used.

2 George Seferis, *George Seferis: Collected Poems, 1924-1955*, trans. and eds. Edmund Keeley and Philip Sherrard (Princeton: Princeton University Press, 1967).

3 A cross-reference in the next *cahier* suggests that some of the sketches may been done by Howard Engel. In *Cahier* VII, Engel notes that Howard has been stung by a bee [20]. A sketch in *Cahier* VI, dated 22/9/63, is annotated "shape of my bee-stung arm."

1. Narrator
1. Larnaia Tis Lapitver
2. Mammós shop
3. Reno
4. Street & vendors etc
5. Clito & Sabri
6. Collis
7. (Pat & Willis)
8. (Ronah on women)
9. Chris
10. (Steve)
11. (Mickey & Ruth)
12. (Big Three)
13. Prison stuff.

2. Durrell
3. Foley
4. Excerpts Cypria

[p.2]

[illegible] H. Engel

Makarios →	Maurnios →	bourgeoisie life.	
Political	Bourgeoisie	Pastoral	Historical
(Mick)	(Ronah)	Mammos	(Kargeorghus)
(Keetah)	(Steve)	Collis	(Mickey)
(Cebrides)		Aristides	(Ruth)
Reno.		Hemles	Reno
		(Steve)	(Steve)
Bosses			
(Nick)			
(Mickey)			
(Willis & Pat)			

[p.3]

[Drawing of an organist playing in a church]

[p.4]

[Drawing of a cat sleeping]

[p.5]

[Drawing of a person sitting]

[p.6]

[Drawing of a chair]

[p.7]

[Drawing of a woman taking a bath]

[p.8]

[Various drawings: profiles, a cat, etc.]

[p.9]

Page 9

[Various drawings: feet, a Chagall-like woman, etc.]

[p.10]

[Upside down drawing of clothes with caption:
shape of my bee stung arm
22/9/63]

Page 11

[p.11]

[Upside down drawing of a girl skipping, clothing, shoes, etc.]

[p.12]

<u>Rules & Regulations</u>
Parking—2 hours only
Substitute potatoes 10¢ extra
Please wait til hostess seats you
Gentlemen are requested to wear suit jackets in the steakhouse.

How do I write normally?

Pop 38,000
Babcock & Wilcox
Dobbies—old P.O.
Stauffer
Galts Towels
Galt Knitting—Tigerbrand
Underwear

Hon Wm Dickson
Absalom Shade[4]

[pp.13-16]

[Greek vocabulary]

[p.17]

Helen
ΕΛΕΝΗ

"The nightengales[5] won't let you sleep in Platres."[6]

Shy nightengale, in the breathing of the leaves
you who bestow the forests' musical coolness
on the parted bodies, on the souls
of those who know they will not return.
Blind voice, you who grope in the
darkness of memory
for footsteps & gestures—I wouldn't dare say
kisses—
and the bitter raging of the slave woman
grown wild.

"The Nightengales won't let you sleep in Platres"

Platres, where is Platres? And the island—
who knows it?

---

4 These people were business associates instrumental in the development of present-day Cambridge, formerly Galt. William Dickson (1769-1846), who owned land along the Grand River, contracted Absalom Shade (1793-1862) to erect the sawmill and gristmill that became the centre of a new community, Shade's Mills, settled largely by Scots from Dumfries county in Scotland. Both men prospered and proceeded to various legal and political offices.

5 This is the spelling Engel uses throughout the *cahier* for nightingale.

6 This is a mountain resort town in the Limassol district, central Cyprus.

I've lived my life hearing names I've
never heard before:

[p.18]

[Greek vocabulary for the words: nightingales, breathing, shy, coolness, know, return, blind, voice, memory, bitter, island]

[p.19]

new countries, new idiocies of men
or of the gods:
my fate, which wavers
between the last sword of some Ajax
and another Salamis
brought me here, to this shore.
The moon
Rose from the sea like Aphrodite
Covered the archer's stars, now moves to
find
the Heart of Skorpio, and changes
everything
Truth, where's the truth.
I too was an archer in the war:
My fate: that of a man who misses
his target.

Lyric nightengale
On a night like this, by the shore of Proteus
the spartan slave girls heard you &
began their lament

[p.20]

[Greek vocabulary for the words: sword, shore, moon, here sea is, like, archer, change, truth, lyric, poetic, shore, lament]

[p.21]

and among them—who would have
believed it—was Helen.
She whom we hunted for years by
the banks of the Scamander
She was there; by the lip of the desert
I touched her, she spoke to me
"It is not true, it isn't true" she cried
"I didn't didn't board the blue—
bowed ship."
I never went to valiant Troy.

High girdled, the sun in her hair &
that stature
shadows & smiles everywhere
on shoulders, thighs & knees
the skin alive, & her eyes.
with large eyelids
She was there & on the banks of a delta
and at Troy
At Troy, nothing—a phantom image.

[p.22]

[Greek vocabulary for the words: among, believed, of the desert, touched, she cried, ship, hair, eyes]

[p.23]

The gods wanted it so
And Paris, Paris lay with a shadow
as if it were a solid being
and for ten whole years we slaughtered
ourselves for Helen.

Great suffering descended on Greece
So many bodies thrown
into the jaws of the sea, the jaws of the
earth
so many souls
fed to the millstones like grain.
And the rivers swelling, blood in
their silt
all for a linen undulation, a bit of cloud,
a butterfly's flicker, a swan's down
an empty tunic, all for Helen.
And my brother?

"The nightengales won't let you sleep in Platres."

[p.24]

[Greek vocabulary for the words: solid being, souls, river, blood, swan]

[p.25]

Tearful bird
on sea-kissed Cyprus
Consecrated to remind me of my
country
I moved alone with this fable

If it is true that it is a fable.
If it's true that mortals will not
again take up
the old deceit of the gods.
If it's true
that in future years some other Tencer
or other Ajax or Priam or Hecuba
or someone unknown or nameless
who nevertheless saw
a Scamander overflowing with corpses
isn't fated to hear
news bearers coming to tell him
that so much suffering, so much life
went into the abyss
all for an empty tunic, all
for a Helen.

[p.26]

[Greek vocabulary for the words: tearful, bud, deceit]

Geo Seferis
Collected Poems
1924-1955
ed. Keeley & Sherrard
Princ[e]ton 1967

Cahier VII[1]

Seeing myself again & for the first time in a long while as a writer [4].

This is one of Engel's more traditional "diary-like" *cahiers* in that, on balance, personal introspection outweighs draft fiction, philosophical reflection, social observation or lists! Its entries include descriptions of friends and outings in Cyprus, which the Engels were preparing to leave towards the end of 1963. On the challenges and demands of being a writer, Engel pondered: "Will Canada be good to write in? It <u>must</u> be!"[6].

[p.1]

And the school teacher went out to meet Life.
Hello schoolteacher, said Life, come and play with me.
Who are you?
Nobody you'd recognise, said Life, and hurried away.

But it wasn't that way at all.

[p.2]

I've lost a lot of poems in my day.

I was born, and became the victim of a bucolic childhood—lived in lyricism beggaring the question. I can be endlessly sentimental about it too—and can show you my cut-off braids (14)

I threw out two pins this morning—a bad omen.

1 1963, khaki green notebook, with "M.E." and "II. Monodromos" handwritten on the cover; 28 pages used.

[p.3]

Things to consider—

1) our passivity
2) how I've fouled things up here—by talking too much?—by aggression
3) our reaction to heat
4) sorting out the levels on which things reach one—Auden's ego-analyses
5) the vicissitudes of the married state:
    1) conventions—how do they affect us?
    2) real changes....

WHAT WILL PEOPLE THINK?
Cf what will people DO.

For me thinking = action.
No wonder I'm static.
Imagination stronger in effect than action.

[p.4]

The Long Dry days to be put in

When TO THINE OWN SELF BE TRUE really is the advice of an addled old man.

Loyalty

Have I written down about participating in another's unhappiness?

—

Aftermath of a long dry day—

Spent that Thursday morning finishing a John Wyndham[2] & reading Maurois' The Quest for Proust.[3] One quotation hit me and I started sliding down, down, seeing myself again & for the first time in a long while

---

2 John Wyndham (1903-1969) was a science fiction writer whose works include *The Day of the Triffids* (1951), *The Kraken Wakes* (1953), *The Chrysalids* (1955) and *The Midwich Cuckoos* (1957).

3 André Maurois, *The Quest for Proust*, trans. Gerard Hopkins (Harmondsworth, Middlesex: Penguin Books in association with J. Cape, 1962).

as a writer, then [...]

[p.5]

[...] worrying about H's having said "Don't run away from Cyprus in defeat." The extent of the defeat is incalculable, the possibility slim of turning it into a victory & yet so much of the story is unborn.

By the time he phoned & I went to John Odger's, it was bad, but that gang cheered me[...]. Home again—and H. wakes me out of 10 minutes sleep into depression. Coffee at Fiesta

[p.6]

which he hated. Then Chris's and a long slow warm-up to a new idea about a novel and an invitation to a farm in Paphos. Liver kebab—weary weariness & Willis phones at 7:45 when I am dreaming about Cat, who is chewing me.

Will Canada be good to write in? It must be.

[...]

[p.7]

Cat—hearing grown cats mating in the street—stares thoughtfully at me—then looks chilled & frightened.

The week:

Saturday—We have steak[?] in the moat—I still sulky, moody, deprived. H. struggling desperately on—drinks w. Rhona who weeps. Sunday—Rise early—bus to Kyrenia—Zephysos; good swim & staring boys. Aphelia for lunch—v. good. Howard & Pat talking wildly, I a little bored & sleepy & physically as usual complaining. On the way home, failing the Kents, we go to some tombs in the hills—those too being stoics in flipflops under sun on stone. H. crawled into a tomb & was seen prehistoric

[p.8]

Thro a spy-hole—then confessed a fear of bats. Site excavated by Australians 2 yrs ago. Landscape—Queen's Wardow[?], Ayios Georgios, sea, terraced olive groves, beach goats, groves of pine, satisfyingly lush. We rest under a tree—I am childish & vain as they talk history & I wiggle in my tight bathing suit. Home. H drives cannily thro TRIMITHI where the villagers move their chairs out of the way & guide him thro' cobbled lanes. Back to Pat's for a drink, then walking (SORE HEELS) thro' Kyrenia back rd. to main road. Ride with Eng-Turk couple (HOW can you call a baby Mehmet?) to cheese factory bridge. Walked to Donner Kebab place—sparks flying, ate. Home painfully—but we

[p.9]

saw a tiny shrine in ΟΔΟΣ ΛΙΣΤΕΡ w. candlelit ikon and terra cotta pot. H. a little afraid of being accused of interfering? Magic Armenian

Quarter. New vows to explore.

Monday: Paphos plans

Ramadan invites us boating but I hold out for Steve—we carry him off to Mitsero—cook chops under a pine tree on a hill near Phoenician slag heaps. [...] Home at 4.[...]

TUESDAY—Released from office—read in bed while H. did business.

[p.10]

S. called. we go to Odgers & then Mahedonitissa—all money spent on lunch—then ice cream. Crazy sex discussion ending in squeezing phallic cacti. Ice cream, then Odgers(?) Bed. Then David G. J's dull party. T.V. Nothing doing. Plans for Platres.

Wed

Up at 6:30—Platres trip w. both (?) Helliers—v nice in sections—H. bitter about boy-scouts—NORMALCY they are to him—any uniform [illegible] his bitterness. Hunger. Good lunch. Flat evening—Robin comes—then good reading. G[ood]night.

[p.11]

A MAP of Cyprus

Magic Places— Agenon
Pera
Old F[amagu]sta at Night
Old N[ico]sia at Night
Parts of Illyria
Chris's Studio
LAMBOUSA Vouni–perhaps
MYRTHOV Kantara & coast & eagles.
AGRIDHAKI Orounda

NOT QUITE places: Mitsero, Asinon, Polis, Boghaz, Kythrea, Rahopetria, Lannaca
Night = Snow for glossing over.
How often have I deliberately spoiled H's pleasure?
A dream of Dhoulis[?]
Is the dissatisfaction only in us—No

[p.12]

On Going Away

All summer I have been shouting, pleading, screaming to go, yet even now I cannot without moral assistance. I must be told to go, and helped to go, otherwise, confronted by action, I fade into dreams. Now, when it is almost too late, I have incentive and yet I hang terribly about the telephone, much preferring, as usual, the dream.

But then there is the practical idea that I cannot go unless H. says I can spend the money.

[p.13]

Last evening

After a frantic day with all the C's and a frantic rush, got breathless to Bellapaix for harpsichord music lit by a church candelabra, with bats, lanterns, Cyprus.

Found, at the end, Pelleg, lonesome in the refectory. I, since it was my awkward night, was taken back grudgingly by Armstrongs.

On Being Away—

Another pleasant, inconsequential morning with Christiane. We swam together—she lent me her mask for a bit. Beautiful things, she lives for.

[p.14]

Then buses, connections, Davlos.

[...]

[p.15]

The relief of being away will soon degenerate into boredom. But to be simple & selfish for five days.

Is there a future? 25
When will we betray each other? 8
200
£ 10
£ 11

Must go Tues. A.M.

Davlos perfection.

It was as if I was communicating with something very big. The clear serene. Work, discipline, the sensuality of merely lying—not sensuality—simplicity on a rock.

But O I am a liar—passing basic truths to and fro' am I? I am only deceiving myself. I dare not love, except in this bucolic way. The need to be loved is still so all-consuming that one day it will be the death of me.

[p.16]

Certainly it has greatly harmed my writing—I cannot be ruthless. But perhaps I am learning.

How quickly adoration palls.

We are all traps for each other. Trap & be trapped. The biter bit.

How true is it that a woman must be made to submit her will before she can have a relationship? If it is, I am [illegible]

18/9/63 Utter despair at the thought of having to go. The moment doesn't seem right. Nothing seems right. Hopes of confiding in Tommy. But it must be obvious what's wrong.

Coming home: The nest is very real but somehow out of tune. How long can I stick it?

[p.17]

One must somehow learn to live in a newer freer way. Decide what is most important. Be ready to die inside for it.

20/9/63 Random thoughts after a randy day—The luncheon came off [...] Why not a series of letters from under the net?

21/9/63 Always the aftermath of intensity is serenity.

We went there—met M. on the way—later blackmail? We went feeling guilty and shy & necessary. Oh, the painful small talk! Then comments on that other day. Of course unsuccess. He is half heartbroken, savage. "Why not leave well enough alone" sort of thing.

[p.18]

JOE[4] oh the misery and the anger! We could almost have had a quarrel. I felt weak and sad because so ready to have any scrap that was thrown to me—this always gives rise to a trampish feeling. But oh it wasn't the same—we couldn't talk! And suddenly he was domestic, the way he touched me. And I wanted to cry. But—taste of skin—lemony. Feel of knotted forehead. Oh, children, let me think, so I can have the hour again (shadow of a man in a

4 A character in *Sarah Bastard's Notebook*.

museum case).
Bracing ourselves for the return—we talk business: marriage. So I must learn to be subtle with my strength and hide it from everyone but myself—heretofore the reverse having been the case.

[p.19]

Getting out: "I think I have been a sentimental fool."
"I have never been so irresponsible before."
Misery slides away.
So he says we are both on the verge of something very big.
It is a question of using strength and power in the right way—of exploiting the right things.

23/ A pleasant weekend by the sea eliminated panicky obsessions—but brought schemes for reunion.
Melancholy Jacques. Restaurants: Lapithis and Karavas

The following week:
Monday?
Tuesday?

[p.20]

Why can't I remember writing after catharsis.
Monday we must have talked—ah! God—Monday was the day I came in furious (sand in the sinus) to greet Howard's bee sting & Steve silent & unsympathetic—and I was kept late by a staff meeting. June Griffin brought me home—O splendidly null.

Anyway—home. Cross. No beer.
Silent men.
Then H. holds up a repulsive puffy arm.
Then Steve takes us out to the workmen's place for lunch & gets depressed too.

[p.21]

Tuesday—to Salamis for AJAX. H cured. Weather bad—lovely dinner—Christiane splendid. Play exciting & closeness—"Later we'll talk about the book"—and—Wednesday—later turns out to be a morning he thought I had off. Terrible heartrendings but he does not press the not-parting and I DO MY DUTY. And Oh God the morning. H. is late for lunch—we talk a little. He goes to get Kebab (Gas is out). Then Oh Lord the donkey saddle incident when we show too much and <u>such</u> an afternoon. I decide to go to Rhodes. Instead I go to Rhona.

[p.22]

Thursday: H. has found out about boats. The 9th is decided upon.

Max & Jas for dinner. Nicole & Jack. Good.
Friday: Steve—Mahedonitissa

The origins of our marriages. Were we both talking nonsense. [...] The truth lies as usual....

[p.23]

The truth **LIES**

Home so early—but no H. So I houseclean & get more & more depressed until he calls me to go to the Odge. Then I stay on w. Jack Young—go to Chris's—talk, talk, talk to all the men. Robin brings me home—So tight—I make a fool of myself, which Robin seems to enjoy—then won't go to bed—leap about, cut wrists, run baths—finally H. slaps me about & I sleep.

[p.24]

Saturday—Famagusta for some odd reason—and Sunday—rather domestic. Ambelopoulia in that particular village—fat little, drooly beasts and me half sick. H. loves them. Sunday—[Chris]tiane cooks rabbit, we go & get the boat—S. strains his back—a little drama (she is so far from recovered: hysterically resentful—give her any issue like his not reading her mind) (he doesn't care to any more) Georghiou stories of Pol; his 2 sisters; Mrs Calam .. the father of the dwarf & his 3 wives.
[The weekend: trying not to show tension, everyone told very long stories—

[p.25]

But how can I remember all the conversations we have had—the subjects have been sex & marriage & ourselves. He must have been living on illusions about himself for much longer than I have—but then he married much younger & in a way more easily.
Biography—the MEAT bit—(not sentimental about childhood—a little glowing about places, but why not? Kantara, Famagusta beach ... but you can't in the end share a paradise.) Grew up being like the others—at
[...]

[p.26]

first the good boy (but always) wild.

Left-handed

Our 4-cornered relationship.

But the conversations: when did we squeeze them in?

1) Yialousa day

2) Myrthou[?] day

Wednesdays in July

Thursdays in August (before Pat)

So very, very seldom ... and often because of a plea to H to leave us alone.

The children.
No—conversations
love
marriage
partners
labour
power

[p.27]

[...]
Friendships between complementary couples; the needs & dangers are to be examined. Wives & husbands approaching in different ways.
[...] [p.28]
Ah, mon cahier, écoute...
Singing together—charm of voices...
Why can't I get back to individual days—the final one is so important—were there eagles?
I feel like a b—.—D1
D2: If nothing had happened today it would have been finished between us. We should have become more & more depressed.

Voice: rather high & rasping.
Gestures: Large & definite
(father)
Coarse pubic beard.

Ah, mon cahier, écoute --
Singing together - charm of
voices...
Why can't I get back to individual
days - the ~~final~~ one is so
important - were there eagles?
'I feel like a b—' - D1
D2: If nothing had happened today
it would have been finished
between us We should have
become more & more depressed.

Voice: rather high & rasping.
Gestures: Large & definite
(father)
Coarse pubic beard.

Page 28

Cahier VIII[1]

On se raconte la vie [21].

A writerly notebook par excellence, *Cahier* VIII is primarily draft copy of the two books Engel was working towards in the early 1960s: her unpublished murder mystery, "Death Comes for the Yaya," and her first published novel, *Sarah Bastard's Notebook. Cahier* pages [1-7] concern the latter book and include an outline for the novel; draft dialogue and description; a first reference to "bloc notes," a technique that would be used in *Monodromos*; and a writer's instructions to herself.[2] Beginning on page [8], material for "Death Comes for the Yaya" includes an outline, draft dialogue and descriptions for the book. Draft character Liz discusses notebooks. As seen in *Cahier* III, earlier draft material for "Death Comes for the Yaya" ascribed a role to diaries belonging to the murder victim, Barbara.

An insert towards the end of the *cahier* lists prices for a variety of consumer goods, including alcohol and cigarettes. The *cahier* closes with an intriguing note, written upside down and in French. Here, as elsewhere in the *cahiers*, Engel's use of French recalls her facility with the language and her knowledge of the culture and literature.

[p.1]

The only way to handle it was to decide that the place was a mediocre chateau—the salon was all right (Empire)—the sedan chair in the corner certainly very good—but she had to school herself to look at it with a good French critical eye: somebody had let a cat in at the brocade. Somebody had, in fact, stopped caring, probably the hostess, the predatory correct little blonde talking to Louis in the corner. Finished marrying for love, she had married for—what? That great handkissing clot in the corner with the thirsty romantic brunette. Oh, chateaus—anyway, interesting people in the room? Lucie de Campol's brother—the blonde Regnier—a fairy—but he was helping de Campol cultivate the brunette—who had lustrous green eyes &

[p.2]

1 1963-64, faded green notebook, "Engel P." handwritten on cover; 28 pages used.

2 "Early on shoes can be the big symbol" [4]; "Must put in props"[9].

a super—elegant Greek husband.

De Gambroie—very minor provençal title involved in that name once. The art historian from Paris: Louis-Pol Santorini—posing in a window, hoping to attract Regnier. Pathetic to be so wistful at his age. The jeune-ménage was happy at least ... a young & very correct & probably very broke English baronet with his French wife. She had the money. Later, there would be fireworks there.

The old lady was the only interesting one: many rings, many marriages.

[p.3]

It was one of her nights for not being able to talk, except with malice—for loathing people. Perhaps, truly, these were loathsome? Louis liked them but he liked anything that passed for society & why not—

"Ethamy"—a voice above her spoke her name slowly & distinctly. She twisted in her gold-clawed chair. The elegant Greek. She dropped her cigarettes.

As offensively as possible "My mother got it out of a movie."

"The name?"

"The name."

If he had asked to join her she might have roughly slashed him away. But he sat down & gave her another cigarette; flat, loosely rolled. Black tobacco.

[p.4]

"And so you are bored?"

"No."

"Obstinate, though."

"These French women make me feel nervous & deformed."

"Shall we walk in the garden, then?"

"Not yet. Cela ne se fait pas."

Early on shoes can be the big symbol.

[p.5]

The Wrong Year

1) Mrs Bastard's notebook
    Intro—identity
        1) the chateau
    Mr Bastard's article & reply
    Invocation to Lyle

2) The funeral & abortion
1) Stel's primer
Leda's visit
2) Leda's elopement

[p.6]

* Main image

Time travels in Mrs Bastard.

I— <u>Present</u> immediate—the week after the funeral—
⋆ cat dies
Joe & Egon visit
Lyle visits
The stuff is sold
Visit to the cottage
father dies
II Present: quits her job
⋆ goes to funeral

III Present external—Pembroke street
—drunken Indians
PAST

I Childhood. The beach*
Peeling houses
II Leda's elopement—* the lake
III France & Joe—* wet landscapes
France & Leah * the chateau

IV Venice—⋆ grey hunting

[p.7]

VII Past Toronto: Lois & Joe

V The islands—bedding in the * landscape

VI London or Abortion?

Themes: The background to choice.
The puritan ethos vs reality
The influence of romanticism
—people caught up in their own legends. S[arah] as healthy, Canadian,

Leah as princess. L. as prince (as others want them to be.)

But—Sarah feels like a lumpy intellect, Leah like a beaten bride, L. a cuckold.
[Doodles]

—Bloc-notes: what Helen says to me.
P. street
Fire halls.

[p.8]

OUTLINE

I	Harry to Beirut. Yaya gone	
Day 1	Brigadier: INTRO	
Sunday	Lunch at Trimithi	BEA
	body	
II	Discovery of Yaya ①	
III	Paul & Sandra. overnight (2-3)	
THURS	Afternoon—Brigadier—speculation ④	
⑤	Motive: Boredom? (buried clue)	
	To Af's—Barbara. Decision to travel.	
IV	Brigadier: FIROS—Bea-travelling	
am	BARBARA KILLED	
	THURSDAY NIGHT FRI. SAT. SUN. MON.	
	TUESDAY. Barbara's body.	
V	Police—then back to N[ico]sia.	
	Tony—hands	
	Paul—Home	
VII	Tuesday night remembering scene over Barbara. Tony calls.	
	Gives diaries. Suggests Bill	
WED.		
VII	Cyprus—drive to Davlos.	
Wednesday	Confesses	
	himself as 1) Barbara's lover	
	2) Signer of FHS in register	
	3) Harry had been B's lover too	
	Delivered at Davlos.	

[p.9]

Must put in props from Af & Firos
What happened to the kitten?

VII The notebook lovers
1) Colin Sandhurst
2) Cypriot—not Bill
IX Harry & Nora there too!—Wed & Thurs.
Decides on blackmail
X Fri Home but first to Bill in Nora Saturday
Then
Sandhurst's quarrel—Tony
Dr Stavros—Bea's body.
XI Action: Suspects knocked out.
Colin, Stavros, Bill-Nora
→ Paul, Firos—only Af & Harry ← } but she might have been killed the day before
remain! Bea's letter.
XII The wake: Russian Embassy car
New diary. The abduction.
XIII Waking up

[p.10]

XIII Harry: Come home & sleep.

I tossed, turned, protested, but Harry's stating "whatever you think of me, Liz, I'm still your husband."—forced a sleeping pill down me & patted my painted head until I dropped off. The new diary was under my pillow, as if I hoped to absorb it thro' the feathers ... as if I hoped it would make me dream the answers.

Instead I dreamed of making love in a grain store to a famous conductor's younger brother—careless by the cider press, and the neglected kitten licking my cheeks.

Which it was, when I woke, none the better for my adventure since the conductor's brother had turned out to be passive, afraid of Harry & only seventeen....

Harry heard me thud the kitten down & appeared with coffee. "Feel better?"

"Somewhat. God, I hate you."

"That's an improvement."

[p.11]

Colin Sandhurst on Thursdays. (There was a long complaint that Colin is too afraid of Guinèvre to take Barbara anywhere really nice and far away—like Davlos). Records of conspiracies with Af to rope someone into a beach expedition, when terrible Tony has hogged the car. Bill & Harry are not evident until early July—two names repeatedly & neatly excised with a razor blade; mention of one blank cancelling a date to go to Beirut. "If I were that Liz I'd find out what he does there—but perhaps she's too busy watering her aspidistras to care." Then on the 25th of July—a threat. "Heard from Harry that Tony is being considered for something big. The question is—am I a suitable wife? Harry says it would mean a lot if I made an effort. He asks if I hate Tony. I do, but I see what he means."

So Harry is dishing out advice.

And Harry knows about Tony.

[p.12]

And Tony is in intelligence.

Ergo....

I stared for a long time at our dark rush ceiling. A rather too large spider stared back. For the first time I felt definitely unsafe.

What was Harry doing anyway, letting me hold onto a document like this?

Why was it the Russian embassy the car had been pinched from?

If she could be orderly, I could. I got up & dressed, put a face on, and tucked the journal in my bag. Public places are best. Yesterday in my house.

I jumped when the telephone jangled. Paul telling me Bea Wender had been dead for at least 24 hours when we found her.

That meant that everyone who had been busy drinking beer

[p.13]

with me yesterday—and Bill & Nora—and Af & Harry—was in the running again. One of us was up to something & it wasn't me.[3]

Five minutes after I received this information I came to grips for the first time in my life with the idea of power. And instead of spending the rest of the day mulling over the splendours of recognition, I went out of character and into high gear.

A call to Paul, and two watchdogs were guaranteed for the night.

A call to Papadopoulos on Ledia Street and a supply of little green notebooks was commanded.

A call to the Brigadier: Guinèvre was there, and would come.

3 Above this sentence, in the top margin, are the words "Cyprus Bill: Paraskerides."

[p.14]

A boy with a bicycle & three half-shilling notebooks arrives first. I send him out for beer. Then I get told of Harry's fat felt pen & label those notebooks:

ON DETECTION
ON BARBARA'S BOOKS
ON THE MURDERER.

There were things to be thought about.

When Guinèvre came, I was half-way through the first quart of Keo and I'd filled the first two pages of the first book. Not bad, Liz.

<u>Guinèvre</u>: (High Giggle) I hear you wanted to see me, Liz.
<u>Liz</u>: Sit down & pour yourself a beer. How are you feeling after last night?
<u>Guinèvre</u>: I should think you're the one to answer that. I hear Bill abducted you!

[p.15]

<u>Liz</u>: Relax. It wasn't sensational. I didn't know you were gunning for him.
<u>Guinèvre</u>: I know you think he's <u>your</u> special territory.
She is as brittle as a box of rice-krispies.
<u>Liz</u>: Look, I want to ask you something about Colin.
<u>Guinèvre</u> jerks her head back stiffer than ever—defensive.
<u>Liz</u>: (stoney stare) Why do you think he killed Barbara?
<u>Guinèvre</u> (gurgling): I may have thought that—once —
<u>Liz</u>: I heard you accuse him of it...
<u>Guinèvre</u> (slyly): Then you must also have heard him say where he was that day—
<u>Liz</u>: What day?
<u>Guinèvre</u>: That Thursday...
<u>Liz</u>: She was killed on Friday—Friday night—I heard

[p.16]

from the police.
<u>Guinèvre</u>: I forgot you had so many spies. Nevertheless, Liz, he couldn't have killed Mrs. Wender: he was working yesterday morning.
<u>Liz</u>: She was killed the day before. What was Colin doing?
<u>Guinèvre</u>: He worked all morning & we took the kids to the beach in the afternoon.
<u>Liz</u>: Still on the way home from the base.
<u>Guinèvre</u>: Liz—what are you trying to do? I know Colin didn't kill anyone...
<u>Liz</u>: And yet you thought so—
G: When I was in a panic, yes...

L: Is it any better now she's out of the way? Or has he found another grass widow—
G: Liz—I consider that unfair & rude. What is it you want to know?
L: Were you blackmailing her?
G: No.
L: Who was?

[p.17]

G: She wouldn't tell Colin.
L: What was it about?
G: Why don't you ask Colin?
L: He's too much afraid of me to answer ... he'd only cry.
G: Why should I tell you—anyone who says such things...
L: He's not much, but he's mine, eh? Tell me & protect yourself, Guinèvre—and Colin.
G: Well all I know is that someone was trying to collect twenty pounds a week. He—
L: So it was a he?
G: He was going to fix Tony's promotion.
L: How?
G: I've been over & over this with Colin. He didn't know how!
L: What do you think.
G: She must have been indiscreet.
L: Did she tell Colin anything compromising about Tony?
G: Ask your husband—he's

[p.18]

been interrogating Colin—not me.
L: Very small o.
G: But of course if you're not talking to each other:
L: Have another beer...
G: I don't think she knew anything to tell.

There's one girl I'll never manage to grind down. She left after her second beer, as proud & fiery as ever. There's something to be said for being born French & proud of it.

I should have bought another notebook to mark "HARRY."

~~My observations about detection were not profound, but I thought them nevertheless necessary. My methods were flawed...~~

[Insert: price list for alcohol and cigarettes]

[p.19]

[List of people to whom to write letters]

[p.20]

Liz's Notes
On diary—
New info—List of lenders
Wld like to be trounced by Bill
Gets advice fro' Harry.

On detection: Who for Dr Watson
On self-protection.

On the Murderer—strong wrists (Harry's weak—jars)
car—Phlamouthi

<u>Dates</u>

12 days	3 drinks—H3	H 36.
Cigarettes		7 50
Beer	20 @ 70	14 00
		57 50
		4
		$15
		3 20

[p.21]

Shopping—matches
bra
l'Express
Wine

Une nuit dans un chateau on se rencontre en miserable—on se raconte la vie—lui qui est plus fort l'a fait haïr son mari. Le matin arrive. C'est tout?

Cahier IX[1]

June 2nd [1964].
Scrambled journals indeed [23].

Engel herself flagged the importance of this *cahier* with the following notations on its cover: "Very Important" and "Collections from other *Cahiers*." Much of *Cahier* IX's interest lies in the author's reflections on her evolution as a writer. She shares her thoughts upon rereading her work, an activity she conducted with the highest of standards. "How can I get rid of the crap," she demanded. "Comment! Question everything!" [15] Engel turned her critical eye on herself as well, and the *cahier* records feelings of depression related to what she judged to be the poor quality of her work and comportment.

Cahier IX introduces Engel's second published novel, *The Honeyman Festival*,[2] with a sketch of its opening scene, in which a very pregnant Minn lies in the bathtub contemplating her enormous belly [28]. Interestingly, Engel sketched this scene before her own pregnancy, the novelist's imaginative powers here preceding personal experience.

At the time of this *cahier*, Engel had four manuscripts in the works: *Sarah Bastard's Notebook* (1968); "Death Comes for the Yaya" (unpublished); *Monodromos* (1973); and *The Honeyman Festival* (1970). In the early 1960s, these manuscripts were still in their formative stages, and some of the characters, scenes and techniques travel back and forth between manuscripts. Others were emerging that would recur in Engel's work right through to her final novel-in-progress, "Elizabeth and the Golden City." Engel's final manuscript twins Elizabeth and Frances Doubleday in scenes remarkably like those Engel sketched for Betsy and Liz on page [20] of this *cahier*.

Hindsight reveals that in the early 1960s Engel was going through an incredibly creative phase, though she may not have felt so fortunate at the time inasmuch as she did not yet have a published book. If she could have known

1 1963-64, light blue notebook, with "M. Engel III" in the top right-hand corner, and "Very important," "Collections from other *Cahiers*," in the centre of the cover; 37 pages used.

2 Although Engel started *The Honeyman Festival* well after she had undertaken *Monodromos*, it was published three years earlier.

that five years later, this would be a fait accompli, she may have found it easier to deal with the moments of depression and lack of confidence that were troubling her. At such times, Engel often took out and reread letters she had received from Hugh MacLennan. The older writer's words of understanding and encouragement helped boost the younger writer's morale. Engel's thoughts after the rereading of MacLennan's letters are especially interesting.

This *cahier* also contains compelling proof that Engel anticipated readership. On page [28], she inserted an explanation for a series of apparently unrelated lines, each with one of three initials: M., P. and H. As the insert explains, Marian (P. for Pass), Howard (H.) and a friend named Michel Euvrard (M.)[3] experimented with "automatic writing" at the time. This is the practice of writing without conscious volition, the words on the page expressing the writer's subconscious—its lapsed memories or half-formed impressions—the stuff of dreams.

[pp.1-4]

[One-line notes for *Sarah Bastard's Notebook*]

[p.5]

August: In order to survive, one must act on certain presumptions—
1) that one is fairly good
2) that one's husband is
3) that one's friends & relations could be

There must be people who know without having to presume, but I always have to juggle the facts to get the presumption because I have no way of knowing the false from the true exc[ept] by my belly—which makes trouble.

To be noted: <u>Sensations</u> of handwriting.

[p.6]

You cannot finish a story, we say.

I have never come closer to knowing so, & yet I know nothing
A spider in a web? A Ulysses figure?

3 Euvrard had been at McMaster and had made the trip to Montreal with Engel when she was organizing her graduate study plans. Euvrard later taught in Montreal, where Engel visited him on occasion.

I identify—& believe he is innocent.
Since I am not, this is ridiculous.
Father-figure: hands & feet

On s'ouvre, l'un à l'autre.
Howard: love of triangles.
The Confidante.

But was not Ulysses a spider in a web?

And have I not planned my life with this sort of calculation?

USING people (when one cannot love them quite enough)

[p.7]

[...]

[p.8]

Absent lovers → security + convenience.

Since my cowardice is supported by intelligence, I shall never have the courage to run away.

Notes For a Novel Based On Aphrodite

The net is love—an overwhelming dependent-protective love which keeps them from being alone together: they make love in his presence & fall more & more into his power → claustrophobia & defiance.

Note: Unwillingness to play "All For Love"

Details of Frustration: amenable meetings
bright conversation fading into despair as the boys pick up magazines.
A. feeds them & they feed on her.

[p.9]

A Fruitful Conversation

—loss of innocent joys: ties w. family—[Fidgety man upset & thirsty].[4] Between great chunks of laughter & cries of despair.

4 Square brackets appear in the original text.

Marriage—cruel because it makes R[elation]ships mundane & complicated.

One is poorer for losing touch with simple joy. One can have a relationship compounded of simple joys but not within marriage. But by "participating in another's unhappiness" one is bound to one's partner in a way that rules out having a guiltless, simple, joyful relationship with someone else. Therefore with marriage the simplicity is lost. esp. after having children. There is deeply valuable tenderness, and a marvel of children, but what can the searching romantic do until his desire for wholeness fades into content, but continue the guilty chase for eternity. Which is the relationship which cannot be mundane.

Age can wither. Custom does stale.

Physical mundanity sets in early, mental very late in happy arrangements.

[p.10]

[On the right-hand corner, the profile of a man's head has been cut out and pasted in]

Themes: SHE ALWAYS DID WHAT SHE WAS TOLD
(esp. by her husband, who went gleefully mad)

SHE HAD NO PRIVATE LIFE
(She talked too much).

I feel like a boool
Just call me Europa

We are free to give our best to each other: the tragedy of marriage.

H: The only man I like better in presence than in imagination. I went away to restore his freshness. But I do not think he has any feeling of obligation towards the world. N[.] would like to be this way—but he has no real quality.[5]

[p.11]

December—On rereading my own work.
How to get the cheapness out.
A trashy form.
How trashy is the mind behind it?

5 See *Cahier* III [5] for an earlier expression of the thoughts on [10] here.

SUBJECT
The conversation between Cal and Edyth is good but ought not need to be written.

Help Help

[p.12]

Hanna has beady eyes & gave up painting.
Pass[6] pretends to be glamourous, looks like Heather.
The old lady wears Pass's hat.
Pass photographed the foolish virgins in Strasbourg & pinned them up.
The desk was real Empire & wouldn't close—FRANCE.
Pass took photographs of her desk.
Pass brought Mimosa & photographed it on a hotel room chair by the bidet.
Michele was ugly at 2.
Barbara sent a postcard from Yugoslavia.
We ate oysters at Oxford & liked the castle with toilets.
Janet sent a congratulatory postcard.
H. climbed to the Tour de Cesar & took a photograph.
Pass was shown picking her nose on a store bench.
Pass wore an Ibiza shirt & a fat smile (pigs nose).
The tide went out at Petit Port St Philippe.

[p.13]

Johnson sent a photograph.
Pass jumped with airbundles.
Pass rowed a boat crookedly.
Pass climbed into a bell.
Pass let him take her in the mirror.
H. wrapped up his head & scratched his nose.
H. read on the port with wine.
H. woke smiling.
Marie-France woke with oursons.[?]
Pass read in bed—[CONCERN with my own image.][7]
Pass went to Pevensey & was pretty.
STILL LIFE NOTRE DAME F. VIRGINS Hanna
HANGED MAN CEZANNES STUDIO

---

6 Engel's nickname—from Passmore.

7 Square brackets appear in the original text. If this comment was not added after the fact, it at least suggests a certain critical consciousness or distance on Engel's part.

Pass posed.
Domestic bliss—Is that what you're good at, P?

[p.14]

If I say I have a cheap mind—what is cheap?

1) subject matter
2) conversation } melodramatic stories
3) behaviour—sloppiness & neglect
4) dreaminess

WHY do I want to write? 1) because I can
2) because I like stories
3) because I want fame.

admiration of 1) artists
2) BIG people
3) drunkenness

<u>OB</u>
Careless writing. Many clichés. What does it say: that people can only live together in a very small way.

[p.15]

When I explain things I go all squashy and cheap. What do I want to say? or do? What is valid?
Cracking up.
The wrong end of the stick.
Purposelessness: reading about writers.
Taunting H, who is MORE.
POWER. Outlet for strength.

How can I get rid of the crap.
Comment. Question everything.

<u>The Monday</u> after that Sunday.

Howard came home comforting—you could see he was afraid my depression would prevent his working, and he was right. He convinced me that self-destructiveness was an escape, though I felt wearily that <u>all</u> his reasons weren't altruistic—and why should they be?

But this afternoon, writing Xmas cards, I felt the feeling again—had phantasies of leaving H.[...] it was a mood to be taken seriously because it accompanied a very complete sense of estrangement: I was cut off from the reasons for things. Why had we come here? Why was I writing a thriller? Why hadn't

[p.16]

I gone out & got a job? Why was I chafing so unrealistically against my [shackles]?[8] Then, feeling that it was perhaps dangerous and sentimental, but again perhaps helpful, I got out Hugh's letters.

He is a <u>good</u> man. I could see my own story in those pages, but nicely put, and feel an enormous effort on his part to tame my hysteria and lack of direction. Men will give me hell, he said, because I have talent. They will want mothering I can't give—and I will want fathering they can't give. I am to suffer & struggle & win.

How often have I heard from men this story? You are strong—you need a strong man, though perhaps you would like a weak one.

Wonderful Howard who is always strong for me. I despise him a bit for it—but that is my nasty side. If I were really honest I should have missed him and faded away. I am now determined to shut up and stop underestimating him.

And get off this women-reading kick.

[p.17]

What's to read? The new books.—M. Spark, I. Murdoch. The Ott. Henry James. G. Eliot.

Reread Hemingway, Joyce.

Analyse abstract writing. There still should be another way to go. Read analytically. Read Greek tragedy.

Kazantzakis

Get glasses! Where is that picture of Pia?

Another Sunday—Dec. 15th

Back from the Armours[9]—upset abt housekeeping.

Read Fanny Hill in bed & had a delicious dream about our apt.—it was in Paris beside the [illegible]—there were woodcarving merchants & nice young clerks involved. Phoned Helen [Engel's sister] [...]. Then—made the screen, ate some potatoes, got depressed about the house [THINGS WILL RISE UP & GET ME!][cf H & little white stones][10]

Read Pat L's book on Tennessee Williams—badly written, but even skimming over his themes is encouraging—he's real & alive.

8 Square brackets appear in the original text.

9 Leslie and Kathy Armour. Leslie Armour was Engel's "office neighbour" the year she taught at the University of Montana (1957-58). They collaborated on "The Pink Sphinx."

10 Square brackets appear in the original text.

[p.18]

Real Meat Writers

— Williams Ibsen

— H. James Chekov[11]

— LAWRENCE

Then I wondered what should I do (the nag nag nag of the ego) & of course it finally occurred to me that the Death ... Yaya book could be used as an externalisation of another book which deals with the same problem—marital boredom—in a less frivolous, more abstract way. Heard it as a radio or stage play—Liz on telephone, Adrian in sitting room—hopeless cross seductions. Lack of CONTENT in women's lives. Only those things felt very strongly could be used.

Three main women, perhaps.

LIZ—schoolteacher
Barbara—
Nora—Christiane
Rhona—Sandra...

} No split personality

Facets of weakness, boredom & great loving. The emotions of those who refuse to reveal them. Again, cannibalism.

[p.19]

— fear of promiscuity
— dashing towards self-destruction.
— maudlin idiocy of MP on balcony.[12]

. . . . .

Strong feelings:

fear of mother, jealousy of sister, (what were my early feelings there? Simply a determination to hog the limelight)
Desire for praise.
Embarrassment—sex, writing, religion, adoption.
The farm: tremendous warmth of all those men (they are supposed to destroy one, no?)
Passionate hopeless friendships wh[ich]
started very early [...]
Jealousy of pretty conventional girls.
Elation at being alone [...]
(Search for surrogate parents NB)

11 This is the spelling Engel uses throughout the *cahiers* for the playwright Anton Chekhov.

12 Reference to *Cahier* VII [23].

Unsatisfactoriness of the real world—it was never a) easy b) explicit enough.

Enough for tonight.

[p.20]

Boxing Day Feels Like Sunday 1963

<u>depressed</u>
But have ideas for a new book:
<u>the Yaya Externalisation</u>

The frame could be written quickly—Rahman—Novella—Sword Theme.
The split personality — Good Betsy
Bad Liz
Harry comes on strong about her liking for Anna, his first wife. She fears & adores Harry, is dying to be thrust aside (self-destruction).
Good Betsy — great cook & house-keeper
— dresses (unsuitably) for husband
— hates herself.
Bad Liz — loves men
— is sloppy, unpunctual
— hates Harry

Bad Liz of course comes out in drink.

[p.21]

But good Betsy always restrains bad Liz until they come to some casual place—with Anna.
Harry — fussy — uncertain
— debonnaire — v. devoted.
[much older][13]
Carefully build it up to either running away & ruining several people, or suicide.

<u>A Geography of Saying:</u>

Like Antonia Gilbert, who is my best friend in addition to being the possessor of an elegant name, I have never forgotten anywhere in Europe where I have peed. Likewise I remember what was said by landscapes of feeling & texture: this is the real pathetic fallacy.

---

13 Square brackets appear in the original text.

ISSUES & Scenes Where Stel justifies his cruelty to Leda.
Where he tells Sarah to marry Oliver (or v. v.?)

[p.22]

Monday 27 January [1964]

Two years to-day.[14] Complicated & very happy. I will fix it to survive! Only it can't be after anyone else's pattern & it will hurt more.

Skimming through [Morley] Callaghan's book: the quality of a person is so terribly important. This country hasn't made first-rate novelist[s] because it hasn't made first-rate people: no other reason. Viz politics.

Wednesday 21 April[1964]

Time [Magazine][15] like an ever-rolling stream tries this week to shoot down Golding & Penn Warren criticising their inflated reputations as if they were their fault.
The up & down game.

[p.23]

For Weaver:[16] Robt McAlmon or Miller-Durrell.
Grandpa's letters

Deception: Everything must happen to Sarah at once.

The week of her father's funeral:

1 Leda returns
2 She abortion—hunts (Stel)
3 Ol's wife comes to claim him
4 Mr Bastard interview
5 Inherits cottage
6 Abortion
7 Retreat to cottage
~~8 Falls for Mr Bastard~~

14 27 January was the Engels' wedding anniversary.

15 "The Art of Darkness," *Time* 24 April 1964: 74-75; and "From an Aeolian Cave," *Time* 24 April 1964: 75-76.

16 Robert Weaver, CBC senior producer of literary affairs; founding editor, *Tamarack Review.*

Long
Speculation on fate of My Antonio[17]

June 2nd: Scrambled journals indeed—always untraceable.
Mr Bastard has now become that callow spotty castratable youngster we met at the Hellenic Banquet. Therefore as a lover unthinkable.

Cut out Egan's deflation where it now stands.

Fantasy on castration: hostility to men.

The fire stations of Toronto.

Toronto thy beauty is to me....
Like some Hellenic???

[p.24][18]

People: shoot down Sheila, MacLennan, Us. Admire if they fit:
Moos, Sarah,
who could teach people to write prose, not sentences, prose.

Westminster Abattoir
Lay off the parents

My mother-thing—terrible STILL! sense of { resentment / deprivation
—trying to make family over

Joe's wife, like Ronah, perhaps—drink & fairies. He goes home to squeeze her out.
I had an idea about Joe & Sarah & sex the other night—her confession of lack of freedom ... likes it gutsier can't get it. Thinks possibly Lesbian but is then approached by (?)
(Bull Dykes with shucked-back peroxide greasy hair, driving taxis)
Were [illegible] & Betty?

Why is Howard so diffident about inviting people here?

[p.25]

I should just go. But I haven't the courage to live alone. I should only rely on someone else. Better the person who has voluntarily taken you.

Which makes me a nice piece of garbage.

I was always garbage. Let someone take me.

I am tired of being this fat ugly opinionated woman.

When they tried to make me over why didn't they give me a sex?

---

17 See *Cahier* II.

18 In the crease between [24-25] Engel has drawn a line of arrows.

No one here I can run to.

What would Howard feel? I wanna go back to Jesus & I see myself wanting this & I hate myself more.

[p.26] [19]

The Old List

Blow your balloons at dusk —Michel Euvrard
Remember the spider under your pillow — P[ass]
Stand on one foot at every opportunity — P
Do not sit between the camel's humps — M

Freedom of grace Howard
Many's the time & off — H
Has it begun to sprout? — P
Wherefore rejoice? — H

Don't just do something — P & H
One ceiling for every 4 walls — H
Combed your socks this morning? P
Little girl, what now? P. & H

But circles are better. H
Have you tried water? H
Suzie does. P
Try our fried scissors. M

Slow, slow dry not. M
The Rhyme is on. H
Sawdust for hire. H
Lack lustre? H

[p.27]

Blue is the time to dine. H
Don't forget to cream your spats. M & H
Fust in us unused. H
Any old sardine. H

Smuggle closer. H

———

19 This page is headed up by the following notation added by Engel in 1983: "We filled up the Muse in 1955 with [Michel Euvrard] these slogans & automatic writing."

Lines:

For all your cleverness, Lady Jane....
Parrot voice in the night
Some way to acquiesce in the inevitable....

On wife as monster: Does its knees
knock?
Giving up birthdays.
Notes on womb-making.
Turn left at Mars.
Charlie Cox as character.
An expiation.
How to forget your origins.
The Orangeman's Saturday Night.
He was always distracted by the weather.
Sinister skins—and love.
Houseful of bloody harpsichord.
The people of Eurpheria live on peanut
[...]

[p.28]

Survival: Minn's Book [20]

Minn surrounded by objects—pyjamas, socks, nightgowns, overalls, jodhpurs, tights, training pants—the infant equipage that haunts her—"Bobby."

Minn, enormous—bloated in the bath; hairy—if she could reach over her belly to shave her legs. She wouldn't waste the energy. She'll have stretch marks, this time, she's in bad shape, she's been boozing—gently—but enough to sap her enthusiasm for exercise. The baby heaves inside her as she slops in the water—"Bobby—I don't think it is twins this time—look at it." The top of her belly is exposed in relief—it quivers—"Distinctly one baby—but a big one."

Fourth in four years. Nestor has paid dearly for his enjoyment of the elastic hairy corridors.

---

20 This is the first reference to what would become *The Honeyman Festival.*

Bobby in the bathroom? At this stage she is as sexless as she thinks I am. Gone beyond femininity

[p.29]

to a state of permanent motherhood—a moving Moore. Her lack of pudeur may also be accounted for by the fact that she can no longer see her pubic hair, which she associates (profoundly) with the shame of nakedness.

She has another week—ten days—perhaps, to go. "Bobby"—I come back to help her out of the tub.

I love her.

So would Nestor, if he saw her now—pink, shimmering with water. But Nestor has to work. He comes home late—at nine, or ten, or after, furrowed, smaller every day, fierce from Grub Street. She makes his dinner, something fried, or a leftover, a salad, a good piece of cheese. Sometimes he talks, sometimes he reads. At this stage he is dispirited—sees the approach of two months without conjugal relations—it is the only relation they have—groans for the 100th time "why didn't Bobby remind you to take your pill."

She is reading Meredith—now—as a sort of penance—and though she is too cowed to concentrate manages

[p.30]

to scan her book & look angry. "He was on his holidays & so were we—remember?"

"You should have had him do the packing."

"Yeah."

When I am being sensitive I think he comes home later in order to avoid me; but that is only my self-importance talking. I am the only one who affords him any peace with his wife—and sometimes he, too, calls "Bobby."

Nestor—which is not his real name—I disguise all of us, in case you have heard of the case—is a free-lance journalist. He works hard & is reasonably successful, but lacks, in my opinion, imagination. He is overwhelmingly earnest, and earnest about facts. For that reason—because he is honest & serious, orderly & punctual in both his contracts & punctuation—a great deal of work comes his way. He has an office and a part-time secretary, even, upon occasion, and when he is not too particular about the typing, Minn's help, and still works half the night. He is not as happy as he was when things began to fall right for him, but still he [continues on second half of p.31]

[p.31]

Infanticide? Minn might accuse Bobby, but have done it herself

1) Intro
2) Bobby—how it was when he came to be State Eunuch
3) Minn's background & Bobby's
4) Minn & Nestor—pre-marital glimpses (Peter Robinson & Irene?)
5) Bobby—why he is State Eunuch
6) The new baby 7) The case 8) Finis.

wears the look of a man satisfied by the work that harries him.

And I like to think that he is happy with the few hours he spends at home.

Sometimes, as I say, I catch resentment—even hate—in his eyes & his voice. He can't like to have someone in his house. It's not a tradition in this country. You put your wife & children in their pumpkin shell & expect to find them there, alone, at the end of the day—not playing ring-a-rosy—with an elderly beatnik, not working on the second bottle of beaujolais with the state eunuch. Married women are supposed to do their drinking alone. They do, mostly.

[p.32]

Not Minn. Minn is the exception, that's why I love her. Minn's a mess, but she has something—force—bottom—that, without me, would never, now be seen by the world. I get my self-respect by helping Minn. Show what she is by however small a world she lives in & am justified by the fact that it is a larger world than it would be without me.

All this for half the housekeeping.

But what's a woman like Minn supposed to do? She was a reporter before she got married—that's how she met Nestor—a passionate muck-raker. And, until she went to Paris, a professional virgin—determined more to avoid children than to avoid men—for she had a strong intuition of her appalling fertility.

[p.33]

Monday—No, this won't do because it's another paean to MP—stupid.[21]

21 Once again, Engel is being critical of her own work here.

Minn because of her BG is still good but Nestor is a direct hit at Howie.

Noon: a gt moral & spiritual victory.
Teatime: Why on earth do I need it?

14/4 [1964]

Writing in tub. Le Bonheur—only film view of the domestic & sensual pleasures—real happiness—flowers & spring in the step. [illegible]—gone off the wife

[...][22]

[p.34]

Muezzin

Graphic
Photos of street } bouzouki
Mr Zavallis
Mammas Aristides & Costas } singing
Phaedra—bouzouki
Fighting pictures?

[p.35]

Where do the public pee?

Same suspicion of beards & late risers.

[p.36]

Because though the suburbs had grassy gardens, and 10 room bungalows (for $200 a month) they didn't have a water-cart horse called Patrice Lunumba, Phaedra, The Cyprus Mail, Captain Flores, Mammas, Costas, Haji Parkerides or the Nero Sisters.

~~It's an ordinary day say a working day in early summer I dash down the street waving to my~~

[p.37][23]

I used to pack up and move every year with never a look behind me and think I was cracking up at the first nostalgic twinge. But now when someone says "I guess you're glad you're out of Cyprus" I straighten up like a Dowager Duchess & shout "of course not."

---

22 Inserted here is a notice from the Ministry of Pensions and National Insurance, regarding Engel's Contribution Records (incomplete).

23 This page presents an entry where, as mentioned in the Introduction, it is very difficult to determine if it is written as "fact" or as "fiction."

We left Nicosia two months ago after a year living in a town that had most of the advantages of home—& the best one was that it felt like home without home's problems & realities. Let me say right away that I do not overestimate the Greek-Turkish influence in my own native land, but Cyprus is a divided country, a middle-class country, and an essentially loving country—just like home.

Our street ran under various names, from the southern Greek [on] one side of the old walled city to the northern Turkish area. It was surrounded by suburbs banal enough to be part of Mimico or Oshawa—but let's talk about our street.

Cahier X[1]

Our conscious views of what life ought to be seldom correspond to what life really is [32].

Cahier X spans the last months of 1964 and the beginning of 1965. The Engels had left Cyprus and settled in Toronto. Back in Canada, Engel missed the people and life she had come to know in Cyprus, England and France. She shared the critical views of Toronto expressed by her protagonist in *Sarah Bastard's Notebook*, draft versions of which represent the bulk of this *Cahier*.

In addition to excerpts of the future novel, the *cahier* contains the familiar lists of books and note taking—this time on Joseph Campbell's *The Hero With a Thousand Faces* [2]—as well as plans for future projects, including details on "Minna's Book" (later *The Honeyman Festival*), a radio programme or article on Ottoline Morrell,[3] and a magazine or newspaper along the lines of *The New Statesman*. Finally, it offers some interesting reflections on superficiality.

[p.1]

Marian Engel
10/7/64

Title for Howard's biography
"Batman's in the First Folio"

1 1964-65, hard-cover, burgundy notebook, "Cunard Line Tourist Class" sticker on cover; 48 pages used.

2 Joseph Campbell, *The Hero With a Thousand Faces* (Princeton: Princeton University Press, 1949).

3 Lady Ottoline Morrell (1873-1938) was a British-born literary hostess and arts patron of the First World War era. Her circle of friends included D.H. Lawrence, E.M. Forster, T.S. Eliot, Bertrand Russell, Aldous Huxley, H.G. Wells, Siegfried Sassoon and Virginia Woolf. They often met at her country home, Garsington Manor in Oxfordshire.

The Wrong Year[4]

Sunday: Mrs Bastard's Notebook.

Monday: How to tell about things that matter.

Tuesday: Affinities: On looking back over 24 hours.

[p.2]

Monday:

How to tell about the things that matter.

First of all, what does? Whose new flag (three spots on a Kotex, garni)? Whose funeral? Whose thwarted birth?

Life and death—and these from the inside.

Ma's loss, yes, if communicated.

Pa's death, yes, but they tried to take it away from him. Fancy waking up dead, having missed it. I should wait for my death like a frightful birthday—is it today? They said "don't tell him—let him be happy." Unhappy he was & the Christless protestants not allowing him to prepare. He holds my hand in his great paw, only one to make mine small—"What do they say?"

"What do you want them to say?"

"I want to live."

"Go on then, live." Nerves kept his old ma alive until 96. She turned blue 6 times before. And he only 62. Pouchy, shrunken. Skin like onion-paper.

"Look, are you afraid."

He shakes his head. "I don't know."

"Live by what you taught me. Brave & respectful. You can't lose."

[p.3]

I was a liar. There I was lying again. Respectful you lose—we had learned that together. You have to be rude. It's a great, friendly dogfight this life. Respect is no longer a learning stage. If death doesn't, why should life?

(This is how I used to annoy Sven.

"You should respect me," he thundered, "I'm a great writer."

"How can I respect you, saying things like that—maybe next year

---

4 At one time this was a working title for *Sarah Bastard's Notebook.*

you'll be <u>out.</u>"

Afraid his rage would penetrate his dignity, he shut up. Another story.)

"Actually," I told my old man, "You only have to respect God. Everyone else is human." He looked disapproving but proud. You could see his drowning man's life careening across an inner screen: the irrepressible country boy, terror of the two-holer, at whom they threw the trenches of the Great (my) war, the military hospitals, the engulfing St. Lawrence, the welcome of the Depression—my good years, these

[p.4]

last twelve, since leaving home, were his rotten: Canadian Tommy marches off to war, eminently & irreverently Christian soldier & is told he's a subject people slotted into a trench with the rest, he survives & in a kind of resurrection becomes a flyer they were machines, too, bat-winged & rat-tat-tat from behind the joy stick ... goggles, fur boots—little Winnie Churchill takes an interest. No parachutes: crutches, slings, nurses with husbands in Hyderabad. That too could be poetry—but soon enough it's home and no job but limping to school, no pension for the wog-Canadian limp—will my life become the kaleidoscope his was—suddenly not classics master, just Latin teacher & four daughters—thank God no dower houses to build.

Why did they want to take away his death?

[p.5]

Perhaps in those antipathetic hospital places they are ashamed not to be able to sterilize the unknown. That's not it: they are afraid to admit the unsterilizable unseen. Here's your hypo and don't tell me the angels of God come flying through those ethylene compounds (dreamless nylon sleep) to get you. You have to wait up for the angels, Pa. Don't miss them now. If you drug away the pain there can't be any meaning.

Doctor calls me an unfeeling fool.

"He's a grown man, my father."

"You want to make him suffer."

"I want him to know where he is, to have a good death. A religious man deserves it."

I was, of course, overruled. A sort of euthanasia prevailed. For him, the joys of consciousness had died a long time ago—perhaps, even, in the trenches, though he was snapped in a flying helmet, once, joyful. But after

[p.6]

Latin set in he became a good kind frightened man. Damned unlucky generation, half of them killed for dead England, the rest, cowed. Victoria was sent victorious in this country long after everywhere else. Respect.

Even for us, the keynote was never "enjoy" or "live" or "be aware." No, the sentence for us was "Advance carefully to go & collect $200." That's all that happened, too.

The pee-or old slee-ave is ...

Not the first death in the history of the world. Only in my world...

[p.7]

Affinities—Tuesday looking back

It is of course dramatically—in both directions—unnecessary that I should have had an abortion because of my brother-in-law. Stel[5] for me was complicated enough without any family tie. But the affair was part of the ludicrous exigencies of ordinary life: melodrama and farce are truer to most peoples' existence than they admit →

[p.8]

Stel and I, that year, that day—had a real affinity for each other: we were ready for each other. An affinity like that is rare enough to lead you into hell for the sake of carrying it through. I have felt it once before—with Sven—& both times it was the same as if he opened my mouth & poked the uvula at the back of my throat, which is why it has such a sexual name. The gag reflex in the mouth leading on the destruction—but a strait gate.

Watching people in their couplings I am more & more fascinated by the symbolism of relationships ... how the dark calls one to the fair—and the fat to the lean: these are the platitudes of wedding photographs. But there are subtler marriages and these we go on seeking all our lives, selling as we do our own identity. Alice & Gertie, what was in it for them? On the mad presumption that sex is knowledge (sex is rest)

[p.9]

my friends screw their own reflexions or the obverse of their ideas about themselves—or mate with their own hopes.

But even I—no Cleopatra—am another person every day. Incapable of change though I be, I go on melting and reforming so that the hope I see in one man's balls today may never operate again.

Thus Stel—his power.

I met him three times & he was thrilling by the same. Since, however, we are now separated by two varieties of death, that static element in my

---

5 A forerunner of the character Sandro in the published version of *Sarah Bastard's Notebook*.

life—& in his, since something has been done about affinity—that kept me tied to him 5 years has been destroyed—finished the love affair.

It was like this.

I CHATEAU
II I could write ... Stel talks in Sonnets
III Island—Sexual release
Domestic reality

[p.10]

Stel opened his life up for me to see as no other man has. Crouched naked on the sand, palms outstretched between his legs, he showed me the nut of his existence. Not quite banal—a reasonably superior biography—and freely offered. And because of the day and the year & the tide it was such a gift.

Poor washed-away Antonio!

[p.11]

I had more, I think, but without knowing it, from a sailor who picked me up at an international soirée in Montreal ... I was very raw about sex & didn't know what to do—he had 4 days leave & spent it showing me. He was clean & there didn't seem to be any good reason for guilt so there wasn't any. Anyhow, he was a ship's officer, & as I said, impossibly clean —never was such a white ass & he moved through & around and into me like a soft white inexhaustible cupid hardly a word said—after the first night I stopped even thinking Hemingway thoughts about good simplicity & after 4 days when he had to meet his old lady at the airport & I had to go back to Toronto, there was no sense of loss.

[p.12]

I have not come to a solution or an end; there are none until you are dead. The station on my personal Underground I stand in now is named Shock & Blandness. Death. Disgrace, mutilation, loss—these have eliminated the personal inessentials (You can say too—ah yes, I was born on the defensive—you can say "cut you down to size—Lady Jane") and I stand clear, knowing perfectly well what I am. There seems to be no point any longer in hating what I am. So I am going.

Egon's effort to recoup the family pride stands isolated. He bent [illegible] until she offered me a renewal, but I cannot respect him for it—or her. A wounded sense of propriety sends the pseudo-Englishman rampaging through delicate fields. This was his act for himself. She understood when I declined, but he was despairing, a honking walrus in suspenders—"Why?"

[p.13]

Some years sit in a scrapbook, others are built upon, Egon. You've got to sit and stare until you know the nature of things.

Yet I feel gentler about him. His bathos[?] no longer makes me scream. I do not think of his handling Joan, for I have seen flashing across the background of the year & pictures of her internal stability and know that the valuable things in her cannot be vulgarised by him. We each keep our own silences. I think, now, that she knows he is a horror and likes him for it. Her work is aesthetically satisfying. She understands no need for trimness or propriety in her life: let Egon roar & wallow: he is feeling things her restricted life has never let her feel. He is ugly, sloppy, foolish, juvenile. She has had enough of age, weakness, carefulness, virtue.

[p.14]

Egon is capable of crassness she cannot imagine. She likes to watch him piss out his life on the television screen. Well, god is love. She'll wash away his tears over me.

Now Ma and I have let each other go—admitted we cannot understand. We can be crotchety to each other.

The job? Always a part of me will stick in the academic. The library is home.

[p.15]

But I think I'd like to marry. Somebody—not like Joe—somebody real & complex & enjoying & poor like all the good people. To marry & make a proper Antonio. Live in Hampstead or Highgate in London, or suburban Paris or Rome & be like the other women, library books in the buggy, placidness inside & a mess of potage on the stove. Not someone I understand too well—not Joe—just a challenging pseudo-simple man with big balls and a decent library. If they're all gone, I'll have to settle for less, won't I?

I do like some things about this town—one day when the ghosts are gone & it's fit to live in, rather—I'll come back ... I like the fire halls.

[p.16]

I

Ottoline Morrell[6]

KM: Letters 71.2:6.4. 80. 90. 102. 157. 163.176.204.5 78 211-6 224 230-2 241

What was the "Garsington Chronicle."

---

6 See *Cahier* X, footnote 4.

"Your wonderful letter which seemed in its spray of verbena to come flying thro' the gold & green Sept. air dropped in my lap & I read it & sniffed the sweet spray & put it at the bottom of a blue jar."
80

She caught chill w. → TB going to Garsington

II 89 96 115 121 158 169 176 191 243

[p.17]

Books & attitudes:

Gorey Alphabet—	a document of fearful words.
The Rule of Folly —	presume we are always ruled by fools & work from there—brakes on an ideal world.
Hardy—his premises—	that the world grinds down women who defy convention—are surely defensive
Graham Green—	after Joyce—flogging a dead horse
Orwell—	Exciting but still the upper class describing the lower. You can see why he was attracted & repelled by Miller

[p.18]

Read

Jean Santeuil[7]
More Balzac
↘ Peacock
Moore—ave arque Vale
↘ Dorothy Richardson
↘ Freud

[p.19]

Pretensions—my dirty word—I am so afraid it is true.

[...] Wish I could move into the simple, conventional cage but it is too late. I have tried to see H. from too many angles—so many that he hardly exists ... but he is more real now than ever before. But how glibly we all hand out characters to each other. Without knowing. Still now we are making a really true marriage—bolstering. I can't break it.

But I still see people in a very childish way.

[...]

[p.20]

[...]

7 Marcel Proust, *Jean Santeuil* (Paris: Gallimard, 1952).

[p.21]

On the Carmania: Remembering what Howie said: "When the alarm goes for God's sake remember to go with the women & children." A Bible-reading roommate. Suitcase contains dirty laundry & coils of rubber—enema or douche?

There is an athletic clergyman, and a man with a yellow T-N. sweater. The children are beautiful—or am I getting soft?

Anyway, free kleenex.

I had a thought this morning that might have saved me: thought that my chatter was a taking refuge behind superficialities instead of being superficial. When I tried to write a letter it didn't work.

[p.22]

The Machiavellian man—don't think of him, think of the novel—and of Aphroulla. How Edward will be included, because of Sarah, but insulted. Does she side-track the story.

A person who is cavalier about reality.

Now don't turn yourself to reality, you know I can't stand it.

Look behind what is said. That's how you lose your innocence. NOT looking is the superficiality.

Innocence of superficiality.
Lola.
End of ch. 4—Innocence. (The Italian Girl)

[p.23]

Ruthie Lowther "You live for excitement."

This grim Scotswoman.

I wish I had grown up in the sordidness of my own life instead of someone else's. The endeavour was all innocence & practicality but somehow did not wash—did not "take." I should have had concrete reality to fight against rather than "unpopularity," "laziness" etc.

Stelios & Tommy Trinder.

Aphroulla should plan to re-open the Br. Council school and half-promise a job to Edward.

Two nuns.

[p.24]

Plans for a Magazine or Paper.

cf New Statesman. v. thin at first

Books Politics (?) Law
Theatre Articles
Poetry Art

Sark Solly Brown Bennett
Carscallen Armour Frazer Engel
Vichert Williams (Pattice too?)
MacLennan? MacNamara
MEAT
Patrons—Pauline & Don?

O. —a Hogarth Press

Do an article on Ottoline.

[p.25]

The Heart To Artemis: (Winifred Ellerman) 6.1894
BRYHER
Harbrace & World

I look at the cover. Poor Queenie of a Woman. Then read: she has come through my life & a thousand others. Paradise of childhood, then convention, stifling, the practical marriage. Analysis: which I begin to think of (the CRACK in me!). What she has learned—compassion, the uselessness of both conventions & material objects, necessity of devotion to facts.

But she was a practical child, a dreamer after facts & details, always precise, hence more dreadful to her elders. Her reading was wide. Sw[iss] Fam[ily]—Robinson the favourite book because of the FACTS. As I read this it struck me that W.T.A. [Women Travelling Alone][8] was a rewrite of Heidi. Is it Miss Rotterweir I am searching for?

[p.26]

She & Meadow Nurrel[?] are real whereas Clara (except for the recovery)

8 Engel's (second) unpublished novel, written the year she worked in London, England, 1961-62.

& Peter are false smiles. Maybe I could never believe boys came looking for one.

Odd, until Bryher's parents married she had quite a magnificent free life! Then, at 11 or so, the vise of convention was screwed on her.

Encounters: Norman Douglas (cf OH & Munthe) [illegible] Sachs, Freud, Dorothy Richardson. HD, H. Ellis

Queer? Is sexuality really irrelevant? Odder not to have any.

I should be the King....

Bargaining—the Middle East—looking behind—loss of innocence again (David has innocence.)

[p.27]

The Last Day of February.

> The long winter beginning to be over.
> Coming out of its tunnel to clean windows, I wonder what went on in it.
> I read Jones' autobiography, Sartre's autobiography & Jones' life of Freud.
> There was the week at the Mill.
> Script on Leonard Woolf—almost an 18th century influence.
> Fruitful encounters—Hamiltons & friends
> Hana & Arthur Nancy Kenyon
> Larry Zolf
> O'Mahoneys
> Vera Frenkel.

New Yorker introduces Mario Praz & Marshall McLuhan.

Good programme on Mavis Gallant—Telescope

<u>Venture</u> article.

[p.28]

In the McLuhan review—artist is after new juxtapositions, new metamorphoses. How to make the reader accept these. Oh, if one could draw!

Superficiality in art: women who draw agonised faces, eschew colour, still do not often hit on any technique showing depth of feeling. Perhaps because the story behind the agonised face has too often been told.

[p.29]

3/11/65

What Michel said.
The bravura works.
What doesn't work.

The intelligence of Sandro, Lyle & Eldon [characters in *Sarah Bastard's Notebook*]—why she [Sarah] is upset by the latter two not quite clear.
Second Boja scene—let Eldon hang himself.
Clear up Lois & heroine business.

All the effects come off but there are character problems—let them speak more for themselves.

How to end it: how many more people does she have to see.

CAPSULE BACKGROUNDS must either go or be left out.

Canadian parts are best.

Theme: Why one becomes an expatriate.

[p.30]

[...]

Nov 14/15 [1965] Joseph Campbell *The Hero with a Thousand Faces.*
[...]

[pp.31-32]

[Notes on *The Hero With a Thousand Faces*]

[p.33]

[...]
"The hero is the one who, while still alive, knows & represents the claims of superconsciousness which, throughout creation, is more or less unconscious. The adventure of the hero represents the moment in his life he achieves illumination."

[p.34]

Titles:[9] Waiting for the Evaluation
|| Dark Passions Subdue—Mrs Bastard's Notebook
|| The Narrow Norm

Alcomo's appeal must be as a hope for entry into superconsciousness—drugs & LSD etc. cf "Doors of Perception." But this is not realized by foundations who would not dream of diagnosing causes as in the society [illegible] the individual. Poets have been shouting about this for generations.

Outdated—Leary now.

Melody Melody
Mervyn

[p.35]

Minna's Book

Minna called them Alice & Gertrude, hated them. They were in reality Bertilla and Edie

The old Lady's priorities

A lady is:
A god-fearing person is

<u>Appearances</u> very NB

Get in Ma as a friend who can never get over her astonishment that the outside world is different from her—that anything is. SHE is the norm.

Ref: mythic structure of Edie's world

[p.36]

Marion	Orla	
Maude	Albert	
Emily	Tom	Arthur
Mary	Wellis	
Elizabeth (Betty)	Vernon	
Anna	Bill	
Henrietta	Ernest	
Bea	John (Jack)	

9 These were titles considered for *Sarah Bastard's Notebook*.

Vernice		Roy	Richard
Genevieve		Neville	Alan
Lola		Ray	
Jennie		Lloyd	
Vida	Orpha	Mait	
Laverne		Torrance	
Leila		Alf	Forneri
Lucille		Fred	Will
Edna.	Edith	Dick	Clure
Juanita		Edward	
Ruth, Ethel, Alice			

Fletcher, Jamieson, Watson, Wier, Flynn, Falconer, Stirling, Gigot, Richardson, Leene, Maitland

[p.37]

9th April: On Reading DHL [D.H. Lawrence] after having given a disappointing party.

Minor intellectuals—mismatched: drinking and dancing was their aim. [...]

But I still despair for strong feelings here. How to bring up kids in this milky atmosphere? Oh well, our social life shouldn't mean anything to them. But never to feel anything but domestic sentiments?

[...]

[p.38]

Only satisfaction is work—but need now literary stimulus.

Nancy K. this is a town where people are so wrapped up in their own private lives they can't hope to communicate.

[p.39]

The Housewife's Neurosis—
absentmindedness
fretfulness
vague hostility to children

—a passion to go "out"—on getting there a
firm desire to go home & set
things to [illegible]; be protected
by the children, square one's
conscience
or
a complete absentmindedness

—Why am I here?
inability to make decisions
or make up a grocery list
feeling of being a great executive
in other fields!

[p.40]

[...]
The acceptance sensation

1. Hysteria
2. Hypochondria
3. Insomnia

Flattered by the people, then distrusting them. They leave a bad taste. One does not like things to be out of control.
Better the book under the bed.
[...]

[p.41]

[Drawing of a floor plan for a living room]

[p.42]

Rejuvenation theme—she sees in the store window this pretty girl—not a woman of thirty, a girl. Like Violet Leduc[10] but backwards.

I begin to understand—if I—who see myself as a kind of toadstool—am in fact from time to time this pretty girl (whose existence I had of course suspected but squelched as prejudicial & imaginary....) I am twice as pretentious as I feared, twice the figure of fun I am. A remark in a train occurs—a student sharing a reclining seat—he is 6 years my junior but attractive—we are intimate because we knew each other at school—he the smallest boy—I the dashing editress of the school magazine. This boy, now enormous & above all independent, with only one complaint returning to reed. "Why," he groans "do women with brains think they don't have to wash their hair?"

[p.43]

Hard to explain. I went through the grooming stage as a teenager struggling with pincurls—like my sisters, like everyone else. But gave up for two reasons—A. I wasn't any good at it and B—the better looking I was, the less real life I had. Fifteen years later it is hard to recall the exact process but a ratio was in operation between the effect of my appearance and the effect of my real life—which consisted of, at that point, the

10 Violette Leduc (1907-72), author of *La Bâtarde* (1964).

absorption of K & the production of temperance essays & romantic novelettes. My face was round and common, and inadequately ringed with corkscrew curls, the face of a flibbert gibbet. A poor imitation of the successful girls like Leah. And even then I hated amateurism. Better be a straighthaired oddity than a bad imitation of a stupid ideal. And pretty women are not taken seriously until they are <u>far</u> older than fifteen. Thought Sarah. Then.

Now? Now I'm incapable of the life of a pretty woman, but still envious. And I understand disgust.

Nonsense—the kind of face that came in with Vistavision &
stayed with Swedish films & Sophia Loren—IN STYLE.

[p.44]

She goes walking, hoping to experience a "Ulysses in Nighttown," but finds herself uninterested. Flits mentally from one meagre treasure to another, hopes one car will be a friend; would like to be not raped but overwhelmed—or simply rolled over. Lacks emotional intensity for anything else. Observes that she drinks often to generate this cf "A Name to Conjure with" → fatal K that she will never be anything but romantic & barnacled. Will start collecting things & people in the next place but it is still OK to leave because one does get to the bottom of the well. People will die of cancer & TO. will march into Lake Ontario (how one longs to say "the sea") on cockroach legs but the need to know goes on. Some experiences are shallow, others, for other reasons, unfathomable. Sarah is cut off—only depths to pursue—Eldon—a self-invented hell—

[p.45]

teaching—long ago cut off from that. Mother—door shut (interior)—she has taken her life back. Joe—destructive of both Joe & Lois. Other people—oh, a party of them—2 or 3 men, a taste for doctors & lawyers —pick their brains in bed; Desmond—but one would come to the bottom of him (faith, hope & charity). Poet friend: lesbian tendencies. Well one <u>could</u> — as a child, the active partner in doctor—brothels with stirrups—no, not really Sarah. Carry this earnestness otherwheres.

Letter from Sandro at end—his then admitted humiliation—one victory —she has made him be <u>sincere</u>.

That's eno'. I should have a party—the hell I will. Who wants a party with me?
Better to go.
Party.

End.

[p.46]

After Rosemary & the Auctioneer—
a respite with a deadline

Sarah thinks about selling her books to Marty—Aust[ralian] Canadian deal.
Thinks about possible attitudes to Pembroke Street & falls asleep.
Dreams of going to bed with Eldon. [illegible] is in car with Bob sleepy & startled.
Talking with mother feels like early morning under water.
Sees mother in a gentler light.
(Mark's wet dreams)
Talks about going away
"I'm leading a wrong kind of life & can't change here"
Sees Mother exhausted & withdraws—a baby's fierce interior concentration.
Takes a taxi home & gets out & walks—remembers
garbage picking bravura.
plans a party.

[p.47]

Goes over acquaintances
—their compromises or lack of them to live here.

[p.48]

It's always been the same old world—
"In for a penny out for a pound."
Power corrupts on this merrygoround
Absolute power's a myth.

Give me intensity any old day.
(But adjectives rise from the steamy ground).
Give me a man whose true love can be found.
Show me the people he's with.

I'll show you how absolute [*sic*] anything goes
Watering wet in the daily round.
Power corrupts, out for a pound
Your marrow my love for my pith.[11]

11 Unidentified poem—possibly Engel's own.

Cahier XI[1]

Writing in so many notebooks—
as ever disorganized. [23]

"Must make the days count," Engel wrote on 4 March 1965, on the first page of this *cahier*. The author was nearing the end of her pregnancy—twins Charlotte and William were born 30 April 1965—and was conscious of the fact that there would be less time for writing following delivery. After several pages of note taking, she admonished herself: "You are busying yourself when you should be writing." Conscious though she was of the time that went into note taking, Engel's attention was gripped by theories about the modern novel and its protagonists. She expressed her irritation with the "little man" of the contemporary novel, who reneges on responsibility and "can't act." "NONSENSE!" exclaimed Engel. "This whole concept is an easy way out. He could do something but prefers to suck his thumb & pretend that the big bad world is insuperable by little guys. [There is] no real desire to conquer" [10]. In notes taken on Mary McCarthy's essay "Characters in Fiction,"[2] Engel recorded the view that the "novel & short story have lost interest in the social" [18]. "A dissociated outsider" is what the contemporary writer liked to be, in keeping with the twentieth-century sensibility that McCarthy suggested was one of "paralyzed grief" [18-19].

Engel's thoughts on modern writing are interspersed with others on her own writing. Upon finishing "Death Comes for the Yaya," 11 March 1965, she recorded: "reread it with respect—something in me had been released. The writing was, though often frivolous & slangy, looser, freer: still with condensed images" [5]. The author instructed herself to "keep the focus always sternly on the inner life" [24] and raised a question over which she puzzled without finding an answer:[3] "How do you deal with the idea of a middle class?" [17].

This *Cahier* XI depicts Engel's recurring struggles with poor self-esteem for which she invoked an image that would prove meaningful in future: "Today I feel like a hunched, old bear—can do nothing but play cards, pick bones,

1 1965 (March-June), bright blue notebook, "Engel," handwritten on cover; 27 pages used.

2 Mary McCarthy, *On the Contrary* (New York: Farrar, Straus and Cudahy, 1961).

3 In *Cahier* XXXII [12] Engel concludes that most literature is middle class.

devour cookies, dream—Why go out? The world is ugly, I am ugly. Hair like bread. Fat cheeks, warty feet. Feel like drinking" [7]. Like her character Sarah Bastard, Engel seemed to feel the need "to rage and do. Else I am not alive" [24]. Sarah's rage helped make Engel's novel come alive: it met assessors' approval[4] and was published in 1968. With its release in the United States and Canada,[5] the author broke through the "first book" barrier and entered the North American literary scene.

[p.1]

Not much joy in the Welsh—Methodism? Does Catholicism WORK?

March 4th [1965]—Must try to make the days count.
[...]

[p.2]

Finishing the Thriller[6] :—

PLANT CLUE IN BEA'S LETTER

"I'd been sitting on the info. All the time...."

[p.3]

Turn left at Mars.

Rewriting the book [*Sarah Bastard's Notebook*]

It is not, at the moment, man-centred. Rather—a dream of hate. Humour might save it.

Previous concepts—a Hamlet (during Hamlet)
A Genêt study (without knowing G.)
A paranoid study with 2 sisters & reader not knowing which dies: original concept.
An expiation of sin.

---

3 In *Cahier* XXXII [12] Engel concludes that most literature is middle class.

4 For the enthusiastic assessment of one of the novel's readers, see Verduyn, *Lifelines* 74.

5 Under different titles: in the United States, *Sarah Bastard's Notebook*: in Canada, *No Clouds of Glory*. See also, Introduction, footnote 47.

6 This is a reference to the unpublished "Death Comes for the Yaya."

Good elements: YP's dream world. But that's about all. What it must say is that you can buck a background but by enormous sacrifices. Might begin AFTER the scandal.

Mr Bastard & Milo are good ideas.

The Orangeman's Saturday night (now SHE married....)

Sinister skin diseases & love.

[p.4]

The people of Euphoria live on peanut butter sandwiches & brandy. They raise cats, rise early and are, fortunately, considered socially unacceptable.

[p.5]

Threatening someone's unhappy home.
—[illegible] is something else

13th March

Sometimes there are whole issues of the paper for Mrs Bastard's Notebook.

On the 11th I finished DEATH COMES FOR THE YAYA and reread it with respect—something in me had been released. The writing was, though often frivolous & slangy, looser, freer: still with condensed images.

On the 10th, letter from Diarmuid returning WOMEN TRAVELLING ALONE.[7] COMMENT "Somehow it does not come together." TRUE!

Family: Father—a much underestimated man, who, however, gave in to a steamroller wife in favour of comfort & peace → amateurism.

Mother: strong, but unwilling to accept the darker side (she experienced it but refused to integrate it) mere prettiness, gentility, became

[p.6]

the aim, "nothing stronger than tea" a whole philosophy. She <u>reneged</u> on her education, on logic, on any interesting concept of womanhood—retreated to the farm.

---

7 This is Engel's second unpublished novel.

Was she ever more than a good farm girl?
Will I ever be?

Interested in outside world—
but believes any[thing] established is good.

Interested in languages
—takes some French course every year

Feelings Intelligence Actions
all divorced.

Father is more integrated.
[...]

[p.7]

13th
Today I feel a hunched, old bear—can do nothing but play cards, pick bones, devour cookies, dream—why go out? The world is ugly, I am ugly. Hair like bread. Fat cheeks, warty feet. Feel like drinking—have to go to Esther's & Jane Tobias's party. How can I meet people? Perhaps in a shroud or a new dress? Life is a bowl of shit & today I am in it.

14th Last night's party: confessions from John of the liquid eyes. Have never met a man so up & be-set. IS his wife going crazy—all is so quick—ulcer, appendix, abortion, sterilization—incipient schizophrenia, or do they need a rest?

People will stay in their cages.

The need to hope, like the need to believe in God.

Muckraking: battered babies.
poor population.

Use EGAN as a target. Compare him to Sarah, expl[ore] hostility thus.

Reading I MURDOCH'S UNICORN[8]—why panned: but has taken a direction.

[p.8]

Pip Lejour—Pip Emma!
Allice Emma

8 Iris Murdoch, *The Unicorn* (London: Chatto and Windus, 1963).

MYTH. FIGURES THERE
1) STRANGE LESBIAN WOMAN
2) schoolmaster
3) homosexuals w supernatural power etc. Think this through later.

[p.9]

[...]

—— . —— . —— . ——

April 4. Canlit again—why not?
1) lack of standards of excellence
2) challenge is foggy—

Idea for a play—
Junk shop
Nobody is a symbol but
2 people pretend to be
free.

[p.10]

Sunday 12 April [Beer wars]

Necessary Books[9] The Dyer's Hand
On The Contrary
Miller's Watercolours

Ideas to deal with

1) The "little man" is one wrong thing with the modern novel—a reneging on responsibility—he <u>can't</u> act—NONSENSE—poor in spirit—meek = EVERYMAN.

Why MEEK? Lazy, unrealistic.
This whole concept is an easy way out—He could do something but prefers to suck his thumb & pretend that the big bad world is insuperable by little guys. No <u>real</u> desire to conquer.

[p.11]

2) Enquire into our **<u>psychic</u>**(?) need for modern Greece—brashness—violence (innocence).

9 W.H. Auden, *The Dyer's Hand, and Other Essays* (New York: Random House, 1962) and Alfred J. Miller, *The Miller Collection of Water-colour Drawings* (Ottawa: King's Printer, 1951).

3) The Leduc case—necessary to combat bastardy by est. fund. Red Feather Agencies can't act: Parkinson's Law (humour is **vile**—leads us to accept things). They now exist as (1) sop to conscience (2) self proliferative entities independent of purpose.

[p.12]

i.e. dykes in Red Cross.
Wild self-deception of **Go**od **Pe**ople based on romantic concept of [Christian]
Service = Help poor NOT
LOVE poor

What is love? We can't act because our idea of love is now so tinged with EPOTIKO[10]
that we are guilty & fastidious.
↓
The Mrs Bastards!

[p.13]

We are all, in this country, great critics of each other's character. This is something other than Greek suspicion of motives. It is a real concern with weighing the amount of virtue in our friends. Sincerity must always be weighed. This takes so much time that non-Puritans (aristo-English, Gks, Armenians, Jews) are the only ones who have TIME to create anything or do anything UNEQUIVOCALLY. Arises, therefore, enormous conflict between idea and action—preoccupation with few things we are SURE of—church going, cleanliness, tidiness civil & legal.

———

CRIMINALITY & Insanity

We want to believe in existence of pure evil
Though we give lip service to belief in "mental illness"
∴ although we know that a large percentage of

[p.14]

murderers & robbers can be proved to have damaged brains we 1) go on hanging 2) refuse to est. neurological & psychiatric exams because the truth would wash away our catharsis. Jesus has to die every day so we can go on sinning.

10 This is the Greek word for eroticism.

The world has need of Jesus
To give the shower of blood
Showers of blessing around w
the Christians sweet brain food.

[p.15]

Oh little Jesus
With a pain in your brain
Die every day
Die, go on dying
Jesus boy
So I can go on sinning.

My Daddy says,
Boy shed no blood
The time for that is gone.

Jesus boy
I need catharsis.
Go on dying, Jesus
The way you used to do.

Psychiatry is bullshit
I need your hanging form
And not on any eikon—

You were born for me to kill
Weren't you? Die everyday
I need your blood my Jesus
To whiten[?] (oh!) my whey.

[p.16]

Civilization is progress.
We don't need centurions now,
We have our B. Jesus
To crucify every hour.

The lady washing[?] the pain
Who did her children in
We watch her on the teley.
To remind us there is sin

Sin is all around us
Even in our homes.
Protect our little bones
And we'll crucify Mrs Jones.

[p.17]

We don't like pain & sorrow
We don't like sordidness
We just give in to a little blood lust
To take away the mess

How do you deal with the idea of a middle class?

Mary McCarthy   On The Contrary "Characters in Fiction"

There is no "one clear recent photo" of a real character in recent Am[erican] fiction though there are in real life. Our exterior lives are very rich right now. Why are they not chronicled?—Social workers, slot machine kings. Bennington girls. What glorious conjunctions—sociologists but they no longer become archetypes.

[p.18]

In England there were Gulley J. & Lucky Jim.[11] Wilson has people but Joyce was really "the last gt creator of character."

Novel & short story have lost interest in the social—impasse as a result of progress & experience. Arts have aged. It is impossible to "go back."

Experiments C20 — 1) sensibility — England
— Women & Forster
2) sensation — USA
H[eming]way, Dos P[assos] Farrell
G. Stein, Joyce, merged these

Today 1) Green, Sanson
Porter Welty Stafford McCullers.

2) Beats, Cain, Hammett, Chandler.

11 Gulley Jimson is the artist/protagonist in Joyce Cary's, *The Horse's Mouth* (New York: Harper, 1944) and Lucky Jim is the main character in Kingsley Amis's novel *Lucky Jim* (London: V. Gollancz, 1954).

Through both these the sense of character is annihilated—starting with our own ("In violence we forget who we are")—these are at their height in the child—who cannot act to any purpose or talk expressively—is a dissociated outsider which is just what the current writer likes to be.

[p.19]

Occurred before in Stendhal. Inability to feel or say appropriate thing & faculty of noticing also in Tolstoy—but world of C20 sensibility is one of paralysed grief—shimmer of consciousness occupies whole field of vision. Modern novel of sensation is almost mute, confined to subtitles & pix. Nothing happens in novel of sensibility.

Way out for character—inside-outness of Joyce.
Joyce—ventriloquist of the novel—sustained power of mimicry which V. Woolf lacked. Nearly all gt modern novelists rely on mimicry alone...

This is wrong! You are busying yourself when you should be writing.

Think—how it might be the day to decide whether to be tied up in T. Town.

[p.20]

16th April. Rose early—8.15 started to read The Representative[12] in the bath—v strong—I hate to go on.
Then after H. left automatically phoned Helen—Jennie having a party on the 30th.
Whole family issue rises again.

What sort of world do Howard & I live in?
1) We don't recognise ties exc. sentimental outside immediate family.
2) We scorn the need.
3) But feel guilty.

Also want them to be as self-contained as they brought us up to be.

———— . ————

Two books here

Sarah vs Canadian society which is so incredibly credulous that anything could happen behind the facade.
1 Very Ibsen play
2 I book

---

12 Rolf Hochhuth, *The Representative* (London: Methuen, 1963).

[p.21]

Domestic preoccupation—can[n]ot make a coffee table from a picture frame?
What sort of coat?

Opening—Sarah playing w cat
Rosemary comes in—very upset—housework not done—Sarah skipped family party
"Egan is a scapegoat."
"Why don't you give it all up, Sarah?"

TWIN STUFF OUT!

22nd May Giving up birthdays[13]
An Outing: To CBC—[...]

[p.22]

[...]
Lunch at a café
[...]
Things to put in [*Sarah Bastard's Notebook*]. Allan Gardens
Firehalls
Outdoor cafés
Orange Hall
Spadina area (rooftop party?)
Colours of Pembroke street—hunchbacks etc.
fights (I've got a razor in my purse, go on, kill me)
Social workers

[p.23]

June 4th

Writing in so many notebooks—as ever, disorganized.

[...]

Last night we dropped into the 4 seasons [...]. Exchange of information leads to supper. Insane beery conversation about Patriotism—old thing. If the good people stay the country will become something. On the contrary—the good people become mediocre.

13 Engel's birthday was 24 May.

[...]

Fuel for Mrs Bastard

[p.24]

Keep the focus always sternly on the inner life—the multiplicity of events & scenes outside to be on the surface....

Pembroke Street—brutalising.

I could stop being a bastard but that is my function—to rage & do. Else I am not alive.

"I am riding my own character like a horse these days—disobeying orders—living instinctively instead of logically. But riding high. I've bashed a great hole in the year—through to the destructive reality of the other side. The brass band plays of God in the Gardens. The Victorian glasshouse."

[p.25]

17th June.

Howard is gone [on a short trip] & I feel more lost than I ever have—getting old, frightened of leaving people & resisting it. He's dead scared too.

25th June. [..]— among the kindly trolls, confessions. Pretensions among the Dutch.

[p.26]

[Greek sentences]	21. Harriet Monroe	A Poet's Life 1938
Food for beast	22. Samuel Putnam	Paris was our Mistress 1947
[Greek sentences]	23. Leo Stein ↘	Journals 1950
Place to sleep	24. Michael Strange	Who Tells Me True.

[p.27]

A bibliography of the 20's
From: McALMON & The Lost Generation. R.E. Kuoll. Nebraska 1962.

[List of books]

Cahier XII[1]

The Texture of Women [34].

Following the publication of *Sarah Bastard's Notebook* (1968), Engel became deeply involved with "Minn," the manuscript that would become *The Honeyman Festival.* Most of this *cahier* is draft "Minn." The protagonist's home town of Godwin is presented through the humorous narration of excursions to local beauty parlours for 1950s-style hairdressing. Parental struggles to transform their daughters' stick-straight hair into crowns of curls is a recurring theme in Engel's work and no doubt a reflection of the author's own experiences with stubbornly straight hair! Here, Minn's thirteenth birthday present is an outing to "Stardust Salon," from which she emerges, six hours later, "a stranger to herself, smooth-curled, light-headed & hating it, only having acquired a taste for confession magazines" [13-14].

"Diary-like" entries of personal introspection include notes on the Passmores [2-5] and a chronology of events around the launch of *Sarah Bastard's Notebook.* Engel is next to silent on response to the novel. An entry dated 8 February 1968 reads only, "Cutting one's hair, thinking of Fulford's review" [12].[2] In her next notebook, Engel mentions "loss of self-esteem [...] since book came out" [*Cahier* XIII 28], and in *Cahier* XVIII she admits disappointment at not having been nominated for a Governor General's Award.[3] But for the most part, *Cahier* XII is devoted to Minn and "items" about her—Engel's word throughout the last pages of the notebook for the various "ingredients" to remember in writing Minn's story.

---

1 1966-68, black notebook; 64 pages used.

2 Robert Fulford, "A War Inside Sarah's Head," *Toronto Daily Star* (Tuesday, 6 February 1968): 23. "No Clouds of Glory is less a completed fiction than a series of notes towards a definition of a personality," Fulford wrote, "but the notes are often illuminating and memorable." Though he judged it "unsatisfactory in many ways," Fulford thought Engel's novel had "the smell of life about it." If the critic was of two minds about the work, the author, it seems, was of two minds about the review.

3 "Not nominated for G Gen's award—upset." *Cahier* XVIII [36], 18 March 1969.

[p.1]

Passmores and Minn

[...]

[p.2]

Frederick F. Passmore C.E. (deceased) was for many years a well-known c[ivil] e[ngineer] of TO. where he died in 1892. He was born in Devonshire, England, in 1823, the son of Frederick & Mariah Passmore.

Mr P. grew to manhood in his native country, & there received both his literary & professional education. When a young man he came to Toronto & shortly thereafter formed a partnership with a Mr Tully, under the firm name Tully & Passmore, civil engineers & govt surveyors. In this, his professional work, Mr P cont[inued] for a number of years. He then secured the appointment to the registry office of the city of TO. & served in that capacity until his death.

[p.3]

Mr P. married Miss Isabella Rankin who belongs to a family long identified with Cy York, being a daughter of Wm & Mary (Mahoffey) Rankin, natives of Ireland who came to TO at an early date, settling on Yonge St, where Mr R owned a track of land & where their 13 children, Mrs P & her sister Mrs Cunningham & 1 brother, Abraham Rankin, survive.

To Mr & Mrs P. were born 4 children: Alfred C., Frederick F., Isobel (deceased) & Blanche Ellen, the last named the wife of Robert Tickey, a well-known barrister of Toronto. Mr P was a member of the C[hurch] of E[ngland], a faith of which his widow also adheres.

[p.4]

[Passmore family addresses]

[p.5]

Things couldn't have been better than they were as Norman put it.[4] "Minn's OK. just slightly allergic to things that go bump in the night."

"And Mother," Minn would say ruefully, and not tell the story. So everybody was relieved.

Mother, since the break, was, according to sources, also relieved. She was not missing her grandchildren. She was not missing Minn.

And Annie, the sister, who was more than "not quite right," who was a hydrocephalic idiot, died in the Home, a further relief, since her original sweetness had long ago worn thin.

And Minn had these children, & this house, and, in the absence of Norman, this friend to watch over her—an arrangement that smelt awkwardly of the passel of women at home,

---

4 From *The Honeyman Festival*.

[p.6]

but that Norman thought was better, that therefore, he having in the past oftener than she proved right, she accepted....

[p.7]

22 Sept.

There was on the whole no point in talking to Frank, they had [illegible] they were establishment vs bohemian and it was boring to even think of the battles in exchange. But they were both there in this big dead white house, which was as dead as the white skin of an old woman, (old men's she had avoided—she was no genius at genetics) and—well, there had to be talk.

"Can we?" she asked.

He squirmed—or did he? Perhaps he thought pleasantly of her now. He'd had women but he wasn't queer on the 8th month, he was safe with her.

"What do you think of it?"

"What?"

"All this?"

"Oh—what do you want me to say?"

"Do you like it?"

"The house. Oh, yes in a

[p.8]

way. It stands for something."

"I did, once, too?"

"You knew it."

"Yes. I made you stand for my father."

"That was obvious. I felt a little young or wanted to."

"That really wasn't what I wanted to talk about?"

"What was your subject, then?"

"Aspirations."

"Are we being so abstract? Is there a subject for each night?"

"Until I find them help—imagine—me—the housekeeper."

"Not your line?"

"Hate the whole woman bit. Always your obedient servant. Promotion subject to servility."

"I read Norman, I respect it."

"But you've got it right. I'm not very servile ergo

[p.9]

he's not high up."

He chuckled. "You. I can't imagine you servile."

"That's why we didn't marry."

"You're being unfair. It was the no breakfast—the disorder—"

"That's—god, you're profound."

"Not profound, practical. Fool—I've never married for one reason—

I've never found a woman who showed any sign of being able to organize a household I could live in."

"The socks."

"The unpressed pants!"

"Oh—you're right—Poor men, putting their physical welfare in our unwilling hands."

"How do you manage."

"Chaos. But I make him do for himself—it's the only way with kids. Papa's wash goes out, he pays."

"Journalism doesn't."

"We manage."

"Children are beyond me."

"And me!"

[p.10]

"What do you do?"

"Hope to survive, fail to control. But you see—control is fascism."

"Don't believe that."

"Depends on who."

"Ah, hmmm...."

Ah, love to lollop into his arms once more. He knows. [illegible] to bed.

Jan 18, 1967

I must record the night & then the day

Father was tired; Charlotte[5] happy in his lap. Mother was late. Pa went to nap. [...][6]

[p.11]

[...]

Morning the same—nice, but they march urgently off—don't they understand that urgency kills me? [...]

[p.12]

Feb 8. 1968.

Cutting one's hair, thinking of Fulford's review.[7]

---

5 Charlotte was 20 months old.

6 The remainder of the page is smudged.

7 See *Cahier* XII, footnote 2.

Mordie had told her to run along to the Beauty Parlour—to be thus dismissed was ... low. Pip, she said of him, and hacked crossways with the scissors at her hair, which was blacker and coarser than before—a sign, perhaps, that it was soon to be pepper-and-salt. There was a satisfaction in chopping it, making her head neater, cleaner, and in throwing hunks of it in the toilet, & in flushing the evil stuff away.

In Godwin there were the *Beauty Box* and the *Stardust Salon*,[8] one run by Laura, who was fat & fifty & the other by 2 bleached blondes wearing tickets "Miss Linda" & "Miss Carol." They cut her hair off one spring-combed out her braids

[p.13]

and, carefully, scissored the locks, saying "good thick hair, it will take a curl," combed & scissored and then stuck her head backwards in a stainless steel basin with a tray with a neck-plate, deriving no doubt from Spanish barbers' plates with bites out, and sopped her head, then made her sit under a tin beehive for five chapters of *The Big Six*, then combed it excruciatingly with dirty metal combs & rolled it on hairy cucumbers attached to an octopus. It was her father's present for her 13th birthday, she was going to be a lady now and have strangers put their fingers in her hair & cook it & her under the heavy machine, its bound cords sending her neck awry. She came out combed & curled, six hours later, a stranger to herself, smooth-curled, light-headed & hating it, only

[p.14]

having acquired a taste for confession magazines & proud of herself for not having hit anyone.

She was much praised for being beautiful, as if she had not been good enough for them before.

When she stuck her head under the tap, her hair went into little ringlets & dried into frizz. She cried, & began to chop—but Miss Carol & Miss Linda had done their job. Alice had to do it up for her, every night, in curlers that looked like silver clothes pins, had rather pleasant dragon faces, & fell out in the middle of the night. Gertrude hid the scissors—the job had cost $10, by God. Father absented himself when it looked too bad, she tried to stay away from school,

[p.15]

but, Gertrude being Chairman of the Board, did not succeed & went late, red-faced, blotched, frizzed & if this was the lady's crown of thorns, wearing it gracelessly, coming to the conclusion that if ladies had to spend all their time on their hair, they'd never have time to read, which, she found

---

8 Engel made a note to herself in the margin here to check the names of the beauty parlours.

out at university, was true, & which the lads upstairs were finding to their annoyance now.

The consolation was that Annie, finding her crying, would comfort her. And the first time Louisa her daughter said "Mummy cry, I kiss," she discovered in that healing sensation that it was Annie who had taught her how to love.

Afterwards, she grew her braids again, learning to plait them neatly, gather in the black stray back hairs, find her own elastics, brush every

[p.16]

morning. She wore a proud crown then, until she was 16, & fell prey to fads & home immersions in ammonia & hydrochloric curling acid. Now she thought of Miss Linda & Miss Carol, retired into baby-making by the home Mr Toni, and pitied them—ten dollars for a day with her being small fee.

She went about once a year now & always to a big one, always in the hope of meeting not pink plastic but some sort of glorious women's brothel, that was their promise—the city now being full of them, fancy ones with gilt mirrors and velvet carpets, strutting little men—once an Italian with sworls of hair on his forearm had clicked & giggled over her hair. If there were justice, there was a sliding door

[p.17]

in the back, containing therapeutics, legalized adultery. Alas, she was always disappointed. Pastel nylon uniforms rustled ineffectively aware. Hairdressers told her about the children. Her neck looked dirty. There should be—she kept saying—but she doubted there were any for men, that there ever, really had been. It was just an idea, something from Westerns & novels about Edward VII. If there were any, they'd be tatty, diseased. If she were running one, it would be surgical. Maybe there were in Paris. What kind of clientele would you get? What kind of help? Would the Mafia move in? Maybe men couldn't do it on demand. She always thought about it in the hospital, where they were a rude lot anyway. But thought it a public

[p.18]

service to create a house for rude dreams, as in Chinese literature. Better than having your hair tied in knots & fried.

When she thought this she sang to herself, high & thin & childishly, "Where have all the morals gone?" Then supposed it was hereditary, her father never had any.

He had a wonderful speech he gave in the '40's—the mothers of Canada—the war effort—sacrificing their strong sons. Gertrude, curled

Minn, and, before he was killed—though a passive verb didn't seem right for Alan it was right for war-Alan. "Now," he would shout prancing, while Minn squirmed & Gertrude & Alan held their big chins high—"I want to pay tribute to the biggest single force for good for strength and—yes—for victory.

[p.19]

To the people who are making our war effort not only possible but also—victorious—we will win, we shall win, and we shall win because of their efforts—Ladies & gentlemen, 3 cheers for the Mothers of Canada."

At least he wasn't parochial, at least he didn't say Godwin or Ontario. But as weeping Willie's popularity thinned on the wane, at the back there was often a beer. Which meant he would get awfully drunk that night, & stay away & that her mother would be even more rigorous about propriety & she would cry a lot & Annie comfort her. And she would hear on street corners "Well, in his way, Willie's a mother" too. And "ssh" because she was passing.

[p.20]

As a childhood, it was, however, painful, beautiful & rich. The cosmos was Godwin and, though Godwin had its shortcomings, Godwin was the right size for a child & contained enough variety for a child & in its politics, taught her both escape & innuendo....

Extra cash
Don Sims – 25
NY Times [9]
Advance 250

<u>Prime</u> the
pump

[p.21]

When <u>the book came out</u>

No Clouds of Glory

31 Jan— out in U.S.—Telegram from Dan
1 Feb— took kids to Helen's (they rubbed shit when getting ready)
— Longman's Party—e<u>very</u>body there & talking to each other. Austin most fun.

Dinner for 14 downstairs—me sick on way out. Bob sends back his oysters, Arlene wipes me up.

2 - late rising, big head. Lunch at Czardas—shop, get

9 Engel frequently reviewed books for the *New York Times*.

kids—Armours arrive, 3, 4 — Sears come over.
Late nights
Engels Sunday. — Gert's party—autographs. "I hear you wrote a horny book," from
All kids good. — Rickey Marx. Awful Corinne. Gert does a bit with the lamp cord & endears herself.
Back to our own party too tired to take it in.

5 - Don Sims show—putting in the evening—finally, w Taras Bulba

[p.22]

Maddening

6. Fulford's article: Lew Gloin & Tom Dwan got in touch. Sylvia Child phoned—details on having chubes blown by Bernie Ludwig

8 - Dinner w Hohnstocks at Brysons.
Awful evening. 9. We SKIN RABBIT

10 - Hamiltons—no dinner. I pass out, H. goes to Mars.

11 - Cold. Rabbit cancelled

12 - Elwood Glover—easy. Susan Clarke there. Lunch w. Weaver.

9—also—visit from Jennie & Lola who are much loved by W[illiam] & C[harlotte]

13 - Ratty tempers all around.

14 - Warren Davis interview. The Ivy League
—Marg Morrison & Danny Callendan call. [...] spoils it with references to Jews.

[p.23]

20/2/68

Arthur came last night to sign the picture. He was still & shy at first but when we talked books & boats [...] it was ok and he did his job.

Marvellous insights—The Frenchwoman's sand house N. of Maple.

Vietnam conversation—I suddenly realized that Minn's refusal to deal w. the idea of Norman's being in VNam is a refusal to live on the profits of war. Hence it is a Vietnam more than a baby novel.

[p.24]

John Barth in the Atlantic

What advances can be made in the novel?

Surely, an advance in self-consciousness, in awareness of layers of reality.

Hence Minn can dissect the reality she is in vs the externals her family lives in, comparing realities.

Castles built: Katmandu
Gertrude & Alice
Rufus' life

[pp.25-28]

[Lists of names, for possible use in writing]

[p.29]

25/10/66 On reading Maurois' life of Balzac[10]—

The multiplicity of the man, the love of chaos, hugger-mugger. Junkshop or splendid museum of a mind? Versailles & Highgate cemetery. Means of knowing people—prolific intimacy.

How many peoples' stories do I know this way?[11]

[…]

[p.30]

[Inventory of names and places.]

[p.31]

Life before & after children
the empty self-absorbed house
the wife distracting herself until husband returns

later h[usband] is almost an intrusion
(in cond[ition] of weariness & impatience)

The intensity of the living from day to day w. children has created an amnesia in Minn. She has forgotten the details of her life b.c. [before children]—living with Frank, frantic dependence on Lucy. Lucy is both wounded & amused—& rather drunk. Living it all over again with Barney—it also interferes with her sex life.

Minn has forgotten she was beautiful & clever—& is glad of it.

[…]

10 André Maurois, *Prométhée ou la vie de Balzac* (Paris: Hachette, 1965).

11 An inventory follows [29-30] of individuals Engel knew in the various places she had lived, including Sarnia, Hamilton, Cyprus, Montreal, London and Toronto.

[p.32]

Lucy— Yr mother used to be sick with worry about you. You should have seen yourself & you'd know why! I would have been too—all that—girl, everything. All freshness & volupté. Beautiful. And, smart as a whip. And innocent—my god you must have been the easiest lay in 7 counties. What did you think about?

Minn pictures Minn.

— About whatever I was doing. My work. It puzzled people. It puzzles them now—though I can't think at the moment.

[p.33]

Minn confronted by her own beauty at last finds the pattern in the carpet—laughs.
Then feels Nastiness.
When did she learn to use it?

when I looked
"And I took walks at night ^ like that!"

Knew it partly, but not all along, vanity had been well discouraged.

"No wonder I got jobs."

[p.34]

Feb 2. Thought a while ago of calling it [*The Honeyman Festival*] "The Texture of Women"—keeping it narrowly sensual.

Joe is dubious. She would have to have some guilt.

Meg Sears last night & to-day.
On adoption: Children's Aid's & parents' attitude wrong.
Letters from adopted children: "It's not the same."
To-day she said she'd like to hire someone who'd say to all arriving expectant mothers:
"How marvellous!"

What I learned in House Ec[onomics]
"Glass, silver, china, etc."

Minn—sits on steps swathed in guilt,
a time of erotic fantasies: playing doctor.

[p.35]

[...]

Next

In short, Jellicoe was irrelevant to the present Minn lived in, because Minn had grown up.

It was with some sense of wonder that, patiently drowsing upright with one hand on Jane's rubber bottom & the other hand on the new lad's buried one, she realized that she had at last acquired an armour. She had marvelled at Morgan & Lucy, in the old days—indifference.

It must be being 35—at an age when you begin to pare your

[p.36]

passions to match your energies. She had no strength to worry about these people. The job in hand was to placate them. Beyond that, they did not interest her—Alice, her mother, Lucy—even Morgan, particularly Barney. They failed to exist.

Oh—once they had. Once she had been Juliet—"take him & cut him out in little stars"—even Alice had had a corner of her affections. Now—no. Too late. Sleep was the thing. She lived in a dream of sleep.

Sleep. The children, Bernie, Norman. Intimacy.

They'd had their chance. One by one they'd had her heart at their feet—had had no time to pick it up. Other loyalties? Perhaps. Intimacy is in the end also wearying.

Bev—had she flung herself on Morgan because rejected by

[p.37]

Minn?
Was Morgan's desire for Bev a reflection of his guilt for Minn?
—Explain
—Well—until 4 a.m.—
house rules

Next morning

Katmandu.

The Queen Empress of Fecundia

Get the kids to myself & scream at them

Annie—lost

[p.38]

Break no hearts this Xmas[12]
All interior monologue!

My husband Harry mourns virginity. Dreams? Does she? And worry after, struggling to interpret? No, says humph & gets ON with it.
Inquisition:

Why do you bite the hand that feeds?
My husband Harry is away in Katmandu. Living out my dreams.
Why do you have to do with nuns?

—Building schools, organizing work parties, preserving the toad of tradition. What we once were shall be, the same & ever after.

How can she face you?

Ah—there's our history. The mistaken generations change. Once a young lawyer married an old schoolteacher.

[p.39]

As his old brother married a young wife, the dynasty was assured—but askew. What generation are we, we grew up to ask?

You carry on your shoulders that load which you are given. Alpha. Omega

A Ʊ Minn Heriot
Heretic
Harriet
Harry

I wanted to be a boy—when I was one. Now?

Shut yo' mouf.

Could use rude words.
Why? It hurts your mother?
She hurts me—whalebone in my soul.

12 From *Inside the Easter Egg*. See also *Cahier* XIII, footnote 5.

[p.40]

While having the baby—she hunkered away from what she was doing—sideways—a crab afraid of its shadow. It was the end of body-think, this first conscious confinement. Body does not think, body does. Body hurts. Body betrays. Its insides sink & lurch. There is no heaving like labour except the slow churn of a ship's engine, deep down at which writers talk of screws.

[If we become disease-free will we become sterile i.e. unable to expel.][13]
(OR integrate)

[Freedom from Sex?]

Katmandu
    The mind has mountains
    Everest—The Great Penis
    The Top of the world -
    Shangri la the country of the orgasm.

[p.41]

Nepal—more ideas.

[Does your passionate nature lead you to entrapments?][14]

She's buried in the mother-concept
        —serial responsibilities
He's **climbing**—his cumulative—is the pattern different?
        Not so involved with time?
        How is the lead to carry?
        Surely larger things
        —not so much detail
            woods not trees.

—Katmandu vs hospital.

[p.42]

March 2.

13 Square brackets here, and on the next line, appear in the original text.
14 Square brackets appear in the original text.

—And what am I accused of now?
—Mothering.

——— . ——— . ———

These cold stone towns.
These cold wood towns.
Wood, stone, yellow brick.
Genteel sufficiency.

My little nun I left behind.
I fled unto my mother.

[...]

Bev & Morgan[15] go!

[p.43]

Home: cold stone, corsets.

Louisa making a snatch
(Cut out Jane)

Turnstiles in subways won't admit me—the TTC considers pregnancy obscene—public transport obscene as well. Respectable people drive chauffeured limousines.

Braithwaite on women today

The Katmandu theme—up the penis to where women are beasts of burden?

[p.44]

The marriage was going well. From time to time she committed an assinity, occasionally she was less than kind to the children, but on the whole, her life was more successful than she thought she deserved. Pregnancy, for instance, suited her—she was lusty & healthy during it, and on the whole no more vague than when she was not pregnant. And to be encircled by happy children, however maddening, made her feel that she had changed her luck—crossed a hurdle into a brighter world.

Norman was wonderfully protective, read her mood, directed her mind, arranged things. And since they both liked the hugger-mugger of

15 These characters were envisioned for *The Honeyman Festival.*

domesticity—since both could find respite in a better-ordered cerebral world—and neither cared about the finish on the furniture, they were happy.

She had work, as well as the children—her own corner of information

[p.45]

to be consulted on. She compiled lists, wrote articles, on a subject far from her heart and close to her experience and smiled anarchically when a cheque came in.

She had, in fact, almost every satisfaction.

And help—help with 3 children & 1 coming—was important. She had Bev, and even Bev was special, having used to be a nun & now regaling Minn with information about a world that fascinated her.

She liked the idea of a convent, peace.[16]

Though now she lived in luxury—to a degree.

[p.46]

She—repeat—had everything. The first psychiatrist hadn't been any good, he hadn't understood anything & seemed to be even less well read than herself in his own subject. But after haggling with Norman—who had had burdens to bear—had she realised what she was doing to him, she might not at that time have tried to commit suicide—she had gone to a second who bore but her own conclusions and reinforced them in the best possible way. It was a point of logic she had missed, there was a logical reason to go on living—so her immediate problem was solved; she was pronounced, in addition, not schizophrenic. Norman stopped looking at her with dread—love, always almost unbearable love—but mixed with dread—she had got pregnant & discovered beautiful vacuity—she had everything. Her life was, because of that fundamental mistake, now manicured.

[p.47]

Not that she was entirely happy. Not that she really did have everything. But she had more than any woman could reasonably expect—liked what she had.

But there was a strain of pessimism in her that denied life itself any absolute value. Psychiatrists, Norman, her obstetrician—they were all life-lovers, shocked at her gloomy attachment to death. If lives begin, she would say, they also end. If you like the beginning—if it excites you—doesn't the end—NO! they shouted.

Thought her paranoic?

Kaisermann, the psychiatrist, had taken another tack. Live for something.

16 There are early signs of *The Glassy Sea* here and in preceding lines.

Hobbies? God!

No—aren't you useful?

Anyone could do what I do?

She was a frightful housekeeper and, now, often so neurotic that

[p.48]

it was physically impossible for her to make love. There was no fluid in her. And she had been, in addition, & of late, unfaithful. She found men at parties.

She expected him to be impressed, but he found it on the whole, normal for her.

But I'm not like that—

When aren't you?

When I'm—ME.

What are you. Earnest. Knowledgeable. Good at things.

True—too—once. But, then, that was school. A protected frame. Life-as-it-was, unprotected she failed. "No point staying in."

"You could be useful"'

"How?"

"To your children."

"No."

"Why?"

"We've no money—and there's—well—Annie. My father."

She told.

[p.49]

"Pish-tish. Fiddle faddle."

He said this in her mother's voice. She laughed.

"If you want to stay with him—positively—have kids. If not, go. Don't use him."

"Oh—never!"

"Everybody does!"

So here she was. She had a function. She was high-priced talent. A mother. Still, she liked the option of death. But it was something in a contract she could not sign because of other obligations. Norman was still difficult. Still mixed up with dread. More nervous because he, now, had to deal with things he feared—to hustle—for their bread. But compared to others—they were Utopian—they had their reasons.

[p.50]

So she sat in the bath feeling (-resolved-) satisfied? No—content. Human. Animal

Human - - - -

the entirety beautiful.

Yes. Beautiful.
Up to her arms in belly & pubic hair & pushed out navel. But in that state which, when viewed from outside, is called beautiful.
There was just enough—that was it—just enough divine discontent—to shut hubris out.

And hubris, being no stranger, being, in fact, the wolfe [*sic*] at the door, had royally to be shut out.

[p.51]

Divine discontent.

Item—Husband. Norman
Earnest
Absent
Unwilling to admit her equality

Earnest i.e. ______

Item: Friends—
None, or many—at intervals—like the hare—and Bev. who had her limitations—i.e.

Item: Weariness.	Louisa—	3¼ —	32 lb.
	Ben—	2—	35 lb
	Jane—	1—	18 lb
			85 lb.

Item— Snowsuits—N.B. to-morrow bomb the manufacturers for poor design.

Item— Toronto Turnstiles in Subways. So arranged

[p.52]

as to prevent the very pregnant passing through sans pressing with buttocks of unborn against gate.

i.e. back doors of buses—if bus too close to post, no room for pregnant to dismount.

Item—America—Cars —
foetus in extremis blows horn of car

Item— Taxis
Chers.

So—you see?

"Tell me more about the convent—I love it."

"You talk the way we used to. We were always getting at the ones who'd had real mothers & fathers."

[p.53]

Item—Mothers' helps. Work to keep them from boring.

Item—Viet bloody Nam. Where Norman is.

Item—Greasy hair

Item: there's the rub—Item N.B. item, fool, item, Minn—fool—(pelvic rub?). Attempted suicide four years ago had unforethought about the result—I am never to be taken seriously again. "You're cross Minn, take your pill."

Tranquillisers—diuretics, sleeping pills. All for Meshega. No heart-to-hearts—you're special—take your pill

.

Item: Life lacks salt.

[p.54]

Item: A telegram from Ma.

On my fine gravestone?

Norman—come home!

Why do you have as closely connected as possible with the natural history of the human race. Before them—I carried this great ball of love in my arms, trying to get rid of it. Take, take, I said. Even my mother, esp. my mother, thought me a grotesque. "Carry it yourself," they said sharply. "Cut your garment to suit your cloth."

Norman said "Pass it on!"

Now—look—they play with it. Love, shit, jam & plasticine—all the sticky things are the same to them—they know what to do—muck it up &

scream "More!"

They took my load—

[p.55]

I don't do it because I get much from them. Just the birth, just that excitement. And—normally—the pregnancy. But oh, hell, babies are boring. They stare, they pucker—their eyes are unfocussed. Toddlers are worse. No, it's not the mothering, it's just—they use me. I could be anybody, they don't care, but I'm there—useful, you see. I'm no imposition on them. After all these years, I have a function anyone else could do it—but only I will.

Intellectual ideas about populating the world? Not my burden. These won't be a drag. They'll earn & learn & feed.

No other job—oh, acting perhaps—gets rid, like this, of the excess of emotion over cause.

[p.56]

IUD's flow out.
Condoms itch.
Pill takes away libido.
Dutch caps fly across the bathroom.

—

She found herself jabbering uncontrollably to Frank in her head; incapable of speaking downstairs.

—

The vocabulary of the thing—had to be played with to be endured—bags of waters, plugs of mucous, show & afterbirth—no, that's a logical one.

One never minded the Latin words, except vagina which sounded downright wrong.

& uvula which is at the wrong end.

[p.57]

Weeping Willy Willis, the sage of Godwin Town

She was in Branksome Hall when he got in. Hush

Went, on a dare, to hear him defend himself on scandal charges.

Minn   on her father's career.

As far as I know he was just a cheapjack cracker barrel politician who drank like a fish, did as little as he could, kept the land preservation lobbyists off his back & used his "high office" to keep his legal fees high. But you see, I didn't know him very well—I was only his daughter, & home was a front. His life was his office.... He even died there—towards the end he got so he'd just crawl

[p.58]

out of jail & go there & jabber at the Tom Thomson. The dentist next door would phone mother & she'd send Bob Comstock round to bring him home.

How long did that stage last?

For years—five, six—I don't know. He was defeated in '49—once the Vets got home & saw through him—God, even I saw through him long before that, he used to kill me when he spoke at the High School, not a straw of logic in anything he said—but anyway he was a youngish man then—only 50, and he lived till he was sixty-two, long enough to see Louisa. I don't know whether it was gin or the cops got him, I never liked to enquire. They found him dead.

The cops.

The wet towel brigade. They used to beat him,

[p.59]

dear.

What on earth for?

Oh, they'd get him in on drunk & disorderly & a couple of the older ones had scores to settle. He had to take it because he'd always start the fight—remember, he'd boxed a bit—ach, he was a fool. I knew this later from the boys on the paper. I hated the thought of it happening—of him twitching & flinching in his droopy silk underwear—but I couldn't get anyone to do anything. Apparently, it happens in places like this.

You love this town, I see.

I shit on it. I wish I'd tried harder, though. But I felt—it's her job, not mine. There wasn't a lawyer who'd help me. Mother wouldn't believe me—and—you'll see, I'll get flowers from the police ass[ociatio]n.

[p.60]

You're not going to turn all this into a book, Frank—a book on him! He was a scourge—the way you got a job in this town during the '30's was to let him screw your daughter—even I knew that. He's not a historic figure, he's a cliché fake—the little guy to whom politics is you scratch my back, I'll scratch yours—that's bloody well all. And Gertrude—she's not paying you for it, is she? She hasn't got a thin dime besides the house & the pension & some investments she gives mostly to the church.

No, dear, I'm the archivist, remember?

Thank God—no, I hadn't heard—I obliterated you—I censor things—but listen—

[p.61]

Gertrude hasn't had a easy life—imagine looking like that & having a personality like that & being married to him. Well, she took it all as God's will & forged ahead in her Clapp shoes, it saved her thinking anything through. She accepted institutions & went on to make damn useful improvements but she had a brain & a will—she could have done a lot more. She needn't, for instance, to have blamed Annie on him—that was in a birth injury, not V.D.—her fault, if anyone's, I mean, her own physical fault, to take too long giving birth & not to have better medical help. And then—me. I'm nutty as a fruitcake, Frank, but I'm NOT Original Sin. She might have smiled at me. He did—I kind of loved him for it.

That's them—don't make history of them—honey, don't you ever dare.

Frank took it all with an amused, Olympian smile.

[p.62]

They're busy embalming him—making him out bigger than he was. When he was only a little, crummy politician who tried to live big. He didn't know his place, for God's sake—& she doesn't know hers or his. The William Willis Museum for Chrissake. His spittoon? The police hoses? The rubber gloves of the doctor who cured him of clap? At least I know my place—I live small. I am small. I've got their big ego but I'm damn well not going to donate it to the Nation.

Storefronts that were alternately Millinery Shoppes & committee rooms.

[p.63]

Calling Mordie

Don't take the kids.

Who's going to look after them?

I dunno—can't you get a housekeeper?

Norm isn't back. I don't think I've got the money.

To hell with that....

We can be away for a long while yet, Mordie. I have to be careful.

Listen, you....

OK, I'm sorry I phoned.

You should be, it's the steaming middle of the night.

OK, Mordie

Listen Minn, it's your old uncle Mordie talking & what he's saying is for Chrissake don't take the kids. If things are bad at home, it'll be too much for you & besides you spend too much time with those kids.

Oh, Mordie come on! I have to.

You don't have to. You've been

[p.64]

stuck at home for so long with them you feel insecure without them.

Like going out without a coat in summer, for the first time?

If you say so. Have you got anybody lined up for when you to the hospital?

Only vaguely.

You women! Listen, there's a Mrs Robinson at VICTORIA 4-4096 who's a practical nurse. Got that. She's good & she likes kids & she's just home from her holidays. She should be free. I'll put fifty bucks in the mail for you—no I'll make it out to her....

Mordie!

Don't be coy—I'll put it on my bill, don't worry. Now you call her & you go off & when you get home if your belly aches get in touch with the old guy who delivered you ... have a good trip, sweetheart and for Chrissake don't take those kids!

Cahier XIII[1]

Push ideas further.
Throw out furniture. [17]

A lengthy entry in *Cahier* XIII presents the characters Mrs Titivant and Roger. The former is an elderly woman whose housekeeping and style of dressing are disorderly but delightful; the latter is a drinker with a talent for insight into modern abstract art. These pages seem to have been written in a single sitting and are highly satisfying prose as well as testimony to Engel's writerly talents. Although the characters were mooted for inclusion in *The Honeyman Festival*, they do not appear in the final published version of the novel. Their names and character types turn up in later work, mainly *Lunatic Villas,* which features a Roger and an Oliver as well as old and endearingly odd Mrs Saxe.

Passages near the beginning of the *cahier* explore the subject of pregnancy (Minn's in *The Honeyman Festival*) and the "gentility" of the language associated with childbirth. An entry dated 22 October 1967 shows Engel again at grips with depression. "Low for many days [...] I see no reason to go on. It is silly not to be able to arrange one's life efficiently. One might as well be dead" [22]. Finally, budget calculations on the last page of the *cahier* are a reminder of everyday reality and the need to make ends meet while writing and raising a family.

[p.1]

Order for Minn's book.

She woke with a start. She would not dream that dream any longer. So, even The Babes in the Wood was a wish fulfilment fantasy, the perfect disposal of the irksome reality of children—parents die suddenly & are taken to heaven ... a genteel escape. Children handed over to wicked uncle—removes idea of wickedness from parent, another cleansing. Children abandoned to starve by Welsh murderers—you get farther &

1 1967-68, red, coil notebook, with "Minn" handwritten on cover; 59 pages used.

farther away from being the cause. The birds cover the babes with leaves. The birds are kind, the babes are dead. Everyone is in heaven. Sic transit.... William & Jane.

Her dream was less sophisticated—she had been rifling through a marked-down counter of emeralds, silks & eskimo soapstones carvings in a great dept store. Then she had flirted with a fishmonger who had watercress in his hat. In the back of her mind—I'm late, I oughtn't to leave them so long with the painter, it's 12, he has to go, will he leave them alone? I'm late as the white rabbit. I'm late, aren't I wicked, shall I

[p.2]

have to apologize gaily, charmingly, does the fishmonger like me? I'm late....

She was suddenly home, in the manner of dreams—& they were not with the painter at all. They were all, all drowned in the bath. "No!" she cried, "I didn't mean that at all." And woke herself up, knowing she had.

That was a mad dream, but the sort of thing women did who were too much alone & burdened & sick of the kaka-universe, walked out & left them with matches or hot taps on or full baths or open windows. Or, worse, wrote novels & killed them off, which is less bloody, but less honest. She hadn't done anything yet, & possibly never would, but there was her mother's tea set to think of, the gift of a woman who subsequently killed her babes with an axe, and her

[p.3]

mother's firm— "How well I understand."

One in the stroller, one on foot, one on the breast, one on the way. She couldn't say she wasn't involved in the world. Still, she hated the dream.

Usually Norman found someone to live with her while he was away. This time they'd sent him, however, to Saigon in a hurry, and, anyway, pregnancy calmed her down. She hadn't thought she minded as much as her subconscious said she did....

[p.4]

But this trip was hurried, ill-timed—he was to replace another correspondent in Saigon, who had been shot down by intestinal disaster. Norman was not addicted to aeroplanes, Norman was not attracted by Viet-Nam; there was, however, money involved. He went off in a sulk, gloomily hoping she would be all right. It was to have been a six-week trip. He had been away six weeks & 2 days. She had forty dollars & the baby-bonus left & she hoped that if his plane crashed—as he always expected it would—he'd taken out one of those silly insurance policies. She couldn't see her kids working their way through college except by cleaning lavatories.

[p.5]

What irked them most was that they had missed the best part of her pregnancy when she was perpetually lusty & there was no worry, no fear. It made up for all the rest, the mental vagueness, the weariness, the irritability & sloppiness, the condition pressed upon her. Not to make love, now, not to be able to, when one was hopelessly & permanently ready—she ached for him.

—She had fallen asleep over the evening paper & a bottle of warm beer ... <u>Penelopé moderne</u>.

[p.6]

MESHEGA-WORLD

Reality: shit, pyloric stenosis, wailing, shoes

battle	drowsiness	} pregnancy
house-battle	cumbersome-ness	
food-battle	irritability	

figure-battle- Mordie[2]-battle

Compensation: Making love ___ Gone.

Fantasy life: Norman & the beautiful hairless women of Katmandu.
Mordie & his best cow.

Physical: SHAPE coarseness
brown line Stretchmarks
hairy legs
INSOMNIA

Fear— this time.

DREAM— Babes in the Woods—
She's had ENOUGH.

[p.7]

In Michel's apartment— the same impression as there ought to be in the book of a life <u>lost</u> because one cannot be that kind of person. A terrible wistfulness for the orderly person one is not. Here, for the books in rows, neat, well cut, existing in order in someone else's head.

There for the pincushions on the dressers, the starched lace, the ironed underwear, the things that one is not, the things that Norman would like to have but hasn't because she's not. But he can't have them & Minn.

---

2 Minn's doctor.

[p.8]

10 July The sympathy of mother is, this time, good: She knows how it is learning how to use Henriette. When Howard left, so did uneasiness. But then he travels <u>very</u> badly, he can't settle, he wanders in a haze of fear & criticism. Do said he was beautiful.

[p.9]

Her belly—white, water-repellent, gleaming.

Stretchmarks like snail trails.

A diet of beer & peanut-butter sandwiches.

How we used to say "N. years of...."

Mordie—relations less cordial than before—he has a doctor's double vision of fertility: in its place, it's profitable & compelling. Overworked, it's a problem of plumbing. Risk of no text-book or instruct answer.
[No pelvic last time—impossible to perform while Ben was hopping on his septic toe.][3]

Pills get lost, condoms wither & diaphragms shoot across the room.

[p.10]

<u>Discharge</u> words (are there anymore?)

Show.

Genteelism used <u>esp.</u> by doctors.

[p.11]

<u>Getting rid of the kids tales</u>:

(Fantasy on both sides?—Cheap thrill, anyhow)

Hansel & G[retel]
Babes in Wood—William & Jane

Moles—say something about moles!
Hanging moles.
Brown, flat, lovely moles—beauty spots.

---

3 Square brackets appear in original text.

[p.12]

Parents' Fantasies	Children
Babes in Wood	Cinderella
Hansel & Gretel	Rapunzel
\	Frog—Prince Stories
not very many of them. I guess but isn't the wicked stepmother a transference?	Ugly Duckling

[p.13]

Minn was born immediately before the crucial campaign of __. Her father was re-elected, but not by dint of showing off his children. There was Annie, the dark shadows, to hide, and though her mother did the tea-circuit faithfully, she took no Minnie with her. She could not, in fact, bear babies.

At least, Minn thought, surrounded by her own, she's sincere. But unforgiven.

[p.14]

Faces —Mervyn Johns—weeping Willy
Dr Roscoe.

[p.15]

Structure

Try simple chronology

1. Minn — dream
   — bath
   — telegram

2. Mordie phone—housekeeper

3. Trip home

4. Confrontation & **<u>being</u>** home

5 About Alice, Annie, & Gertrude

6. About Frank

7. Sounding Lucy

8. Having the Baby

9. Sowing

[p.16]

On seeing Frank:

No, I won't have those emotions any more. One makes & has children, in fact, to avoid just those emotions. I won't love that burning, childlike way, I won't hate with that scrape-kneed spite, I won't play; your mother's a rotten egg, Frank. Hanna, your father runs a manure machine, and you can't play in my old house to-day.

Goddamn children for deserting me.

[p.17]

Push the ideas further.
Throw out furniture.

Their house—a nest of late Victoriana—birds under glass bells—better stuff than at home. Norman grew up in an apartment. Minn hated home— they were creating a new past together.

[p.18]

August 29, 1967

Talk with Mabel—she is sceptical of Minn's mentality. Likes childbirth as sex act but v suspicious of childbirth having to do w. sex on part of doctor. [...]

[pp.19-21]

[Speculations about friends' childhoods]

[p.22]

[Doodle of a cat's head in top left margin]

22 Oct 1967

Low for many days. Then to see Nancy & Gord & how good to be in that house tho' H. stiff. But I apparently have sworn too often there. So though it was good it isn't good any more. Nothing is.

Why does one put up with it?

Why do I ask to be punished.

[...] Last night—an attempt to put things right.

I think we have had enough.

My mother ran away. It's very hard, not to have the courage to. I see no reason to go on. It is silly not to be able to arrange one's life efficiently. One might as well be dead.

[p.23]

So I said, I've got to go away & he said, yes, go away & then we were so happy & I am sorry now to be away. Must make up a sort of emploi du temps.

But it was so good for us to be happy until today. Instead of fussing, we lived. Then, again, we fussed. [...] Hell. Never mind....

Sarah preached the inadequacies of the Ontario norm. Minn must-show them.

[p.24]

Pattern it.

Themes— Mouse's nest
Katmandu—home is like rancid yak butter anyway.
Flower children—psychedelic cheques & sitars.
The home nest—different in its quality of feeling—feelings have been suppressed until they exist only as a hard part supporting rather than undermining duty. But no flowers grow.
Lucy—a sounding board.
Arden—extension of home
Frank~~—is he necessary~~

[p.25]

Morning she took the Flower children's psychedelic cheque to the bank—surprisingly it cashed itself. Decorations could be money after all.
[...]

Bev. As Minn grew monumental & her skin stained brown, Bev did more. Bev was religious & prayed in her nightie & at night wore her hair in a braid. Bev had a sense of duty—which Minn had thrown away with her sexual inhibitions—and was capable of tending a child in the night. Minn knew she was screwing Bev—the child was tired, tired. She also knew that, women being women, Bev would screw her good & proper in return.

Bev came to them from a cocktail party, though she didn't approve of drink. She was, at the

[p.26]
beginning, introduced as Harry Shaw's new wife. By the end of it she was being slapped in the kisser by Harry Shaw, & Lou, who had a lengthy acquaintance with Harry Shaw, picked her up like a kitten & brought her weeping home.

[p.27]
More Patterns, more themes:

[...]
[p.28]
A Peep Show with the Silent Companions in the foreground.

Minn as
Ottoline Morrell
—

Change Roger's name to Morgan Plant—painter

Action: The Bath
The Reception of Regina
Washing Roger's hands
The Visitors: Morgan, Christabel,
Jane, Bill & Oliver
The let-down—walking the house
The visit to the hippies
Walking the house again
The onset of labour
Dawn—the onset of sanity
The birth

[p.29]
<u>The Peep Show</u>
[Ongoing one-line notes]

[p.30]
$7000

housekeeper
nursery school
give up freelancing

Weaver
MacLennan
Hunter

Harry J. Boyle

[p.31]

lemons
other fruit exc. apples/oranges
eggs

Throw it all out, Pass

Begin: Saturdays, we do our visiting.
Calling on creatures whose
lives we think are manqué

Saturday afternoons, we go visiting, calling on those unfortunates whose lives we think are manqué like Mrs Titivant, who lives in an unpainted frame house within easy reach of the Heliconian Club. All the houses around here have been white-painted and turned into boutiques, not hers. Her [illegible] husband, Mister Titivant as she so charmingly calls him, was only a little clerk. Her son is an engineer in California. As Oliver says, what she should do is sell the house at the

[p.32]

enormous profit that is now possible; or at least do something about the hippies camping out on her lawn. But not Mrs Titivant. She grew up in the house and brought her husband to live there when they married. She's staying there. In a way, she's very resistant to change; and money doesn't interest her. We think she doesn't eat enough. Her pantry looks stale and unused when we go to help her with the tea. And what she does eat, she seems to share with the so-called Flower Children who infest the neighbourhood like stray cats—really very bad for trade.

When we go, we try to wear relaxed clothes, so she won't feel uncomfortable herself. She's getting shabbier

[p.33]

and shabbier in her old age. It must be a blessing that her sight is getting dim.

The house is—or was, no work has been done on it for a long time—very prettily decorated. You'd think from the outside that it would be a dark, damp velvet nest. However, Mrs Titivant has always preferred pastels, and the drawing room is white—getting fearfully grimy, but what can you do about living down town? All the overstuffed furniture is slipcovered in pastels, so we feel as if we are standing among a herd of colour-washed elephants. Her treasure is the imitation Aubusson on the floor—really a hooked rug, but the colours are very nice.

She, for her age, can be considered very active, though when she comes to the front door all the way from the back yard, wearing her husband's enormous, antique galoshes,

[p.34]

there is an edge of exhaustion on her face. But she welcomes us nicely and takes our coats and makes us a cup of tea.

Not many people come calling, or make themselves so easy in her elephant chairs. All her old friends are either dead or disabled, so there's only us and the elders of her church. Her son in California keeps in regular touch, of course—he sends photographs of his children who are always graduating from things—you know how they are down there, cap & gown in kindergarten. We hope he sends her money, the way taxes are going up.

Oliver sits down & leafs through her family album—they were a handsome crew, the Titivants, though most of them died in the war. Mrs Titivant

[p.35]

and I discuss the weather, and supermarkets, and what our children & her grandchildren are doing now. Then I go to the pantry with her to help reach down the blue tea-set—I don't know how she gets it back up, I hope she doesn't stand on her rickety stool. It's rather sweet, Worcester, I think, with spidery indigo flowers, and Mrs Titivant dusts the cups with an honestly grubby tea towel, while the kettle boils on the high-legged old gas stove.

I can't honestly say she's a very good housekeeper. I've seen an insect or two scuttle across the pantry floor. But everything's in its place when she comes to see us, down to the ginger nuts she keeps in the tea-caddy specially for us. They're inclined to be stale. After Oliver cracked his bridge

[p.36]

on one we gave her some Huntley & Palmers the next week but she must have given them out to the hippies because we never saw them again, not even the tin, which was a particularly decorative one.

She has a strange relationship with the "Hippies" as people call them. We're quite prepared to be broad-minded but we're glad our children aren't old enough to join that particular spree. But she seems to think they're the greatest thing that has ever happened, and annoys her neighbours by not signing petitions in favour of getting them off the street. In fact, she's in favour of legalizing marijuana—she thinks it's a much lesser evil than drink, and signed a petition

[p.37]

in favour of it that was hanging in one of their junky stores. From time to time odd things appear in her parlour—tin lampshades & peacock-feather fans, I suppose those generations have rather a lot in common, though as I said before, her taste is pastel & post-Edwardian rather than ornate. At any rate, she likes their psychedelic posters and says next year in her garden she'll make a spiral flowerbed.

We've never seen it but that's her particular pleasure. She calls it her "secret garden" & doesn't let visitors in. But in the summer her house is a bower of roses and shasta daisies & sometimes she answers the door smelling horribly of manure. She's also fond of foreign-looking clumps of pinks & sweet William, and bunches of sweet Alyssum & Candy-tuft Daisies

[p.38]

she grows out in front to show she's a friend of the Flower Children, but they never do very well, there are too many cats & dogs.

So, we load the tea-tray with Worcester & the old brown Betty and bring the kettle in and make it properly by the fire—an elegant weekend <u>divertissement</u> for Mrs Titivant. Her silver service looks reproachfully from the dining room. (It's black as your boot, she says she doesn't believe in public displays of Saran). Oliver tells her the latest news of the market, and she nods quite happily, though she hasn't a cent to invest. And we chat. We like to feel we bring her the news of the world. She won't have television and it's not good for the

[p.39]

elderly to live too much inside themselves.

She doesn't talk much, in fact she is rather laconic. You'd think from her spryness & dark eyes she'd be a regular canary but she's a listener; we keep the conversation going.

And then, precisely at five, by the grandfather clock on the landing, we all sigh, & get up to say good-bye. Oliver loads the tray & takes it to the pantry. Then we put on our coats & go to the door & say good-bye. Mrs Titivant looks gratefully at us. Oliver drops a five-dollar bill in the umbrella-stand, which is never either acknowledged or returned.

From there, because, frankly we need the change, we spend an hour looking for dear old Roger, another senior citizen whose life is a bit more than <u>manqué</u>.

[p.40]

[The words "The <u>beitches</u>" are written in the top left-hand corner of this page]

We have the feeling that he didn't miss his train, he definitely jumped off it. But nevertheless he's worth a visit now & again.

Besides, it's always fun to start in the pubs near Bloor Street. We find them deliciously dowdy & gay. There's usually quite a crowd at the Pilot which is black & chrome with a terrible abstract mural which purports to describe the war. There are all sorts of artists there, and tough-looking regular drinkers and loads of people in very fashionable leather clothes, all jammed together in the most uncomfortable way. Roger is sometimes there, winter or summer deep in his overcoat. He gives us a loud hail over the other drinkers & always very kindly offers to buy us a beer. I've never got over my

[p.41]

mother's prohibition—beer is one thing ladies just don't drink—so we pay for our own & I have a sherry cocktail.

Most often, however, it is a long, long search for Roger & I stand outside while [Oliver] combs those vast tiled beverage places where men do their drinking alone. Usually, at the fourth or fifth place he hauls him out & we all go for a drink or an early dinner—in one of the Italian places where they don't mind Roger's coat.

I'm very fond of Roger; no matter how low he sinks you can see the gentleman underneath. He came from a very good English family & joined Oliver's business here just after the war. He didn't mind you flaunt[ing] his old school tie as so many of them do, he rather hid it. Maybe he started to drink because he found out how snobbish,

[p.42]

really, Eton was, and it made him ashamed. Of course we weren't in circulation then but we found out from Oliver's father that he hadn't much talent for business. Numbers, he still says, don't interest him worth a damn. He seems only interested in surviving now.

He lives with a dreadful, painted widow—one of the kind who always seem so amusing in the movies and are mean, suspicious & rude in real life—in the absolutely worst part of town. For a long time he kept this hidden but one Sat. Oliver felt obliged to drive him home, he looked so ill, and though with a drunkard's craftiness he took us on a circuitous route, he did have to give us the address & later we looked it up on the map. It's only a few blocks from Rosedale

[p.43]

but you'd never know from the people on the street, drunks & what Roger calls "hookers" and poor little children in ragged clothing & bare feet, all doing perfectly dreadful things, like putting broken bottles in the curb to wreck one's tires. We had to help him, one on either side—into his awful house—which actually wouldn't be awful with a lick of white paint, it's just like ours, and when we rang the Gorgon answered the door. She accused us of getting him drunk again, "and him a sick man, too" she said, and made scurrilous remarks about him & "his toney friends." Next time we saw him—it was three weeks later—he was dreadfully embarrassed. He said she was good-hearted & didn't make him pay much in the way of rent. He was bitter because of being exposed in front of us, & very careful of what he drank in front

[p.44]

of us. We took him to a little Portuguese place in the market, where we stuffed ourselves with the most gorgeous, crackling fish. We brought our own wine and mixed it with glasses of Italian pop to make a kind of Sangria. It was fun—rather like Prohibition in the movies. Of course, the proprietor didn't know what to make of us, but we were quieter than most of the people there.

Roger calls all of the foreigners "Wops" & "Wogs," though we've tried to convince him that it's not a proper attitude for the new world. He fits into the area—alcoholics have to accept anyone who'll accept them—but he keeps this edge of superiority by using those really very unhelpful words. Compared to him these people seem honest & hard-working—

[p.45]

certainly they're buying all the real estate in sight. The children are lovely with their olive skin & their dark, and heavy-lashed eyes. We think they ought to make an effort to speak English, it's hard on the children to bring them up as little Europeans in a new world. But I suppose they'll learn soon enough to accommodate themselves to our ways. The whole neighbourhood used to be Jewish & look what's happened to them.

To get back to Roger—I don't understand why we like him. He's a contemptible object, more tattered every time we see him, but he seems much freer than us. Almost anybody is, of course, who doesn't feel our obligations, but he's particularly charming with the vestiges of the country gentleman showing through his mumbling chat. Politically, as you'd expect, he's awfully conservative, but he's

[p.46]

more appreciative than us of modern art. I know this because occasionally we find him early & make the rounds of the galleries which haven't closed their doors. I think most of it is the most inane doodling. I'm not prepared to collect it, just to be fashionable. But Roger laps it up, especially Sculpture. He straightens his shoulders & puts his head on one side & mumbles & puffs—and then offers us some awfully good explanations. He seems to think that through this we have our perceptions widened. If there weren't all this fuss I'd rather have LSD for that.

But I know my taste is "kitschy." I don't have an eye at all. Neither did Mother, but she had dealers to help her spend all her money. She's had to give up her chauffeur

[p.47]

but she has some awfully good art.

Roger, it turns out, was an art student once himself, though of course old Etonians aren't encouraged at that. His family thought the whole idea disreputable but after the war he spent a couple of terms at the Slade. He just wasn't good enough, he said—though there must be something in him, he couldn't have tried hard enough. I mean that most alcoholics have something in them, some discontent that makes them throw their lives away.

We talk to him from time to time about treatment, but he assures us he's happy in the company of "bums"—which could be taken as a slight to brokers, but we're not really sensitive that way.

So on either side [of] his rather noble profile, we throw another

[p.48]

piece of our Saturday away. But we feel we ought to keep in touch with Roger. He's depressing but we feel more fortunate when we get home.

It makes for an early supper, but we like to [be] home by seven, the hour when Nanny is putting the children to bed. For one thing, if I don't watch her she screws Victoria's hair up in rags, which breaks the ends—she's English and she thinks our curlers are too mechanical. I don't see why the child can't have braids as usually, but Nanny has her routine burned into her soul, and that means curls on Sunday, and curlers on Saturday night.

Nanny doesn't believe in stretchy pyjamas either, though I must say the baby looks sweet in flannel & lace.

[p.49]

But since I'm to have him on Sunday I usually change him.

And then, if we're staying home, we go to the library and put on records and open a bottle of brandy or champagne—the cheapest drinkable kind. It's the ideal setting for our kind of evening at home—a place where all the most pleasurable things can happen, which is too serene for a quarrel or ugliness. ||| Oliver lately has taken up tapestry; after a week at the office he feels like working with his hands. It's not a thing for which I thought he had any ability, but he's doing beautifully (he should be, he sends me all over town for thread); he's both careful and ambitious. He has really got infinite patience. He did his design himself—I'd call it abstract—mediaeval. Mind you, I'd like it better if it weren't sick green.

I spend home-evenings keeping

[p.50]

up with my reading, although when I say it, it sounds absurd. George—we'll tell you about George, he's another of our favourite people—says, in everything I've got determinedly unsophisticated taste, but this winter I've set myself Turgenev and at the moment I'm reading Chekov, I don't think that's bad at all. He accuses me of never having got past Anne of Green Gables.

George is one of the people we see out of loyalty rather than liking—and one of the few who just walk into our house. I don't know why he comes—maybe it's just that we make enough money for booze and he's a terrible toper. Unlike Roger, he's anything but an alcoholic. He doesn't depend on it—he says it makes him radiate joy. He's a funny little man, he works in

[p.51]

advertizing. And very bitter, he's cross-eyed & has a withered arm. Sometimes the things he says are quite insulting, but we don't mind because he's invariably rude. He's an "idea" man—they bounce like ping-pong balls when he's in the room. They're mostly negative. They're very anti-us. He can't stand stock-brokers & he certainly doesn't like women. And he's always breaking in on our Saturday nights.

Now, I think it's important to improve your mind. I don't have much time, with the children & the house all the length of the day. Oliver likes to go out a lot, I haven't much time for reading, and sometimes, I confess, he finds me reading something—well—unsophisticated. Like Mary Stewart or Somerset Maugham (which it's all right for men to be seen reading or—well—Harold Robbins—you know.)

[p.52]

So, Oliver's stitching & thumping away his tapestry, which he weaves, then re-embroiders as he goes— and in bursts George if we leave the front door unlocked. He snatches my book & looks at the title despairingly, and says, no matter if it's light fiction or Plato "Crap, unremittent crap!" And, then, seizing Oliver, begins to tell him the latest, while I'm supposed to be getting him a drink.

"That woman of yours is getting out of hand," he tells Oliver. "Now listen to this—I was down Spadina to-day and I met this guy...." If I don't hand him his drink he'll cut into the B & B at this point (and, given George's capacity, I ought to say we're well off, but not rich). And then he goes on to tell long pointless stories

[p.53]

about the evils of the Establishment.

"Nobody asks to be born there either," I say.

"Have you tried sincerely to get away?"
"I'm not even sure that we're in the Establishment."
"I am."
"Well, have it your own way."
"That wife of yours, Ol, she's spoiling you. Are you going to make a killing in real estate?"
He thinks we're such terrible capitalists, when everything we have is tied up in Government Bonds.
He's not like Roger, there's nothing to recommend him, except that there's a good deal more of him there. He gets by because he's a bully & a bundle of energy. George makes Chekov seem almost intolerably sweet.
When we've had enough we go out & look for a party....

[p.54]

often we do it even if George isn't there. And often, of course, we're invited. After all, we know a lot of people in Toronto—we were born here and went to school here—though I was in Switzerland for an abortive year. People say we're always off to Europe, but whenever Oliver goes on a trip, I pack & go along. What else is Nanny for?

On Saturday night someone is always giving a party. As Oliver says, you can walk in anywhere. We tried it one night—put a bottle of Scotch in a paper bag & drove around Rosedale looking for lights, parking problems & open front doors. George knocks & if anyone comes he asks for Sylvia. I don't know why, but there's always a Sylvia there. Sometimes it's not a very amusing party and theres always the problem of running into someone you know __.

[p.55]

(They say we have an eclectic circle of friends.) But if all else fails I corner one of the girls & whisper "Who's the host? We're only friends of Sylvia." It would be awfully embarrassing to raid any clients of Oliver's, but so far we've had very good luck.

If there's no one we know, Ol and George go around doing put-ons—Russian ambassador, Orangeman, Insurance man. They love acting as a team. It's a little bit childish and I can't go along, I always break down & laugh. But it amuses them & keeps dear old George out of my hair.

Getting your liquor back and getting out is the problem. Parties you aren't invited to often prove to be duds. But my fur coat is old-fashioned and has enormous pockets. We sneak it in there & parade out feeling tremendously gay. Square citizens like us need some little form of rebellion.

[p.56]

The Annex is usually very much better than Rosedale, but a little less safe. Sometimes you walk into things that are terribly artsy—and once we went into a shabby old house & found them all in boiled shirts. We said "Oh, but it's not OUR Sylvia." George was annoyed. But we fled.

Oh—parties. When they sparkle, when there's just enough wine & good food, when you know most of the people & like a lot of those—when you get home at two, and flop, the feeling is good—if you've driven George firmly to his apartment door, if he comes in, he plays chess with Oliver for hours. I take a hot shower, do my face & go straight to bed. Sunday I have the children to do by myself.

[p.57]

The Magic Primer.

The Glenholme Primer.
The Cythera Primer.
The New Cythera Primer.

One for sorrow, one for joy.
The Magpie Papers.

[illegible]

[p.58]

The Deception of the Thrush
To Carthage Then I came.
Go, Said the Bird.[4]
The Whole Wide World.
Freedom of Grace
The Marmeluke's Shebeen

Break no hearts this Xmas.[5]

The Puritan Primer
The Cythera Primer.

---

4 Lines from T.S. Eliot: *Burnt Norton*, line 024: "The deception of the thrush? Into our first world"; and *Burnt Norton* line 042: "Go, said the bird, for the leaves were full of children," and line 044: Go, go, go, said the bird: human kind"; as well as *The Waste Land* line 307: "To Carthage then I came." See *Cahier* II, footnote 8.

5 Short story in *Inside the Easter Egg*. See also *Cahier* XII, footnote 12 and *Cahier* XIII, footnote 5.

One For Sorrow, One for Joy
The Flight From Mariposa

[p.59]

Fares	$12	
Hotel	29	
Xmas cards	6	50
Post.		50
Taxis	5	
Meals	12	
Booze	2	75
Toys	2	
Books etc	5	
Fags	3	
	77	75

Cahier XIV[1]

And the broken toys & the bottles of Beaujolais & the why bother & the must, and the "what will people think?" [33]

In an early entry of *Cahier* XIV, Engel grapples with a catch-22 familiar to many women. This is the dilemma whereby the work women do is seen to be without much value precisely because it is women's, as opposed to men's, work. This seems especially true of housework. Housework is necessary and important, but because historically it has been done mainly by women, and mostly without pay, it is widely perceived to be less important and less valuable than other types of work. Engel's entry records her sitting "idle surrounded by muck and utterly unwilling to cope with it. Unwilling to believe that it is important because it makes me unimportant" [4]. The devaluation of women's work is not limited to housework. That it could extend to women's writing was a possibility of which Engel, like many other women writers, was well aware.

Much of this notebook is dedicated to further thoughts, outlines and draft passages for *The Honeyman Festival.* Particularly effective are passages between pages [33] and [37], where Engel the list-maker and Engel the *dialoguiste* are in full flight. Engel the researcher is also in evidence, this time taking notes on Marshall McLuhan.

[pp.1-3][2]

Bibliography

[...] [p.4]

14 May\67 Someone in the house to clean.

It is not encouraging. One's dirty secrets are exposed & seeing is guilt. Better to shove it under the bed! I sit idle surrounded by muck & utterly unwilling to cope with it.

1 1967-68, black notebook with a sticker on the cover that reads "Minn & Others"; 41 pages used.

2 Pages [1-3] comprise book lists and ideas for CBC programs, e.g., "The Life & Death of Propaganda," "Freedom & Decency" and "Energy."

Unwilling to believe that it is important because it makes me unimportant. How many patches of truth (is dirt truth?) do I thus avoid? (Well, then, reality?) How can I do it for more years?

[p.5]

Minn Book

Minn arrives carrying her case up the steps feeling for all the world like a visiting nurse—brave, competent, slightly heroic. She hits her head on the hanging pot & takes in the row on the verandah. And her mother says "Well, Minn! What a lovely surprise!" Alice, ashamed of duplicity, giggles down at her rumpled elastic stockings & her buttoned kid shoes. The old are the young.
Frank Hanna & Morgan Plant are the responsible in betweens. And they, too, are embarrassed for separate reasons.

[p.6]

January 1968

After the Howes' party?
Why these public emotional purges?

To shock oneself into the guilt of reflection—into the imaginary world? Mind needs blasting—this is best done alone.

Now— the shape of the book.

All the characters at her imaginary party carrying their images & pasts like cartoonists' conversational balloons.

Shape of book

I BATH + DREAM + Reflection on kids
Thursdays

II Silent Companions
Proust, CHURCHILL
Gertrude & Alice
Norman—yellow
MY HERO

The necessity of Katmandu

[p.7]

III Jane-Regina tells of Mrs Titivant

IV Minn does her card-file

V Bill & Oliver come for Jane-Regina
VI The night is silent
VII Edward comes

VIII Minn washes Edward
Minn talks
Minn naps & dreams again

IX The other Edward—the cautious hippie

X Minn walks in the yard & almost has the baby

[p.8]

Jan. 28—6 yrs over— contract renewed[3]

Want to get my mind off alone but find I haven't any more got one. [...]

[p.9]

Things about Minn

Expand consciousness about Godwin without rancour—the family was isolated, had a special status in 3 ways—but this gave Minn an observer's position.

——

Have to keep them in hand because they're getting at me: old H.G. about the house—manor, Victorian, unhealthy, sort of thing he campaigned about—knows we can't afford to budge: won't accept this; Winnie for sloth—propped as he is—propped, stuffed, wire-pulled—he manages 20 pp per day; P. mourns, they will never see me as a lovely mummy—always in black drapes or jeans, not rose-scented— the others—my food from cans, my Elle houses tacked on walls—what indifference, what laziness—Norman among the golden hairless bods of Katmandu. If there is a God they smell of yak-butter.

If this one, like the others, also

[p.10]

sends my shoulder cuds of curd—I, too.

Even the imagination offers no escape. And I have failed to master the new nomenclature of Africa. Specifics save us.

Godwin in the Western of Ontario, wearing its station like a sequin.

3 The Engels' wedding anniversary was 27 January (1962).

[p.11]

April 26 1968. A Friday

Start further back.
Friday—checked nursery school, went to Britnell. Last Saturday—William & Howard went to Yorkville—Blow Up & the Fire Station—Charlotte & I to market. Same experience—extremely good at first, then impatient for home & each other.

[...]

[p.12]

[...]

[p.13]

The Heliconian club sale

The dusty minds of elderly career women, overtones of that raw green so much used then even by Emily Carr & Henry Lamb. Old art books, old art music. No really good taste.

Books for England—
Anthony Shiel }
Archie Ogden }
McNamara
Forster & Davies
Vosburgh
Solly

[Insert: newspaper article about Lila Kedrova who starred as Madame Hortense in the movie *Zorba the Greek*.]

[p.14]

Minn's book:

The mythos of modern

Work superstition, myth, for texture
The mother
The daughter
The friend
Morgan Plant
Arden
Mordy

After Reading McLuhan

Man is thought, woman is intuition—or Jas Stephens would have it that way

—Men's cunt fear—being sucked in by one's pleasure. Now with freedom—Penis—fear? Yes.
—Back to the small world after the larger experience of attempting to live with universals rather than specifics, which makes for a furious physical cosmos among intellectuals & much baby-having, but also a [illegible] rudimentary self-consciousness & world consciousness.

[p.15]

Here in the village spiritual & intellectual values are codified by the church—that department is one you don't flounder in you're busy instead keeping house—or ordering your universe. Provide, provide. It is <u>immoral</u> to think for yourself ∵ it means neglecting the ordering of the community. A few individuals fight but eventually are ground down—i.e. <u>have</u> to keep village house.

Pre electric light mentality prevails
—authoritarian society
—unquestioning "natural order" is obeyed though in reality it hasn't kinship with any order anywhere.

Minn has dealt only with the non-conformists in it— Morgan
Arden
Mother

Alice, conformist, has taken her mother over.

[p.16]

Mother as non-conformist—a woman of automatic authority on whom specialness conferred by "Annie" & then widowhood.
Then into local politics.
But she believes in values of village—in fact MAKES them.
[...]

[pp.17-26]

[Notes and Draft for *The Honeyman Festival*]

[p.27]

A man marries, desiring to conquer the <u>web</u>? of the female genitalia with gifts instead of his childish ribaldry. Hoping to discover the mystery there. The pubic clamshell fastens on him; he finds his life determined by it. He becomes nest-minder, nag. And there is no mystery there?

Expand.

The pubic clamshell—oysters' teeth—oysters' feet—mussels, barnacles—things of sea-fuzz.
But after all—you called the sea—Mother! Aphrodite had no hair!

menstruation white règle
menopause unnecessarily ugly words?
How to take an attitude?
Why take an attitude?
Just march on—
Some have to live step by step love step by step.

[p.28]

Sunk into a private emotional world.
Incapable of taking the world of events seriously—because it can't be perfect?

21

—She felt at that moment, driving into town, entirely rich & free. A woman with everything—a soft, ripe, yellow pear of happiness. She had found & adjusted a world for herself & found it entirely—to-day attractive & suitable, the complete contrast to her sterile, hopeless youth—the fulfilment of her Thirties, in which fertility & animal communication had reached a degree of perfection she had not hoped for; in which weariness was balanced by joy, isolation by the pleasures of the nest. Norman's closed-cropped head, his thick, bull terrier's neck, his blunted emperor's profile, had stamped the coin of her life with meaning. She had what she wanted—house, husband, help—she was going back wealthy & strong. She sang.

[p.29]

—She was exhausted, burning with a hard gemlike flame wasn't any more her thing, she was accustomed to taking life easy, rolling like a barrel, basking in time. She had to, it was the only way for her to put up with babies. But, after dinner, after the exhausting bedtime, the strain, the effort—they were busy imposing themselves on life while she slopped through it to keep her good temper for Norman, even absent, & the children. She was another generation, the ___ well? She was—many generations from them. Damn Gertrude for being old, old-old. So that Minn was first educated—first sexual **&** first without help. And, it appeared, first, in this family, servant—for mother. No—Alice had done it, Gertrude

[p.30]

had done it but was it to be the final crusher, that they, who had never attempted philosophy, had never gone willingly to bed & had never certainly coped kindly with their own children should expect her to wait table also? Was this the price of escape from committee meetings.

She thought of fleeing naked & hairy & ungainly through corridors screaming "Price is the wrong concept" but it would wake the goddam, kids.

Then she thought of broaching Frank for a drink. If she knew Frank there in his virginal upstairs in her mother's house he had a drink. But broach? Broach was something you did to something friendly like a bottle, not Frank. Bottles

[p.31]

had necks & long, lean, now in his 40's, bottle-shaped Frank had a neck & a penis & had anyone—certainly not Minn—ever broached Frank? Not Minn. Not. Not.

She began to get mad.

Frank.

Minn.

Here

& then she thought it was funny—

& broached the divine anger of weeping Willie her father in the mess of a-piss-a-pail-fulls. —wrong but in a good—no—how could it be good? way? Too complex?

But Alice & her pony are finally pathetic ∵ incapable of tragedy. Thus harmless to child. Ma's gimlet-eyed intensity harmful.

[p.32]

Frank: I wish I could persuade you to give up hating Godwin & the Willises—I feel you're damming off extremely useful information.

M—Why stand for a world of principle & more & more I distrust that old straightjacket principle.

What do you stand for?

Things that widen, not narrow, the world-view. I want my kids to have access to the whole—the big world—uncorseted by stupid rules—oh, I don't know nearly enough about philosophy but, you see, at least I've learned that the big mytho-poetic world—the whole history of man—is the important one. Not the here & now.

It's unsheltered.
It's very hard—but 1 nest is enough.

[p.33]

Anxieties—

Rash, tantrums, cradle cap, mouse—no—thrush-pins, temper, hang-over, slaps, yelling, croup, colic, measle shots, chicken pox, calamine, anti-histamines, aspirin, tuna fish, Raid, radiation, Rachel Carson, Adele Davis, Brewers yeast, honey, ants, trots, white medicine, pink medicine, red antibiotic, yellow anti-biotic, sedative, suppository, vaporiser, supervisor, crap, crud, creeping, creeps, co-ordination, bellyache, teeth, ears, eyes, scurf, scrapes, stitches, navels, toes, nails, cream, oil, powder, starch, out of, diaper service, Wednesdays, socks, shoes, tights, trousers, overalls, smocks, shirts, buttons, snaps, tapes, elastic, ~~Dr Dentons~~

And the broken toys & the bottles of Beaujolais & the why bother & the you must. And the "What will people think."

What will people think—What will people think. Ye ye generation ja ja

[p.34]

So we went to Sick Kids' Hospital him all bruised & me all battered & was it a pin in his inside? They said "he's bruised here & how? And this scratch—how? And the punctures? Are you nearsighted with pins?"

No, he does that—he pulls them open & out.
And his nose?
Curb.
Knee?
High chair—
Back.
Metal braces on crib.
Bruise?
Sister bit.
You have help?
No.
How many others?
Two.
Under four.
Yes?
Address?
On the form.

[p.35]

See myself in court. "Well, actually sir, there was this woman Mrs Marshall, who killed her kids with an axe, see, & she gave my mum this cruet—when she was sane & friendly, like—& every Sunday we use it & my mum says 'That was given me in 1936 by poor Mrs Marshall who later went mad & attacked her children with an axe, poor soul & I well understand how she felt.' But, see, sir, I don't own an axe, though I, too, well understand."

What crimes?

No shoes before noon. No vitamins this week. Dirty ears, (jug jug to you). Lack of vigilance—drinking dishwater. 1 ate 3 matches, 1 crapped on kitchen floor, one fell downstairs while practising initiative, one picked another's scab. Shall I resign.

[p.36]

You are condemned to 20 years of it.
You are condemned to not resign.

Address? The Shitty Palace Hotel.
Husband? In Katmandu—there where there's infinity & hairless girls. Henry Miller's China; raw amber, coral, turquoise, prayer-wheels. The East in the spirit—peace—one hopes.
Profession He has a bull's forehead—a bull's nape. Otherwise small. A journalist. Amber, as in cats' eyes. On rare occasions—brute beauty. A dappled king, like all the best. I love. I think.
Children? Racketeers, man, racketeers.
You beat them? My hand on satisfying rumps.

You live condemned
Til our friend death us part.

[p.37]

Playing doctor!

[p.38]

[...]

Bring out— idleness
tradition
emptymindedness
prejudices

[pp.39-41]

[Jottings on Evelyn Waugh. Telephone numbers]

Cahier XV[1]

Aug. 30 1968 Fragmented is the word for my mind [16].

While *Cahier* XV contains more notes on "Minn," by its end Engel had "turn[ed] Minn in" to Longmans,[2] and had begun a new book—the unpublished "Lost Heir and Happy Families," featuring characters such as Stanley, Verity, Faber and others. Engel envisioned her next project as a "new comedie humaine" [41] in which she wanted to draw upon what she argued was the vast, overlooked wealth of Ontario social history.

The *cahier* also records Engel's state of depression at the time ("It takes me half a day to make up a grocery list" [29]). Feelings of failure seemed to stem from more than one source. She was critical of her writing, her physical appearance and her performance as a mother. Reading Gordon Haight's biography of George Eliot [3] at the time did not help. "Life of Geo. Eliot was very bad for me," Engel recorded [32]. "I keep saying to myself 'Writing has changed so' but know that if I had that mind, I would have that affection" [26]. Engel compared herself to George Eliot with whom she shared a similar name, as well as a talent for languages and writing.[4] She also thought they had similar upbringings—"strict (but valuable) against-the-grain [but] no outlet for normal rebellion. Sexual squelching" [29]. But in Engel's case, "it didn't take" [26]. "What did?" the author mused, reprimanding herself for "reverting to a belief in my family's values that cut both Howard and myself out" [31]. Returning to her thoughts on George Eliot, Engel exclaimed that "if someone said [Eliot] was a bad writer [she]'d be relieved!" [32], then added: "Well, if she rewrote as much as I do. Well, if I worked as hard as she does!" Considering the possibility that a more disciplined work routine might help, Engel—reading Harold Nicholson—noted: "I must keep a diary, keep it regularly as an act of self-discipline & sanity & labour" [18]. Knowingly, she added: "my pen will run out."

1 1967-68, black, coil notebook, labelled "Minn"; 50 pages used.

2 Engel submitted her manuscript to Longmans, her publisher, on 19 November.

3 Gordon Haight, *George Eliot: A Biography* (New York: Oxford University Press, 1968).

4 George Eliot was a pseudonym for Mary Ann Evans (1819-80).

Engel's pen, happily, did not run out, even if she never did adopt the traditional "disciplined" approach to diary writing. She filled many more notebooks and finished several more books.

[p.1]

On the lam—Sally Ann for a bed
library
coffee in two places

Jeweller
Butcher—steak for tonight?

What did they say about KP

—sick
—brilliant —clever
—flawed

[p.2]

Dear Morley Callaghan—who are you?

[p.3]

June 15/68

Le Vietnam voulez-moi, je ris Ma-o Ma-o

cf La Chinoise to Honeyman films

Honeyman filled the gap between Philippe & Belmondo. It was [as] if Gary Cooper had come over to work with Losey or Abel Gance.

A book with strong rhythm in b[ack]g[round]
Bouzouki
Beatles
Jeanne Moreau
Ma-O, Ma-O
Folk-rock
Vaginas on buses

[p.4]

<u>Stuck Records</u>
<u>Structure</u>

Minn: + Monologue

Must have both alienation & intimacy

Cut out <u>the</u> furniture again
be brave

—

[p.5]

Vignette: A woman with her belly in her hands waltzing to the brouillard theme of Jules & Jim.[5]

—

If you're going to San Francisco[6]

[p.6]

The Honeyman Festival

1. Minn
2. Jane-Regina—Bare & Naked
3. Minn
4. Alice
5. Minn
   Woman at Party
6. —women & domesticity & novels—See <u>NOVA</u>
7. Minn
8. Max
9. Minn
10. Edward
11. Minn has baby

(Articles between—Minn & Norman?)

[pp.7-10]

[More rapid-fire notes for *The Honeyman Festival*]

5 This is François Truffaut's 1962 film starring Jeanne Moreau and Oskar Werner, about a love triangle between two friends and a woman.

6 These words are from the popular 1960s song "San Francisco," written and performed by Scott McKenzie.

[p.11]

Pattern, pattern

The Honeyman Festival gives
structure. Where to bring it in.

Honeyman's "Klootch"

Elements Missing

Visits to law courts.
—wallpaper
—shuffle system. 23 court?
Housekeeping—stuff from manuals

[p.12]

Thomas Rogers: Pursuit of Happiness

Style: bland, conversational
Matter: Defeat of conventional
happiness by accident
ordinary student becomes an "outlaw"

Characters: His conventional family
—the [illegible] & father
—His baroque grandmother
Jane & family
Lasher & the gang—perpetual students
Values: young

[p.13]

After school behaviour:

Monday. Glad to see me but not overwhelmed. We go to Russell's store on way home. I give them suckers. On way home William runs on road, then holds my hand. Charlotte trails quietly behind with lollipop, wants to cross road 6 feet behind us alone but comes when called. I promise a tea party on arrival home. Chris & Kevin are met along the way. They beat us to backyard.

I go in & get 4 plain cookies. While I'm there Wm has movement on grass. Charlotte sits on potty but will not pull pants down.

Kids can't decide whether to play indoors or outdoors. I go out, they go in. Want water after I tell Charlotte "No more water" (she's spilling)

[p.14]

she gently drops glass & smashes it.

Wm runs away once.
Has tantrum when not given bottle—then gets milk out of fridge.

Runaways etc.

———

The man reading the 11 p.m. news always reminds me of my Father.

[p.15]

Books to Get & Read (from A. Burgess's bibliographies)

Wyndham Lewis: Tarr 1918
The Childermass 1928
Apes of God '30
Doom of Youth '32 Snooty Baronet '32
Roaring Queen '36
Count Your Dead 1937
Revenge for Love /37
etc.

Thos Mann—Try more. esp. Dr. Faustus
T.F. Powys
Firbank
Beckett
Flann O'Brien— The Hard Life
The Dalhey Archive

Henry Williamson
Compton—Burnett

[p.16]

Aug 30. 1968.

There is a sudden feeling of risk about taking a holiday—a fear of the unknown, but also a feeling of being compelled to enjoy ourselves, so much is being attained at others' expense.

I must pack picnic things. Might well have bought a basket.

Fragmented is the word for my mind.

Matthew Arnold is comfortingly solid though.
Wish I cld read aloud to H.
Feel intellectually alone—so does he.

[p.17]

Old Tiger's Book of Practical Pussy:

Max: In the ruins of the home-made pleasure palace, pablum.

Private lives, unstructured time. In someone else's pockets, intimacy, inconsistency. There ... lands.

This is Erotika, lady.

(The Honeyman Festival as title)

The house—full of propitiatory gesture—torn slips of towelling where doilies in another generation sat. And yet I thought of her once as a "scion of an old family"—with their fear of violating the upper class code—wrong on both counts. Family not old, only staunch.

[p.18]

10/10/68

Reading Harold Nicholson. I must keep a diary, keep it regularly as an act of self-discipline & labour & sanity. Only my pen will run out.

I have been so upset—by what? Loss of Helen, sleep, worry over kids but I am too tired to find [illegible]

[p.19]

The Week—

Not good—fear, guilt, this loosely-used term paranoia—always I fight against the grain of my upbringing—as now—Embassy room drinking beer alone, smoking—how low.

[...]

Mention this to Mother, she is horrified—mention "reputation," "position."

What I miss in our house is something that used to be called "high seriousness."

[p.20]

Tuesday after Thanksgiving [1968]

The beautiful weather sobs on—trees golden, sun beamish—we infected with horrid viruses so it only makes our noses run more. Squirrels grow fat on my daffodil bulbs.

Dreams—[...]

[p.21]

[...]

Need father—& mother figures very badly these days. Feel orphaned. Why? Want the kids to love me more, but do not treat them v well—or they me. (They are WICKED!) Have not had dreams for a long time. Perhaps that's what's bothering me.

Reading Tom Wolfe on Ken Kesey v interesting[7]
Harold Nicholson III
Balzac—Beatrix—this I love
Haight's—George Eliot
—find myself there

[p.22]

same day

Cyril calls & is immensely comforting—talks about creative depressions—loved H's programme—wants us to party 18th
[...]
Damn why can't I have kids [illegible] & securely

Reading Haight's Geo. Eliot—in some ways profoundly identified
—others not sympa.[8]

Still thinking about escapes—[illegible]—thinking at least, dammit. Jean [illegible] & I blast at domesticity (husbands?)

Now I have Pet[ula] Clarke[9] on—she washes ideas away but the rhythm, jerking waist & hips in opposition, is good.

7 Thomas Wolfe, *The Electric Kool-Aid Acid Test* (New York: Farrar, Strauss and Grover, 1968).

8 This is the short form of the French word *sympathique* meaning nice, agreeable or pleasant.

9 Petula Clarke is a British singer and actress best known for her 1960s hit singles "Downtown" and "Don't Sleep in the Subway."

[p.23]

So I avoid thinking—how to widen & deepen it? Obviously Bill's right—more Minn better.

[...]

Longings to escape, understanding of Mother—politics even small, Good causes.

[p.24]

Remember—because of the Hippie movement you don't have to go to Europe any more.

Read more T. Wolfe jr.

Party music Get Ella Fitzgerald
Country-western
Get Scotchguard

Dead flowers.
Won't you have another dream on me.
Rich sodden happiness—rum cake.

Some people evaporate when they become memories—mostly when they are inappropriate to our present lives. Rub the magic lamp → Honeyman—but wrong.

Men's cheap endearments—doll, sugar, honey.

[p.25]

Somewhat drunk, something running into the veins—waters!

Images of songs—
The Sun Shines Out of Your Shoes[10] on perpetual motion

She jerks around the house to it. Cake-walk?

Do a bit on lyrics for Bill.

Monday: Sewing machine
bits
Lunch w. Selena Appleby
(?) What time?
Food.

---

10 Song by Petula Clarke (1968).

19 October [1968]—The brilliant weather continues. October is usually my happiest month. This one is

[p.26]

challenged by Howard's almost complete absence. How much easier it would be if he were r<u>eally</u> away, instead of a shadow of a presence one has to defer to. But I am becoming cold & cavalier.

George Eliot—The reading has been the jealous event of my week. I keep saying to myself "Writing has changed so" but know that if I had <u>that</u> mind, I would have that affection. But I was raised almost the same way. On me, it didn't take. What did?

Sickening to have, still, only oneself to rely on. But what would the story have been from Lewes'[11] point of view?

[p.27]

[...]
End of book—go <u>very</u> deeply into Norman.

To the cops she[12] points out Marvella as her mother's help[er].
[...]
Whom to dedicate Minn to?

[p.28]

Oct. 22 [1968]

Sit down & write it all down.

The past two weeks have been awful. It is as if something inside me had putrefied—the ensuing loss of self-esteem (which may perhaps be bald ego) has been paralyzing.

But it has been going on for a long time—esp. since book came out—esp since children were born etc. But not always so self-punishing & acute.

I grow uglier, smoke more. Don't buy clothes—can't go into fitting rooms.

Howie now too busy (& bored) to help. [...]

[p.29]

But the same critical voices that have been in me since childhood (AM I MAKING ALL THIS UP—NO!) grow louder. Is this trip necessary? It takes me half a day to make up a grocery list. I am sure people are staring at me. I feel enormous & very ugly.

11 George Lewes, with whom George Eliot lived for twenty years but never married.

12 This is a reference to Minn and a scene at the end of *The Honeyman Festival.*

Origins: a strict (but valuable) against-the-grain upbringing. No outlet for normal rebellion. Sexual squelching. My twin, perhaps?

I feel the same pattern in Will & am probably creating it.

I want help. But I am desperately afraid of

[p.30]

having my stories taken away. Yet I so much want to think clearly again. And would love to remember my real childhood.

I am very full of fear except when I drink.

I must not spoil things for Howie. One of the fears is of getting close enough to someone to talk & then "falling in love" which hurts too much & is an unfaithfulness. I long for the romance but can't take the reality—any more than I can.

Haven't I been on about this for years?

Withdrawal of parents over the years—age—detachment.

[p.31]

"You can't change the world."
"No, luv but you don't give into it, either. So you crack a little at the edges, you still hang onto what you know is right."
[...]

Why am I reverting to a belief in my family's values that cuts both Howard & Myself out?

Singing hymns.

[p.32]

Life of Geo. Eliot was very bad for me. If someone said she was a bad writer, I'd be relieved!

Well, if she rewrote as much as I do.

Well, if I worked as hard as she does!

Friday 1 November

Razor blades in apples.[13] Well, the idea of the poisoned apple isn't exactly new, is it?

Dreams: Balzac—surrounded by Duchesses
Prousts too.
Mine: surr. by distinguished men. Hugh's, too.
Must find his letters.[14]

[p.33]

Song images:
My shoes come walking.
The sun shines out of your shoes.
I wish his arms were in this shirt.

My wearing of men's shirts is a kind of fetishism.
[...]

Dancing to Pet Clark—a limbering of the legs

Bach à la Mooy—the things we do together!

Sudden memory—Edmondo Branco & his diving outfit.

Edward is Howie's Greek name!

[p.34]

The Honeyman Festival

Ch. IV is v. bad because not done with conviction. It is embarrassed & ashamed. Reflect the Glory of the whole thing—do 30 pages on that & the whole book will be O.K.

> "There had been two good things in her life so far, Godwin & Honeyman. They had their virtue in their uniqueness, romanticism

---

13 This refers to a fear of razor blades hidden in apples given out at Hallowe'en (31 October). The observation "Well, the idea of the poisoned apple isn't exactly new," is vintage Engel. Poisoned apples are common in fairy tales.

14 For Hugh MacLennan's letters to Marian Engel, see Verduyn, ed., *Dear Marian, Dear Hugh: The MacLennan-Engel Correspondence.*

in their baroque extremes. It was nothing to run from a small town into the arms of an older man, something precious to be given those terms to do it on. But contemptible to let this past cause one to fail to enjoy the placid present."

How did the affair **work**? What was it like in A-M? What was H[oneyman] like in bed or all round? Other people?

[p.35]

How do you feel.
Well, I feel pretty funny.
I don't know what it's like—I mean, what the others will feel about it.
Hayseed, aren't you?
How do you know?
Oh, it's pretty good to speak American again—you do, you know, in spite of saying "out" & "aboot." It brings things back. I know a million of you—& I feel homesick for you.

—By that time of year the little town was bone dry.

[p.36]

Notes 9 November

Re: The Wasteland issue — TLS [Times Literary Supplement] article Nov 7

Seeing this I know what I want, why the book doesn't work. There have to be "burnished throne" passages amongst the dialogues—there aren't enough of them.

J[ane]-R[egina][15] make her look like thing Gilmour—incredibly like Shirley Temple—not enough nose[?] to be taken seriously. In fact there is something vaguely syphilitic about the lack.

[p.37]

11/11/68 On the one level I was seasoning some pans, on another reading about Warhol when I began to wonder if it were really necessary to be dull. What if one just pushed off? To a farm.

15 A character in *The Honeyman Festival*; a social worker whose house calls make Minn feel insecure and untidy.

But there still exists the provide-provide. How close can one come to dreams?

But we are organizing something we do not wholly value, taking refuge in the material when we really want something else—aren't we? On the other hand, we can't live with ugliness.

[p.38]

Fulton
50 - - Davisville

19 Nov. 1968

The psychedelic day.
[...] worried about myself & booze. Is it a bribe or a treat I use for myself? Anyway pain in the tum at 6 is a booze pain & hairs of dogs don't help.
Thence to empty meeting w. Audrey at Longmans to turn Minn in. Managing weakly to outstare the gorgon in the lobby. Gadzoolis. Good Goons for kids tho'

[...]

[p.39]

[...]

[p.40]

Must make notes for the new book ["Lost Heir and Happy Families"]

Stanley—the old man

Verity—the new girl

V. turned on, lots of conversations.
A map w pins.
Almost [illegible].

Get IUD
Take driving lessons.
Dentist Basian

---

21 Nov [1968] Turned on—beer & music & children's aspirin crisis. <u>LOVING</u> Joe because he refused to let me panic. Says, "for arthritis they give them 15 & 20 at a time, keep calm" [...].

On being turned on. Liquor? I think, move, being free of
that g.d. book ["Minn"—*The Honeyman Festival*]—and the

[p.41]

splendid idea of a "new comedie humaine"—wanting Burke's Peerage very much—then deciding that after the Stanley-Verity book I can start on one—"A nous deux" Toronto.

Thought: "but I want the sponges to grow in my head."
Picture: glorious submarine forms. Got Sgt. Pepper record back from the bottom of a wrong envelope: HAPPY. So someone else is going to the cemetery down our street.
[...]

[p.42]

In which Verity asks Professor Porlock about Stanley.

"What is it, exactly that you want to know? Something negative?"

"It's just—that—a lot of us go to him for coaching, you know."

"He's very good. Highly recommended, a real polymath."

"Yes, but—lately—I've had a feeling."

"Are you sure yours isn't a problem in semantics?"

"I can't get any closer to it than that there's a suggestion—the vaguest—of—fishiness."

[p.43]

"Aren't you being romantic?"

"I'd think so—but it's not only me."

"Your brother? Mightn't he be jealous?"

"Oh—he's—difficult. But his instincts are fine, really."

"What kind of fishiness—sex? intrigue? politics?"

"Oh—very much the latter."

"Is it important to you?"

"Well, rather—bothersome."

"He's got a good reputation. He's very solid—at least very 'in.'"

[p.44]

"There's political freedom here. If you think you're fishing in troubled waters, quit."

"Yes, but."

"Child, I don't think I can afford to hear more."

Stanley's Steamer

After Faber died, they thought they ought to do more for young people. They were too old to adopt children, (and, really, Stanley did not want children about, they were too disruptive) so he had worked in an early version of the Big Brother Movement while Frieda continued her teaching. From time to time, they took a homeless teenager in & only one had worked out badly.

With his retirement (early, under the then new, rigid rules)

[p.45]

he had turned the tutoring into a business. A lot of students were referred to him. "There's a man called Stanley Markham who will probably help you."

So that now, when he looked at his charts, he felt almost satisfied.

He and his house were shabbier but he was not lonely. White hair became his big, white shovel-shaped face. The chart was nearly full. He reflected that he was, finally, a powerful man. Frieda would not have liked it, she said he counted on the outside world too much; but she lay beside Faber under the idiotic but apposite inscription, "Gone but not forgotten" in the Necropolis. He felt power in

[p.46]

his grip, he sat for a moment and savoured it, thought, I must be very, very careful about my will. With so many children how can I hope to be fair?

He was seventy-four.

Last week what he called "The Toronto Connection" had given him a party. He had looked around (he was very short-sighted now & peered like a cat or an owl, swivelled his head) and was very contented. Even taking into account the decline of the critical faculty with age, his young people could be emphatically said to be doing well.

These days rather than old he felt world weary. He had lived through an indigestible amount of history. He thought, this is perhaps why they die younger in Europe—the diet time offers is too

[p.47] [16]

rich. Here, the wars have been on foreign soil. The battles have been almost theoretical. The expanse of time still wearies me. Am I a weak man.

He thought, on the whole, not. The one weakness he could recognise (though there were people who said his politics were his weakness) had led him exactly where he was—a man with power, with the discretion to have it unexercised. It was there if it was needed—but he would wait until the need was great.

WHAT IS POWER?

The possibility of using groups of people as instruments. All clubs are power. All clubs are lobbies.

[p.48]

The cult of the Mackinaw.
(the red-headed boy in green Mackinaw shirt who passes sulkily by)

Stanley: boiled blue eyes & a long, spade-faced paper-white face, a white tonsure—old, farmerish clothes.

His house—near the university. Huge & shabby. Upstairs rooms let to draft-dodgers & served by old char & separate entrance.
Rather thuggish neighbourhood

[pp.49-50]

[Party invitation list]

16 Barber Fairley is written in the top left hand corner of page.

Cahier XVI[1]

How to make a novel—toujours le problème [51].

The bulk of *Cahier* XVI consists of notes for, and draft passages of, Engel's unpublished novel "Lost Heir and Happy Families," variously referred to as "Stanley's Novel," "Stanley's Book," "Stanley—Verity" or just "Stanley." Random "novel notes" are interspersed among others that would eventually work their way into the novel *Monodromos*. They concern questions of colonialism and authorial (as well as authoritative) voice. Engel had an early sense of the contemporary debate about who is and who is not best placed to write about the peoples and experiences of Africa. *Cahier* references to Algeria—many in French—suggest she was aware of the country's political struggles, while others indicate she knew there were limits to what she could write about developments and individuals in Africa. Thus for example, Engel acknowledged that she "couldn't begin to go far enough" in any writing she might do about Africa [15]. Draft text for the "Stanley novel" ("Lost Heir and Happy Families") became a vehicle for further explorations of one's limits in the world. Given these, but at the same time given all the interesting material the world presents, the issue remained "How to get it all in without parentheses" [53]. "How," Engel asked again 1 August 1970, "to get it all in?" [54]. Many *cahiers* would be filled trying to answer these and other "writerly" questions!

[p.1]

29 Dec. [1968]

Le Mythe de Sisyphe a la main, Howie sounds terriblement enfermé, Theodorakis[?] sur le phone.

John[2] et Sisyphe:

There are some people who would give anything to live even with a pig's liver inside them. I ____I.

Is it because of the child's expression—in a pig's eye?

1 1968-70, bright blue "Hilroy Exercise Book" *Cahier*, "Stanley" handwritten on cover; 64 pages used.

2 A character in "Stanley's Novel."

I—no.

I don't know what the value of living is. If Stanley really knew me, he'd be disappointed I haven't worked it out. For me the big "abstract" life has no more value than one of those enormous hard-edged geometric acrylic paintings that fill a whole art gallery wall. It is too big & too blank to take in. If I want to go on living I have to go to London to the National Portrait Gallery—where things are smaller, more specific

[continues on p.3]

[p.2]

The most miserable—because mediocre but complicated week I have lived through. Loving the children & hating H's withdrawal.

[p.3]

in order to have any fate or any idea of [illegible] life, purpose.

You see, I like details.

One wonders whether nihilism began with the big Italian paintings.

Where love of detail leads is another problem.

However—life—whether to choose to live it.

When I say yes I can only return to the outworn concept of DUTY. I can only say I admire Silly Sisyphus. Though I am not sure I shall last.

If death is endless sleep, no phone-calls—one embraces the idea.

Hell must have been a deterrent.

Whether it is better in the mind to suffer—whether one could nail the [illegible] & run down the [illegible] of suicides against [illegible]. What string? What arrows?

Emptiness
caused by busyness.

Logic commands increased business in aid of a holiday.

Shit, man. You wan live that way?

Oui, monsieur, I was conditioned and am most pleased by

[continues on p.5]

[p.4]

If I hit a big theme
from a man's pt of view it
will be a big novel.
From a woman's

[...]

[p.5]

children's sighs of perpetual motion. Not that I fail to value contemplation, but action is still sacred—sometimes.

[Faith without works is dead][3]
John printed every year in small G[ree]k letters in front of his diary.

Stanley's ideas
distract me, damn him, from my death
As no other has:
Wife
Ma & Pa
work
What else?
Elsa.

Elsa likes it upside down & backwards but not in captivation I want her always → death wish.
Father & mother—one exchanges pleasantries.

STANLEY symbol of progressiveness wh[ich] one can't drop: Scots GRIT

[6]

There is no help
What book is now?
Hopkins

[p.7]

but not—internationally or imaginatively up to much.

On a[4] — a man who would commit suicide exc. for Stanley's demand

On a— a group of female commandos working for Tory Dean
Ferreting out outmoded
Get—Stanley
On a— Sarah
On a— Elsa
On a— des idées
On a— les "apôtres" de Stanley
Les Funeraires

3 Square brackets in the original text. Biblical quotation from James 2:26.

4 French for "One has" or "There is." What follows is an inventory of ingredients for the new novel.

[p.8]

Camus et
Sahara

[p.9]

When Karl Jaspers, revealing the impossibility of conceiving of the world as a unity, cried "This limitation leads me to myself, there, where I can't hide myself behind an objective point of view, something that I can represent, there where neither I nor anyone else's existence can become an object for me" he evokes, after so many others; deserted places, waterless; where thought reaches its boundaries. After so many others—yes, but how many were in a hurry to get out! To this point where thought vacillates, many men have arrived, and many humble men. These left behind the dearest things in their lives. Others, princes, of the spirit, left behind their will also, but

[p.10]

it is in their suicidal thoughts, in the worst revolt of the spirit, that they proceeded. The real effort is to hold onto, to will the contrary, as much as is possible and to examine closely the baroque jungle of these distant contrasts: tenacity and clairvoyance are privileged spectators of our absurd, inhuman game, death & hope exchange replies. This dance at once elementary & subtle, one can analyse its steps before illustrating it and living it out.

[p.11]

[...] Joe proletarian intellectual [...]

[p.12]

Toi tu devrais vraiment décrire le monde étroit de Carscallen et d'Elisabeth et de Don.
FOR FEAR of meeting devils on the wayside?

Have I met all the Devils?

Ends of years are sacred.
One can't underline to Howie.
Patterns— Hajijakis, persian carpets.
Low tastes?

[p.13]

Al-gé , rie Francaise[5]
Af ri ka libre

5 Engel's thoughts in the next few pages are more relevant to her project in *Monodromos* than to the Ontario-based "Stanley" novel. As usual, she had more than one manuscript in mind at once.

An image of the Western imagination
Whereas all Africa has known is 1) beauty
2) Slavery
Bringing up children—one wants beauty & one is always a fascist because cf beauty ← order.

If African & Western order can meet? Ever? Good western things ← very suppressed people.

[p.14]

[...] Camus & Algeria [...]

[p.15]

How suppressed are Africans aside from slavery (always keep in mind Arabs, Turks).

Theme: The Conquests.

(but I couldn't begin to go far enough could I. What a weak mind. Not even a colloquy with Leslie Fiedler could I stand. Logical conclusion

Africans I have known }
W I I have known } N O N E
U.S. negroes I have known

[p.16]

Well it pays to ask questions.
(and man I have always need of these.)
Greek music, Algerian themes.
What has North Africa? Greece? Kypros? Mexico? [...] we have need of thee!
[...]

[p.17]

[...]
Colonialism.[6]
But where is English conscience English guilt?

[p.18]

Ecrire à Solange
Chaput-Rolland.[7]

6 See *Cahier* XXXII [13] for further thoughts Engel developed on "voice appropriation."

7 Solange Chaput-Rolland, best known for her non-fiction writing on Canadian politics and Quebec nationalism, is author of *My Country, Canada or Quebec?* (1966), *Face to Face* (1972) and *Où es-tu?* (1996).

Et pourquoi pas?

Whenever I have drunk a lot of rye (vin du pays) French seems very much more profound

[p.19]

We were taught, reading(?) (<u>Punch</u> (not knowing about the penis) in the Pub.Lib (after all mother had met the Queen of Romania, who <u>smoked</u>) ((Why do I always K[now] people who respect Butlers?)) that the preserving thing about the English was that they had a sense of humour about themselves. But no comparable anti-colonial stuff has come out, has it? Due to Labour perhaps?

[p.20]

References to Ferragus &
bad French
blotting

Ferragus—Ferrago

[p.21]

John ["Lost Heir and Happy Families"] at the staff meeting: [...]
doodled his only doodle—a MASONIC EYE. Put him in mind of Stanley and as always of dark, dead Faber.

Looked around, counting heads. Which were Faber's men?

[p.22]

Old boy network vs how Stanley operated.

Wondered if, now, Stanley was as sublimely unimportant as paper clips vs Bostitch pins.

No, he was saved because of his politics. He had awarded interest on the basis of concern & to him concern was political concern. He was still in closer touch w the students than the rest of them ex[cept] poss[ibly] Draycott & Schachter. None of the rest of them even believed in the Roman Engagé. (Why not marry the Fr[ench] & English depts?)

Just here, Sylvia Bamard is sick in his lap.

[p.23]

[...]
[Line of written music notes]

[p.24]

John on receiving Stanley's call.

Guilty, guilty.

The students now were beautiful & many, despite the fact that they refused to deal with anything between the 14th & the 20th century, were well read. But principally, when he saw them, he felt elderly & ashamed & dead.

He was alive according to his way of living as they were according to his. Ideally, the two ways in scholarship would fuse but increasingly the best of them were drop-outs or cop outs and Faber haunted him when he saw them & made him angry & confused.

Guilt, guilt. Faber looking like a cross between Mailer & Dorian Gray saying, "Listen, Johnnie, tell Dad...."

[p.25]

Meyer said to
read
S.M. Lipsett
AGRARIAN
SOCIALISM[8]

[p.26]

Meeting towards the end of the book: all in a distinguished circle, on small chairs—and—there is roll-call and everyone answers "Present" as in Grade One.

Verity & Charles— he squirrels around with her pants & sends her running away.
Is she an icicle?

Kath Keamey— a good character but don't let her take over.

Oh she's developed.

Long evening of Marx (4 paras)
Gin, [illegible], + Alexander Levesby

↘ Also letters to the editor

8 Seymour Martin Lipset, *Agrarian Socialism: The Cooperative Commonwealth Federation in Saskatchewan* (Berkeley: University of California Press, 1971).

I can see John in front of a group of "Distinguished" men. ("as long as you're up" realizing that what they have is CONFIDENCE.)
Marx: The DICTATORSHIP of the PROLETARIAT

TORONTO
Where are TRUTH & BEAUTY

[p.27]

Donald Barthelme[9]

[p.28]

Sentimentality = Feeling 〉cause = BOOZE

But really where are TRUTH & IMAGINATION now?
And aren't they the things children need most? The cause of the defection of the children of the '50's?

Why is it EVIL to create TRUTH & BEAUTY? [...]

Why do the mothers throw them out?

Why are the old anti-platonic Beatles better than Philosophy?
[...]

(How much sophistication does it take to say "I poop on it")

Without Booze would I have any Emotions? (what about 18's without Drugs) (Southern chimes?) (they all booze)
WHAT IS NATURAL?

[p.29]

I'm a leader rather than
a follower but I don't
know how to lead esp
in a strange country

[p.30]

[...]

Am I really married to booze & feelings—I don't respect either.
But I'm out of nervous depression.

---

9 American writer, author of *Come back, Dr. Caligari* (1964), *Snow White* (1967), *Unspeakable Practices* (1968) and *City Life* (1970).

Need a holiday.
[...]

[p.31]

22/1/69

At the core—at the heart
of things we so terribly
worry about—is
something—utterly simple.

Or is there?

<u>6 Feb. 69</u>

Paris review interviews—Waugh the funniest.

STANLEY—why not make him madder?

The man I saw yesterday going into the Park Plaza—looking for entrance as if he hadn't been there since it changed.

V. tall, holes in sock, no rubbers, long limp overcoat, reddish tonsure, small grey-red beard—long man, long head carrying superbly—one paper shopping bag, one <u>petit point</u> suitcase w air label!

Was it his old mother's? Was he a poet or an HEIR?

JOHN!

[pp.32-39]

[Character sketches (e.g., John, Verity and Stanley) from draft of "Lost Heir and Happy Families"]

[p.40]

Feb. 24 [1969]
Reading NY Review of Books—(cf Making it)

Mary McCarthy on Orwell:

See Orwell's self-destructiveness as John's but of course for much nobler reasons. Same desire (unexpressed) for <u>real</u> feeling & observation, same quasi saintliness.

D.A.N. Jones on novels: Use of "freaks" in Junie Moon & Janet Frame's book covers up sentimentality. He says this too of Salinger & McCullers.

He likes prose to be transparent, honest; so do I.

[p.41]

More plans

1. Gen Intro
2. Stanley
3. Chas & Verity

She is cool, says little, hates a lot—<u>never</u> honest.

He has <u>a</u> <u>fit</u> when he finds out who her father is.

When he fires her, she asks John to take her in. He won't—she perseveres.

4. Other characters
    Kath sees herself as Mother to the Group.
    Ronquist
    Bligo the diplomat
    Other man—Roger Meyer?

Use faces of writers from TIME article

5 Stanley's death
6 John
7 Funeral & Inquisition
8 Verity follows him
9 Sorting of goods by Kath & ___.
    Verity's pursuit.
    His illness.

[p.42]

[...]

20 March '69. Comments on re-reading:
Level of language is bad—too many prepositional suffixes: e.g. ended-up; all the NDP & economics references bad because over-simplified & stupid. Think more deeply or leave out.

Importance of good, cold gray ability
must emerge from the text.
<u>Then</u>, the importance of decent aims.

[...]

[pp.43-45]

[Notes on CRTC Air-of-Death[10] hearing, 18-21 March 1969 and observations of people in attendance]

[p.46]

[...]
Use this kind of close observation.
[...]
Don't want a realistic novel—must get at psychological (?) truth too.

But no great woman-centred spasms either.

Simenon does realism very well but leaves one always feeling blank—he doesn't go far enough inside people. Self-satisfied, undisturbing writing.

John as self-made philosopher.

What does Verity represent for him?

A Sexual fury?

[p.47]

[More notes on characters]

[p.48]

Left right & centre she wanted it and there, a little to the side and what was he doing here—she shut up the question.

I am innocent stranger.
She swore by the rood/rude & other blasphemies she'd had no one since him—but where had she learned it all, out of a bloody book? How did his pecker keep up, it hadn't been any Albert Memorial before? Here—God. She had it she was it—but, no lass, not there, that

10 On 22 October 1967, the CBC television network broadcast a program on environmental pollution entitled *Air of Death*. The program was controversial because of its discussion of the effects of pollution on human health and because a number of groups argued that the producers did not represent a balanced approach to the topic. The Canadian Radio-Television Commission held hearings to determine if the research presented was valid and reliable. Canada, Canadian Radio-Television Commission, *Annual Report* 1970-71 (Ottawa: Dept. of Supply and Services, 1971) 42-43.

"I'm an old man for godsake."
"Not bloody likely."
"Look here—not that."
"Why?"
"It's ... illegal."
"Are you really that hung up?"
"Yes. Yes."
"You don't look it."
"There's enough to be had out of it in the ordinary way."
"There's never enough, you're marvellous."
"I'm twenty years older than you, and twenty years less free."

Hangdog by the window of a filthy provincial hotel. Not by exact choice.

[p.49]

"I thought you liked me ... and this."
"I do."
Roles were ridiculously reversed—he the pleading virgin, "Don't touch me ... there."
Though why not plunge into certain seas? The others had been tried?

But it seemed to him that there would be anarchy if something was not taboo. This she would not understand ... her generation.

"Hung-up. Old. Not free. Do you find me ridiculous?"
"I love you."
"You're not old enough to know what that word means."
"You never use it."
"No."
"Why can't you just enjoy me?"
"Because ... you will want to come live in my house."
"Well—why not? Look—I'm <u>some</u> use to you—I'm there for your bed."
"I feel old—God, when you talk like that I'm a thousand. Has no one ever told you, dolt—daughter—darling—that that's not honest?"

[p.50]

"Earning my keep?"
"Earning your keep in bed."
"My mother does."
"She's married."
"Only because of us."

"What do you mean?"

"Oh god, Maureen was born 6 months after the wedding—you know, all that crazy old-fashioned 'and don't tell' stuff. Anyway—I don't want to marry you, I just want to live with you."

"No"

"Why not?"

"Much as I value your company—no."

[p.51]

How to make a novel—toujours le problème.

Think of psychodelia [*sic*] in terms of the rocking-horse winner.

I'm too lazy to like clotted reading.

so—eschew

NOTES for a <u>new</u> novel [*Monodromos*]

The Retreat

Nicosia— in a [illegible] sort of house w her mother who gives piano lessons lives Eleanor who is practising a game called "The Circles of Hell" & retreating further into herself. She has reached 2nd last stage & is locked in her room. This makes the outside world more real for her.

How she got there: when she was 14 her mother married an Englishman who took her to England, then Kypros. He has been inconsiderate enough to disappear on a sailing exped'n.

= Edward the snail factor

[pp.52-53]

[Notes for *Monodromos*]

[p.54]

8/1/70

If you love them too much they will never become anything—except "the salt of the earth."

People who want to accomplish in the highest degree are those who are unsure of their own value & need "the world's" confirmation. Yet they know in their hearts that "the world" is inadequate so they either believe in God or in absolute i.e. historical standards.

Therefore it is evil to teach one's children that history i.e. man is evil. One should teach them that "the once & future king" is both inside & outside them. The divinity is the mystery, the good. Evil is not mysterious—it has been described & re-described throughout history & remains constant. It is the cramping withholding of love, the love of power, sadistic power of death, unreined ego, the corruption of children: sexual drives & religion & death & collectivity encompass it—& also the good. Greek logic codified it but is not the only means.

On writing about Cyprus— the rich vs the poor environment.
A novel called Byzantium.
How to get it all in?

[p.55]

[...]

The transplantation
of American ideas is a
curse. Everywhere is not America
(US in France, England, here)

75 house
75 cash
25 car
175

[p.56]

Could one join those elements in a big novel called Byzantium?

Thoughts (?)
Heroines are not important.
Environment is.
Flesh is.
Relationships, people are.

The voice. Must not be jokey.
[...]
Byzantium—a one day thing.

[p.57]

grins at
the word

Sold "Amaryllis" for $250 [11] bump
Write some more.

Orlo Miller:

black turtleneck, ministers boon

Sarnia —ugly but practical.
low standard of aspiration in middle class?

---

25 years—Donelleys.

Man with what looks like a cork in his car.

"Sheesday" Lucan. Mention means no coal.
Miller on Kelly

[p.58]

On reading the Niagara of Michel Butor [12]

Here he separates out the "tracks" of an experience.

I am trying to show in synthesis the tracks in Minn's mind.

These are
1. Pregnancy
2. Marriage to Norman
3. Motherdom
4. Gertrude } sometimes tog[ether]
5. Alice
6. Weeping Willie
7. Godwin Town
8. Rebellion
9. Honeyman—v. subdued now
10. Hippies & house.

I am a large, pregnant mother of three; I live in a large oozing house with hippies in Toronto; I once lived with Honeyman; Gertrude & Alice raised me; Godwin was my town I left.

---

11 "Amaryllis" is a short story included in Engel's first collection, *Inside the Easter Egg.*

12 Michel Butor (1926-), French novelist of the *nouveau roman* period and author of *Niagara,* trans. by Elinor S. Miller (Chicago: H. Regnery, 1969).

Symbols— raw amber
mountains
old people
fish?

[p.59]

At any given moment we are many things—if we are too many things at once there is static in our minds, we fail to communicate.

Characters.
Jane—Regina—marriage & motherhood
Richard—being mothered.
Marvella—Rebellion
Sam—Minn's Rebellion
E.E.—Godwin, Willie
Annabel—Pregnancy (give her the Mrs Tachaberry role)
Reiner—Honeyman

[p.60]

[Doodle]

[p.61]

[Party Invitation List]
The Lonely Ones[13] —Jim Bacque
—incompetent writing
—subject—impossible sans sentimentalization.

Tales of the Quarter[14] —fine—good writing exactly as it was.

The Edible Woman[15] —v good
fiancé as two-dimensional as fiancés are
I. Murdoch-ish—apt building etc
the "poetic" touches
But names are wrong—Clara

The Chain[16] powderpuff w serious themes

best themes are not consciously chosen.

13 James Bacque, *The Lonely Ones* (Toronto: McClelland & Stewart, 1969).
14 Lawrence Garber, *Tales from the Quarter* (Toronto: Peter Martin Associates, 1969).
15 Margaret Atwood, *The Edible Woman* (Toronto: McClelland & Stewart, 1969).
16 Hélène P. Holden, *The Chain* (Don Mills, ON: Longmans, 1969).

[p.62]

Best themes are not consciously chosen out of patriotism or a desire to please—but because they are natural to one's perceptions & style ∴ theme becomes transparent.

So also with characters—once they are thematic they require extraordinary treatment. Garber is the one who knows this.

The Chain—almost hypnotic chant w censors; it is so poetic—but the style carries her too fast, she can't stop for details, to go into things. Therefore book seems more superficial than it is.

Checklist of what is to be done in Can. Lit—possible points of view.

The Lonely Ones

[p.63]

Kermodey References.

1. Beckett's book on Proust.
2. Dante's "Belagua"—who had to relive his slothful life before entering purgatory
3. Descartes René 1596 né LaHaye, RF
   Founder of modern philosophy—invention of scientific method—

CARTESIAN METHOD: "In order to reach the truth one must once in one's life divest oneself of all received ideas and reconstruct anew all one's systems of knowledge."

4. Look for puns in names of characters. Still? Certainly in Nabokov & Beckett.

5. Sartre: What are Paradigms? Examples, models (e.g. of conjugations) "eidetic imagery of bad faith"
   bad faith = taking one's paradigms from the past, from illusions left over from childhood i.e. an era that is finished—passéisme.

EIDETIC??

Iris Murdoch—profoundest task of the novelist is to create irreducible & opaque persons.
Form interferes w this.

Robbe Grillet is against the retention of any paradigm which may suggest that the world means something. "Quite simply, it IS."

[p.64]

John & Verity

The Dance—	John lets Verity in as a refugee from Chas.
	She heals him.
	Refuses to go—becomes sexually necessary to him.
	He refuses to send her away.
Put Galt into	He is to be prosecuted.
John's dreams.	She goes, then returns later—it is a boarding house.
[Doodle]	She muscles in on him & is dissatisfied, moves upstairs w a negro.
	Then her family really crashes in.

Cahier XVII[1]

L'écrivain en toute honnêteté,
parle de soi [16].

This *cahier* opens with notes on Galt (present-day Cambridge), Ontario, where Engel spent part of her childhood, and reaffirms the importance of the small-town Ontario background she wanted to mine in her new novel, "Lost Heir and Happy Families," provisorily referred to as "Stanley." Small-town settings were a feature of Margaret Laurence's writing as well, as Engel observed in notes she took on Laurence's novels in this *cahier.* "Manawaka," she declared, was "absolutely accurate" [5].

The late 1960s and early to mid-1970s were a period of intense intellectual exploration for Engel. She was particularly interested in the work of French theorists, not only because she could read them in the original, but also, as the notes in this *cahier* suggest, because "in G[reat] B[ritain] [there was] no nouvelle critique" [7]. Moreover, British experimentalists did not, in Engel's view, go in for the blend of philosophy and criticism that so appealed to her. In *Cahier* XVII, Husserl and phenomenology are her focus, with additional notes and comments on Nathalie Sarraute, André Gide and Alain Robbe-Grillet. Like the writers and critics she read, Engel was concerned with literary realism and romanticism, subjects she explored in more than one *cahier.* The Marian Engel Archive contains an undated notebook that is likely from this period.[2] Its cover reads "Notes on Auden & Proust" and its contents comprise thoughts and quotations from W.H. Auden's *The Enchafèd Flood; or, The Romantic Iconography of the Sea* and André Maurois's *The Quest for Proust.*[3]

---

1 1969, teal-blue notebook, "Stanley" and "Fifth Business" written on cover; 19 pages used.

2 MEA, Box 6 File 25. Mentioned but not reproduced here, the *cahier's* entire 24 pages are notes.

3 W.H. Auden, *The Enchafèd Flood; or, The Romantic Iconography of the Sea* (New York: Random House, 1950) and André Maurois, *The Quest for Proust* (Harmondsworth, Middlesex: Penguin, 1962).

[p.1]

GALT
Slow train.
WASPS— middle middle class.
Station— at the end of Rose Street—unchanged.
First?
Ride down—close, cheap— past Central United.
Marvellous architecture somewhere between Edinburgh & Woodbridge.

Remembering: there are **no** lions on the library, just columns.

Bridge over to church is beautiful
Dickson School & St Andrew St are up that way.
Very solid little town centre.

But are the hearts cold stone.
CORBELS—You look up, they
form a lacy roof.

Where's the action now?

[p.2]

Social forms in Margaret Laurence

Literature is:
"the creation
of imaginary
gardens with
real toads in them"
Marianne Moore[4]

[p.3]

Margaret Laurence B-RD.
Jest of God[5]—GG
"woman's perceptions of a woman's frustrations"
not sympathetic
cynical Rachel

Stone Angel— R[obertson] Davies liked it.

4 Marianne Moore, "Poetry," Poems (London: Egoist, 1921).

5 Published by McClelland & Stewart, this novel received the Governor General's Award for Fiction in 1966.

Good reviews
Trilling on Casamassina

Intro—historical

Analysis of story type—Hyacinth Robinson, Rastignac etc: "It is to confront … Freedom & ease, K[nowledge] & power, money, opportunity & Society."— the story of the young man from the Provinces combines legend & actuality. From it we learn about class & its strange rituals, power, influence, money … the hard fluent face in which society has its being.

Jean Jacques Rousseau is the father of all men of this type inc[luding] Napoleon.

[p.4]

The Women vs The Men
Real lovers— hard-fucking non-Calvinist outsiders often cruel (Shipley).
BUCK May not be hung-up but also not manageable. Drinkers— drink = freedom from Mrs Grundy.

Good husbands—the dull blankness of reality
Complex of Stacey: She falls apart when confronted w ordinary Thor Thorlakeson: the anglo-turned-angel

social situations wh. represent oppression of her ma's propriety

Elements

Women's life: hard-driving, cynical

Small town— clubby
prying
layers & groups
Stacey
Hagar & Rachel— their desire for the dark "outsider"
corseted
Freedom from Calvinism
—but he is free too of their domestic aspirations
They know that this sacrifice is too painful

It is one of the Tonnerre girls who tells her why—instinct has forbidden her to conform to Vernon Winklers jumped-up aspirations.

RICHALIFE— worst phoniness

Richest } associations are lower class
Realest } Val
—Tonnerres, Buckle Fennick
Luke?

[p.5]

Figuring out these women
Stacey
Rachel
Hagar— early, clear—absolutist absolutely tough, acting according
Will to a morality—a personal
Lioness rule that is based on the sin of pride—yet, spunky anti-social Old Mrs Cameron—a watered-down faceless woman w Hagar's pride but not her character. <u>Social</u> convention is all she sees, not personal satisfaction—but then, maintaining her place.

ERRANT H U S B A N D S (DRINKING,
} Cameron & Bram escapist)
Shipley
Sense of Family—the Scotch ones were the good ones.
Manawaka
Wamaka or whatever it's called—Sense of place as in "Our Town" & "Main Street"
Manawaka—absolutely accurate.

Fires imaginary lady-bug ones

Stacey—settled & fettered
satisfied—almost.

[p.6]

The crisis before the fact is faced.

The awful stone grimness in us women.

The fear of "spoiling."
Another ego scrabbling through the
bracken to be reformed.

Love—Mothers must be a well. Well, I've gone & sopped up a lot of other peoples'.

cf Main street

Elements of small-town life.

propriety—putting a good face on it
doctoring—
drinking
church
school—Rachel
funeral parlour—Camerons
dairy—Nick & Julie
Farms
Stores—Curries
French-Canadians—Tonnerres
Bank

the dark
forbidden
foreign
lover—other
side of the track

Woman— cooking
kids
bed
covers
illness
work

[p.7]

French
<u>The Nouveau Roman</u>—Times Litt supp
<u>Claude</u> Simon, M. Butor, A[lain]R[obbe]-G[rillet]: By John Sturrock[6] misunderstood in G[reat] B[ritain]—people cannot shed old habits of thought.

part of general 20th [century] breakdown—breakthrough to
non-Arist[ocratic] non-Euclidean way of thinking—
only the novel lags behind this
in GB no nouvelle critique

GB experimenters borrowing old tricks
" does not go in for schools of philosophy & criticism

---

6 John Sturrock, *The French New Novel: Claude Simon, Michel Butor, Alain Robbe-Grillet* (London & New York: Oxford University Press, 1969).

But by avoiding these England too introverted.
∴ this book welcome.

3 figures— earliest clearest representatives in work & in crit[icism] of phenomenological [method?]

Passmore

Phenomenological method

Husserl at first describes it as "descriptive psychology"

wants to arrive at a pure theory "independent of contingent empirical facts"

Historicists say a pure truth cannot exist.
Husserl says they have to act as if their
own theories are true ∴ there must be truths.

Empiricists: we are directly acquainted
only with "particular existences"
general theory must be
constructed by generalization
out of them
a non-empirical theory ∴ a fabrication

[p.8]

<u>Houses</u>

On attaining the "Other Island"

[p.9]

Museum

Husserl: it is a presumption that we are directly aware only of particulars "Everyone sees ideas 'essences' & sees them ... continuously; they work with them when they think & they also pass judgements about them. But ... people explain them away."

—any philosophy which is worthy of the name ... must shake itself free from all metaphysical presuppositions: it must investigate what actually confronts it, not allowing any metaphysical fantasy to distract it from its general analysis of "essences" or "general structures."

to proceed thus is to be "phenomenological"

a statement as event in the lives of a particular person

a statement as what a person means

propositions & universals are not entities, not things that exist here or there: they are the unity or essence, of a set of entities:
redness of red things, propositions
of statements.
We have direct experience of them.

"Consciousness in itself has a being of its own which in its absolute uniqueness of nature remains unaffected by the phenomenological disconnexion."

i.e. consciousness does exist & is not a "natural" object

(Br. philosophers reject this)

[p.10]

(Logic and maths are deductive.
Physical sciences are inductive)

There are such things as "acts of consciousness" which have as their object q.c. which is itself a "mode of consciousness"—acts which would still exist if everything but consciousness was wiped out. Existence of such acts is the primary certainty.

We cannot "think away our
consciousness"—it is the
one Absolute.

Moving back from that absolute we move back to the world of objects & approach them from the standpoint of transcendental phenomenology—"As they declare themselves to consciousness," & not taking for granted the conclusions of natural science ∴ we preserve the purity of our inquiry

phenomenology of time—as it appears to consciousness

(Later he was thought to revert to idealism)

[pp.11-12]

[Notes on legal terminology and process]

[p.13]

Nathalie Sarraute: L'ère du soupçon[7]

It appears today that the novelist does not believe in his characters any more
AND NEITHER DOES THE READER

∴ the fictional character, deprived of this support, which allowed him to stand up solidly, vacillates & is destroyed (undoes himself)

In the time of Eugenie Grandet[8] he was in the position of saints among donors in It[?] primitive pictures. Since then he has continuously lost ground—everything: even, in places, his name.

Today there are books which pretend to be novels—lots of them—narrated by an "I" who is a reflection of the author; with characters who are visions, nightmares, or dependences [*sic*] etc.
This evolution shows that readers & writers are now very sophisticated.
They now mistrust both fictional characters AND each other.
We are in the era of suspicion.

[p.14]

Everything in art comes down to, as Gide said, "the intensity of **life** which dictates the value of a thing." This quality of life (conviction?) has deserted forms otherwise promising & broken the old boundaries & useless accessories of the novels—characters, intrigues, reading glasses & smoking jackets can continue to exist but no longer reveal anything to us about reality.

PROPS are gone—Balzac.

Now we have read Joyce, Proust & Freud—the interior monologue, the psychological life, and the K[nowledge] of the unconscious—have tumbled down the HERO—he is now terribly limited—not there for writer or reader—any more than a whole person is there for a medical specialist—for the external world now speaks of internal meanings.

---

7 Nathalie Sarraute, *L'ère du soupçon* (Paris: Gallimard, 1956).

8 This novel by Honoré de Balzac (1833) is part of the *Comédie Humaine* series.

So if writers no longer believe in the reproduction of realism, it is because the character is like a surgeon: the body exists for him but not the personality.

Time has ceased to be the {current / container} of plot & is now still waters which cover slow, subtle acts of decomposition.

Our acts have lost their moving currents & obvious significance—new sentiments & meanings have appeared.

[p.15]

Real vs Ideal
Reproduction is
OUT exc. as parody

[p.16]

No-one now believes that the product of the novelist's imagination is as rich as a real object.

Loss of Faith — And since realistic writers feel that it is vain to try to reproduce the whole complexity of life, & it is up to the reader to bring his sense of life to the book & interpret its mysteries—he prefers now to deal with real facts.

The "petit fait vrai" has incontestable advantages over stories.
1. It is real—has conviction
2. It is beyond the editorial bounds of "good taste etc"
3. It is audacious—it doesn't have to be within the bounds of credibility. No writer quite dares reality as reality does.

It is now impossible to begin a story "La marquise sortit à cinq heures"
Claude Mauriac

Also—narrator—now we want to know WHO?—don't believe omniscient author (—college prof?)
The 1st person narrator ∴ better now.

Conventions are dying

NOW—l'écrivain, en toute honnêteté, parle de soi.

[p.17]

Robbe-Grillet

No attempt at new writing has yet enthralled the public as much as the old bourgeois novel of Balzac, Dickens—still THE form.

In those days, lay psychological analysis was the basis of all prose.

A GOOD novel = study of a passion
conflict " "
absence " " in a given situation

Most writers who still follow old forms could paraphrase Pere Goriot & get away with it

> Well, language hasn't changed.
> Society hasn't much.
> Our minds are still the same & our upbringing.
>
> Everything has been said.

Can there be a literature of Revolution?
(Pagan suckled by a creed outworn)

[p.18]

Margaret—I've just told my creative writing people to write a 50 word beginning for a novel—meanwhile leafing through this old notebook I find notes on a) Galt b) Margaret Laurence c) Husserl, phenomenology, the new novel. That was a winter.

[...]

[p.19]

[Fragment of notes on *As You Like It*]

Cahier XVIII[1]

Resolutions
Learn to dance.
Take care of teeth.
Write Stanley's Book. [1] [2]

Cahier XVIII is the second of three traditional date books Engel attempted. Like the first in 1962, and the third in 1977, it is convincing proof that the author's *cahiers* were much more than conventional diaries.

Engel did not do very well with the fixed form. Scarcely a week into the year of this date book, she was adding information after the fact. Many days passed without an entry. There are no draft passages of novels or short stories, and only an occasional reflection on writing (28 June: "Nothing much doing—exc[ept] book reviews"). For the most part, the entries are short and "factual"—names of visitors, appointments with dentists and doctors, social events, travel itinerary. These are only noted, not reproduced, here.

In point of fact Engel was, as she herself observed, "writing in [so] many notebooks" at once. A cross reference confirms this. On 18 March 1969, Engel recorded: "CRTC (on "Air of Death") hearings begin." *Cahier* XVI contains the notes Engel took on the hearings. For her *cahiers*, Engel reserved her characteristic lengthy drafts of text and philosophical musings. To the date-book style notebook, she committed observations of a different sort—those mentioned above, as well as financial worries or concerns about her comportment with the children. On 21 March she feels "mean and adult" for "automatically" siding with another adult (William's teacher) in response to a school incident. She still feels "mean" the next day when she removes William from a theatre, where the family has come to see the movie *Swiss Family Robinson*, because he is running up and down the aisles.

Not quite four years old, the twins were at an active age and the date book logs efforts to burn off some of their energy—a walk to the cemetery on a winter afternoon (22 February), an excursion to a sugar bush near St Catharine's (8 March), various outings to the movies (*Yellow Submarine*, 4 January; *A Hard Day's Night*, 22 February; *Swiss Family Robinson*, 22 March). It also

1 1969, dark green date book; 89 pages used.

2 New Year's Resolutions for 1969.

records instances when Engel disciplined in ways that troubled her after the fact and that led to discussions with Howard. At bath time on 1 November, "I hit William too hard (he has run full tilt down the hall & knocked my uterus into the sink) & H sulks. Long talk later—lately I have been harsh & unsubtle"; 2 November: "'Discipline' etc is discussed."

Engel's fondness for her father, Frederick Passmore, emerges on visits with her parents (8 January and 19 January), as does her upset upon hearing that "everyone was sorry for [her] mother when Sara.no.clouds [*Sarah Bastard's Notebook*] came out. This hurts," Engel wrote 5 November. The author also expressed disappointment when *Sarah Bastard's Notebook* was not nominated for a Governor General's Award (18 March).

Two final items from this notebook are included here. One is a "camping list" for a trip the Engels made 1-16 July 1969 through parts of Michigan and Ontario. This was the trip during which the author "discovered" St Joseph's Island—the setting for *Bear*'s Cary Island—and Major William Kingdom Rains—a key character in her final novel-in-progress, "Elizabeth and the Golden City":

> Our family was camping that summer [1969]. We went up through Michigan, interviewing people who had known Hemingway. We decided to return through Sault Ste Marie, spend the night on St Joseph's Island, the largest of the arching group that fills the shipping channel and the mouth of St Mary's River. We dropped in on the mother of a friend who said we could put the tent right over there on the lawn. "I'd love to know whose log cabin that was, all covered with wild roses." "Haven't you ever heard of the major?" she asked.[5]

The "major" was William Kingdom Rains, who settled on St Joseph's Island in the 1830s with two young women left to his charge upon the death of their father, "Mad Jack Doubleday of Milford Haven."[6] The Doubleday sisters, Elizabeth and Frances, became central characters in the novel that Engel was working on at the time of her death, "Elizabeth and the Golden City," a fictionalization of the story of real-life Rains and his companions Elizabeth and Frances.

---

3 *Cahier* XI [23] 4 June.

4 See *Cahier* XVI, footnote 10, for details about the CRTC hearings. In the present *Cahier* (XVIII), Engel signaled, to herself or a potential reader, that notes she took on the hearings were in "Stanley's notebook" (*Cahier* XVI). See *Cahier* XVIII [37], 19 March 1969.

5 MEA, Box 33 File 86.

6 This is Engel's expression in a three-page description of the novel, accompanying lengthy draft sections of it in MEA, Box 34 File 36.

Cahier XVIII ends with a second item of note: a tally of Engel's 1969 income from reviews and articles she wrote for newspapers and magazines such as the *New York Times*, *Saturday Night* and *The Globe & Mail.* The amount is not insignificant but still not enough to offset worries such as that she recorded 7 November: "v. worried abt money tired."

[p.1]

Resolutions[7]

Learn to drive
Take care of teeth
Write Stanley's Book

[p.2]

N[ew] Y[ear's] Eve [...]

[p.3]

Wed JANUARY 1, 1969[8]
Snowed in & hung over
We walk to the milk store

Thurs JANUARY 2
Kids back to school

[p.4]

Fri JANUARY 3

Sat JANUARY 4
Take the kids to <u>Yellow Submarine</u>[9]

[p.5]

Sun JANUARY 5, 1969
Doug Fetherling[10] invites us to tea—
which is pop—& it makes us
all happy

---

7 Teeth were a constant concern for Engel, and she never did become a driver. She did, however, finish "Stanley's Novel," which she retitled "Lost Heir & Happy Families," though it remained unpublished.

8 The year 1969 appears irregularly throughout; days of the week are written both in full and short form.

9 This 1968 movie starred the members of the British band The Beatles and was directed by George Dunning.

10 Author of more than 40 books, including the recent *Travels By Night: A Memoir of the Sixties* (1994).

[...]

Mon. JANUARY 6
↑H. to see "The Fixes"
Worked on Stanley a bit
[...]

[p.6]

Tuesday JANUARY 7, 1969
I must have gone shopping
But I also worked
Then H. sent me to Dr Shivago [*sic*][11]

Wednesday JANUARY 8
Mostly, read Pat Grosskurth's John Addington Symonds[12]
Dad for lunch w. his fish & chips.
Enjoy Dad so much, w. his talk of books & places, his reverence for things.
Worked out plot-end of Beatrix.
Evening—good dinner—porc truffé w white wine.
We read & sleep.

[p.7]

Thursday JANUARY 9, 1969
OK let's do that, yaya, I'm making fire....
We are colouring on the dining room table
[...]
The past 10 days distinguished for not unpleasant dullness—but where are the people?

Friday JANUARY 10
A good evening—play working HUNG
[...]

[p.8]

Saturday JANUARY 11
Alie Fischer for lunch—vol au vent & salade Nicoise & martinis—an enormous effort
Murray's party:
at which Maman goes on drinking & talking too much.

11 A 1965 film directed by David Lean, based on the 1954 novel by Boris Pasternak.

12 Phyllis Grosskurth, *John Addington Symonds; A Biography* (London: Longmans, 1964).

Sunday JANUARY 12
A very long hangover day—the kids were furious & destructive! I washed the bathroom walls, though.
Me to bed fairly early after reading NY Times. Had to spank Will.
They had a terrible weekend.

[p.9]

Mon JANUARY 13, 1969
Worked on play 10:30–4:30
Will made awful scene a.m.
came home good as gold.
Feel as if I had <u>never</u> been so mentally active.
Phoned Lola, who says she has a photograph album for me.

Tuesday JANUARY 14
[...]
Lousy day to begin with—sore from typing—
But now it's OK—have ideas, will travel.

[p.10]

Wed JANUARY 15, 1969
Welles & Bill to lunch
Then an awful Engel visit at 9
Kids disorganized for the rest of the week.

Thur JANUARY 16
Finished the play!

[p.11]

✗ Fri JANUARY 17, 1969
[...]
Fetherling for dinner—he upsets me, he is exactly what I would like to be —a male poet w. long beautiful hair. Had curse, got drunk fast & couldn't stop talking.
[...]
Satisfaction painting bathroom.

Sat. JANUARY 18
hangover day
But in all this WHAT IS THERE TO KEEP ME ALIVE
What do I **<u>need</u>**?

(Jan 27—nothing!)
Shut up.

[p.12]

Sunday JANUARY 19, 1969

Passmores' wedding anniversary

Country w. Dad: Altona meeting house, mill at Utica, Goodwood antique shop, wild drive. Home to find my article p.4 in NYTBR[13]—not bad. Early to bed w wild dreams of escape & freedom—how can I manage a small escape to prevent a big one? Want to go on the [illegible] for a while. How to arrange it?—Oh, I won't, not probably ever, lack courage & ability.

JANUARY 20

Monday—blow of school softened by cookies & a monster game—then they see Paul, Jonathon and race down the street. I come back to chaos. None of us are living right. <u>Can</u> anyone?

[p.13]

Tues. JANUARY 21

Wed. JANUARY 22

Liz's birthday

[...]

[p.14]

JANUARY 23

Incredible energy

[...]

Friday JANUARY 24

Teeth at 2—library before

IUD at 2:30 IT HURT

labour pains at night!

But he also gives me a diuretic

[p.15]

JANUARY 25, 1969

Sat:

Howes for tea.

Belly still hell & temper bad

Sun JANUARY 26

Ouch still: but to Parsons in afternoon.

---

13 Marian Engel, "The Girls," rev. of *Les Jeunes Filles* by Henry de Montherlant, *New York Times Book Review*, 19 January 1969: 4.

[p.16]

Mon JANUARY 27, 1969
Wedding anniversary & a dreary one.
Bill Casselman calls
Charlotte sick
kids won't go to bed.

Tues JANUARY 28
I do the bills etc.
Charlotte still sick—on front porch
Razie calls in afternoon—tells me all about insides.
Nice evening—books & back to bed.
I have at least slept & slept & lost 5 lb of water & feel good again.

[p.17]

Wed JANUARY 29
No Engels tho' Lollie calls.
Bennett?

Thurs. JANUARY 30
I was supposed to go to Kirsten's literary group but someone had died & she cancelled. Thus we were able to take advantage of 1st night tickets to Good King Charles' Golden Days. Lovely dialogue—bad scenes & acting. [...]

[p.18]

Fri JANUARY 31
Wanted to go to Vichert's coffee party. H said no & I didn't blame him but still wanted to go—how I cast him in the old & dull role!

Hagbard & Signe: Marimekko, ponies, Iceland—& heads cut off! Ugh. Before—a <u>beauteous</u> Italian pastry <u>shoppe</u> Cassatta & Expresso. H. v. uncertain, me, too.

Sat FEBRUARY 1
H to work, us to Clery's on streetcar. Too much. Pooped. W. puts on own pyjamas.
Bennett at night.
We are <u>so</u> tired!

[p.19]

SUN FEBRUARY 2, 1969
Still pooped—bitchy with it. Legs hurt. [...]
Evening—H. watches films

<u>Mon</u> FEBRUARY 3
Good day—why? Played solitaire.

H. stayed out—came in lit up by <u>3</u> movies! Love his lights. Even tho' resentful of isolation.

[p.20]

<u>Tues</u> FEBRUARY 4, 1969
Finished wine & Sybille Bedford review. Then resentful of H went upstairs read ____. How we really do love each other!

Witneys & Sue for dinner. Will I be sober? No! Shall buy Pernod. There was no Pernod but the dinner turned out to be superb [...] S<u>kinne</u>d chicken cooked à la rabbit!

Wed FEBRUARY 5
A day for opening the eyes. We explore Queen's Park—Cleve Horne's Mitch Hepburn, the best portrait. All those group photographs....
I lose my tam

Funniest thing —elevator to basement—THEN: doors open on ugly brick walls & sign "Provincial Police"
—we shoot right back up again.

$17 w. books at Surtees, lunch at Le Coin. Litho[graphs] at Gerald Morris. Couldn't cross Avenue Rd. Then Pascal where I bought a little Silverberg. Then Loblaws, home, kids AWFUL. Paris Review Interviews v. good & useful.

[p.21]

Thurs FEBRUARY 6, 1969
Selena phoned
Bill French sent <u>Melinda</u>. <u>Must</u> read Saradove.[14]

Fri FEBRUARY 7
Masquerade?
—and it was great
Remember Josi dancing

14 William French, *The Globe and Mail* literary critic; Gaia Servadio, *Melinda*, trans. L.K. Conrad (London: Weinfeld & Nicolson, 1968); Bertha Harris, *Catching Saradove* (New York, Harcourt, Brace & World, 1969).

[pp.22-25][15]

[...]

[p.26]

MON FEBRUARY 17
Lunch w Weaver—good
[...]
Parents' Night

[p.27]

Tues FEBRUARY 18
[...] Shrove Tuesday party
H. to the movies

Wed – FEBRUARY 19
Back home w lots of scrubbing to do
Did **I** go out? Where?
Did radio program—matinée

[p.28]

Thurs FEBRUARY 20, 1969
Did floors etc

Fri FEBRUARY 21, '69
Harry Pollock—[...]

[p.29]

Sat FEBRUARY 22, 1969
Kids restless
To cemetery in p.m.
Watched "A Hard Day's Night"[16]
Hazel phoned

FEBRUARY 23
Visiting in PM— [...]

[p.30]

Mon MARCH 3
Much work on Stanley's book during this period—& much unhappiness when this is not possible

---

15 From Saturday, 8 February to Sunday, 16 February, the entries are minimal and not reproduced here.

16 A 1964 comedy/musical, starring The Beatles and directed by Richard Lester.

[pp.31-36][17]

[...]

MARCH 18

Tuesday
CRTC[18] hearings begin
Not nominated for G Gen's award—upset
Bennett pulls me out of it
Sark & everybody's sexuality
Much beer

[p.37]

MARCH 19

Wed: CRTC hearings on "AIR of DEATH"
Notes in Stanley's notebook

MARCH 20

Thurs
CRTC hearings
Good news at bank—we are in the black at last.

[p.38]

MARCH 21

Friday

The day Willy ran away from school. Charlotte came home by herself while I was collecting him—and I proved I was mean & adult by automatically choosing Mrs Hoff's side.

[...]

Sat MARCH 22

To Jen & Michael's for dinner w. Liz & Christopher Barry
Swiss Fam. Robinson—I yanked Willy away because he ran around the aisles. Was I mean? He was broken-hearted. I bought a broom.

[p.39]

Sun MARCH 23, 1969

Kids play out doors
Howard [illegible] & then cooks a great chicken.
Bennet came.

17 The fortnight between Tuesday, 4 March and Tuesday, 18 March is minimally described. On 12 March Engel notes she is reading Margaret Laurence but adds no comment.

18 This is cross referenced in *Cahier* XVI [43-46].

Mon MARCH 24

[...]

Stanley must have made an earlier will in favour of the College
Later will has revisions & decisions—unwitnessed. Must be some grounds for his being senile. Kath can testify he confuses Faber & John.

[pp. 40-74][19]

[...]

[p.75]

OCTOBER 30

Thursday—H. brings home Earle Birney[20] & Doug Fetherling
A scratch dinner & I am nervous.
Fetherling stays late. My back is ugly-sore—I retire early.
Exchange of books—w. Birney
[...]

[p.76]

OCTOBER 31

At this point we are agonizing over money.
But it is Hallowe'en night. I am as usual intensely lonely & left out when the kids & Howie are out.
[...]

Sat. NOVEMBER 1

H. to work early—Mum & Dad come. I am stiff & short-tempered. They help me set up the beds.
At bath time I hit William too hard (he has run full tilt down the hall & knocked my uterus into the sink) & H sulks.
Long talk later—lately I have been harsh & unsubtle.

[p.77]

Sunday NOVEMBER 2, 1969

Programme a.m.
Then, drive to Claremont Farm
Then, Jennie
Then, dinner, then Marx Bros
General exhaustion
H. very tense & cheesed. Ma has sided w me about Wm. I like this dangerous sympathy, but it is grasping & evil. "Discipline" etc is discussed. I

---

19 Starting late March, entries are cursory, the diary serving mainly to note the comings and goings of family and friends and travel itinerary. Entries become more regular and longer towards the end of October.

20 Canadian poet Earle Birney (1904-95) won the Governor General's Award for Poetry for *David* (1942) and *Now is Time* (1945).

think it is OK to hit, but not as I hit. She wld drive a wedge & love it if she came to live with us. cf Lola & Ray. Dad good, tho.

NOVEMBER 3
[...]
I work on Stanley
I take kids to buy shoes & to library.

Advice about marriage—tidy better & lose weight. Always the same. I feel like Martha, yet do not comply.

[p.78]

NOVEMBER 4
Letter from Bennett: he loves London. **Good**
H to work late.
I work on Stanley a while then go to library, research Wilton for Pa.
H. off to [illegible] with Dud.
I am nervy with the kids—beer?
Fowles review—reading of Agar on law

Wed NOVEMBER 5
A.M. many letters—Russell, Woods, family
Fowles review
Then—lunch out, reading Sir John Rothenstein
Kids won't eat

H [...]—home tomorrow. Girl Marianne Neville has told him everyone was sorry for mother when Sara.no.clouds came out.[21] This hurts.

[p.79]

NOVEMBER 6
"Her poor mother" begins to be funny.
H. back

Fri NOVEMBER 7
V. worried abt money
tired [pp.80-86][22]
[...]

---

21 Here Engel blends the novel's two names: *Sarah Bastard's Notebook* (the title in United States) and *No Clouds of Glory* (the title in Canada).

22 From here to the year's end, entries are few and short.

[p.87]

DECEMBER 25

Jolly, jolly

[p.88]

MEMORANDA

1969 Income

Henri de Monterlant	$100	Jan
Sybille Bedford	$100	NYT March
Festival	$500	Play
Globe—"Melinda"	$ 35	
Matinee	$ 80	
Saturday Night—Marg Laurence		$100
Toronto Star	3 x 65	
Telegram?		
NYTimes P Gilliat	$100	

[p.89]

Camping list

bread	pail
bacon	whisk
meat	mugs
potatoes	
rice	
carrots	
celery	
butter	

Cahier XIX[1]

C'est un beau métier [4].

Cahier XIX opens with a draft manuscript in which Juno Fraser[2] is trying to circumvent doctor's orders to remain three weeks in bed to treat a case of jaundice.[3] The doctor's French-language background, in contrast with the protagonist's English-Canadian background, is the springboard for several amusing comments about Canadians and their work ethics. The story is also an opportunity for observations about writing ("un beau métier," the doctor remarks [4]) and the writing process: "Theories of genius had always annoyed her [Juno]. [Genius] was the flowering of a particular seed-talent in a particular soil. This soil was fertile for the seed in certain circumstances" [13]. Whether these circumstances existed in Canada remained a matter of some doubt for Engel. She viewed the Canadian literary scene as "pretty political now—I don't know what will happen to me if I admit to having always liked Irving Layton.[4] Am I a feminist or a nationalist copout?" [24].

Cahier XIX also contains notes on the French writer Stéphane Mallarmé, who exalted the autonomous text "purified of origins and free to exist" without its author [19]. Arguments and theories about textual independence were disseminated in France and Europe throughout the 1960s in critical movements such as structuralism. With her ability to read French, Engel encountered these ideas early in their evolution.

Other entries in the notebook introduce the Heber family and return to small-town Ontario, both of which feature in Engel's 1978 novel, The *Glassy Sea*. Finally, the *cahier* contains two recipes, reproduced here, since writing and day-to-day living were not separate spheres for Engel.

---

1 1970, black notebook; 29 pages used.

2 Juno Fraser is one of several characters Engel presents who keep notebooks much like their author.

3 During her year in the south of France (1960-61) Engel too had jaundice, as she recounts in a biographical sketch she includes in *Cahier* XXXIV.

4 Layton's poetry was thought by some to express unacceptable and outdated sexist attitudes towards women.

[p.1]

National Geographic, $12.95 per year. N.G. Society Washington DC 20036

[p.2]

Red-green. Red-green good bad good bad.
In those little towns there were no yellow lights.

The people had long faces. Whenever they started making something—axe handles, ships, apple juice, berry wine, smelt paste (and why not put Erick bay herring up in pots & jars?—the Norwegians did & had the gall to send it here) the bottom fell out of the market & left them again stranded on their tidal flats, arrested in their progress to the status of Ladies & Gentlemen. Demi-peasants. Front-keepers, Do-withouters. Tryagainers. It showed on their faces which tended to be long & gray & set into deep lines of self-control. No rebel-rabble—but severely tried.

[p.3]

Good-bad   good-bad
Tourists in sticky station wagons come to pick amethysts out of the cliffs at low tide. Much good may the tide-rotted stuff do them.

Mrs Craigie has an elephant's foot in the hall.

Sun today sucking the damp out of the ground—oozing it up your ankles.

A lady with a parasol … my grandfather.…

Tide. Hats. Small time. Small town. Three weeks in bed he said. Who['s] he? Romanian. Queen Marie we talked about. If love is a glorious cycle of song.… I didn't think him up to Dorothy Parker. Liver, he said.

Canadians don't have livers, they have gallbladders.

But they are not the same.

[p.4]

We talked much, for the pleasure of it, the unfamiliarity.

Not that in this place no one can.… Someone in a house with a tower, someone in a cottage … but we were the first we.…

I can't spend three weeks in bed.

Why not?

I am hear [*sic*] to work.

What is your work.

I am working on a book.

C'est un beau métier—

Mon dieu, I have arrived.... C'est un beau métier. Monster mister (why? Vlad the Impaler—that's why—those eyes) divert him.

"And what brings you from Romania to this place?"

"I have been practising in Montreal—qualifying to practise—that is— [p.5] and I am looking for an opening—meanwhile a friend says that his friend in this town is tired out—weary to die—there is no one to replace him.

Is there much practise in this town?

Oh yes—they don't come unless they are very ill—but they have things one doesn't normally see.

[p.6]

Three weeks in bed. No one ever....

Here is a mirror. Do you not see? Your face is yellow. Your eyes. You have palpitations of the heart. You weep—you cannot eat.

Jaundice?

Coup de foie—yes, a mild jaundice.

In this country, mon docteur, one does not go to bed.

One works, eh? Summers in high school, summers in university.

At the grocery store during university.

And after—work work work—then one is forty & very tired & yellow. Three weeks in bed.

Two.

Oh, alors, two ... I will give you this injection, you will get this prescription, then you will sleep.

Could it not be the emotions?

[p.7]

My speciality is not the emotions. You are yellow, go to bed....

Strange hooded eyes—missing one fold? Lashless. Bald. Sinister Vlad, the Impaler.

I will call on you after—tomorrow, to make sure. You are chez Mrs Craigie.

Yes.

Good. Bye.

Good— bad
Good— bad

Pharmacy. Drug store. IDA. No wait for the prescription. OHIP number all my own.

Still now on the corner. The sun burns. For a change. <u>Coup de soleil</u> now, not <u>foie</u>?

[p.8]

Home. Home to bed.
The devil finds work.
Wait—presentable, one must be… "LINGERIE." Not a laundry.

"I would like a nice nightgown."

The lady has blue hair & a marcelled face. "Well, I don't know.… What size?"

Arnold Bennett's wife was hated. The corsetiere. Those women who size you up & gird you—make your spirillas. Me ungirt, lumpy, large.

"It's that you're rather tall."

Two Scots meet, breed raw bones on one another. Poor Ronald got the smallness, me the size. Juno, Colgate called me, when I was young. Now it's all rattier, collapsed. I find I care.

Yellow nylon. The only thing she has.

[p.9]

Mrs Craigie. She walked up the walk. Between the trees, the hanging New England or Niagara Parkways looking sign.

"Well, Dr. Fraser, how are you?"

"It's the most astounding thing— he says I have to go to bed. Can you look after me? He gave me a diet sheet— simple enough— no coffee, no booze, no tea."

"Up with you then."

Weak beside her.

[p.10]

She felt she owed him something, for calling him Vlad the Impaler.

Mrs Craigies' rent goes up.

Parker did not want to part with the MS[anuscript]. He was, of course, quite right. It would have been easy for both of them to have it copied mechanically, but there was no copying machine in the town. The library & the Post Office were still benightedly purely library & post office. They had no truck with the new hardware. They decided to rent a car & drive to Halifax. Lobster was out of season so she had no qualms on going there about Vlad the Impaler's Diet.

They left at dawn and drove across the province against the grain, through misty valleys. Not the tourist route. They passed through slatternly villages.

[p.11]

Parker stopped once at a hamlet where, he said, a poet named Fanshawe was born. Fanshawe wasn't on her list. She saw only a chipped dealer's sign swinging against a sulky sky. An unpainted store, guarded by a one-eyed fleabitten black & brown collie. A few moulting tamaracks behind. Parker finished his leak & said of course he wouldn't take the tourist route—authors deserved to see what the reality was.

She wondered what Parker's Halifax would be, but Parker, as soon as the notebooks were conveyed to the Xeroxer, commandeered the car & said he had to see a sick friend, could he pick her up at four in the churchyard?

[p.12]

She went at once to the stationers', bought a map, set out to explore. But the sun came out, her legs betrayed her, suddenly she was in a dingy café regaling herself with dry toast & soda water. She felt light-headed. She could barely stay awake. She convinced herself to stay upright by promising herself Skade's manuscript.

———

Wasn't Parker the ethereal soloist in the U[nited] C[hurch] choir who left under a cloud?

And what would the cloud have been?

[p.13]

Speculations about Skade:

Always, everywhere, there was to be found an animateur.

Where genius grew there was always some kind of animateur.

Theories of genius had always annoyed her. Manna did not descend from heaven. Genius was not manna, and not merely hard work. It was the flowering of a particular seed—talent—in a particular soil. This soil was fertile for the seed in certain circumstances.

[p.14]

Remarkable among them was always the presence of some sort of fertilizer, some sort of animateur. In tracking down the animateur she had been called a prosaicizer—sobeit. But she knew that it took three or four gathered together—not a wound and a bow (a theory that works by hindsight but not inevitably beforehand—else every cripple would be an artist) but—talent, certainly, but also soil & nourishment. Often, a family, that cared to nurture talent—but often, too, in the insalubrious milieu of the 19th century in Canada, one person in a community who had clung, sometimes stupidly, to the belief that

[p.15]

whatever the field—this activity was of value. A parent, sometimes, often in these communities.

It was a strong village Homer, in other words, who did it on his own. And in these villages the fathers plunged into commerce, farming—practical survival exercises....

[p.16]

Le Livre à Venir [5]

1. Ecce Leber.
   In 1866 Mallarmé was preoccupied by this idea that there was One Book (?)
2. Many books—
   but also one book—
   maybe 5 vols. Why plurality?
   A book of many faces—going towards Beauty, Nothing, etc.

Must stack up creative space. He meditated on its structure. Must be architectural & premeditated, not marvellous inspirations—limited, hieratic. Everything outside this "Œuvre" for its author will be null & void.

3. Without chance—
   What does he mean by "premeditated"?
   —made by extreme reflective powers which can organize this ensemble.
   —must write well and with mastery over his own spirit & also—so well calculated that individual words lose their colour & become part of the whole.

[p.17]

—Natural things disappear in vibrations of words.... The book will hold chance in check by attacking concrete reality—poetry becomes music.

The tension w. chance implies Mallarmé's struggle to transform language + a mystical quality.
His r[elation]ship with chance branches off in 2 ways:

1) work oriented to absence, negation, where nothing narrative[?] real or fortuitous has a place.
2) but from these negative powers which are also working in the language we know that he comes through to immediate precise experience.

5 Maurice Blanchot, *Le Livre à venir* (Paris: Gallimard, 1959). Engel's notes on the book follow.

"La destruction fut ma Beatrice."

[p.18]

Im<u>personalis</u>ed

The Book exists among books but is multiple ... avoids chance and accomplishes the essentials of language by transforming them, in using them or using them in their absence—w. rhythm (Beckett). Also anonymous as if it was written in nature. Here he is giving into the occult a bit but writing was magic for him exc[ept] that he saw magicians as impatient, artists as patient, & rejects Wagner & Novalis. The importance about anonymity AUTHOR MUST CEDE HIS POSITION TO WORDS, give up "elocution."

<u>Fait, etant</u>

Book is without author ∵ it writes itself when authors talk, disappear. It needs author as absence or *absence-substitute. Book is a book

[p.19]

when it is purified of origins & free to exist & has its existence in the reader's mind. The individual finds himself as <u>reader</u> not <u>writer</u>
"IMPERSONNIFÉ, le volume, autant qu'on s'en sépare comme auteur, ne réclame approche de lecteur. Tel, sache, entre les accessoires humains, il a lieu tout seul: fait, etant"[6]

Very far from both esoteric & romantic theories here—this is an eternally true book wh[ich] could put the reader in touch w. eternity.

Time is escaped & affirmed.

[p.20]

[Notes for "Stanley's Novel"]

[p.21]

White ash

Dalgety owns the ferry & the Thistle
Rubber Printing works
Showed us a glassy [*sic*] from Scotland

No Hebers about
Spokes in archways

6 In the margins Engel wrote "Ego—[illegible]."

[Drawing with caption "like wheelspokes"]

Lines all named W. of Sydenham
River
County
Lambton
Point
Ward
French (deGuerseys?)
Smith
Church
White
Stanley
Town

[p.22]

Becher
Terminus—no trees, logged off
Heavy sticky clay soil. No water.
Are the Chenal Ecarté
Sydenham &
Snye the same?

The old house still heeled over.

Marshalline[*sic*][7] writes from Paris...

Send Elfords some French books.

[p.23]

On The Train

Man with harmonica going to St John's

Mockingbird Hill

Cacahuètes. Christopher Golden

Story Club Car

7 This is the first mention of the character Marshallene of the novel *Lunatic Villas* and various short stories.

[p.24]

Story—Man w Harmonica

The Canadian literary scene is pretty political now—I don't know what will happen to me if I admit to having always liked Irving Layton.[8] Am I a feminist or a nationalist copout?

[p.25][9]

Gino Empry's Marineland Picnic

Stifling heat
Performing seals & tigers
Dressed up bears.
[...]

[p.26]

Bear on velocipede
Longs for Winter
It loves the adulation
of the crowd
Who knows?
The philosopher fisher king?
He is the performing bear.
[...]

[p.27]

Reading Pynchon[10] gives me a feeling I can after all do a new book.

Boris—who looked like Apollo Belvedere & ran the library
Ruth—who is Ruth
The tenants of { Annie Laurie &
Laura Secord?

Barney
Wanda Van Horne
or La touche
Marshallene
Hilda MacRae.

[p.28]

Gumdrop Cake

1 c sugar
2 eggs
1 tsp salt
3/4 lb raisins
1 heaping tsp b.p.

1/2 c butter
3/4 c milk
1 lb gumdrops
2 c flour

Cream b & s and add eggs.
Add salt, milk & flour alternately.
flour gumdrops ([illegible]) & add.
Then raisins & b.p. Bake 1 hr.

[p.29]

Lemon Bread

1/2 c. shortening
1 c wh. sugar
2 eggs
1/2 c flour
2 tsp b.p.

1/2 c chopped walnuts
1 lemon rind, grated
1/2 c milk (?)

Cream s & s add eggs
Sift dry ingred. add alternatively w milk.
Add lemon last
Let rise 2 min
Bake 45-60 min 325°.
When still hot pour over top mixture of 1/4 c sugar & juice of one lemon.
Store.

Cahier XX[1]

> Hearing MacLennan on the novel—the old beloved voice.... This is the real Proustian feeling—elements combining to a gentle explanation of what one's life had been about [63].

This *cahier* contains copious notes Engel took on the subject of memory as explored by Freud and writers such as Proust, Borges, Cortázar and Beckett. Sample excerpts are presented here for the light they shed on Engel's work, in particular *Monodromos*. This novel was informed by the enormous amount of reading that Engel completed during the early 1970s. As Kathy Garay has noted,[2] of all Engel's novels, *Monodromos* seemed to have involved the greatest amount of work. Certainly it takes up the most space in her *cahiers*. Many later notebooks contain drafts of, and references to, this novel. *Monodromos*'s extended and complicated gestation was related to the pressure Engel placed upon it to reflect the numerous philosophical and theoretical concepts she was processing at the time. Thus, where previously (in *Cahier* XVI) Engel had considered her novel in terms of the question of colonialism, here she set it up against an exploration of the function of memory—"the mother of the muses" [41]—and dream.

The relationship between philosophy and literature, a subject broached in earlier *cahiers*, resurfaces here. Engel recorded William Gass's contention, in *Fiction and the Figures of Life*,[3] that philosophy and literature are much the same. Both are obsessed with language and both create worlds.[4] From Ernest Schachtel's *Metamorphosis* [5] Engel took notes on taboos, in particular taboos of smell and taste, both "proximity senses" as opposed to the "distance senses" of sight and hearing. "Distance is a means of imposing authority, dominating [therefore] taste & smell taboos stronger in upper class—esp. body odours—discouragement of proximity sense." "Very important!" Engel noted, storing the idea away for later use in *Bear*.[6]

Marian Engel was clearly an "ideas person," someone who enjoyed letting her mind wrestle with concepts, abstractions and intellectual proposals. That

---

1 1970, light green notebook, with "Engel" written on the front cover; 66 pages used.

2 Garay, *The Marian Engel Archive* x.

3 William Gass, *Fiction and the Figures of Life* (New York: Knopf, 1970).

4 For more points in common, see [60-61].

5 Ernest G. Schachtel, *Metamorphosis: On the Development of Affect, Perception, Attention, and Memory* (New York: Basic Books, 1959).

6 See Verduyn, *Lifelines* 132.

this caused her some difficulty is suggested by an entry "Early one morning":

> Women's Lib: Have I always been put down for having ideas? Or does everyone deal with ideas by opposition? Loneliness of the writer.... Needed literature. Do I really flit as Bennett said[7] (also that I am hung up by belief in narrative). Novel should proceed by self-linked (naturally linked by subconscious) images. [49]

Further highlights of *Cahier* XX include a transcription of Rudyard Kipling's poem "If,"[8] and notes on a trip Engel made to France with Howard in 1970. Kipling's poem was familiar to Engel from her childhood, when the British writer's work was readily found on Canadian public school curricula. In outlining admirable behaviour for upstanding young men—young women presumably intended to follow suit—"If" was a particularly popular choice for school texts. During her trip to France, Engel's delight is palpable at being back in Europe, taking in art exhibitions and museums, listing French words—one suspects for the sheer pleasure of the sounds—and feeling generally stimulated and alive in a world of art and literature. "I am full of vague ideas," the author recorded, "there are subtleties here of shape & colour. Brightness falls from the air? No—all good & happy. Rue Campagne" [10].

[p.1]

To read: Arthur Yannoj: The Primal Streams [*sic*][9]

Perigueux—arrive after melting 2 hours in local market day train from Bergerac. Hotel du Midi. Bathed in sweat—r[oo]m w shower Fr 20. Nightwalk—souper à 47 F heat—melting—sweatbath—benison[?] of water. Sleep. Everywhere one gets tinned pâté.

Les grandes villes tristes de Provence!
Les musées—Astérix faces among byzantine capitals. Arrowheads but not Indian crocodile skins from Indo-China, stuffed artifacts from Madagascar, bits of Limoges & bad Dutch paintings
Boules contest in the [illegible] [p.2][10]
Dans le chateau, Pierre et Caroline qui plaignait [*sic*] tout [*sic*] les ouvriers

7 See entry [47].

8 Rudyard Kipling, "If," *Rewards and Fairies* (London: Macmillan, 1910).

9 Arthur Janov, *The Primal Scream: Primal Theory: the Cure for Neurosis* (New York: Laurel, 1970).

10 Engel's use of French accents throughout these travel notes is irregular.

qui ne voulaient que se balader dans leurs 2CV.

Chateau de Fontvielle

↘

Real estate ads in Bergerac
gentilhommière.
maison.
chateau avec dependences.
chartreuse.

[p.3][11]

Velosolex — Tabac—Royal—Menthe
Mobilette — Interflora
Pachard — Coiffure—diplomé de l'etat
Peugeot 404 — Knapsacks & guitares
Simca — Patisserie—gold letters on marble
Hotels particuliers with lush gardens

Quelle transpiration
Kronenbourg à la pression
Slavia
Croquet le Perigord—Membe
Martini—l'apéritif à base de vin.

Huber & Boisevin—Fleurs St Martin

Street signs in porcelain
ferrovierre— 18—fine
19 stamped

[p.4]

On passe son temps à regarder une femme dans une voiture.

[Addresses]

[p.5]

Cotes de Bergerac (Makes [?] Byrrh[12])
Domaine de Violet
Chateau de Fontvielle: chichi—something they do with red gingham mansards
Pierre et Caroline—grandes armoires

We have friends in Angers who have bought a chateau & installed a

11 In the margins there is a series of numerical calculations, possibly a budget:
9/33 = 5 62 + 32 = 95
61/3 x 9 54 + 3 = 57 + 32 = 89

12 A French apéritif that is a blend of red wine and tonic water.

swimming pool in the cloister. A trip in a boat to Corsica. Children, <u>Sidonie et Adelaide. Anne who is enchantée par tout.</u>

Rational France—Zip codes are licence plate numbers

---

motocyclette, fishing rod, beret, plastic pail

Hertz man: big moustaches—we v. nervous—would think it was the register office.

Sarlat →

[p.6]

Sarlat—Plein de Touristes—Specialité de la [*sic*] Tourisme—men with shaved bald heads. Everyone hot & greasy. Bldgs de plus & plus sand-blasted w boutiques. Rooftiles—split stone m.q. slate or tile. Again this yellow Cyprus stone. Perspectives de vieux quartiers—one begins to think in French again. Pots of petunias & geraniums. Siesta & nightwalks.

[p.7]

<u>Martel</u> cathedral [illegible] has horrible painting—Victorian re-plastering & colouring—stripes, fleurs- de-lis, pierced hearts—plaster over old plaster—dramatic false marble—windows asymmetrically placed to justify a 19th century love of false-Gothic—but it was a fortified church—magnificent exterior now being cleaned.
Town hall—inside broken & neglected—mag[nificent] mixture 13th century & Gothic (dates?).

[p.8]

<u>Paris</u>— café beside the Louvre near where we came that morning with the Cypriot who recited Homer at Dawn.
To-day—met at the Dome for breakfast—**<u>cher</u>** 3^{20} the coffee. Wandered to Fleurus, Luxembourg, down rue de Seine lunch at Gk place in rue Serpente (48 Fr!) then to Delacroix studio, place Furstemburg
Hier—Proust show (H. drinks <u>Suze</u>)

More than ever, with its face washed, this is a city for poetry.
Dreams: vie de chateau—shapes, carved edges of armoires. The straight line disappears from memory. Doorways, arches, jardins d'hotels particuliers. Hier, Palais Royal—great abandoned arcades, Grand Velour & its painted flowers—bergères du dix-neuvieme.

One begins to float—

[p.9]

Delacroix et les fauves

Paris II Delacroix exhibition
[...]
One has more & more the feeling that Delacroix is the great interpreter of the feeling & imagination of his epoch (a man passes—grey hair, chemise Lacoste, Eisenhower jacket). Mixture of heroic, classic, oriental. N. Africa delighted him but this is a very thin exhibition

Proust
Exhibition Musée Jacquart-André—Maison de grande epoque 1852—with a curious circular wall around the garden & the grand staircase at the

[p.10]

back [Engel includes a line-drawing sketch]

Good bldg for the show. H. has sore foot. We do not go upstairs.

Mais il y a la robe noire de Mme de Greffulle! Et les portraits de Philippe de Lazlo et de Blanche. Et le Sarah Bernhardt de Clairon. In the grand salon one sits on the pouffs blue velvet. The old cahiers—fold-outs (account of restoration in the guide). I am full of vague ideas. My imagination, when it is not caught up by flanged armoires, goes back always to the children. Bright faces I miss. But there are subtleties here of shape & colour. Brightness falls from the air? No—all good & happy. Rue Campagne—P
Rue Christine.

[p.11]

garcons—white shirts black vests & pants white aprons

[p.12]

Place des Vosges Cinderella to be here
[...]

[p.13]

Mais on se querelle: "You are like your mother, once you decide on something nobody can stop you."

Paris—dragging him round with a bad foot.

But what's different in France?
You don't have to pay for the chairs. Everything's cleaner.
Hardly any clochards.
Have taxes on home improvements been lifted?
Beaucoup de nègres & Chinois.

Marais—worst streets—Couscous
Patchwork!
Things to make—patchwork tunics.

[p.14]

[...]

Ruthie & Ziggy & Pinky (Bunny? Honey?)[13]
Ruth —sliding out of the marriage
—sneering Pinky on the way to be converted
—sitting shiva the day of the wedding
—consoling her mother in all directions
—meeting them later in Paris

And then there is Matisse who m<u>ov</u>es out to clarity & lets the process show through.

Progressions: Leger. Soft—disorganized
Very hard & political
Soft & sure.
As for Matisse—growth = clarification
Picasso adds games.
Chagall → softness with time.

[p.15]

Le type barbu costu [et] viellâtre qui cherche une femme le long du café.

[p.16]

the mental & spiritual process is that the spirit enlarges with confidence—but middle-age softens the ego. Then colours are clear as ideas. But for painters there always seems to be more time.
Picasso the magpie—speed, certainty always. But are all the results good? Much prefer Matisse now: sweetness of line. Not as full of ideas as P, though. How prolific they all were. Enviable.

Monodromos: put it together fast & well—how? hell, it will take years. But perhaps one could work a little more carelessly.

[p.17]

Drink at the Closerie de Lilas
Mardi 18 (?)[14] Smiles again—reunion, money & good dinner chez maitre Paul Beace de l'Odeon. Snails & coq au vin, salade, fraises du bois pour lui; pour moi medaillon du

---

13 These are names of characters in various Engel short stories.

14 Engel is uncertain about the date here.

lievre, rognons de veau, salade, framboises. Coffee & peace & a great Beaune. Puis—St Germain des Pres (un monde fou—Lipp & Flore fermes) bookstore open. Then the Select—[illegible] pas très fine. Then home.

[p.18]

Ideas for articles: Galt.

Why one goes there is no child's business. The first chip on the shoulder.
Ella /Ella
Grace Grace
Hungarians—rainbarrel.

[p.19]

[Doodle]
Letters to Max [in *Monodromos*].
The best thing was
the Proust exhibition

Title: The Laughing Stock of Lithrodonda

[p.20]

28 July—and the devil take the fountain pen!
Revision of the letter to Max ch. 4.
Account of Bishop more or less OK.
But instead of waffle about imagery you want dream, history, botany & art.
The ownership of the house <u>may</u> be important. But it could belong to a Gk who bought it from the Erkaf[?]

Dreams:[15] as I perhaps mentioned, ludicrously Freudian. Partly as a result of a journey I made by bicycle in early spring to a village perhaps 20 miles to the south. Although we are reputed to sit dead in the centre of a plain, the fact is that in almost every direction it displays a different geography—and five miles out of town—oh—perhaps [illegible], ten, to the south west, one begins to pump & pedal first on chalk ridges, [illegible], with lurid white & purple (why purple? the light?) [illegible]. In
[continues on p.22]

[p.21]

This could be

[p.22]

between the hills & valleys of ancient river beds. I must have told you that perhaps because of the light, the spring colouring is lurid, hysterical. Here

15 The dreams in question are Audrey's, protagonist of *Monodromos*, recounted in a letter to her lover, Max.

you find jasper—red & yellow—in the river beds—[illegible] occurs where there are copper mines, the name of the soil in much of the plain is terra-rosa. The uplands appear unimaginably quickly—by some trick of perspective—perhaps my eyes are permanently adjusted to the North American scale—one is suddenly there—into relief. And the vegetation has, after the trudge—changed—one is in deep gashes of stone & curiously oriental pine, in long hanging pictures, on ivory, the colours are milk-white & terra-cotta, milky green-blue. Some sort of suffusion—why—there is no mist, the air is clear?

Why not?

One dreams of chasms, after.

To the north—going merely, in the heat, to the beach—sweat trailing

[p.23]

like insects down the thighs—already it is hot—one passes through a curvous region of mudbrick farms, poor poor—this is dryland, shut off from rain by mountains—then a section of bared uplifted strata—something one has forgotten from geology—nude geosynclines perhaps—like corrugated cardboard. Above, looming, are the pass, the range, the castle. One attacks the pen, and at the top—flip, flop, the inwards (oh my love I cannot write beautifully) the liver, lights, kidneys, unmentionables—attention: this is Illyna, today—the sea, suddenly. Bursting blue. Proud sailor—buttons Penis envy—if I had one I would [illegible]

[p.24]

always, to salute this sea. Or grovel?

So the dreams are chasms—caves (the story of the troglodyte gypsies? I find there have been some here.) Heartland. Why should one not dream.

Lovers? Go not tactless into the.... The desire has been unaccustomedly vast. I do not know if I am (a) shy (b) cowardly (c) virtuous, but most invitations have not seemed attractive. Men are attractive but I doubt possible to know. Laddie[16] watches (why not? I watch him!) Young Will Pender has an odd attraction but one feels one would have to teach him, lacks the art of say, Jeanne Moreau. At least, there is choice. I suppose I feel the tart's path too easy. No. I don't think most of them would be physically kind. Good perhaps, but ... sex is so much in the air, but we puritans are as usual full of reservations. One has a feeling that they are fairly brutal. One doesn't want to fail to experiment, but ... choosing Wm Pender is on the other hand choosing not to be. Perhaps one day you'll know the [?]

[p.25]

Like you, in your poems I have much sexual imagination & no sexual courage. I do not feel loved. I feel watched, I am, except under the influence

16 Laddie is Audrey's ex-husband in *Monodromos*.

of much wine, reasonably indifferent to this.

How can one be so demanding as to ask of men both balls & tact?

Lie
You lie
He lies
We lie
You
They lie

Under the willow ______________

Megas & Maro are lovely & must be developed.

[p.26]

Metamorphosis—Ernest G. Schachtel—Basic 1969

Ch.12—On Memory, Childhood Amnesia

1. Mnemosyne—goddess of memory, bore 9 muses to Zeus. Centuries later, Plato banned poetry, the child of memory, from his ideal state, as idle & seductive. Quote—Morris's Homer—song of sirens invokes the past, he blocks his ears.
2. Ambivalent att[ention] to memory, esp in form of story, characteristic of history. Both expression & repression of story-longing exist today.
3. Fascination of memory most NB for Proust & Freud—most-sig[nificant] contribution here.
4. Both aware of antagonism inherent in mem[ory]—conflict past & present. Proust would renounce active present for truth recaptured. e.g. of Venice, Combray—inaction of dreamer necessitated by need to remember—different kind of memory from the voluntary instrument we usually use & it is unsatisfactory to Proust.

[pp.27-38]

[Lengthy notes on Freud, Proust, memory and childhood]

[p.39]

Mode of exp[erience] changes. Consciousness of self begins & with it memory. In child this starts with recognition of states of body-feeling (comfort, satisfaction, tension)—a re-sensing ∴ early memories tend to be called up by re-sensing of body memories (i.e. [Proust's] Madeleine) "Procrustean bed of culturally relevant schemata" needs this to grow into his culture of course—but has huge range of sympathy & no vessels to preserve it.
Development of senses limited—esp smell.

Autobiographical memory—ability for voluntary recall of one's past life—is one of the latest developments in childhood.

Child's life reoriented to present & future.

Fact that autobiographical memory devel[ops] late puts into question its usefulness in W[estern] K[nowledge]. It is not encouraged. Ulysses can't give in to the Sirens.
Dreams—amnesia—or transformation in dream, logic subsides, psyche is free.

[p.40]

Discuss dreams—lewd ones.
Inability to talk to Laddie.
Why in this place.

Dream amnesia & early childhood amnesia are due to related causes—experiences & thoughts which [tran]scend conventional schemata; aschematic quality makes them hard to recall.
How do we recall childhood—
in hypnosis
dream interpretation
drug recall

Proust describes the quality of these lost memories. He sees these experiences as isolated untouched vases.
Freud: "becoming conscious & leaving a memory-trace are incompatible."
Genuine recovery of the past elating
possessive recovery is egotistic & proprietary about one's character—fetching up of spurious treasure (= event perceived in pre-conceived clichés.)

[p.41]

End [*Monodromos*] w silently, I followed him along the shore.
[...]

[pp.42-44]

[Notes on memory, myth and childhood]

[p.45]

Re Cortázar & Borges:

Both inhabit the world of dream, myth, symbol & archetype.
Borges appears to do so automatically, naturally. Always to have been there or to have started publishing after he got there.
Cortázar is in someways more interesting because he approaches it through careful recording—at ironic distance but with a close-up lens—of the naturalistic (i.e. social, surface) world. So that you get both distance & denseness & the dream-world.

[p.46]

Re: Bloc-notes[17] —begin one—I know what I want from this place: that it should be the world of a dream, an erotic dream at that—that the dream should be maintained—even at the expense of the inhabitants. I hope my wish is defeated—otherwise I am on the side of the Imperialists & prey to opium traders.

Cyprus navy.

[p.47]

Nov 5 Reading Symbols[18]
Jung

A woman who makes the closets into boxes.
Bunty—the dream—comfort person. A black Turk belly-dancer—mobile Venus of Willendorf. "I will show you fear in a handful of dust."[19]

Con III is I is 2

Bennett—Discussions re sexuality.
great pudeur in all 3 of us.

I can't quite grasp what he thinks my limitation is. He thinks I'm best when autobiographical but too hung up by narrative values.

[p.48]

[...]

I went to tell Charlotte a story. "Oh, no, not one about a fairy ... one about when you were little."

Luigi on our poems: "I can see you like to play & you do not."

[p.49]

[...]

Early one morning:

Women's Lib[eration]: Have I always been put down for having ideas? Or does everyone deal with ideas by opposition? Loneliness of the writer. Should have been in the sciences or [illegible]. Needed literature. Do I really flit as Bennett said. (Also that I am hung up by belief in narrative.)

---

17 This is a structural device used in *Monodromos*. See *Cahier* VIII Introduction and [7].

18 Carl Jung, *Man and His Symbols* (Garden City, NY: Doubleday, 1964).

19 In the left margin below Engel notes the names of people she must write. She also jots here "SCM [Toronto bookstore]—Freud, Jung."

Novel should proceed by self-linked (naturally linked by subconscious) images.

[p.50]

Paravisions: Cortázar: brief <u>outside</u> instincts = moments of detachment when one knows what one is not, what one does not know, where one has never been.

Hassled by time.

Women are too realistic to have visions—Dudley.

"There are imbeciles who shall believe that drunkenness is a way, or mescaline, or homosexuality, anything magnificent & inane per se but stupidly [illegible] into a system—Maybe there is another world inside this one, but we will

[p.51]

not find it cutting out its silhouette from the fabulous tunnel of days & lives, we will not find it in either a trophy or hypertrophy—that world does not exist, one has to create it like the phoenix."

"Everything can be killed except nostalgia for the kingdom."

The essence of bourgeoisie—settling back into a very comfortable car & watching one's belly expand.

Giving a woman another name to remove her from her mother.

[p.52]

> Once long ago I used to sit with the boys making up long incredible stories about what we were not. Now I find myself at an age where I'm in long incredible stories & they tie me & I wish they would stop.

(At coming out of anaesthesia—eyes dilated. Head shaking. Full of fear. Can't see right. Tongue out. Disorientation—eager to **<u>see</u>** where he is. Paws relaxed, like hands.)
[illegible]

[p.53]

[...]
This middle of the night drunken isolation—Whose is it?
[...]
It is always better to be making things. But in world terms like Women's Lib it is a luxury.

That beach is nice, it's full of fossils, but I still want to [illegible] my mum.

[p.54]

IF [Rudyard Kipling]

If you can keep yr head when all about you
Are losing theirs, & blaming it on you;
If you can trust yourself when all men doubt you,
But make allowance for their doubting too;
If you can wait & not be tired by waiting,
Or, being lied about, don't deal in lies,
Or being hated, don't give way to hating.
And yet don't look too good nor talk too wise;

If you can dream—& not make dreams yr master;
If you can think—& not make thoughts yr aim,
If you can meet with Triumph & Disaster
And treat those two impostors just the same:
If you can bear to hear the truth you've spoken
Twisted by knaves to make a trap for fools,
Or watch the things you gave your life to, broken,
And stoop & build 'em up with worn-out tools;

[p.55]

If you can make one heap of all your winnings
And risk it on one turn of pitch-&-toss,
And lose, & start again at your beginnings,
And never breathe a word about your loss:
If you can force your heart & nerve & sinew
To serve your turn long after they are gone,
And so hold on when there is nothing in you
Except the will which says to them: "Hold on!"

If you can talk with crowds & keep your virtue,
Or walk with Kings—nor lose the common touch,
If neither foes nor loving friends can hurt you,
If all men count with you, but none too much:
If you can fill the unforgiving minute
With sixty seconds' worth of distance run,
Yours is the Earth & everything that's in it,
And—which is more—you'll be a Man, my son!

[p.56]

Panofsky Meaning in the Visual Arts[20]
Iconography & Iconology

[pp.57-59]

[...]

[p.60]

Fiction & the Figures of Life: William H. Gass.
[...]

[pp.61-62]

[Ongoing Notes from Gass's book]

[p.63]

6 Nov. This is good stuff

Last night: Reading FMFord by Frank Macshane[21]
Night before: A. Anderson's Canadian novelists' tapes.

Ford's life made me want to weep but I was glad for it—nothing worked for him but yet ... he did have a good meat sandwich of a life.
Hearing MacLennan on the Novel—the old beloved voice: things fell together for me like a sudden snowstorm—Ford—Montreal—Literature. Great soft explosions went off inside—doughnuts of emotion—no, but I began to float. This is the real Proustian feeling—elements combining to a gentle explanation of what one's life had been about.

[p.64]

Ford—in his doctrine was always true to himself. I find him sympathetic because of his one-foot-in-Europe attitude.

One foot-in-Montreal—helps me here but detaches me from TO [Toronto] scene. Good, though.

Then the idea came to me that I must integrate the last chapter.
[...][22]

20 Erwin Panofsky, *Meaning in the Visual Arts: Papers in and on Art History* (Garden City, NY: Doubleday, 1955). Notes on this book and William Gass's *Fiction and the Figures of Life* are interspersed throughout the final pages of the *cahier*. A couple of sample excerpts only are included here.

21 Frank MacShane, *Ford Madox Ford: The Critical Heritage* (London: Routledge & Kegan Paul, 1972).

22 The last page of *Cahier* XX [65] notes the names and titles of a few Québec writers (e.g. Jacques Ferron, *Contes* and *Le Ciel du Québec*); the back inside cover [66] lists two names and telephone numbers.

Cahier XXI[1]

Women's Lib: Many good points best because
it deals with how we live now & not how we will live [14].

Cahier XXI comprises notes on books read as well as outlines, draft passages and Engel's instructions to herself on work in progress.

Engel's reading list at the time included David Lodge's *The Novelist at the Crossroads*,[2] Naïm Kattan's *Le Réel et le Théâtral* [3] and the Summer 1969 issue of the review *Critical Quarterly*.[4] The *cahier* also contains lengthy notes on Aphrodite. These, like the notes on books read, appear in abbreviated form here, but still amply demonstrate Engel's simultaneous struggle with theories about the novel in general[5] and work on her novel in particular. Outlines[6] and draft passages[7] for the future *Monodromos* are accompanied by a series of instructions Engel gave herself about the novel: "keep foreign drama out" [1]; "each chapter can encapsulate a story" [4]; "the surge of action is subtle" [4]; "Remember: Keep Audrey's feelings out & help her from getting slangy. She is a pair of eyes, NOT a camera. All references to her should define her eyes or her existence—nothing else" [15].[8] Slowly but surely, Engel articulated her

---

1 1970, blue notebook, with "Engel" and "Monodromos 1st" handwritten on the cover; 38 pages used.

2 David Lodge, *The Novelist at the Crossroads* (Ithaca: Cornell University Press, 1971). Engel's notes, taken in 1970, are based on a preview excerpt of the book, published in *The Critical Quarterly* 2.2 (Summer 1969). See [11-13].

3 Naïm Kattan, *Le Réel et le Théâtral* (Montréal: HMH, 1970). Notes on this book are found on [25-32].

4 Vol. II No. 2. Notes on this reading are found on [12-14].

5 For instance, Engel transcribed Robbe-Grillet's contention that "in describing the world of things we are not willing to admit that they are just things, with their own existence, indifferent to ours. We make things reassuring by attributing human meaning or 'significants' to them" [12].

6 [7-10].

7 "Bert & Rosa," [17-24].

8 See Verduyn, *Lifelines* 101 for a discussion of how *Monodromos*'s Audrey Moore is markedly different from Engel's previous two protagonists—the talkative, self-revealing Sarah Porlock (Sarah Bastard) and the imposingly pregnant Minn Burge. These characters' audible "I"'s become "eyes" in the case of *Monodromos*'s protagonist.

vision of her novel in progress:

> I want very hard staccato penis erectus passages alternating with the soft relaxed past.... This is turning out rather like other middle east books—the foreigner meeting the magician & failing to be transformed—Saxondom being a condition of soul. Mention this? ... But what I want to get is the tremendous Elizabethan vitality of a society released from a form of bondage. It has not yet decided on its true aim. Ergo: confusion of aims. Charm of handicraft society for artists & foreigners. Backwardness of those inside. Necessity to make a living or go to Camden town. [35]

Even as Engel worried whether she was "aiming high enough" in her work, she harboured "fear [of] being called pretentious" [35]. This echoes her earlier concern about being perceived as a woman with too many ideas. Such anxieties notwithstanding, Engel knew she stood apart from the crowd in a number of areas. This is manifest in her thoughts, recorded 17 November 1970, on Pollution Probe [24], and on the women's liberation movement [14-16]. They confirm Engel as an independent thinker—"not a joiner" as she wrote [15], though not unsupportive either. She was "intellectually for [women's lib]," as her *cahier* notes attest, but she remained critically analytical. She wanted, for example, anthropological perspectives on the various issues [16]. As for Pollution Probe, "Well, fine, good: but it is intolerable for me to join a nation of paper-savers again. [...] Mea culpa" [24]. In the final pages of *Cahier* XXI, Engel made notes on letters sent to and from Cyprus. This was part of her work towards *Monodromos*, and demonstrates the link between life and writing in the author's work.

[p.1]

Monodromos
The city
The city walls
The street
[...]

[pp.2-6]

[One-word, one-line notes for *Monodromos*]

[p.7]

X's [Xanthos] questions [to Audrey, in *Monodromos*] in the car, first intimacy—

Your brother is a homosexual.

Yes. Is that badly thought of here?

Oh—we are more tolerant than some people, less than others. I wouldn't send my son to him. But Efy—he seems all right with her. One always has a certain fear of pederasty of course? What was he like as a child? Did your mother favour him?

He was very shy, he cried a lot—otherwise—like he is now: sometimes depressed, sometimes domineering. Like everyone.

And what form does depression take in a little child?

Oh—sulking, tantrums, you know.

I'm not sure I do. What did your mother want for him?

Rosa: flamboyant, cooped, mangled. The dying fighting cocks.
Never a hen.
—"That he should be a musician"

—And for you?

—Oh, nothing. I wasn't musical.

[p.8]

Didn't you have piano lessons?

I hated them.

And you're—how much younger.

Six months older.

Silence. Slip. Damn.

So you're not his sister?

I <u>was</u> his wife.

Divorced?

Long ago. I didn't like his telling everyone I was his sister. But what can I do? I hope it doesn't get me in trouble with the passport people.

Are you responsible for his debts?

Technically, no. Morally—who knows? Did you know Edward?

(Absently) No. Edward who?

His friend, Edward Millington. Millington Sands, properly.

I've seen him. One of our resident English drunkards.

[p.9]

I don't feel responsible for him.

I should think not. Are you going in there?

Yes, I'm meeting a friend. Thanks for the lift.

You're welcome. Mrs ... Mrs. **M**.

[p.10]

Reading:
David Lodge: The Novelist at the Crossroads.

Scholes & Kellog say there are two main, antithetical modes of narrative:

the empirical: primary allegiance to the real
HISTORY—true to fact MIMESIS—true to experience.
the fictional: primary allegiance to the ideal
romance—cultivates beauty, aims to delight
allegory— " goodness, " " instruct

synthesis—in primitive oral epic
renaissance & towards novel

breakup—late classical lit[erature]
European vernacular lit[erature]

"novel has satisfied our hunger for the meaningful ordering of experience without denying our empirical observation of its randomness & particularity."

Scholes claims that allegory & romance are now handled by technique he calls "fabulation."

Frank Conroy: Stop Time[9]

"The increasing demands for social & psychological detail that are made upon the novelist can only be satisfied out of his own experience."

[p.11]

Critical Quarterly
Vol II No 2 Summer '69

[p.12]

"In French experiments with the non-fiction novel the fiction that is purged is not so much a matter of invented characters & actions as a philosophical 'fiction' or fallacy, which the trad[itional] novel encourages—namely, that the universe is susceptible of human interpretation."[10]

Ac[cording] to Robbe-Grillet[11] in describing the world of things, we are not willing to admit that they are <u>just</u> things, with their own existence, indifferent to ours. We make things reassuring by attributing human meaning or "significations" to them.

Metaphor is used in setting up a constant rapport between the universe & the human being who inhabits it.

But language <u>must</u> humanize everything that touches it.

"the pressure of scepticism on the aesthetic & epistemological premises of literary realism is now so intense that many novelists, instead of marching confidently straight ahead, are at least considering the two routes that branch off in opposite directions—the non-fiction novel & fabulation."[12]

[p.13]

Fabulators: Grass
Burroughs
Pynchon
Cohen

---

9 Frank Conroy, *Stop-time* (New York: Viking Press, 1967).

10 Lodge, "The Novelist at the Crossroads" 115.

11 Ibid. 116.

12 Ibid.

Sontag
Some Burgess

Henderson, the Centaur, the Natural, Old Men at the Zoo, Gog.

Inspiration: in order to get wonder wish fulfilment, suspense: sci-fi; porn; the thriller.

Speaks highly of Myra B[13] —as non-fiction novel participant.

Novelists— at the crossroads between non-fiction & fabulation build their hesitation into the novel itself → the novel—about itself

trick, game or puzzle novel—
[...]

[p.14]

Women's lib:

Many good points but because it deals with how we live now & not how we will live: i.e. applies to a democratic, technocratic culture & is usable by these—it has almost no relevance.

abortion

schools as propaganda machines

What is womanhood to become when breeding is immoral?

[p.15]

Women's Lib & Marian E.

Intellectually for provided that physical differences are taken into account.

Domesticity—happy values of oughtn't to be forgotten.

Mothering vs smothering.
Old fashioned background.

Tiger.

13 Gore Vidal's *Myra Breckinridge* (Boston: Little, Brown and Company, 1968).

Not a joiner.

What would women's Lib do for Minn? Except make her hate her life more?

Value of children now?

Anthropological perspectives.

I invented it: no girls in the mounties

[p.16]

Remember: Keep Audrey's feelings out [of *Monodromos*] & help her from getting slangy. She is a pair of eyes, <u>NOT</u> a camera.

All references to her should define her eyes or her <u>existence</u>—nothing else.
explore: "going native"

Do this section with 1) Florinda listening
2) listener's footnotes i.e. going into the closet to smell his mother's clothes (Rainbow Valley) references to South Wind, Brideshead, Little Miss Melody, Henty[?] etc
Kids' books, Queen's books, music, art i.e. the Matisse with the Pleyel

Landmarks or Tombstones.

[p.17]

Monodromos: Bert & Rosa

Bert lasted longer than Florinda. Laddie was in Corsica when he died. Barbara & her husband were living in Australia. He knew it was he who would have to go home.

He was in Corsica with Edward, staying à quatre with a choreographer & a famous composer in the composer's castle, where the piano was in the Donjon, where previous to taking up residence, the composer, who had enormous private means, fame, talent & the friendship of the church, had had the virtual village exorcised by a prince of the church—otherwise no servants would make themselves available. The villagers believed it to be a black, bad place.

He was in Corsica. The composer was possessive about the piano. Edward had bought him a clavichord but somehow ... he had not played for months. The life ... the climate....

The telegram about Bert was forwarded by his agent. He had to motor to Ajaccio, fly from there to Nice, to Paris, to Montreal, to Toronto, (where he found that the time of the train had changed but there was a new airline.) It was February. From the airport at home he telephoned Bert's lawyer, who signed the wire. The funeral was to be in an hour. He took a taxi from the airport

[p.18]

to the house, (he always carried that key) dug out his father's best winter overcoat, which was thin and short for him, but black & warmer than his Corsican machinitos[?] (somewhere—in somebody's flat in London (mine?) he had some winter clothes but how many years? Five? Six?)—and Bert's galoshes, blessing him because if he was a small man he had long long feet, peed, stuck out his tongue at the oleograph of the lady in red at the spinet in the dining room, slammed the door so that the house, which he noticed at that time & for the first time, was barely worthy of the name of cottage, rattled & shook, and arrived in his taxi at the funeral home with ten minutes to spare & five dollars in his pocket.

He was stunned by the journey, chilled by the temperature, and glad that he had enough theatrical training to act [illegible] mourner without collapsing. Stinson the lawyer offered him baked meats in the Crystal Grill after the burial, after the line of mourners, who seemed as simple & remote from his experience as Corsican peasants, whose names & faces he remembered but whose trappings seemed to him (except for their

[p.19]

huge, pastel-coloured cars) unaccustomedly humble, departed.

Stinson said "well," & he said "well" & "what's to do now?" his voice rang out high & foreign in the Grill & he was ashamed. Stinson asked if he had time to come to the office & he said he had. The Moores (most of the mourners had been Moores, cousins & uncles & aunts) & the Lenehans (Detroit & Windsor branch) had treated him with respect & backed away. He half wished they had asked him up to someone's huge plain kitchen in Camlachie to eat black beef & drink weak coffee, tried to picture himself there, failed & went willingly with Stinson.

Who looked carefully at him and showed him the evidence—mortgage after mortgage. Promissary notes. "Why?"

"For you."

"But I thought … the Lenehans … scholarships.…

Stinson shook his head. He leafed through the papers. The names … the fat-faced Moore cousins ... the hideous piano-teachers.

"Some of them are dead," said Stinson. It did not help.

He went home, shocked, to

[p.20]
the empty house. He slept for a week & lived on Rosa's ancient preserves & never thought that corroded gem jars were worth five dollars a piece. Got sick. Met Stinson. Phoned his agent.

He nearly died of the weather, but he got what he wanted by telling the truth to the papers. The old highschool Steinway[?] moved from the gym to the furnace room to practice in.—The auditorium at a percentage of the take. A poster on the never-never from Jim Watny. He sent free tickets to the Moores, the neighbours, the Lenehans & the note-holders, found out from Mrs Morris the community concerts what they liked now, froze at bus stops, gave lessons, ate broccoli casserole with the neighbours, borrowed Stinson's tails from the '30's & gave them the time of their life.

He said he was lucky it was the season. Erlback booked him in Toronto & Montreal. He was amazed when he asked for the minor tour as well. He would have paid them all if he had not taken ill.

Oh, he said, it was crazy to go back, crazy, like stepping into a time machine—& who

[p.21]
could do it, after years of the soft life who could do it. Fried eggs in a million one-night-stand hotels....

But when he saw it on paper—the debts, the notes. Rosa would have gone to call Bert's relatives, one by one—& her telling him she got the money from her father, & Bert with hard eyes nodding.

The surprise was that he sold the cottage for a lot of money. Did I remember it stood on an amazing piece of land? It was a shack, the building.

No, I said. Rosa's taste, grandeur....

Your house, he said, your house, bitterly, still stands—when I last saw it—the rambler roses—your sister....

But his house ... yes, there was the land. The beach & the cedar trees & the land. It was a converted summer cottage that stood on the shore acres of Bert's father's farm. Rosa's trappings had made it something grand & mysterious. But we always thought the land was bad, it wouldn't grow any grass. Eighteen lots—a whole development. We paid off the lawyer, the

[p.22]
mortgages. Stinson was good. He made the bargain & took a commission & waived the fees. I sent money to Barbara.

"But you were ill?"

"Haileybury, the Soo, Port Arthur, Fort Francis ... and damn lucky to get the tour. Pneumonia. I kept hoping I'd meet an Indian, any Indian...."

"Not their shtik, love."

"Poor Bert. He lived on mustard & wieners…."

& I thought of the tribe. People with flower pots for hats, people Rosa was kind to. "Did they come to the concert?"

"Absolutely. I autographed programs after."

"Did you get the Collegiate to provide usherettes?"

"The day of the strapless evening gown is gone. They wore navy-blue dresses to the knees...."

"Oh, Laddie...."

"Oh, tempere … I can't say that. At any rate, I … no—I didn't miss you. I thought of you. Did your mother tell you?"

"Not about Bert, & the money. I should think that's been all over town."

"Moores are close-lipped, it emerges."

[p.23]

Pollution

[p.24]

He leaned on the moon for a moment & said, "you see, I have some morality."

Pollution Probe

17/11/70 Well, fine, good: but it is intolerable for me to join a nation of paper-savers again. Probably because my priorities are wrong—but if I conserve paper I waste energy. I don't know how to be cautious, tidy etc. without reverting or disintegrating. Mea culpa.

On finding two NNRF's at the Junior League Opportunity Shop:[14] Where have I been all these years? Why haven't I aspired to this level?

Because basically it didn't mean anything to me & I still cling to values (bone soup, home, farm) that make it partially irrelevant. Think of Weaver: he has an odd faith that Mr Littlejohn will win through—over experiment, idealism etc. He is shaken, though.

14 NNRF is the acronym for the literary publication *Nouvelle Nouvelle Revue Français*. The Junior League, founded in New York in 1901, is an international association of women committed to community development through voluntarism and action.

Howard inviting Weaver to Dennis's[15] party!

[pp.25-31]

[Notes on Naïm Kattan's *Le Réel et le Théâtral*]

[p.32]

Aphrodite Stories

[...]

b 6 The Hittites make Cronus bite off the genitals of Uranus, swallow some of the seed & spit out the rest on M[oun]t Kansura → Goddess → G[ree]k tale of how Aphrodite rose from a sea impregnated by Uranus' severed genitals.

11 Aphrodite, goddess of desire rose from the sea on a scallop shell, first stepped ashore on Cythera but moved to Paphos. Where she walks, flowers & grass grow. At Paphos the season clothed & adorned her. She takes to the air w. doves & sparrows.

[...]

[p.33]

18 Aphrodite's Nature & Deeds

had magic girdle to make people fall in love with wearer. Would not lend it.

[...]

[p.34]

[...]

It was said to be Aphrodite who turned the Sirens into birds. They were the children of Axelous or Phorcys either by Terpsichore or Sterope—had girls' faces, birds' feet & feathers

Aph. disliked them because for pride they would yield their maidenheads neither to men nor to gods.

[p.35]

Monodromos: Max as Louis

I want very hard staccato penis erectus passages alternating with the soft relaxed past.

In brackish February. "What thou will highly, that wouldst thou holily." Are you aiming high enough? Don't you <u>fear</u> being called pretentious?

---

15 Dennis Lee, prolific Canadian writer and editor.

This is turning out rather like other Middle East books—the foreigner meeting the magician & failing to be transformed—Saxondom being a condition of soul. Mention this.

But what I want to get is the tremendous Elizabethan vitality of a society released from a form of bondage. It has not yet decided on its true aim. Ergo: confusion of aims. Charm of handicraft society for artists & foreigners. Backwardness for those inside. Necessity to make a living or go to Camden town.

[pp.36-37]

Gk mythological names.

[Lists of names]

[p.38]

Notes from Letters:

Lola May: bought terra cotta vase
too hot for maillot bought bikini
teaching 730 a.m. to 12:30
camp 5 miles out of town
beach a lot
sailing
The English couple come to stay
building
Sandals & cotton dresses
26-27 May—rain filled the Pedios
Bolshoi Ballet, Ballet Rambert & Americans
teaching [illegible] us out of Gk community
Snowdons wedding

Lola—Feb H. interviews the "mufti"
"settling involved a lot of sleeping, the sunshine was a shock after England"

no farms w. houses on
"villages" as places to return to.
St. Xaralambous—Feb. 50 buses.
donkey saddles.
dance at Kyrenia
muezzin at 5 o'clock Mecca time.

August Scrawly handwriting
Paphos—very poor & v. beautiful.
no neon, no plastic
Steve—kids

Cat chews knuckles
Zavvo crisis
"one" will do everything.
Swimming with Pat L. near Kyrenia

Marian Engel in 1942

Graduation, McMaster University, 1955

Paris, Christmas, 1960

Wedding Day, January 1962

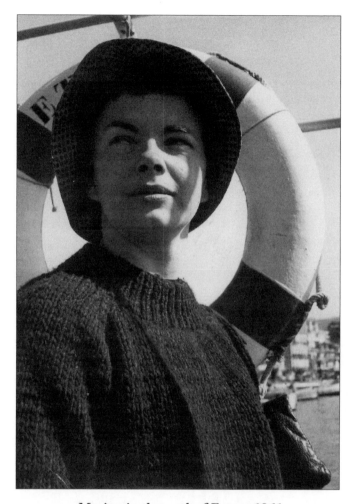

Marian in the south of France 1961

London, England 1962

Toronto 1966

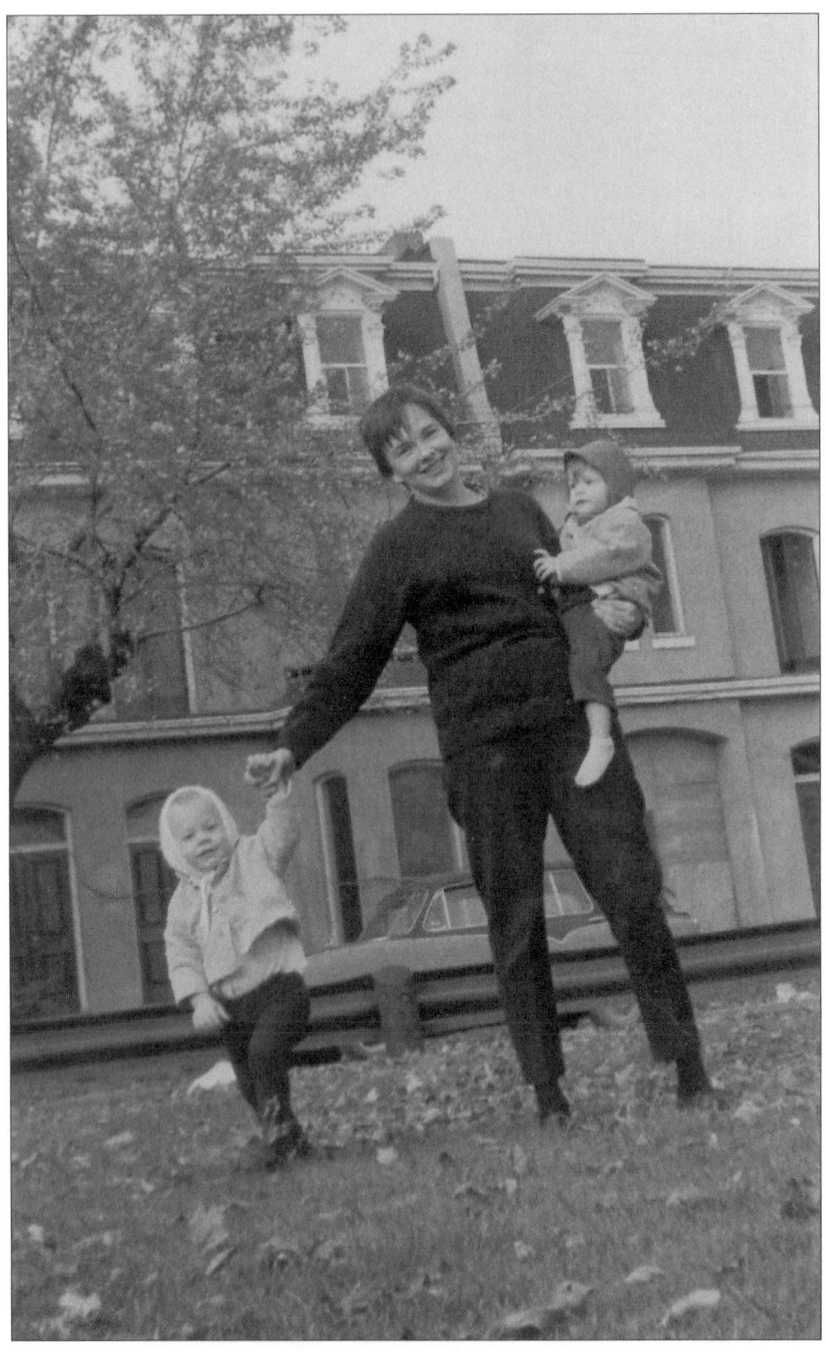

With William and Charlotte, Toronto 1966

1969

1981

April 1984

Cahier XXII[1]

C20 envy of
C19 nostalgia [45]

This *cahier* features one of Engel's most impressive lists. Inspired by a visit, 24 February 1970, to a friend's studio, she delved into Ralph Mayer's *The Artist's Handbook of Materials and Techniques*[2] and proceeded to an alphabetical listing of names of colours. Spanning twenty *cahier* pages, of which only the first two are reproduced here, the inventory far outstrips the colour wheel of the author's first *cahier* and, in its length and detail, attests to a genuine delight in words and sounds.

Engel's explorations of literary criticism and its relevance to *Monodromos* are ongoing: "The Nouveau Roman, the Old Roman & the Now Roman. Straighten out your ideas before you continue," the author instructed herself [5]. Ideas culled from French literary criticism were held up against her project in *Monodromos*: "R[obbe]-G[rillet] is saying ... why try to see what's behind things when we never see things (as they are)? He wants the outside to come first. He may be right but what I want is to place the rare joys of reality against those few elements of reality that seep through to me" [9]. Engel was concerned about *Monodromos* being too "soft," or too centred on "women's worlds," as some critics had claimed of *Sarah Bastard's Notebook* and *The Honeyman Festival*.[3] "Already the book [*Monodromos*] is going squashy and domestic. But the need is to set the island off against a very Canadian background.... I want them to see a place and a reaction to a place" [13]. The following entry, made on her birthday, 24 May 1971, shows Engel's continuing concern: "Monodromos: Synthesis; make a hard surface.... Md ought to be enclosed in eggshell—instead of which there is the worst kind of glaucous white film on it.... Stop things from going squashy" [44-45]. The author's task was not made easier by acquaintances who asked her: "Why does a soft lady want to write a hard book?" [43].

---

1 1970-71, yellow notebook, "Monodromos I" on cover; 47 pages used.

2 Ralph Mayer, *The Artist's Handbook of Materials and Techniques* (New York: Viking Press, 1957).

3 See Verduyn, *Lifelines* 94.

Among her readings at the time of this *cahier*, Engel noted Rose Macaulay's *The Pleasure of Ruins*;[4] Franz Georg Maier's *Cyprus*;[5] Frank Kermode's study of *Durrell, Puzzles & Epiphanies*;[6] a *New York Times* article by David Rounds on "The Education of a Romantic in Backwater";[7] E.A. Craig's Gordon Craig;[8] and E.G. Craig's *Index to the Story of My Days*.[9] There are two instalments of nearly identical notes on the Craig books (E.A. and E.G.'s), accompanied by the notation, dated 21 May 1971, that they have been "recopied from Warped book" [42]. The "Warped [note]book," located in the Marian Engel Archive,[10] contains twelve pages of Greek names, as well as lists of names typical of the author's age group, that of her parents and that of Howard Engel.[11] These pages are noted but not reproduced here.

[p.1]

Titles [for *Monodromos*].
Aphrodite's Realm
Greek in Your House — * History of Cyprus
Romantic Cyprus — Sir Geo. Hill
Island in Revolt
Historic Cyprus
Excerpta Cypria
Portrait of a Terrorist
Cyprus—Sir Harry Luke

Epithets
Rosy Realm of Venus
Aphrodite's Home

4 Rose Macaulay, *The Pleasure of Ruins* (London: Weidenfeld and Nicolson, 1953). See [40-41].

5 See [41-42].

6 Frank Kermode, *Puzzles & Epiphanies* (London: Routledge and Kegan Paul, 1962). This notation is dated 30 June 1971.

7 20 June 1971 edition.

8 E.A. Craig, *Gordon Craig* (New York: Knopf, 1968).

9 E.G. Craig, *Index to the Story of My Days* (New York: Viking Press, 1957).

10 MEA, Box 6 File 23. Small green notebook.

11 Joan, Barbara, Helen, Ardith, Janet, Catharine, Shirlie, Mary, Lou, etc.; Jennie, Jessie, Hazel, Winnifred, Mary, Marion, Genevieve, Lola, Hilda, Ethel; and Percy, Fred, Douglas, Mack, Norman, Bill, Ernie, John, Frank, Owen, Homer, Vern, etc.; Frank, Harry, Jack, Peter, Ian, Garth, Cal, Bill, John, etc. This is followed by an excerpt from Round's article, which was recopied into *Cahier* XXII.

[p.2]

Troubles with structure: I am going on in idleness when I should be working on islanders.

[p.3]

First names

Glafkos
Zenon
Spyros
Tassos
Renos
Costas
Pahodos
Georghios
Andreas
Peter
Miltrades
Vassos
Stavros
Mammas

[p.4]

William: Mummy, where is my thing?
Me: What thing? What's it called?
Wm: I don't know, I haven't given it a name yet.

[p.5]

30 Jan—[1970]

Calamitous visit to Earle Birney in hospital—one of my moments of mental paralysis: not enhanced by embarrassment at a male hospital ward.

The Nouveau Roman, the Old Roman & the <u>Now</u> Roman. Straighten out your ideas before you continue.

Louis Auchincloss: The trick of author as character. NYTBR 1 2 70[12]

problem of regular literary critic—having read too many novels → him a greater than usual need to innovation
i.e. Richard Gilman
Christopher Lehmann-Haupt "Thoughts for the End of the Year"

---

12 Louis Auchincloss, "Speaking of Books: The Trick of Author as Character," *New York Times Book Review* (1 February 1970): 2 and 38.

L-H says in conventional fiction narrator is parent, reader is bedtime child. Novelist should bare his soul, cease sublimating e.g. French loot.[13]

But the novelist in French loot is surely an artifice, a device. A good one, one to be used sparingly— not a radical innovation. Besides, who notices point of view if a book is good? e.g. Wuthering Heights vs Tenant of Wildfell Hall. (The voice for new book—Borges?)

This is a weak argument. Why? Because it down-grades innovation & is anti-creative.

Besides the article is a piffle with someone called Lehmann-Haupt.

[p.6]

Cyprus: for me the experience was novelettish & that conditioned one's behaviour. People seemed to be "characters"—often 2-dimensional ones. Gossip sketched in their backgrounds.

cf. "A Narrow Street"—which is really a kind of glorified travel book. Even Bitter Lemons.

The charm of foreign environments is our superficial relation to them. We can talk about them 2-dimensionally without guilt, oversimplify where we will. But it's cheap, like Durrell's "Mr Honey" reducing a human being to 2 year-old "cuteness."

Is there any legitimate ground for using that foreign environment—yes—it is material that exists.

But use it without adjectives so to speak!

[p.7]

Begin it with the disquisition on the word beautiful.

Borges

I who do not remember, if I ever knew, who the gnostics are, perhaps shouldn't even try to read him—but he says a great deal to me.

His parables deal w what one can refer to as "artistic creation"—or creations or discovery. His labyrinths are tunnels for seekers—and writers are

13 Probable reference to John Fowles's 1969 novel *The French Lieutenant's Woman*, which Christopher Lehmann-Haupt reviewed for *The New York Times Book Review*.

par excellence seekers (if I can't find it, I'll invent it) as are, of course, also explorers, artists, inventors, scientists etc.

Is there cabalistic nonsense behind this? If there is nonsense, he is aware of it.

What I try to make is something beautiful, good, true etc ... the impossible, I suppose. But I try to make out of experience & imagination objects more shapely & satisfying than reality....

Is that true?

Poems, maybe, you try to make, woman.
Why not?

But re Borges vs Robbe-Grillet & the Myth of Depth— what I think
[continues on p.9]

[p.8]

allie
Camille Maupin[14]

[p.9]

R-G is saying is why try to see what's behind things when we never see things (as they are)? He wants the outside to come first.

He may be right but what I want is to place the rare joys of reality against those few elements of reality that seep t hrough to me. Traditional, he said-she said, he went, A B & C narrative & "character" militate against this.

"Character" = cuteness too often.

14 Camille Maurin is a character in Honoré de Balzac's *Béatrix* (Paris: Calmann-Levy, n.d.). In the novel Maurin is the pen name for the character Felicité des Touches. This character is a writer and thought to portray the nineteenth-century French author Amandine-Aurore Dupin, Baronne Dudevant, who wrote under the pseudonym George Sand.

It is impossible to know other people. Or is it?

Mast Is there only the surface they present?

Sails

Deadness

[p.10]

[Two little drawings/doodles]

[p.11]

71?

14 Feb ~~1969~~ [15]

From "MM the analogical critic." Review of The Interior Landscape

by M. McLuhan. Globe & Mail 14/2/70 by Peter Buitenhuis

NB 1 section is called "The Nets of Analogy"

"Essays on Joyce, Pound, Hopkins & Wyndham Lewis all hammer away at the same motif: these writers did not work by discursive method but by the juxtaposition of image & idea thro' imaginative analogy. Increasingly this becomes the method through which McLuhan operates as critic, until we find him in his recent writing on communications working not through logic at all but by mosaic method: the technique of placing concepts and images side by side so that they illustrate each other by implicit comparison."

Vera: "The West is easternising, healing the mind-body split. But it is doing it by Western methods—drugs, products. The movement is coming, as it should, not from outside."

"They had a horror now of the home service, with its harder conditions, severe view of duty, & the hazard of stormy oceans. They were attuned to the eternal peace of Eastern sky & sea. They loved short passages, good deck-chairs, large native crews, & the distinction of being white."

Lord Jim p. 7.

[p.12]

Annie Wilher

Who?

---

15 This is more evidence that Engel reread her *cahiers*: 1969 is scratched out and 1971 is inserted with a question mark.

[p.13]

The bastions of the city are.... It was on __ that I saw the cockfight the day I walked the circumference of the wall.

[Drawing and accompanying question: "What is that shape?"]

The bastions
the walk
hard to get away from Gladys
rel[ation]ship w Gladys
the walk
the cockfight

Already the book is going squashy & domestic. But the need is to set the island off against a very Canadian background, from which D goes out.

I want them to see a place & a reaction to a place & the tremendous vitality of the place.

[p.14]

Tenses?

[p.15]

Dympna [character in *Monodromos*] talked the kind of rubbish she was ever willing to attribute to the lower orders & foreigners 90% of the time—but she was capable of occasional & redeemingly English flashes of sensitivity & even erudition. She knew, for instance, probably all there was to be known on the subject of Henry VIII's wives. And once she came when I was sleeping & I awoke to see her moon face staring at mine. "You feel imprisoned, ergo, ill" she said with brisk sympathy. "Energy fading away. Can't we smuggle you out through Phaedra's for a walk?"

"She won't have it. The old woman can see."

"And you rather like it, don't you? Removed from the cares of the world—secure. Get dressed, though—it's your exercise period. We're going to walk in the courtyard."

"I'd rather stay in bed."

"You're white, you'll atrophy afterward, you can make me a teentsy-weentsy brandy sour. Shall I turn my ugly phiz[?] away while you dress. Whooo—you're nearly as fat as old Dymp. I'll wait outside—hurry now."

I always have a grand abstract conception & write this ↑[16]

16 The arrow here points to the passage above.

[p.16]

24 Feb 1970
Visit to Arthur last night.
His painting has grown, blossomed, & shimmers.
Conversation: dyes, colours.
[...]
He is becoming a **fabulous** painter.

[p.17]

The Artist's Handbook of Materials & Techniques by Ralph Mayer Viking Press 1950

Pigments:
A finely divided, colored substance which imparts its color effect to another material either when mixed intimately w. it or when applied over its surface in a thin layer.
Pigments remain dispersed or suspended in liquid.
Dyes dissolve & stain material.

Classification:

A. Inorganic (mineral)
1. Native earth's—ochre, raw umber
2. Calcined native earth's—burnt umber, burnt sienna
3. Artificially prepared mineral colours zinc oxide etc

B. Organic
1. Veg: gamboge, indigo, madder
2. Animal: cochineal Indian yellow
3. Artificially prepared—anilines
alizarin

[p.18]

Lakes: a lake is a pigment which has been made by precipitation or fixing a dye upon an inert pigment or lake base

term comes from Lac (Shellac)

"The nomenclature of pigments is confusing & un-systematic" p. 28.

Academy blue—ultramarine & viridean.
Alexandrian Blue = Egyptian blue
Alizarin Blue, or Green—

clear, transparent brilliant lakes
indigo to emerald
NOT for permanent use as they turn black
A. Brown—Dull but transparent
Permanent
A. Crimson. Lake. Red. Scarlet.
made from anthracene—coal tar product
Rosy scarlet to maroon w bluish undertones
clear & transparent & permanent
slow dries

A. Violet: permanent. Contains purpurin.
A. Yellow brownish—not reliable as high grades are rare

American Vermilion: a heavy, opaque coal-tar lake—made from
Eosin on red lead base. Not permanent
[p.19]

Aniline cobins—from coal tar
complete range of lakes
not for permanent painting
as some fade. 1870

Antimony Orange & Vermilion
A. trisulfide—bright & permanent
but the sulphur blackens lead pigments. 1847
Replaced by cadmium.

A. white A. Oxide & 70% blanc fixe.
1920 Perment but n.b.q.

A. Yellow = Naples Yellow

Antwerp blue—pale Prussian blue
PB + 75% inert pigment.
Not permanent.
A. red = Light red.

ARMENIAN BOLE = Venetian red. A red earth.

Arnaudon's Green—Variety of Chromium
oxide green.

Arsenic Orange & Yellow: See. Realgar & Kings Yellow

[p.20]

Asbestine— a kind of tale used as an inert pigment.

Asphaltuim—used for <u>scrumbling</u> decorative work to simulate age but not for permanent painting.

Araluen: Cobalt—potassium nitrite. Yellow supersedes Gamboge discovered in Breslau in 1830

Auripigmentuim—Kings Yellow

Aurora Yellow: Kind of Cadmium Y.

Auruim Mussivum—Mosaic gold.

Azure blue—<u>Smalt.</u> —very early general term for blue
see dictionary
Azurite: Native basic copper carbonate
Rare. Replaced by ultramarine, cobalt & cerulean blues. Poor in oil.

[pp.21-37]

[Names and Descriptions of colours, B-Z]

[p.38]

<u>Epigraph</u>[17]

"Facts become art through love,
which unifies them and lifts them to a
higher plane of reality;
and in landscape, this
all-embracing love is expressed
by light."

Kenneth Clark
Landscape into art p.16[18]

---

17 As noted in *Lifelines*, this epigraph, mooted for *Monodromos*, was eventually used for *Bear*.

18 Kenneth Clark, *Landscape into Art* (Boston: Beacon Press, 1961).

If Max becomes Louis...
Monodromos—Strands
1. Laddie
2. Audrey & Max
3. Robin
4. Cypriots (4th place?)
5. Politics
6. Landscape
7. The British

This is not a
good list

<u>Exodus</u>

The book should be about

1. a dying handicraft culture
2. of a dying western culture (Piano lessons!)
3. British colonialism of emergent nationalism
4

[p.39]

[Names of characters in *Monodromos*]

[p.40]

The Pleasures of Ruins: Rose Macaulay

"Layer upon layer of intruded civilizations
stand wrecked."
On pre-historic sites rose Phoenician
temples, classical temples & theatres;
on pavements of Cypriot palaces
[...]
"The enchantment of ruinous Cyprus is
cumulative rather than individual"
[...]

[p.41]

[...]

Cyprus was the
last European
feudal state
under the Lusignans

[p.42]

That night in Max's head
a forest bloomed. He was
sending me to Byzantium.

Conversation about Sepade
hearts (see Heart-Burial) ?

21 May 1971 (recopied from Warped book)
Reading EA Craig: Gordon Craig
EG " : Index to the Story of My Days.

When I first read Index I was appalled by C[raig]'s narcissism—& the boyish attitude to women. Gordon Craig reinforced this, but now, re-skipping through Index, pulling it all together, I am fascinated. He's such a good writer—direct, energetic, honest about what seems to matter. On Isadora he is very fine indeed.
[…]
Other book: I. Malcolm: The Pursuit of Intoxication[19]—dour but admirable in scope. Sallow imitation of romanticism.

[p.43]

Monodromos again—after the Bill Roberts weekend. Why does a soft lady want to write a hard book?
Bill says I protect myself. I certainly know enough to do that.
Thinking of Stan Pfefferman & Helen Hutchison programme—yes.

By indirections give directions out.
Keep the funny bits, the joy.
L. can't have been a good pianist.

Lists of names always work.

Desperate to communicate with Ian Malcolm about his book. Why?

Stop things from going squashy.
Booze, writing is squashy—sentimental.

[p.44]

21\5\71 Reading E.A. Craig: Gordon Craig
E.G. Craig: Index to the Story
of my days

I was appalled on first reading index by the narcissism of this boy's attitude to women. Gordon Craig reinforced this, but no, skipping through Index, pulling it all together, I am fascinated. He is such a good writer. On

19 Andrew I. Malcolm, *The Pursuit of Intoxication* (Toronto: PaperJacks, 1972).

Isadora, he is masterly. He conveys a marvellous concept of love-in-work— raising the relationship above everything.
[...]
Pursuit of Intoxication: a dour volume but admirable in scope. Sallow limitation of romanticism though.

24\5 Monodromos: synthesise; make a hard surface.

"You try to protect yourself, don't you?" Bill Roberts.

Md ought to be enclosed in eggshell—instead of which there is the worst kind of glaucous white film on it.

Does Max have to go? Does Henshaw?

BY INDIRECTIONS GIVE DIRECTIONS OUT

Keep the funny parts.

[p.45]

Quotations in early journal—good
Book of names—good

Stop things from going squashy.

—

21 June: Show as C20 envy of C19 nostalgia

"Of the diversity of urban life in Napoleonic times, of the doubts cast by science on religion, of revolution, of the new tyranny of Machines, the peasants in Wordsworth's poems knew nothing. He thought them lucky in their ignorance."

David Rounds: "The Education of a Romantic in Backwater"

"The city man on tour in backwater America is charmed by the quaintly dilapidated houses, the ancient vehicles, the rocky pastures, the untutored girls, & he does not bother to reflect that what charms him is, in effect, the local population's poverty."

—Rounds NYT 20\6\71

Looking out at the backwater from our aesthetic distance, we conclude that the residents are as pleased to live there as we are to visit—Ibid.

[p.46]

Now what have we:

I Cityscape
Khan
1st relationship

II Meeting Aphroulla
job
letter to Max I

III Bloc-notes —seasons
—landscape

IV God's Place —characters
defense of eating society
church vs archaeology
affair
Aphroulla's meddling

very bad
not on
subject
or stiff

V Bert's funeral (short)

VI Conversation w Maro by the sea.
To a village w Stetros?
Picnic somewhere?

Conversations w X
must be Socratic
m.q. informational.

Subjects
to cover
landscape
eroticism
position of artist
to layman
expatriatism
culture of
island.
music?

[p.47]

30 June 1971 Frank Kermode: Puzzles & Epiphanies

"Durrell & Others" p.214

216 "The major modern novel is a poem, giving the kind of pleasure that the majority of new novels do not even aim at. An exception is Mr D's work in progress, an anatomy of love … undertaken in the conviction that 'somewhere in the heart of experience there is an order & a coherence which we might surprise if we were attentive enough, loving enough, patient enough' to quote its narrator. One must respect the attempt in Justine to … get something analogous to Lear tearing off his clothes in that basic act of sex in the Bazaar book.…"

Cahier XXIII[1]

Every thing is political [2].

In addition to more notes and thoughts on *Monodromos* (structure and method), *Cahier* XXIII offers interesting comments on Ontario and on the October 1970 FLQ crisis in Québec.[2] The latter event, together with her ongoing work on *Monodromos*, plunged Engel into reflection about differing cultural values. An entry made on 3 February 1971 is a reminder that writing was one of many demands on the author's energies: "Dead tired but the head is very much alive" [8].

[p.1]

Notes for Monodromos.

"Do you mind being English? Isn't it constricting?"

"One is always something, except those poor bastards living on ferries."

"I suppose you've got it to fall back on if you don't want to see the truth. That's the sin of pride."

"We all fall back on nationality."

"Some let you down with a crash."

---

1 1971, light green notebook, with two handwritten items on the cover: "Monodromos II and notes for new Stanley," ("Lost Heir and Happy Families"); and, "By the power vested in me by the Criminal Court of Canada, I now pronounce you man and wife," which is the opening sentence of Engel's short story "Sublet," *Inside the Easter Egg*; 11 pages used.

2 In October 1970, the Front de Libération du Québec (FLQ), a militant separatist organization, kidnapped British diplomat James Cross and Quebec immigration minister Pierre Laporte (who was subsequently murdered). The federal government responded by invoking the War Measures Act.

"All the better for you then."

"Not much to choose between the French & the English for chauvinism."

"It's jolly ... convenient to be a foreigner here."

"Good old shitty, soggy, bigoted England."

"The Dominions are inclined to idealize us."

Bloody island. Bloody girl for disturbing it. It had wine & a climate, though.

Bloody colonial nymphomaniac.

His was a planned abdication.

[p.2]

Every thing is
political

[pp.3-8]

["Monodromotic" ideas]

[p.9]

1 Getting there is half the fun
2 And then it isn't there
3 We all have Toronto & they've moved the KCR
4 George Gurney thinks history is something that happens to other people.
5 Ontario Gothic

[p.10]

But I find I have no heart for a totally—AS [anglo-saxon] Canada. Where would intelligence go?

So—I agree with parts of the manifesto but not with the kidnapping—sneaking rebels attitude, though.

But, fundamentally, I don't believe in Ontario—it is an entity, but not one worth making others suffer for.

Blackmail, though—no.

It's too much like the "Indian question." Where's the Indian answer?

[p.11]

Techniques of Imprisonment

Sick "friends"—always when I go; querulous insistence on letters; self-justifying when the others' <u>special</u> nature is revealed.

Jealousy of sibling at advanced age. Is it ashamed or possessive of one?

Other imprisonments:

The kidnapping—since the second one, I am almost completely preoccupied. I find that

1) My heart is with the FLQ
but it will not admit that they will kill
2) That Trudeau, Sharp, & Marshall
are linked in my mind
& I do not like or trust them

3. Add [illegible] to this & you
get something that ought
not to live: wrong-heartedness.
None of them intrinsically
evil but all basically
despisers of women & the French.

Some CBC attitudes are fairly broad but there are sinister elements: the psychologist who diagnosed certain forms of rebellion as paranoia.

Frank Roach looks at Pierre Laporte's writing "doesn't go off the line."

Cahier XXIV[1]

As you fictionalize you fictionalize yourself [1].

In August 1971, Engel visited her parents in Sarnia, and sketched a story featuring the characters Brenda and Oliver. Brenda's background and story are familiar territory in Engel's fiction and anticipate aspects of both *The Glassy Sea* and *Lunatic Villas*:

> She had been considered an imaginative child & a clever one. Perhaps she was in that small world of manses & parsonages, rectories,—but once she left it she discovered (after a period of pretending to be the wildest minister's daughter ever to hit the university & being outstripped by an Anglican canon's offspring) she was commonplace and married Oliver. Her life, now, was exceedingly commonplace: she was the only stay-at-home wife on the street. [4]

Further in the *cahier*,[2] Engel drafted the outdoor theatre scene in *Monodromos*, in which island residents stage Shakespeare's *Julius Caesar*. In this draft version, the protagonist Audrey Moore, reflects:

> How strangely life here is like life in the little town I came from—always personal—punctuated only by events & entertainments. There is <u>never</u> detachment. Yet History, like a big blind statue, is always staring at us. [14]

As these two passages indicate, Engel drew on her own small-town background in her writing.

In characteristic fashion, Engel kept notes on books read.[3] Toy's *History of Fortifications* set up "a screaming chorus of 19th [century] poetry in [her] mind,"

1 1971-72, coverless "Sarnia" notebook"; 18 pages used.

2 Though earlier in the year—the entry is dated 10 January 1972.

3 These included John Updike, *Bech: A Book* (New York: Knopf, 1970); works by Jean Bruller, also known as Vercors, who wrote *Le Radeau de la Méduse* (1969) among others; and Sidney Toy, *A History of Fortification: From 3000 B.C. to A.D. 1700* (London: Heinemann, 1955).

Engel recorded [17]. Sometimes I feel my whole life was filtered through the 19th...." Then, in typical Engel fashion, her critical self intervened: "Stop: Everybody's was, you as[s]" [17]. Reading Updike's *Bech: A Book*, Engel wondered if she was "too egotistic" to see as well as Updike. On the other hand, "I am so tired," Engel observed, "heavy with weariness, as if I am carrying a leaden foetus. I've grown complaining & picky when I'm working. Return to a simplified version of life" [1].

[p.1]

Sarnia Aug 10

Bech: A Book—v. amusing, the point being that the horizon vanishes when you get there, that as you fictionalize you fictionalize yourself. I am wondering if I am not too egotistic to see as well as he does.
Father asleep by the set: young face.
About Galt—how nasty the children were.
Ask more questions.
How afraid people are to be held up to ridicule.

Article for NYT
Writers
Interview & interviewers.
Little mags
Big mags
Newspapers [Drawing of an eye and an ear]
Ministers

TV-addled villagers.
And once he was gone wot
K w[ou]ld die w him? (portentous music). I am so tired. Hapsbings [?] indeed.
Heavy with weariness, as if I am carrying a leaden foetus.
I've grown complaining & picky exc. when I'm working.

Return to a simplified version of life: certain things are left out—sex(?) exc. in horror stories.

Writers in Residence—who—where?
[...]

[p.2]

Claustrophobia—they really would like a poor martyred alcoholic daughter shut up in the kitchen—or would they? Certainly not consciously because they are darlings, but the oppression is there—NOISE & lack of escape—the desire I make up for them is born of adolescent feelings.

Finding a lost
Rubens—why do
we celebrate art?

Write Barbara

[p.3]

Brenda put down the paper. It hadn't worked. The continent was vast and at last she thought she understood its dream: to make it pure and good & simple as nothing ever was. It hadn't worked. They had thought to prevent "evil," first by exorcising it, then by pretending it didn't exist, then by legislating against it. It hadn't worked. Perhaps they ought to have admitted its prevalence, lived side by side with it, held its hand a little, to keep it down. What was that, the manichean heresy. She sighed, thought of her father, wondered what he'd have said if his daughter used such a catholic word.

Oliver heard her, frowned up from his book. "What is it?"

"I am meditating on the appearance in the colonies of some very sophisticated sins."

"Any conclusions?"

"I'll let you know."

She sat staring at the wall across from her and at Oliver, without seeing them (Oliver never had enough time to read) meditating on sophisticated sins. As if the wall were a fire, staring. Not really thinking. Staring.

Something soft passed across her field of vision. Not the real one—the Wordsworthean one she had been relieved to hear about in high school—"the inward eye that is the bliss of solitude" (she had been for

[p.4]

[...]

some time before sure that she was insane, she had thought no one had ever mentioned to her—) something soft.

Then she sat up sharply & said "Really?"

Oliver looked up, startled forth from worlds away. "What is it?"

"Was it tripe or stomach that hung in sheets outside the butcher's in Ravenna—very white & mossy?"

He grinned. "Stomach."

"I thought I had the solution to the world's problems—suddenly I see a sheep's stomach...."

"Cow's."

"Stomach.... Hanging from a line. I give up. I'm going to bed."

She had been considered an imaginative child & a clever one. Perhaps she was in that small world of manses & parsonages, rectories,—but once she left it she discovered (after a period of pretending to be the wildest minister's daughter ever to hit the university & being outstripped by an Anglican canon's offspring) she was commonplace and married Oliver. Her life, now, was exceedingly commonplace: she was the only stay-at-home wife on the street.

[p.5]

[Inventory of objects (in a kitchen, likely in Sarnia)]

[p.6]

And yet—and yet—she had her moments.

She was always angry when Oliver complained she was like her mother, more a parson's wife than she realised. Then she would sit down to the evening paper & read the scandal & think "In <u>Toronto</u>" ___ with a prurient frisson.

And then a sheep's stomach—<u>no</u>, a cow's—only sheep's sounded better in her head, would intervene.

If only she had interesting dreams. She slept like a stone.

But there was a lot of day, to dream in. Her son Kent, like her husband, was apt at the table to cut across her field of vision with scissor-finger motion reaping her dreams.

And they were never, really, about Manicheaen heresies—only silly visions.

They lived, for instance, by an enormous cemetery. Some of her friends said it was bad luck. She sneered at them. Yet, looking out the bathroom window, pretending to scrub the basins, she watched the—jolly—life of the cemetery with interest. (The wall was high but in winter activity beyond it

[p.7]

was clearly visible). They dug the graves with power shovels & pneumatic drills in winter. In summer, noises went on to indicate that they were playing horse shoes. For grand funerals, gay pavilions were erected.... One Halloween night she had looked out & seen jack o'lanterns gleaning & rushed to tell Oliver, & was not satisfied until he took [a] stepladder to [the] wall & helped her confirm to disappointment (disappointment was always necessary, otherwise one might fly quite away) that they were watch-lanterns on sawhorses over open graves.

[p.8]

Every night at five-past five the grave diggers marched down her street: solid dwarves in hard-hats carrying paper bags, not a smile among them, belying the Italian they were speaking.

Sometimes she thought she ought to go out & get a job. That something imprecise was happening to her mind. Oliver said "Where? The dime store." (She had not been what is called "a worker").

[p.9][4]

Sarnia. Aug. 14th. Maude. Marcella. Mary.

The Manly boys sent back my book!
(Undercounter lending)

Maude: Gigot was with the HBC in Nelson. d. 1929. was in the '80's member of the Manitoba legislature. Had been at LePas. Maude taught theory & form.
(Send more cards. Keep up)

Mother: Twice I saw my father cry. He heard Maude had married Albert (a R[oman] C[atholic] he did not know) & I had to tell him Tom was going to die. He had a tragic life. His three sisters died of TB. Emily was his favorite, he called Maude, Emily Maude. His father was a hardworking man, was Reeve of the township & in business as well as farming. He was killed driving a load of timber to the sawmill. The team came back without him. Father & Tom (Nait's brother who died young of TB) went to look for him. The horses had slipped into a pitch hole & the load fell on top of him. So Tom died young too, and Arthur married Mary Jamieson; her mother had Aunt Martha, Lizzie, U[ncle] James, U[ncle] Willie

[pp.10-11]

[Notes and ideas for the story developed in the previous pages][5]

[p.12]

Vercors: Jean Bruller[6] 26/2/02 [*sic*] Paris.
graphic artist—Hugo's birthday

---

4 Engel has written a series of names on the top and left margins of this page.

5 An interesting reference is made to Engel's earlier, unpublished novel "Women Travelling Alone": "Use [it]," Engel instructed herself [11].

6 As mentioned earlier, Vercors is the pseudonym for Jean Bruller; the author of *Le Silence de la mer* (Paris: Albin Michel, 1951).

electrical engineer—mil[itary] service Tunis—began to paint—drawing, etching—satirical drawings.
illustrator
Vercors—WWII fall of France
fell in with Resistance & helped found E.d. Minuit [Éditions du Minuit]
Le Silence was first pub[lication]—attributed to all the gt writers.
you shall know them—what is "human"

Columbia Dic[tionary] of mod[ern] European Lit[erature]

. ——— .

Jan 10/72

Julius Caesar: If one of the monuments of existence is to see Greek classic drama from this stone amphitheatre (one comes with one's cushion), sit sweating lightly in the soft air, hear the strange gutturals of demotic—uttered in a lisping Athenian accent—at the same time attempting to decipher the bourgeoisie around one (the French cultural centre people, all of whom know Greek: the hard core of long term British residents, public school men & their vague, scarved wives, & a remarkably handsome group of people one never sees on the street—formally dressed, their lithe suaveness buttoned down—& a few fat men gustily sighing like husbands in New Yorker cartoons condemned to the Metropolitan Opera),

[p.13]

one of the headstones of boredom is to see the Royal Air Force in Julius Caesar.

If only, one thinks, if only they could have stayed in the Biggles Books.

The theatre they have chosen (there are four in working condition on the island) faces the sea. Against the full moon, headland after headland courts the glistening waves. One can see the shadows of long, moaning valleys, and the silhouettes of little separate trees, as on a mediaeval map.

Why do they do it to themselves & William Shakespeare? Their faces, serious & mournful, open & shout the words in a medley of accents—North, South, Sussex, Wessex, Stepney, a medley of failed Oxbridge imitations (for it is plain from the cast-list that officers, senior at least, in their function of gentlemen cannot be expected to lower themselves to the thespian profession) mouthing, mouthing. Peter Barnes as Brutus AND director is wooden & woeful. It is a long play & one I have never liked much.

Then it strikes me that it would be interesting to have them do it in their own demotic.

For there is quite another drama going on here sitting between a patriotic Florinda & a tight lipped Dympna, edged by William with all his juvenile, public-school superiority showing (when will he grow into what he is?)

[p.14]

and Laddie who is as intent as if his eyes were on stalks—I sense the whole loneliness of voluntary exile. The actors fail in scene after scene to mesh, to become other than themselves, to engage themselves with each other, and the audience—except for a few "locals" dredged out of their jobs on the military bases—sits failing to engage itself with the island. A great rift in communication opens—oh God, if the headlands would reach around, swallow us in their embrace, if some land would absorb us!

So here there are a pack of military foreigners acting a military tale. But all this running about & running on swords is so much without conviction to them: the drama that Peter Barnes could do is the one that belongs to this island, Othello. He and his crew of orphans are not Romans—100 yrs ago they might have been—but exiled, confused Venetians.

In addition, we all here play out the play—belonging without belonging. Aphroulla was right not to come with us—however badly she fares, she does belong.

How strangely life here is like life in the little town I came from—always personal—punctuated only by events & entertainments. There is never detachment.

Yet History, like a big blind statue

[p.15]

is always staring at us.

—

Notes on Toy's History of Fortification[7]

A cold hard night, the wind like steel. Not a night for reading novels or poetry—one would have to have a fireplace, make the place cosy. Better to take advantage of the energy released by a high pressure front & deal with facts.

[pp. 16-18]

[Notes on Toy]

---

7 See *Cahier* XXIV, footnote 3 for bibliographical information on Toy.

Cahier XXV[1]

The continuity of the novel with daily life [10].

The theoretical and aesthetic concerns of Engel's "*Monodromos* period" are further explored in this *cahier*. Discussions about "The Novel" and aesthetics generated the following insights into Engel's ambitions in *Monodromos*: "Without wanting to say 'what is truth?' I want in *Monodromos* to depict but differently— taking on the poets & the sociologists & the painter. But also to admit failure in the end" [1]. She pursued her explorations of French literary theory, reading Butor and Breton, and concluded that the "French have separated the genres too much" [6]. Criticism of the realist tradition in literature attracted her attention. Engel's readings tracked the emergence of the novel that "shows how it produces itself in the middle of reality"; "the novelist is … he who perceives that a structure is showing itself in his surroundings, can make it grow, perfect it, study it until it is legible for all" [10]. "In a great novel," she added, "all the ordinary events become special—the structure integrates all those things which are at first sight unimportant—prosody is interiorised, banality is transfigured by a strong form." In light of these notes, and others on French literary theory, it is ever more clear why Engel struggled so long with the form and shape of *Monodromos*.

[p.1]

August 25\72

Talking with John Bruce about The Novel, aesthetics, etc. Saying I wanted to work out an aesthetic, his saying philosophically speaking an "aesthetic" doesn't apply—anyway artists are no good at explaining what they do. We agreed, however, that style was the exciting thing—I rambled off into nothing, instead of asking him why. But I suppose it's because as a linguist he likes word-constructions—the placement of words so as to suggest new ways of getting at truths.

1 1972, orange notebook, "Marian Engel—Holstein Book" handwritten on cover; 11 pages used.

Without wanting to say "what is truth?" I want in *Monodromos* to depict but differently—taking on the poets & the sociologists & the painters. But also to admit failure in the end.

If one is just lush, one is Pierre Loti.[2]

Try the end of the book as lists, thus,

Concert: Laddie—mountain top, blue evening
Hush of forest
Profile against glimmer of sea
Then the damp wind
Elegances of sound
A dying fall
Women moved to tears—

[p.2]

Chopin himself has stepped
consumptive into their circle.

Driving home with Williamsons—banned from the inner circle & feeling it—winter fog comes down like a great white magic bird. Grouse in the pine forests (are they natural did the Brits bring them?) Road snakes through a hamlet—lights are lit—Jack & Caroline sing Cadet Roussel & the fog lifts.

—Flies fucking on the table as I write. How stupendously unnecessary.

Packing: Damn leg aches in the rain. I would jettison all. Aphroulla [*Monodromos*] (who is above all practical) says: "Costas will make you a crate," which he does, gratis. My pots can be shipped between the legs of van Gogh chairs.

Farewells: All you poets stand & philosophize death.
Today I saw a woman lying
in the corner of her own house
groaning, twisting her hands. Crying
children around her.

---

2 Pierre Loti (1850-1923) was a turn-of-the-century explorer and novelist whose works, e.g., *Aziyadé* (1879) and *Ramuntcho* (1897), are known for their exotic settings.

Her husband, my friend, is impatient.
She has been sent home from the Klinik

[p.3]

There is nothing more that she can do
But pull her dignity around her like a sheet
And die. That's what she's doing now.

Her face is gaunt, her eyes still shine
They [are] dark, dark Irish blue.
She mutters to her daughter. Elbows up
To speak to me, then shakes her head,
Falls back again. Holds out a knuckled hand
What am I to learn from this weakening grip.

"Don't give him drink," a son translates.

In another week she'll be underground.
Here the coffins are coffin shaped
And wear gilt doily paper wreathes.

. ——— .

Dear Max—posthumous—

Why not? Perhaps the Postman too can cross the Styx. Here with a crumb of a brooch you bought me once.

The sea is cold, now. I swam with William Pender & was <u>insulted</u> by its wrath. Big rough cold waves that tear your <u>maillot</u> off.

[p.4]

Afterwards. [illegible] as a kind of dying gesture (the sun sinks I am ready to depart) <u>le comble</u> he took me to meet his <u>gran</u>.

Figurez-vous a six-foot tall albino bloodhound—trampling the thyme in British Oxfords & an ancient much-tucked Chanel suit. Fending off vineyard vipers with a blackthorn stick. A face whiter & deader—liver-marked—than Mrs Pambo's in her coffin. "So you are interested in wine. Have you a palate?"

"No, I smoke too much."

She tests me: I do not fail utterly—I have a gift at least for body if not finesse. She is happy when I compare her dessert wine to Montbazillac—good Montbazillac. We stamp the vineyards. William lopes ahead. "What will become of him?" she asks.

"He will grow wine."
"He says not."
"He is busy growing up."
"He has not the intelligence to be a journalist."
"Could you take him in."
She stamps impatiently, "It is

[p.5]

all here, for him—if he will learn."
"He has to play at being independent."
"He will come to nothing."
"You must play him like a trout upon a line."
"He will marry badly."

- 26. Mary Ann & I sit around talking until the kids stagger to the floor, pleading to go to bed! Her stories of fierce nuns at Assumption are very funny. Good tales pulling W. Ontario together for me.[3]

[p.6]

BUTOR Repertoire II

1. Le Roman & la Poésie.
1. Problem—stopped writing poetry when he started 1st novel—wanted to serve poetic capacity.
Novel more interesting & also he found novelists freighted with poetic intensity—perhaps the novel
was the invention of ancient poetic traditions.
French have separated the genres too much.

2. Example
adj[ective]: poetic is misunderstood w. regard to the novel. What is the ability to transmute a real room to a fictional one if not poetry (quote about room)

3. Glose[?]
Where does it come from—impression must be unified to impress.
made of words
The patterning of detail → intimacy.
If I say landscape is "poetic" it is because I feel "transported" ∴ this is poetry.

3 This is possible early groundwork for *The Glassy Sea*.

[p.7]

When I was
dancing with my
old friend death

Precis &
Appreciation

a farandole
a bagatelle
a jarretelle

---

4 Refus

But to make this trip we have to
go in the company of a character
we accept.
Breton in the <u>Manifeste</u> de S.[4] refuses the trip.

5 Raisons: Breton's opp[osition] to the novel
is one generally used by critics now.

6 Realism is hostile to morality & the intellectual.
It is made of mediocrity, hate, flat sufficiency. It produces work that is ridiculous.
It checks science & arts because it flatters low taste.
It is the life of the lowest common denominator that it describes.
Every novel partakes of it … so we have little novels each with i[t]s own observation. As Valéry said, he could make up an anthology of beginnings of novels about insanity. He said, I'll never begin a novel "La Marquise sortait à 5 heures...."
but then he kept his word.

[p.8]

Breton continues: If the simple information style is almost the only one in novels, that's because authors have small ambitions. Catalogue or description—blandness, the author sends me picture postcards....

Then the Dostoïevsky[5] quote—B[reton] refuses to enter the room. He hasn't time for it or any other.

—

4 André Breton, *Manifeste du surréalisme: poisson soluble* (Paris: Éditions du Sagittaire, 1924).

5 This is the spelling Engel uses throughout the *cahiers* for the author Fyodor Dostoevsky.

At this, all novelists draw back.
B. has chosen a bad example. But he is serious: he wants to have brilliant, not bland, moments.

Prosodie.

—

Def[inition] of poetry
From Lute to Fixture

First poems lute-songs → classic prosody
C19th—juxtaposition of metaphors
& symbols.

Surrealism relies on different juxtapositions. Images the only prosody. Defect: one can't <u>talk</u> about anything. Verse is condemned to obscurity.

Now—we have to invent new languages & secular forms—the classical is dead.

[p.9]

The poetry or the novel

The difference between immediately poetic passages, i.e. where the words are powerfully tied together even if one isolates them, and passages prosaic at first sight which can't reveal all their virtues exc. by continued study ... it is analogous to the difference which separates the work from the crowd of novels, or from everyday life.

That is to say that the novel itself shows how it produces itself in the middle of reality. <u>Novel</u> poetry is capable of explicating itself, of including its own commentary.

In a great novel all the ordinary events become special—the structure integrates all those things which are at first sight unimportant—prosody is interiorised, banality is transfigured by a strong form.

But if structure & banality are separated the book won't pull together.

So the "banality" has to seem singular & singularly important with regard to the other elements—it must make the other elements understandable.

[p.10]

The internal structure must be in communication with reality.

The novelist is ∴ he who perceives that a structure is showing itself in his surroundings, can make it grow, perfect it, study it until it is legible for all.
He hears things around him murmur & leads this murmur to words.

The banality that is the continuity of the novel with daily life, revealing itself as one reads, endowed with meaning, transfiguring itself.

∴ Novel-poetry is that which enables reality to become conscious of itself, criticise itself, transform itself.

[p.11]

Re write—Max's letter.

Edward thinks everything is "good for a giggle."

Cahier XXVI[1]

L'exigence même d'écrire [22].

Cahier XXVI begins and ends with trademark Engel lists: long columns of place names in Prince Edward County and Manitoulin Island; market goods; and flowers—annuals, biennials and perennials. Further instalments of *Monodromos* present an interesting twist in which protagonist Audrey Moore's lover, the English poet Max Magill, visits the Greek island where Audrey has come to bail her ex-husband out of financial straits. In the final published version of the novel, Max never makes this trip; he dies in England before Audrey has a chance to see him again. The draft passage here is a lively read and an intriguing glimpse of the genesis of the novel that caused its author so much work.

As noted earlier, *Monodromos*'s complex evolution was in part due to Engel's extensive excursions into literary theory—particularly French critical theory—during the novel's gestation. The author's explorations continue in this *cahier* with notes on books by Maurice Blanchot and Roland Barthes—names to be added to the lengthening list of French theorists whose work she processed, including Breton, Butor, Mallarmé, Robbe-Grillet and Sarraute.[2] Meanwhile, S.K. Langer's *Philosophy in a New Key: A Study in the Symbolism of Reason, Rite, and Art*[3] was satisfying Engel's lifelong interest in philosophy. She was especially pleased with Langer's thoughts on feelings: "There must be a cognitive element in a mind besides discursive thinking. That must be feeling. [...] FEELINGS HAVE DEFINITE FORMS which become progressively particular." "This," Engel noted, "is a rich theory" [28].

Reading Langer and other thinkers generated more ideas for *Monodromos*. "What I should do is intersperse little case-histories," Engel reflected [18]. "It [the novel] must be more broken—the pieces are too large, bloc-notes scattered. Finish it, then recast. So exciting this book. Gestaltung" [28]. Engel did not waste any time trying out her new ideas. *Cahier* pages 29 to 30 depict the writer and the (self)critic interacting. Following a draft paragraph, Engel bracketed the

1 1972-73, small, gold-yellow notebook, with "Engel" and "Name Game" handwritten on cover; 86 pages used.

2 Engel also read Spanish-language authors such as Borges and Cortázar.

3 S.K. Langer, *Philosophy In a New Key: A Study in the Symbolism of Reason, Rite, and Art* (Cambridge, MA: Harvard University Press, 1942).

observation that her "mind runs ahead," then knowingly commented: "my trouble is I just do Victorian narrative naturally & this, if it is to tell about place, has to be unnatural. What is this book about?"

Another entry of draft fiction in the *cahier* introduces the character Ziggy, a writer returning from abroad "to savour the joys of nationalism" [64]. Ziggy became the protagonist of several short stories.[4] Of interest in this draft is its reference to two previous writing efforts by Engel. Her unpublished novel "Women Travelling Alone" is echoed in the title of Ziggy's (deceased) wife's PhD thesis "On Lady Travellers in the Middle East." The thesis occasioned "some amusing letters from Syria and Lebanon describing adventures with a recalcitrant donkey & a week of virtual imprisonment by a lusty Orthodox Archimandrite named Dionysios in a mostly empty monastery" [67-68].[5] This mirrors Audrey Moore's experiences in *Monodromos.*

Personal entries in this *cahier* record Engel's hospitalization in February 1972 for tubal ligation. "There was a wistful last night when we all talked about having babies," she wrote [12]. The procedure meant a work-slowdown for the author, who had other plans: "It is impossible to work in hospital. There are interruptions & hopes. Concentration's fractured" [12]. In addition to a dream suite,[6] Engel jotted some thoughts about herself ("I am trying to be too much/too many") and about her children ("splaying themselves on rocks like pigeons or gulls—to be loved" [57]).

Finally, and notably, the *cahier* records the beginnings of the Writers' Union of Canada.[7] Some of the early meetings, including one noted in this *cahier* for 8 January 1972, took place in the Engels' living room on Brunswick Avenue in Toronto. The *cahier* also reveals the various names mooted for the future organization,[8] initial thoughts about criteria for membership[9] and the beginnings of a list of members.[10] This is an instance in which the *cahiers* constitute a record of history in the making.

---

4 These include "Home Thoughts from Abroad," "Sublet," "What do Lovers do?" "Break no Hearts this Christmas," "Nationalism," and the stories in the middle section, "Ziggy and Company," of *Inside the Easter Egg* (1975).

5 See *Cahier* V, Introduction and footnote 2 for further information.

6 Pages [50-52] are not reproduced here.

7 As mentioned in the Introduction, the early days and evolution of the Writers' Union of Canada have been detailed in Jennifer Gillard della Casa's MA thesis, "The Author as Activist: Marian Engel and the Writers' Union of Canada," Trent University, 1996.

8 These were "The Canadian Writers Guild, The Canadian Book Writers Union, The Canadian Writers Co-op, Writers Canada, Canadian Professional Writers Union, Quill and Anvil[?], The Burning Pen, the N Writers Union of Canada and Canada Writers" [78].

9 "1 book; 2 good books." "Serious contributions to Canadian Prose Literature Fiction and Belles Lettres Literature" [83].

10 [86-87].

[p.1]

Names:

Prince Edward County

Consecon	Point Petre
Weller Bay	Soup Harbour
North Bay	Wicked Point
Pleasant Bay	Channell Pt
Huyck Bay	Balfour
Wellington	Long Point
Scotch Bonnet	Lighthouse
Yeo Lake	False Ducks
Bloomfield	Timber ls.
Picton	Woodrous
Hillier	Cherry Valley
Spence Lake	Siremanl.

[p.2]

Manitoulin

Points:	Walker	Tamarack	Fanny
Green	Michael	Dutchman	Creighton
Inner Duck	Jenkins	Freer	Dingy
Middle D.	Mutemore		
Girouard	Milton	Sextant	Elizabeth
Blake	Dominion	Mowart	Cunningham
Desert	Gatacre	Jessie	Bayard
Gravel	Preshette	Blackstock	Arthur
	Misery		
	Walkous	Julia	Harold West
Lake Simcoe			Brittomart

[p.3]

Cov. garden market
Orange & Nut Market
Orange & lemon selling in streets

The market

—the old woman
who peddles

Street sellers of Green stuff
Eatables
Halloumopis & Lakmajon Pea soup & Hot Eels
Pickled whelks
Fried fish
Prep of Sheep's Trotters
Street trade— Baked potatoes
Ham sandwiches pumpkin pies

	bread	nuts	halvà
bootmakers	hot gr[een] peas		soujouko
Catsmeat		Sweets	loukoum
Drinkables		Coughdrops	
Coffee stalls		Ices—sweetshops	
Gingerale		Literature, fine arts	
Hot Elder wine		Pallereres	
Milk		Chaunters	
Rice milk—puddings		Lodging houses	
Water carriers Lanuimla		Screevers	
Pastry pumpkin pies		Cutlery	
cadarfi		Spoons at fairs	
Pieman—buns etc		Needles.	
Crumpets		Swag-shops	

[p.4]

After interview with school psychologist:

We would do better if William had more routine & sitting still at home. School is largely 3r's & filler. System requires still sitting.

<u>Bloc notes as in Mayhem</u>

Headings: Street folk
Costermongers
Costermongering mechanics
St[reet] Markets on Sat Nite
Sun a.m. markets.
of Costermonger Habits & amusements
politics
marriage
religion
Uned.[?] state
language
nicknames
education
literature
honesty
Conveyances
Donkeys

Street picture-frames

Capital
Slang weights
& measures
Boys & bunts
Life of lad
Girls
Dress
Diet & Drink
Cries & Rounds
Earnings
Tricks
Street sellers
of fish.

[p.5]

Pachman
Tally-pachman
Conn Salve
Crackers
Cigar Fuzees
Gutta-Parcha Heads
Fly Papers
Cigars
Wash-leathers
eye-glasses
dolls
rat poison

Tea
Petticoat, Rosemary Lanes   markets   Hermes St
2nd Hand clothers.
Dog-finders   Dogs in general
Dog-sellers.
Bird-catchers   sticky sticks
River. Beer-sellers   stalls on the beach
Rags & Bones

[p.6]

Buyers

Rabbit skins.   goatskins
Kitchen grease
Street—Jews
Street finders.
Purse[?] finders
Cigar end finders
Wood-finders
Mudlarks
Dustmen
Scavengers
~~Pachmen~~
~~Tally-Pachmen~~
Crossing sweepers
Rat-killers.
Bug-destroyers
Punch

Countrytrades

screen-weavers
cheese-makers
sweet-making
yoghourt making
spoon-making
lace-making
weaving-alajá
knitting
shepherding
viticulture

	carnival	
Guy Fawkses	people	
Street entertainers		125
Street artists		175
Dollseye makers		150
Cabmen		450

[p.7]

Make a daughter of
an "artist"

Elspeth Grew up
in Angus's room

When Angus was sent
to St Andrews
they moved his
things in with
Allistair & gave
Elspeth his room
No fuss about interior
decorators—

[p.8]

A Quarrel with X [Xanthos in *Monodromos*]:
I was raised on democratic principals & have trouble being humble. (The longer I live the more the sermon on the Mount strikes me as a gloss on the virtues of servility, though as a document & maxim it seems to work)....

Mention King Cophetua & the beggar maid

"If I am Victorian, lady, you are a Tart."
I forbore to say that I was a damn badly paid one.

This grasping things from men....

[p.9]

Historical Architecture—Hugh Braun[11]

[...]

11 Hugh Braun, *Historical Architecture: The Development of Structure and Design* (London: Faber and Faber, 1953).

[p.10]

[Notes on architectural history of Cyprus]

[p.11]

10/2 [1972] It would be interesting to try to explain to the children the rationale of hospital routines—the 1-2-3 of breathing, nourishment, bowels, etc.

Dr D. is probably swish but physically he is terribly like X.—the same allure, enthusiasm. One could see how Aphroulla [in *Monodromos*] would be disgusted by him—he wouldn't put on his charm for her.

[p.12]

14/2 [1972] It is impossible to work in hospital. There are interruptions & hopes. Concentration's fractured. But I have met X & suffered because of him—or perhaps heightened libido is a usual result of the operation. There was a wistful last night when we all talked about having babies.

Stories: lists of generations I II III

Division between N. American & E. European thought probably unbridgeable.

Now, with X: its his hair & his hands—even when she's [Audrey, in *Monodromos*] bored with him as a person (he's basically inaccessible, you can't work your way under his carapace, he's full-grown professional, it's attached) she is obsessed by the thought of his long hands on her body. He makes love with firmness & delicacy, practice, much mental reserve. No desire to be emotional & squashy.
But she finds it trying to wait, anticipate—almost wants to get it over with.

[p.13]

The relationship w X has its silliness—it's superficial—but it satisfies them both.
[...]

[p.14]

Maurice Blanchot: le livre à venir.[12]
Last section: Où va la littérature? vers elle-même, vers son essence qui est la disparition.[13]

---

12 See also *Cahier* XIX [16].

13 Blanchot 285.

Historical proof: Hegel: art is passé
art can no longer carry the need for the
Absolute. Action & real liberty
more NB. Art belongs in a museum or as
a simple aesthetic pleasure.

In a technical world the artist is paid lip-service to, but he is embarrassed because he's not necessary. Apparently art is nothing if it is not supreme.

—

But this historical view is coarse. If art turns on itself it is to have a deeper view. Not in a proud way because when the artist is exalted above ART in a Romantic way, this preference means degradation of art: a shying-away from its real power, a seeking of egotistic compensatory dreams—this happened before 1850 w Novalis & Eichendorff.

[p.15]

With Mallarmé & Cézanne you find no execution of the artist. They were not looking for glory, they were modest & wanted to pursue their research. Mallarmé "Ce n'est pas moi qui parle, c'est le Dieu qui parle en moi"—the poem is independent: not a transcendental creation of a demiurge—not eternity or immutability but the reversal of traditional meanings of "to do"—"to be."

This reversal in art came at a time when man's goals were quite different. But it was not a reaction to "action." It seems that writers & artists had a frivolous retrenchment into subjectivity but Cez[anne] & Mal[larmé] did not seek out the ivory tower as refuges. Art became "realization"—more closely worked, and expressed. The things that go on just before objective & technical progress takes over.

[p.16]

Obscure & difficult research, risky—art, work, truth, language are all put to work. Poet is enemy of THE POET etc. Gives artist a feeling of uncertainty. Art & Lit seem humiliated by the outside world, history. The publicist takes over. The poet is turned back on himself & finds that it is the act of making poems that makes experience possible.

It must be added that historical pressures don't really direct artistic movements or contain an explanation of them. The "modern" movement was created by the revolution of 1848 but Hölderlin a century early was working along the lines of Rilke & Valéry & René Char. Nor do artists ignore history. Even the region of "the absence of time" that artists lead us to is intimately involved in history. But the connections are obscure. So "where is lit going" is a q[uestion] which will get a historical answer which it already mysteriously contains.

[p.17]

Lit[térature] Oeuvre Expérience.

> It is experiment, approach, that excites the artist in going beyond an interesting point. But it is annoying for the non-artist to be inundated with what is essentially a collection of raw material—witness shreds of a false realism. What can we tell of this approach to a region beyond ordinary civilization. Why do we have this authorless writing which would like to pass for books? And isn't it strange that at a moment when books are becoming unimportant <u>literature</u> has become an important activity.

∴ Literature becomes not just a set of forms or an activity—but rather

[p.18]

something enigmatic which one approaches sideways, grasps here & there, by means of researches that have nothing to do with what lit[erature] is <u>essentially</u>, but which seeks to neutralise & reduce, or rather descend, with an elusive movement, into a level where only impartial neutrality speaks.[14]

Non-literature.

Those are the contradictions. Only the work matters—but the work is what takes us to the point of pure inspiration

The book is the important thing: away from genres, rubrics, prose, poetry, novel, eye-witness account, refusing to be categorised. As if it were the "essence" of literature.

But the essence of lit[erature] is to escape definition as essential—which wld stabilise it. Art is always becoming.

To be an artist is to be unsure that there is such a thing as art. Every book looks passionately for a non-book. Every book decides for itself what Lit[erature] is. Every writer answers the question what is LIT[ERATURE]

[p.19]

<u>Looking for Zero</u>

Mallarme divided the territory: useful words—for work, logic, action, which disappear (become transparent) with use || poetic & literary usage, which is not transitory or transparent but seeks to define experience itself. But instead of helping art develop a language, this statement broke down the classic & created in literature a "domaine clos à hauts murs." But

14 Engel's thoughts here generate the following instruction (in the margin at the top of the page) regarding: *Monodromos*: "What I should do is intersperse little case-histories."

Lit. Oeuvre Expérience.

It is experiment, approach, that excites the artist — going beyond an interesting point. But it is annoying for the non-artist to be inundated with what is essentially a collection of raw material — ~~witnesses~~ shreds of a false realism. What can we tell of this approach to a region beyond ordinary civilization. Why do we have this authorless writing which would like to pass for books? And isn't it strange that at a moment when books are becoming unimportant *literature* has become an important activity.

∴ literature becomes not just a set of forms or an activity — but rather

what I should to is intersperse little case-histories.

---

something enigmatic which one approaches sideways, grasps here + there, by means of researches that have nothing to do with what lit. is essentially, but which seeks to neutralise + reduce, or rather descend, with an elusive movement, into a level where only impartial neutrality speaks.

[illegible]/literature.

Those are the contraditions. Only the work matters – but the work is what takes us to the point of pure inspiration

The book is the important thing: away from genres, rubrics, prose, poetry, novel, eye-witness account [illegible] refusing to be categorised As if it were the 'essence' of literature.

But the essence of lit is to escape definition as essential which would stabilise it. Art is always becoming To be an artist is to be unsure that there is such a thing as art. Every book looks passionately for a non-book Every book decides for itself what Lit is. Every writer answers the question what is LIT

though there is a good deal of breaking up, the novel survives as if it contained poison & its own antidote. But it may die of anti-dotes.
But a breaking-up is necessary if literature is to become itself. The artist lives at a tense level where everything is questioned, even the world's horizon. If the world is breaking up, it is

[p.20]

because of the need to question values. Everything is there to be done—but everything is not much when you sit down & write & realise that you have looked into not everything but one period. LIT is perhaps more monotonous than ever before. It is not disunited in its disordered experiments. It is not diversity that makes it dispersed to-day but the nature of its experiments into error, the ungraspable & the irregular.

Language, Style, Writing

L[anguage]: common speech. Always there.
S[tyle]: obscure, linked to blood, instinct, violent profundity (!) density of image, language of solitude where body-preferences speak. It comes from the writer's nature, he does not choose it.
W[riting]: Here lit[erature] begins: an ensemble of rites & ceremonies announcing a literary event. A special rhetoric that announces we [continues on top half of p.21]

[p.21]

Special lit.lang.
now being created in
America

have entered literary space, use of passé simple, for instance.

Barthes—Once, all writers sought to elevate common speech to literature. Now, they seek to make their own special entry thro' language to the temple of Literature—even destroy the temple.
Now that writing is no longer transparent—that literature is a place where one transforms the world—where idols & powers are, every writer must come to grips w this world in his own way & it is a temptation to destroy in order to rebuild—to lead Lit to point zero & then build up something pure. This has silenced many writers.

[p.22]

But the book keeps getting all round & English & jolly—why? Choice of words & of people.
"Nous disons Proust mais nous sentons bien que c'est le tout autre qui

écrit, non pas seulement quelqu'un d'autre, mais l'exigence même d'écrire, une exigence qui se sert du nom de Proust, mais n'exprime pas Proust, qui ne l'exprime qu'en le désappropriant, en le rendant Autre."

The experiment which is literature is a total one: it will not be limited, stabilised, or reduced to a question of language. It is the passion for its own nature. Therefore it must question all forms, all rituals & images, language, conventions of rime [*sic*], number, & story. There are thousands of well-made & badly-made novels today which don't aspire to being literature—not because good or bad. If experiment leads us to zero, it will lead us to the experience of neutralized speech—total impersonality—the spaces in Beckett.

[p.23]

<u>maintaining the impersonality.</u>
letting the <u>content</u> out.

[p.24]

Langer SK Philosophy in a new key.[15]
[...]
Language presents thoughts in a linear way [...] ordinary word order is temporal. Language requires us to string ideas out like washing on a line.

Symbolism [is] the key to epistemology & natural knowledge.
Kant: what can I know = what can I ask
I can ask what language can express.
Anything else <u>is unthinkable</u>.
i.e. emotions, fears, desires
NOT symbols, but symptoms
of inner life.

[Inserted page: Notice of Special Meeting Jan 31 1972—The board of directors of Karma Coop]

[p.25]

metaphysics, poetry ∴ eliminated—they are expressive but not representative—to Wittgenstein, Russell etc.
Well, most metaphysical problems are senseless within the logical framework.
They need to be recast, initial concepts clarified by new forms of knowledge.
Limit is how we think about language
As things stand, nothing that cannot be projected in discursive form is

15 See *Cahier* XXVI, footnote 3.

accessible to the mind—everything beyond this is mysticism, poetry etc—all valueless to K[nowledge].

This assumes that 1) language is [the] only means of articulate tho[ugh]t
2) everything that is not speakable thought is feeling

So long as we regard only sci[entific] & material thought as cognitive of the world—only discursive symbolism as bearer of ideas, "thought" is our only & a narrow intellectual idea.

[p.26]

Without believing in a non-physical world Langer believes there are things in experience outside the grammatical scheme of expression.
Our merest sense experience <u>involves formulation of shards of sense-data</u>. Out of this bedlam we select predominant forms

Sensory appreciation of forms = non-discursive symbolism

Eye & ear have their logic. There is mental life here. "Gestaltung" fills in the gap between <u>perc</u>eption & <u>conception</u>; & allows for devel. of rational forms, symbolic material at a level previously considered pre-rational. Eye & ear make abstractions = "appearance"—patterns of things which we know them. Just as abstract as physics, really, though this field usually dismissed as un-intellectual: full of intuition. Not discursive: visual forms.
Bergson: intuitive K[nowledge] is superior to rational K[nowledge] ∵ It is not mediated by deforming symbols. It is rational but not to be conceived through language.

[p.27]

On meeting people (how to?)
Letters [in *Monodromos*] must have
subjects not just
advance "plot."

i.e. She [Audrey Moore, protagonist of *Monodromos*] doesn't know any Armenian

[...]

[p.28]

[...]
There must be a cognitive element in a mind besides discursive thinking. That must be feeling. How can feelings be conceived of as ingredients of rationality? By their interplay with experience. FEELINGS HAVE DEFINITE FORMS wh[ich] become progressively articulated.
This is a rich theory.

23 March
Talking to Dennis [Lee] about the book.
He didn't understand until I said I was making mosaic. Then I realised that formally what I wrote was leading him down the garden path. It must be more broken—the pieces are too large, bloc-notes scattered. Finish 1st, then recast.
So exciting this book.
<u>Gestaltung</u>

[p.29]

I went back home, to Toronto, to spend 4 miserable yrs finishing a miserable 3-yr degree. I tried everything to make a living & was finally reduced by teaching in a miserable private school (exhausted at the end of the day, failing exams) to saying "what do you really know about?" "Grocery stores" was my conclusion.

Under the cashier's counter, Dostoyevsky [*sic*]. Bagging onions, thinking about Rilke. I finally liberated myself from the idea that being fired is a disgrace. You simply do not tell your Mum. If you have no burning desire except to read, a good job is one that leaves you life over.[16]

[p.30]

(mind runs ahead) My trouble is I just do Victorian narrative naturally & this [*Monodromos*] if it is to tell about <u>place</u> has to be unnatural.
What is this book about?

1) going to new places
2) Islands (not much)
3) Land
4) Knowing novelettish people

Cynical chorus: White Russian twins
(all this can be done by cutouts)

So one has to cut out certain bits of romantic gristle & get on with the images.

→ Feeling that here present outweighs past because past is SO BIG & complicated whereas at home

[pp.31-41]

[Draft of Monodromos]

---

16 Engel comments on this passage of fiction, which draws on her past, on the next page [30]: " → Feeling that here present outweighs past because past is SO BIG & complicated whereas at home […]."

[p.42]

O Max,[17] O Xanthos, O kind Xanthos' wife (intelligent—get to know if possible [?] later) O human race....

Eagle comes in from over the Alps—there is space, silence, polite eagerness & an official party. Max Magill slight, enormously tall (towering over everyone) on the tarmac.

Max on the cover of "Poetry"—1931—with Auden, MacNeice, Spender, Issyvoo—an eery quartet.

Max ambulant. Max official.

She & I [Xanthos's wife and Audrey] are very self -

[p.43]

effacing—I see her eye flicker—turn away—this is business. The British Council out in mohair tweeds; even the French culture [illegible]—the Greek poet who laid Lad instead of me—even Mega Max.

It is superb. My father & mother used to try to explain the Depression away & say "if you're afraid, pretend you're a duchess no matter how your clothes are." They were right.

X's wife beside me, standing tight & proud—a Somebody has come. Anomalies of possession here.

Max, you wouldn't take anything from the queen, would you?

[p.44]

The reception. Yes, she has cards, even for the reception.

"But I can't go, it's such a lousy dress."

She looks ever merry.

"My husband said you were a bohemian, free of such ideas."

———

The Loi—polloi—that means Pall-Mall—The People. ("Istanbul" apparently means STIN POLIS—TO THE TOWN) PIS become Bis easily.

—

Men in business suits. Upholstered women. Mrs Xanthos is the only beauty—Braids around her head—brown delicate features.

[p.45]

Will Max throw his arms around me in front of that awful British Council woman who said we were Beatniks (and it would have been an

17 Max [*Monodromos*] arrives from England.

honour to be a Beatnik?) If he does, what am I & what is Max & what is X's wife?

He is formal with me. He has to be. He mutters tomorrow & takes another drink. Who, concerned with being public today, wouldn't?

X's wife drives me home with a small efficient hoof on the accelerator. "I am so glad I met you. It was a little unsatisfactory tonight but Xanthos was very concerned you should be there."

[p.46]

I feel that I have learned a great deal about marriage.

—

[pp.47-48]

[Draft Monodromos]

[p.49]

[...]

Max ————

"Think of the sun, darling, think of the sun."

[p.50]

Holstein dream Nov. 28/72.

[pp.51-53]

[Dream sequence, followed by drawing of an eye]

[...] [p.54]

28/12/72 Holstein

After reading Quentin Bell's life of V. Woolf[18]

All very much as expect[ed]. One can see how Leonard was impossibly genteel in his account, how the two personalities cut across each other usefully. But what impressed me most was the pace of the life they led—of course she broke down. This is why I have tried to keep ours a relatively non-hectic one. Of course she didn't have to cook & mind children but two or three pets or visitors a day & work between & after—how could she keep her head together!

(I wish this pen would work on encre de Chine—it does sort of).

[p.55]

This is a hard book to write about. Why? Could one write to Quentin Bell?

18 Quentin Bell, the nephew of Leonard and Virginia Woolf, wrote *Virginia Woolf: A Biography* 2 vols. (London: Hogarth, 1972).

The detail is good—better than in some of the other volumes.
[...]

[p.56]

28 Jan
Bounce bounce drinking & talking. How important ego[?] talk is to me, how disgraceful yet—
[...]

[p.57]

[...]

—

I am trying to be too much/too many—

———

Kids splaying themselves on rocks like pigeons or gulls—to be loved

[pp.58-62]

[Draft Monodromos]

[p.63]

I want to cut the novel up in I guess a Godard-ish way—
"One or two things
    I know about them."
Cut loose from conventional plod. [*sic*]

[p.64]

Ziggy,[19] having at last found a ship, embarked, and endured for four days the company of a libidinous lawyer in his stateroom, sailed home down the St Lawrence in style. It was autumn. The rough tree coloured shores reminded him of silk-screened Group of Seven pictures in schools, and then didn't, because they were themselves better. Anticosti loomed with its mysterious appealing memory of geography books and war. It was a brilliant day. He clung to the railing and stared lasciviously at his native shore.

Although he had been listed with several writers who were returning from abroad to savour the joys of nationalism, this was not his motive. He was, like most of his friends, a patriot when it suited him, an opportunist otherwise.

[p.65]

Lord Cookham had sold his gorillas, there was a vacancy in the anthropology department of one of the universities in Toronto, he hated flying—that was why he was standing at the magic railing drinking in the glory of the Fall.

19 This is a draft version of the short story "Nationalism" (*Inside the Easter Egg*).

It made him feel small & childish. He thought of getting off at Quebec City and rushing onto a train to Montreal. But he had flown home to bury his mother, then his father, last year. He stood alone & stalky, blinking like a returning soldier emotionally at the shore coiling past him like a painted pythoness. He was forty.

[p.66]

England had, had not, been good for him. He had lectured at Cambridge, and lived with Ben Spencer-Cookham in a feudal cottage on his grand estate, the gorillas, Susie, Barney, Alice & Tod—romped in Adam drawing rooms, Elizabethan long galleries, and Anglo-Indian arcades. Lady Amande [*sic*] Spencer-Cookham in a specially designed green overall had left her babes squalling in the nursery to drive them wildly round the park in a crested Landrover. Ziggy had studied their social relationships with a view

[p.67]

to helping Spencer-Cookham with a book. He had found their social relationships non-existent, & their personal habits disgusting, though he liked Lord Ben.

His wife had taken advantage of their relative prosperity to finish her PhD, an essay begun many years ago on Lady Travellers in the Middle East. Then, forgetting the retinues that they had travelled with, had attempted to duplicate their feats. This resulted in some amusing letters from Syria & Lebanon describing adventures with a recalcitrant donkey & a week of virtual imprisonment by a lusty Orthodox Archimandrite named Dionysios in a mostly empty

[p.68]

monastery, a renewed interest in architecture on both their parts, and a fatal motor crash in Israel.

He took no pleasure in the fact that she was buried in the promised land. To go to Israel a Jew wishing to bury there a Christian wife was to encounter both religion & politics at their worst.

When he returned to England—empty, genuinely bereaved & cynical—Lady Amanda announced that she was fed up with gorillas. Ben, who had never stuck to anything for more than a year

[p.69]

in his life, agreed that they were tiresome. As Ziggy drove them to London, to the Zoo, the long gallery was already being redecorated with looking-glass & silver paper. The gorillas soiled their crested blazers with ice-lollies and clung to him stickily as he left them, promising to visit them, knowing he would not.

He felt himself funnelled down the St Lawrence, a ghost of aberrations in the past. Aged, silenced, pressed from behind by legions of hopeful adventurers.

When he got to Toronto he took a room in a hotel. Arranged his office & his schedule, and rented a car. Documented the changes in the city since he

[p.70]

had left there, and decided it was improved if you cared about such things. His students, who had seen him on television programmes bought from the BBC, were amazed to find him dull.

Rosebud found him in the St Clair subway station, swooped & scooped. She had remarried, yes, that was all right, but perhaps if he met Aaron's psychiatrist....

Weekend visits with his sons had years ago proved futile. His relationship with them was through birthday presents & sulky thank you letters.

[p.71]

She had made another nest for his boys. Good.

The psychiatrist looked at him coldly. What was he doing here?

"Being a victim," he said bitterly.

"And what kid doesn't have problems at 13?"

"Ziggy's been working with gorillas," said Rosebud.

He stood up & shook himself. He found heavy winter overcoats too much to bear. "I am not married to you any more!" he said. "It is nine years since I was married to you. I am not part of Jake's family. I am part, perhaps, of his complexes & certainly of his heredity, but it is not realistic to have me here. You have seen me—I exist. If I can help Jake, I will take

[p.72]

him out on Sundays. But you wanted those children untainted by me once. I agreed to go, I have gone. Goodbye."

Was it pity or admiration in the psychiatrist's eyes?

He went to the market & stood for a long time staring at the brown crisp carcases of a roasted pig in a butcher's window. He saw a figure behind him in the glass.

"You are thinking," he said slowly separating the words, "racial thoughts," he said.

Alex North laughed & embraced him. "Come for a drink," he said.

[p.73]

Alex's wife Prue was attending her ailing mother in Bermuda. They lived—how un-Canadian, Ziggy thought—in the same white gable where he had left them 5 years ago.

"You look depressed."

"I am."

"I shouldn't wonder."

"Where are you living? I've been trying to get in touch with you."

Ziggy shifted in embarrassment. He had not returned Alex's calls. Why, now he wondered. His oldest friend.

"Listen, this woman I know called Theodora—no, it isn't a plot—has asked me to dinner. She's a marvellous cook. It will take you out of yourself."

[p.74]

Theodora was big and dark, half West Indian, half English. A doctor who taught at medical school, a friend of Prue's. Indeed a marvellous cook. She had a small mustache that outlined her laughter & fine flashing eyes. For the first time in months, Ziggy laughed. And laughed.

At Easter, Jake's psychiatrist asked him to take the boy for a vacation. Ziggy explained that he had no vacation—anyway wasn't that an American word?—The psychiatrist

[p.75]

said that Rosebud's disillusionment had deepened—the bouncy dream of her childhood—to be a brilliant wife & successful mother—punctured, had breathed foul air upon the more sensitive son. There was also the matter of competition with the elder.

Ziggy took an apartment. The child changed schools & took his lunch. He was passive. The principal phoned and said that during a sensitivity session he had grown violent. Ziggy said, "What? Geography?" "No, sensitivity." "Christ," said Ziggy, & grew violent & withdrew the child, who did not need training to be sensitive.

[p.76]

Term finished early in May. Jake had spent most days at the Museum & lunched with Ziggy at Hart House or the Museum. He was quiet, but not more withdrawn than his father. They were whey-coloured invalids together.

Theodora, who did not practice medicine but preached it profitably, had a house in the country. She took them there up a road they had never travelled, & left them for a month.

It was alien, it didn't suit them, living in a house—not a poetic one, just an ordinary farm house in the middle of nowhere, by a barn rented to a taciturn farmer. There was nothing to do until Ziggy found the

[p.77][20]

fishing rods & remembered from somewhere, Hemingway perhaps, a little about fishing. They rose at dawn, put on ex-army balaclavas against the black flies, fished for trout in a kind of canyon that opened out at the back of the property. Stood amongst lacy cedars in general store jeans & rub-

20 Engel included the following in the margin:
Criteria 1) Prose—serious—guidelines for selection

ber boots silent, knee deep in marsh marigolds, feeling, not healed, but occupied, & there were trout, & sometimes they caught them.

Jake found a bird book & learned waxwings from robins & catbirds. Ziggy wrote down the gorillas. They shopped circumspectly in the efficient jumble of the country store & went further afield eventually, using survey maps.

[p.78]

The Canadian Writers Guild
1 The Can Writers Union
2 " " Book-Writers Unions
letter—be Elitist
3 The Can Writers' Co-op
4 Writers Canada
5 C. Professional Writers Union
Quill & Anvil [?]
The Burning Pen
6 The **N** Writers Union of Canada
7 Canada Writers

[p.79]

1
2
3
4—
5
6—
7—

Project Jonah

Not too rigid

Jake was supposed to go to camp. Theodora wanted the house back. They thought of running away. But in Toronto, Jake saw his camp friends at the bus station & scampered to them. (Rosebud was standing sternly by with two labelled suit-cases) and Ziggy remembered his summer course. "Bye Dad," Jake cried. Rosebud cried, Ziggy cried, thinking

[p.80]

Annuals

Ageratum Feb-M indoors ger[minate]: 3-5 days
warmth
Antirrhinum: Feb-M ger: 7 days
warmth
pinch at 3-4 ins
ASTERS RESENT TRANSPLANTINGS
COSMOS: INDOORS—APRIL 5 days
OR SOW OUTDOORS in place 5-10 days
easy.
Delphinium: indoors in March 60 degrees
put in plant-bands
Dianthus: Feb-M. 7 days
or outside May.
Gaillardia. Autumn or May —10-20 days
Hollyhock: Indoors—March 7 days
Iberis: OUTDOORS—resent transplanting
late spring.
Impatiens —Indoors—F-M 14-17 d.
Marigolds —In. April 5 days
Out May 7-10
Petunia. 4-10 days indoors. F-M
do not cover

[p.81]

Scabiosa —March indoors—7 days
warmth.
or outside 10-15 late spring-
Verbena —warmth
March—15 days. Grand flora good
Zinnia —Indoors April—4-7 days
warmth
set out mid May
Don't start too early.
or plant 10 May

Biennials

Hollyhock: March. 7 days. Outdoors 10-15
Bellis March 5-7
Cant. bells. March (early) 14 days
Dianthus B. —Sw. William. Feb. 4-5 days
Digitalis. By 15/3 7-10 days

Fragile
Permanent place by fall.
Much under leaves
Honesty —March 4-5 days
Pansy May or June for next yr.

[p.82]

Perennials

Achillea— F-M 5-7
Hollyhock F-M 7 days
Michaelmas Daisy— FM— 15 days
Delp: Ind—10-17 days
Dianthus—F—M— 4-6 days.
Gaillardia—F-M— 5 days. 12 ins apart
J. Iris—(hill in coldframe—bring in to germinate—14 days. plant in July. (coldframe mid-April.
Lupine: Indoors 3-4 days (Nick)

—

Geranium—15-25 days

[p.83]

Criteria[21] 1 book
2 good books— quality } taste?
value

Serious contributions to Canadian Prose
Literature Fiction and **Belles** Lettres Literature

Appeals

[p.84]

Meeting I 432 Bruns 8 Jan. 8:30 p.m.

[p.85]

Lawyer & Accountant

Mowat:
Co-operative Agency
Owned by us, deals w. publisher
Funding: from better est[ablishment] agents
[Agenting][22]

21 For membership in the proposed Writers' Union.
22 Square brackets appear in the original text.

Graeme

Lorimer

Tests 1) publishing
2) economic?

Austin & Power

[p.86]

Jonathon
Huebsch
Dane Kramer

Bodsworth
Adams
Mowat
Cohen
Garber
Such
Me
Blaise
Wiebe
Engel
Clarke
Findlay
Munro
Gibson
Atwood
Horwood
Lorimer
Laurence
Simpson

Ianhnaru
Faessler
Fielden
Hélène ___.
Carrier
Buckler
MacLennan
Jeann Beattie
Mitchell
Rule
Lampert?
Ross
Richler
Newman
Wright
Bender a Brandis
Watson
Kreisel
Kroetsch

Levine
Hambleton?
Symons

Cahier XXVII[1]

The women had absolute power in our family [21].

At the time of this *cahier* (1973), Engel had undertaken to record her dreams and over thirty pages[2] are devoted to this project. The author's handwriting is large and scrawled, as if executed upon awakening in the night or early morning. This, together with the non sequitur nature typical of dream sequences, makes the recording difficult to follow, and they are not reproduced here.[3] Comments Engel made about her dreams are included, however, together with several personal reflections about herself and about her mother. Of herself, Engel pondered who her heroes were. "The Perfectionists," she speculated, "Proust James Flaubert Balzac J. Austin [*sic*]" [18]—a list that may first seem surprising but then quickly makes sense. All are writers, half of them French, and only one a woman. These ingredients reflect the general context of Engel's aspirations (to be a writer at a time when the profession still seemed dominated by men) and her particular experience (knowledge of French language and culture).

Some sense of social awkwardness or perhaps loneliness seems to underlie Engel's reflection that "perhaps there's a way of being with people I don't know about" [50]. Of her mother the author wondered: "What makes her tick? She's intractable—like me? She imagines what's going to happen & by God it does. Shy, sensitive, imaginative, energetic. Eventually, impulses become needs. She doesn't mean to leave others no freedom but she fills up space" [3]. Captured here is the complexity of both the mother's and the daughter's personalities and their relationship.

With *Cahier* XXVII, Engel's lists expanded to include names of birds.[5] The cahier also develops a portrait of Marshallene in a draft passage that blends

1 1973, lime green Clairefontaine notebook, "Holstein" handwritten on cover; 53 pages used.

2 [14-50].

3 As mentioned in the Introduction, the decision was made to set aside the dream recordings, which became frequent in later *cahiers*, and remain, not untypically, difficult to follow.

4 Mary Elizabeth Passmore, Engel's adoptive mother. This *cahier* also mentions Engel's biological mother [38].

5 This is found on the first page of the *cahier*; entry dated July 25 [1973?].

characters, such as Ruthie, John and Christabel, with the small-town Ontario background envisioned for the unpublished "Lost Heir and Happy Families" and, later, *The Glassy Sea*. An interesting inclusion is a list of books and articles about bears, which seems to anticipate the author's 1976 Governor General award-winning novel. The Writers' Union is mentioned, twice in connection with dreams,[6] and once at the end of the *cahier* where Engel drew up a list of "things to do" in connection with the Union.

[p.1]

July 25		L. St Laurent dies
Flowers:	Elecampane	So did last Rabbit
	Joe-pye	
	Jewelweed	
	alerian → going to seed.	
	Campion →	
	Nightshade	
	Herb Robert→	
	Queen Anne's Lace	
	Black-eyed Susan	
	Chicory	
Birds	Gt Blue Heron	Starlings
	Cedar Waxwing	
	Kingfisher	
	Red-winged blackbird	
	Phoebe	
	Chickadee	
	Swallows	
	Nuthatches	
	Canada Geese	
	Wrens	
	Sparrows	

6 "Dreamt I had a grizzled lover called Philip Hope but I wouldn't sleep w[ith] him so he dropped out of the Union ... to hell w[ith] him I thought lets party"[15]; "WU meeting—going there w[ith] people I get Reg Crombs name all wrong & my friend misses joke" [46].

[p.2]

Serial marriage—vengeance
of women expecting to be cast
off

[p.3]

[...]

What makes her [Engel's mother] tick? She's intractable—like me? She imagines what's going to happen & by God it does. Shy, sensitive, imaginative, energetic. Eventually, impulses become needs. She doesn't mean to leave others no freedom but she fills up space.

[p.4]

Father & Son: Read Hugh Miller, & the Age of Creation[7]

[p.5]

Ethel Macrae's Ruthie holding desperately on to silence. So different from her mother. A pretty thing, mind you, but she couldn't stick university.

–

Oppression of silence untimed.
Ruthie's fundamentalism—where did it come from?

–

The church—

Reprimands: "You wouldn't do a thing like that."

[p.6]

Grotty sex-story. Marshallene, say twice a year, feels some kind of call of the wild & goes off. Gil tries to find out where—or is the framework too old-fashioned?

Describe some kind of nostalgie de la boue—Deep Throat sensation she has—a cry far back in the throat that Gil never elicits—that is the opposite of any sensation civilized or educated men give rise to—intellectual & emotional communion is better to live with but there's the other fierce lowing—the wonky taste of sex in the mouth—the afterwards tousled frowstiness as a relief from over-civilization.

She goes down the 401 & takes an exit, any exit and finds a fair-sized stone Scots town, and walks it,

[p.7]

noting first its river core, its mills & factories, then its market, library & post office, its Victorian extremities (Brampton, Georgetown, Guelph, Kitchener, Galt, Brantford, Woodstock, Paris, Ingersoll) then its tacky suburbs & rickety plaza—overlay of modernity—then waited for night &

7 William J. Cassidy, *Age of Creation* (Toronto: W. Briggs, 1887).

went to the pub in the biggest old hotel—stacked quarters & nickels in front of herself. Then & there it would happen if it was to happen at all.

Plaid shirts, jeans. Enormous fat people. Dwarves (why were there always dwarves?) in leather aprons—

[p.8]

Like—dislike did not come into it. Nor even need. Nor democracy (though in this atmosphere everything genteel was washed away). What was there was strong & not necessarily either virtuous or appealing—it was just that if reality existed the others fell in their place.

Or was it a tarty kind of power she tasted there with beer & musky sex—that she could choose it or not. If I lived somewhere else I'd go where blacks go, she thought. Then no.

The men ___

[p.9]

were always faded & pathetic & long storied & short tailed, shy men, much betrayed by women, (because the others had their own women) and caught in the dulling whirl of this cheapest alcoholism. She stacked quarters lea to grey sheets & filthy walls. Often they would do nothing but lie in her big arms. Afterwards, she was always disgusted. She checked into a motel with a suitcase of books, worked, worried and took showers.

She had a feeling Toby knew what she did.

Once it went differently (John).

"Why?"

"I don't know. A greed for lowness."

"More than that, surely."

"Away from Sundays & velvet dresses. Why, John?"

He shook his head. "Psychology's not my line. They know you, here."

"Who?"

"The barman, Jake."

[p.10]

"They know you, too."

"I've worked here."

"What did they say?"

"There's a good one. Don't know where she comes from, don't know what she wants. Comes twice a year."

"I don't."

"He used to work in Carlstad."

"Christ! I thought he looked familiar."

"He said he didn't know what was in it for me but I was your type."

[p.11]

The idea of incest embarrassed her, but she saw at once that he was grey & waterlogged, a corpse on a sea of fear—her type.

She smoked, sitting on the edge of the bed, staring at him. He blushed. She shook her head. "Tell me about it."

"What."

"Life. Christabel. Anything."

"You know it all."

"We're a pair of zombies."

He shook his head. Zombies. No. We both have other lives: "What do we do, now?"

"Stay a while, I reckon."

[p.12]

He was uncomfortable with her, and silent.

"You wanted the dancer, didn't you?"

"Won't get her. She's an ex-student of mine, name of Verity."

"She's wild—but she looks as if she wants bikers."

"You never get into anything you can't handle?"

"I'm big & tough & old, my lad."

"She thinks he is. She's Tom Farris's daughter. Age 19."

"You stand <u>in loco parentis</u>."

"Fifth in another line."

[p.13]

Pot—could be good but I am messing up the lab. Judy is a schoolteacher who will be good to Char. Or is that sister Bev.

[...]

[pp.14-49]

[Dream recordings]

[p.50]

Sunday
woke thinking
"perhaps there's a
kind of being
with people I
don't know about?"

Then thought about
the good times w
Dad.

[p.51]

Bear

J. Van Wormer, The Black
Bear Book, Caldwell
Idaho, 1974

ARTSCANADA Stones
bones &
Skin

Ritual & Shamanic Art
Dec 1973/ Jan 1974

Pearson, Arthur M
The Northern Interior Gr.
Bear, Ursus Arctos L

Canadian Wildlife
Service Report Series
#34 Inform. Can. 1975

[p.52]

liver	1.00	150	
scallops	2 50		52
wieners	50	75	
steakettes	1.10		
steak			
	——		
Divide writers	3.60		
up & dig	1 50		
up appropriate	—		
opp #'s & in NY	5 10		

make an inventory

$7.60 of writers
by category
produce a list of US arts
organisation int[erested] in
Can[adian] writers

[p.53]

agents' lists
    —which do what
publishers specialising
    in Can books
    or interested

inventory of critics
in order to introduce
writers to them

<u>contacts</u>

Cahier XXVIII[1]

Does it take courage to write? [13]

Monodromos, which had taken up so much time, creative energy and notebook space was published in 1973. The Writers' Union had been created, and Engel had already served as its first chairperson.[2] "Lost Heir & Happy Families" was still in the works, while new story and novel plans were developing for characters such as Marshallene. The first of Engel's two books for children, *Adventure at Moon Bay Towers*, was published in 1974, and the following year, the author produced two more books: her first collection of short stories, *Inside the Easter Egg*, and the short novel, *Joanne: The Last Days of a Modern Marriage*.[3] The mid-1970s were clearly a productive period out of which, as this *cahier* shows, emerged the project around the character William Kingdom Rains.

Introduced earlier in *Cahier* XVIII, Rains was an exemple par excellence of Engel's contention that Ontario social history was a literary goldmine just waiting to be explored in more imaginative and, the author inferred, less boring ways than those of historians. As Engel's abundant notes show, William Kingdom Rains had a fascinating life and career. Born in Wales in 1789—the year the French Revolution began—he served in the Napoleonic Wars. While on duty in the Mediterranean, he met the poet Lord Byron. Stationed in Malta, Rains made up his mind to emigrate to Canada, and randomly chose as his destination St Joseph's Island, which is situated some twenty-five miles from present-day Sault Ste Marie, Ontario. Together with the Doubleday sisters,

1 1974, tan Clairefontaine notebook; 70 pages used.

2 *Monodromos*'s 1973 publication and Engel's term as first chair of the Writers' Union were not unrelated. As a volunteer position, the chairship was thought best held by a writer who had just finished a book rather than by one trying to complete a manuscript.

3 *Joanne* was developed from a CBC radio production that Engel had been invited to create in September 1973. Engel was asked to write a "*fictional* diary—that of a woman whose marriage was dying" (*Joanne*, Preface). The text was read daily for thirteen weeks in four-minute instalments.

Elizabeth and Frances, he settled on the island, to whose population they generously contributed in circumstances some found askance.[4]

Engel's notes on Rains, here and in subsequent *cahiers*,[5] display her tireless research talents. Too lengthy to be reproduced in full, excerpts from her notes have been selected that demonstrate the fascinating way in which Engel adopted Rains's viewpoint, perhaps the better to write his story. The author did this quite deliberately, crossing out the letters "re" in the word "re-embarked," and substituting "we" to create "we embarked" [21]. Thereafter, the pronoun "we" recurs, typically in more "personal" moments, as when Rains expresses his sorrow upon the death, 21 March 1827, of his first-born child Lissa, aged fifteen [35].

Productive and busy as they were, the mid-1970s were a time of personal difficulties for Engel, whose marriage and mental well-being were under stress. Only later did Engel discover that it was also around this time that the disease that would claim her life began to develop. "Thinking about 10 years ago," Engel wrote 20 July 1984 (in *Cahier* XLI, her last one), "my weariness, the bad effect of booze. And it was cancer—but there were no concrete symptoms so I simply blamed myself. I would have" [19]. Ten years earlier, the difficulties seemed to call for psychological as opposed to physical treatment. *Cahier* XXVIII contains the first instalments of notes on meetings with Toronto psychologist John Rich.

Throughout the trials and tribulations of mental or physical health that Engel confronted over the next decade, writing, in its many forms and functions, retained its primacy. Thus, on the very first page of the present *cahier*, as she began psychotherapy, Engel declared: "If I am to spend effort going to Rich, I had better *write about* [emphasis added] what I feel" [1]. "I want to be cured of fear, but not of writing," she added [3]. As if to heighten the importance of writing, several entries in the *cahier* focus on the physical act of putting pen to paper. "Why this funny handwriting?" the author demanded [5]. In answer, she jotted: "To defend myself against ... charges of inconsistency & lousy handwriting" [5]. And then, to underscore the part played by notebooks in all this writing activity, Engel "questioned" her use of them ("No good at notebooks at all," [7]), only to confirm her pleasure in that use: "This is a very funny notebook" [11]; "I like using only a little of the page" [14]. Finally, even as she began to map the tricky terrain of feelings and fears, Engel retained an intellectual

4 See Verduyn, *Lifelines* 194, for Anna Jameson's disapproving mention, in *Winter Studies and Summer Rambles in Canada* (1838), of the Rains's household, in which children were said to have different mothers but the same father.

5 Engel's research also comprised photocopies and other material the author collected on Rains, his times and St Joseph's Island. See, for example, MEA, Box 34 File 4.

and critical perspective: "Maybe I am just the perpetual orphan," she speculated, then quickly—and typically—added: "But how sentimental that sounds! How Dickensian" [4].

[p.1]

If I am to spend effort going to Rich—I had better write about what I feel. First, great relief. Not to be laying one's troubles on someone else but for having help.

Yet what kind of help?

Wit?

I talk about my father to him. But I think the father—even though I loved him—is a symbol with me. Don't know, though. Pen & ink refer back to him—everything.

[p.2]

Don't want to think about that yet.

Rich said "You want me to take away the guilt but not the work." I wonder now if it isn't fear I want him to take away. Or is guilt fear?

I find myself now riddled with pretenses & defences—like the glasses, the uniforms, maybe the fat is a kind of armour too.

Early fear—The house creaking
Loud noises

Rejection, of course, always.

[p.3]

Now I am full of indigestion and tender feelings. I want to stay this way but the world intervenes.

I want to be cured of fear, but not of writing. Wound & bow—shall we discuss that? Perhaps some kind of wound is the spring of excellence but surely it's morbid to look for wounds w excellence.

[p.4]

It eliminates the idea of talent.

(I am drinking vervain[6] & it soothes me.)

(But I also feel ill & shall go to bed soon.)

6 Vervain is an herbal remedy for stomach ailments and nervous disorders.

Fathers—I can turn anything into a father figure. I suppose I have tried that with H. What a burden it is for him.

Maybe I am just a perpetual orphan. But how sentimental that sounds! How Dickensian.

[p.5]

But somewhere something hasn't worked for me. I've pretended I'm OKAY ~~(Why not)~~ (don't be flip & defensive.) But along the way I've lost myself.

Why this funny handwriting?

To defend myself against [...] charges of inconsistency & lousy handwriting.

[p.6]

[...] I have never felt so lost as last fall. Margaret [Laurence] played emergency committee & that was good, drunk as we were—like coming home. Being cared about. Having a mother.

Is it that I haven't felt the P[assmores?]s are real or they laid too heavy a trip on me?

Or is that IT? At all?

> Exhausted. Can't sleep. Can't pee. Liver bad. Watch this.
> Downstairs for toast.

[p.7]

Rather than give everything up.

—

What one wants is to feel blessed enough to relax.

—

June 4 No good at notebook at all. Brysons' after all.
What have I been doing all these years?
Talk about imprisonment—all prisoners have the same reactions—disorientation, resentment etc.

[p.8]

talking, talking—what about?

—

Learning to enjoy, to give oneself guiltlessly to happy fantasy.

Marshallene—little gasps of joy—looking in the mirror—blushing, unable to believe.

After meeting someone "You looked like the cat that swallowed the canary." It wasn't the canary.

[p.9]

The penny has dropped. How genteel I am—the last person to know.

Was there ever such a crying out? Sure. Lots.

I've always thot [*sic*] it scandalous for a mother to screw. And for a writer to make money?

Myths are dangerous.

Dad—"I figure I've got 10 good years left & I'm going to use them"

Bang right, he is.

[p.10]

Don't put all your eggs in 1 basket.

Howard are you there?

[p.11]

This is a very funny notebook.
Play it another way—gasps, sighs, great discomfort on his part. When last seen? MacLennan & noodles (USE). Am I still young & juicy?

<u>Shame</u> (not last year)

20 July [1974] Now—was that a transference or an evasion? Evasion probably—that seems to be what I do best. Change the subject.

What my work says is true, isn't it?

Or is it?

I count a good deal [illegible]—on my

[p.12]

I'm hiding, evading. Yet I really don't have anything to hide.

[Now Will is here, I can't talk to myself.][7]

---

7 Square brackets here, and on next line, are Engel's.

[I can barely talk to myself anyway.]

I have evaded being known—
Today's moral was—"Don't be afraid to be loved," it seems, "or to receive." Wonder if it applies.

Yes, because the theme has been—not hiding—

[p.13]

I want now badly to write about Ruth—how she was afraid. The bones are there in the unfinished story.[8] The significances are in the love affairs—with her mother, with Boris, with Mr Galt, with—? With the land. Cut loose, on this, from Marshallene.

Does it take courage to write?

Creative process—ask about it.

Maybe there is no me—I am not there. H. takes this attitude when talking about feelings.

[p.14]

I like using only a little of the page.

Why has my handwriting changed?

Doing things easily on the surface allows the most tremendous guilt to seep in!

When are presents bribes?

[p.15]

Pafsmore [?]

[p.16]

Major Rains' Diary

Born 1st June 1789 at Milford Haven
Went to Looe Cornwall 1793
Went to Haverford west 1794
Went to London, Deptford 1803
Paper examination as Cadet, Oct 1803
Went to the RMC, Marlow, in Oct 1803

8 "Ruth," in *Inside the Easter Egg*.

" " " R. M. Acad. Woolwich 1 April 1804
Received a commission as 2nd lieut in the Roy Artillery 14th June 1805

—— . ——

Went to Warley in Essex on 28th May 1806.
Promoted to 1st Lieut 1st June 1806.
Marched to Tilbery Fort 24 July 1806
Embarked 28th July 1806.
Disembarked at Ply[mouth] 1st Sept 1806.
Embarked 12 Sept 1806
Sailed 24th Sept 1806
Arrived at Titman(?) 1st Nov 1806.
Sailed 6 Nov. 1806
Arrived at Messina 3 Oct 1806
Sailed 8th
Arrived at Syracuse 13th Oct 1806.
Sailed 15 Dec 1806
Arrived at Malta 16th Dec'1806

[p.17]

Disembarked 19th Oct 1806

Went on Detachment to St Angel 25 Oct 1807
Went back to Quadeas in Valetta 25 April 1808
Went on Detachment to St Angelo 25 Oct 1808
Went to Valetta 1st April 1809

—

Embarked 24th April 1809
Sailed 25th April 1809
Arr at Messina 30 April 1809
Disembarked 1st May 1809

—

Embarked in a Felucca 13th June
Disembarked at In Giovanni in Calabria & marched to Milia heights above Scylla 14th June

[pp.18-42]

[Notes on Rains continued]

[p.43]

20 Dec 1815

In transmitting to you I enclose copy of a letter which has been rec'd from the Under-Sec[retar]y of State for Foreign Affairs stating that the Emp of A[ustria] has been pleased to confer the cross of St Leopold on Lit Rains of the RA in testimony of HM's [His Majesty] approbation of that officer's conduct while [assigned to] the Austrian Army I am directed to express the Master General's desire that you will convey the cross which accompanies it to Lieut Rains—y[our] v[ery] f[aithfully]. signed

IR Chapman

[p.44]

Floating Island
Queen of Puddings
French custard
Rice Flour Blancmange
Plain cookies
Ginger snaps
Raspberry vinegar.

Take ra[spberries] fresh pulled but not too ripe & to ev[ery] q[uar]t of berries put a pint vinegar, let it stand 24 hrs & strain the liquid off without bruising the fruit, pour it on the same quantity of fresh berries & let it remain 24 hrs more. Then strain it off & to every pt of liq add a pound—$^1/_2$ of loaf sugar & boil in preserving pans.

[...]

[pp.45-56]

[Ongoing notes on Rains and descendants; brass rubbings]

[p.57]

Major sold Doubleday's house to pay debts in the Soo
F + E's [Frances and Elizabeth]
Their income was from leases

–

Pioneering

Mrs Beethoven was all right, as her son had taken a timber squaring course in New Jersey, but Mrs Proust was peculiarly attractive to Evening Grosbeak & was followed every where by a flock, or cluster, of them. This was quite a problem until Mrs B invited Mrs P to tea & showed her how to pluck them & roast them on hat pins.

[p.58]

Mrs P's son Marcel always threw away the beaks with disdain.

The two widows and their sons were given land on Whiskey Bay.

[...]As both had inclinations towards the temperance movement, they wished to change the name. Mrs B favoured the name of her favourite poet, Isselotte von Sturne—Drang.

[p.59]

Mrs Proust thought automatically of the Abbé Lautreamont. Since they could not agree they called their sons away from their eternal wood chopping. The boys, stooped now in the shoulders from their work, surveyed the brilliant June water. "Rousseau?" suggested Ludwig feebly, having strained to hear what the business was about.

No, said Marcel, who had, after all, vision. I suggest that this be called after its most pertinacious inhabitants.

So Mosquito Bay it was.

[pp.60-71]

[More notes, and brass rubbings of Rains's family crests and arms]

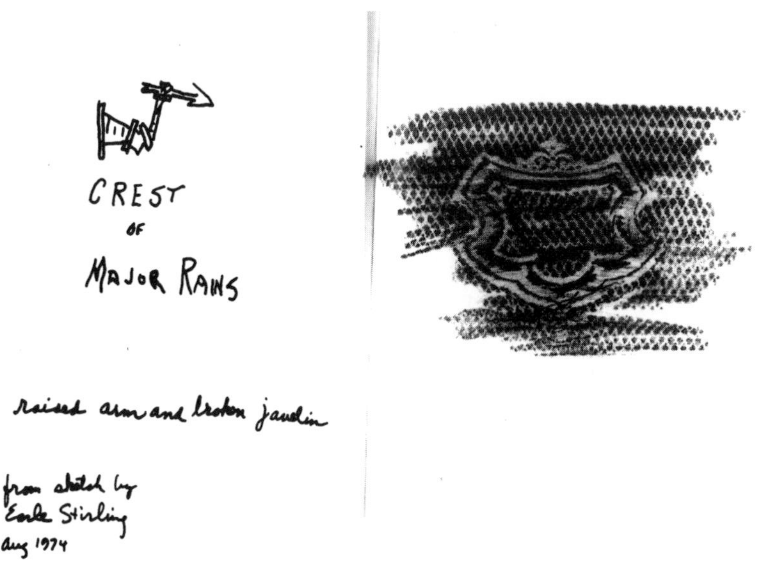

Page 61

Cahier XXIX[1]

5 June 1974 Derby Day.... Thought
Reality was something else [17].

This *cahier* belongs to Engel's "Rains's research" period of the mid-1970s. Over half of its twenty pages is devoted to more notes on "the Major." For the rest, the *cahier* presents lists of "things to do," "back-of-the-envelope" budgets, reflections on Sarnia, references to the Writers' Union, a dream sequence, and thoughts and sketches of Holstein, the Engels' summer place for a brief time.

[p.1]

Things to do—
1. Check CBC reading rates
2. Write [illegible]
[Hugh] Faulkner[2]
[George] Woodcock[3]

Phone Tiff [Timothy Findley][4]
Aubrey—we have to compete with foreign books—how?

Letter to F[rench] C[anadian] writers
Ask Aubrey about Syndicat des Artistes

Huron St School
Mary Lawson

1 1974, notebook with address (N. Tsingos, [Gwendolyn MacEwan's husband] 13 Browning Ave. Toronto 355 Phone 463-8184) on cover; 21 pages used.

2 Member of Parliament from 1965-79, Faulkner held several Cabinet positions. See *Cahier* XXXII, footnote 20 for more details.

3 Woodcock (1912-95) was a Canadian author and essayist. In 1959 he founded the academic journal *Canadian Literature*.

4 Canadian novelist, playwright and short-story writer, Findley is best known for his award-winning book, *The Wars*.

[p.2]

Lorimer
since 1966—increased activity

—

Sarnia—now we know what happens. Undertaker. Astonishingly un-unctuous Irish minister. BK Little—enormous forehead. Newell—John Wayne. School flag. O Donohue—Flowers. Cremation—See burial society material. Put me in a tea caddy in the woods. "Air pollution regulations etc...." Oppression by plastic covers. Sad empty shelves. Cakes without ale—thank goodness.

[p.3]

[...]

Lunch Sun. 6.10	Barrie	
Dinner Sun—	6^{ish} Orillia	
Lunch Mon—Bala—	3:50	
Din B[race]bridge	15 -	
Lunch Tues.		3.50
Hotels	Orillia	$10.^{50}$
Lunch—350	Bbridge	20^{00}
Dinner 15		
Lunch 350		
Dinner 1150	Pembroke	13^{50}
Dinner	Ottawa	22^{50}
Lunch 3.50		

[p.4]

[More budget-keeping; addresses]

[p.5]

U[pper] C[anada] Land Petitions "R" Bundle
16, 1829-31 (RG1.L3, vol 431)

To H[is] E[xcellency] Sir J.C. KCB L. Govt of the Pve [Province] of Upper Can. & M-G Commanding his Majesty's Forces there in ... in council. The Petition of Wm Kingdom Rains Major unattached. Humbly sheweth—that your Petitioner has been in H[is] M[ajesty's] Service 25 years, he has emigrated to this province with his family with the intention of settling on the waste lands of the Crown.

Wherefore your Petitioner humbly prays your Excellency will be pleased to grant him the usual quantity of land accorded to his rank.

and as in
duty bound
(1829-31) will ever pray WK Rains

[p.6]

[Transcription of Deed Paper]

[p.7]

17-34 York 12th Jan
1832

Sir[5]—I have the honor to inform you that I am a resident in the township (of) Thora. I have drawn one thousand acres of land (as a major in the Army) that I have about 50 acres cleared on the lot on which I reside, that there are at present 6 families residing on other parts of my land on clearing leases, who have about 30 more cleared, & this spring there are several more families going on my land on the same tenure. I beg leave further

[p.8]

to state that on several of my lots the road is is already cleared & in some of the others the road runs through an impenetrable swamp—as I am at considerable expence [sic] in clearing land for each of the families who locate themselves on my grant I have to request you will have the goodness to lay this statement before His Ex[cellency] Lt Governor so that he may be pleased to grant me patents for the said land.

[p.9]

as of course I should not wish to expend much more money without having the land Apuru [?](?) to my
family

I have the honour to
be, sir your, ____?____?
WKR [William Kingdom Rains]

—

[...]

[pp.10-14]

[More transcriptions from Rains's documents]

[p.15]

May 23rd Holstein. Today we go to Manitoulin. The valley is alive with birdsong. Today I woke hastily having dreamed I was in Ottawa or somewhere at a big meeting [...]

[pp.16-17]

[Dream sequence]

---

5 On the next page [8], Engel explains in notation that this is E. McMahon, Esquire, writing to his Ex[cellency] The L[ieutenan]t Gov[ernor].

[p.18]

Story—Ruth goes to her mother's cousin's hotel to work for summer.

~~1760~~
1:250 000 5280
62 12
250.000
63,360
1334

[p.19][6]

Northern Cabin—Exposed pine construction, cheap interior wallboard, oil stove, old couch. Mean plastic or gingham curtains (split widths)—everything nice but cheap, socially acceptable—auction dishes, dated (1946 sets maroon, grey, green, green) aluminum pie plate light reflectors. Thumb-latch. Lots of outlets. Corner shelves home carpentry.

[p.20]

[Sketch of a building (Holstein)]

[p.21]

[Drawing accompanied by notation "Sandpoint—water system —possible solution for Holstein"]

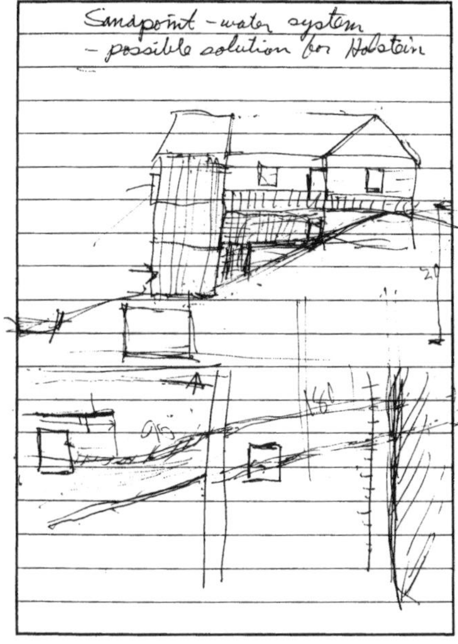

Page 21

6 This page also contains two addresses, one for writer Myrna Kostash, the other for Ted Poole.

Cahier XXX[1]

If this is my Golden Notebook,
I am getting into it a bit late [35].

Of all her notebooks and papers, this is the only *cahier* Engel had embargoed, and then only for a period of five years (until 1988). To all intents and purposes, this was because of the extent and nature of her notes on psychotherapy sessions with John Rich. Some of these are reproduced here and depict Engel at grips with questions flowing from meetings with Rich, as well as questions about the process of psychotherapy itself. Engel examined her "objections to psychoanalysis—telling stories & paying—self-indulgence." She considered psychology to be "an incomplete worldview [...] specialist[s] can't understand some reality" [27]. "As if novelists could!" she immediately quipped [27]. Nevertheless, Engel viewed "making up [a]s more fun than sorting out. Don't want to look at things psychologically—superficial reality too important," she noted [27].

Writing was always on Engel's mind, no matter how deeply her thoughts plunged into personal problems and relationships: "Should have written more," she scolded herself [28]. "Should have written a lot more" [42].

Engel's explorations involved references to the Lady of Shalott and Rapunzel; a sequence about being four feet tall; and a series of thoughts prompted by reading *The Story of O.*[2] about "the question of a lover," and clothing with which to attract or discourage one. These were not easy reflections for Engel, who struggled against feeling "guilty about confiding in anyone" [44].

Buttressing the personal reflections of this cahier are two blocks of fiction. The first is an energetic piece entitled "Bicycle Story" in which forty-year-old Marjorie runs over her elderly mother Irene. Old age has not slowed down Irene and who continues to charge about town on her bicycle. She has darted

1 1974-75, "The embargoed notebook"; the inside cover lists train times to Toronto, and Alice Munro's phone number; 72 pages used.

2 This is the the English title of the translated (by Sabine Estrée) version of *L'Histoire d'O* (1954) by Pauline Reage (pseudonym of Dominique Aury). In "The Unmasking of O," [*The New Yorker* (1 August 1994): 42-50] John St Jorre explores the intriguing story behind this book, its author and various individuals associated with it.

out of a laneway, into the path of an oncoming car, driven by Marjorie, who is distracted by a CBC radio interview with the writer Marshallene. As the police officer handling the accident report suggests to Marjorie, "there's such a thing as a Freudian slip" [2].

The second block of fiction concerns *Monodromos*. Since the novel was published in 1973, and most of the *cahier* contents are from 1974, these entries belong to an earlier period and are evidence once again that Engel moved back and forth between *cahiers*.

[p.1]

Yesterday my whole life rose up & slapped me. I ran over my mother on her bicycle.

Fortunately, I didn't hurt her badly. I ran into Mrs Fern's and telephoned the ambulance, the police, and they took us both to the hospital right away. Buster, who always runs behind her when she's on her bike, bit my arm and almost severed a vein.

It wasn't a nice sensation, finding her lying flat on Cobden Street saying "Child, whatever got into you?" When the police came she said loyally, "Marjorie was always absent-minded."

Everyone was awfully nice about it—they always are in this town unless you're an Eye-talian or an Indian—

[p.2]

and after I was bandaged and she was x-rayed the police asked her if she wanted to lay charges and she looked at me the level way she has, and for a cold minute I thought, it's happening at last, she's going to drown me. Then she said, "No, she's suffered enough." Barney took her back home. She didn't want to stay with us.

I don't know what happened to Buster. She got him when Lucky died. They're both brown-hall-collies, fanatically loyal dogs. I never got on with either of them.

While I was wondering what to do, the policeman said, "There's such a thing as a Freudian slip, you know."

[p.3]

I stared at him. I had never seen him before. He was very fresh faced & intelligent-looking. Policemen in this town have changed. I said right back, "Have you ever seen her, belting out of laneways on that bike?"

He nodded.

"She's a character," I said. "The town wouldn't want to be without her. But she rides like a bat out of hell. We've all always said this would happen to her. I wish to heaven it hadn't been me."

"There's also such a thing as careless driving."

"Don't I know it."

"You're an old family, here, aren't you?"

[p.4]

"Oh, I suppose so. Mother taught Latin at the Collegiate for a total of 36 years. But when you say 'old family' in Rainsville it always implies you're rich. We're not the kind of people streets were named after. My father was a mailman, before the war, and glad of the work as well."

He didn't seem to know what to make of that, so I went on explaining. "In the old days, I mean, when I was a kid, I guess magistrate Warren would have had a soft spot for anyone who was a big paid-up Liberal. But that's all changed. Most of the people are new, now,

[p.5]

and there are a lot more people. I don't even know who the magistrate is & I'd lay you dollars to doughnuts he would know any Anderson from a MacLean or a Heber."

The last name was a mistake. He flinched at it. The Hebers are a big county family. My mother's mother was one: there have been a lot of mediocre Hebers, and a lot of distinguished ones but the one everyone knows about is Byron, who did twenty years in Kingston for robbery with violence, & got out last year & robbed the Bank of Montreal in Godwin.

"Look," I said, "I feel like a damn fool. I am a fool. I'm not trying to get you to let me off."

[p.6]

Because justice in this town has sometimes been odd, but we were all taught carefully in church & school that it would never be corrupt unless we corrupted it.

"I don't really care what you do," I said as he sat there thinking, if that's what he was doing. "It'll mean points off my licence but if I'm going to go around running over my own mother, I shouldn't be driving, should I?"

He shook his head. "I'll give you a lift home," he said. "Your husband took your car."

On the way home he said he had been in Rainsville for 3 years & in some ways it was a strange place. But he wouldn't tell me in what ways.

[p.7]

We live quite far out of town, on the lake. I was surprised to find Barney home ahead of me. "How's Mum?" I asked.

"You've hurt her feelings."

"Oh, if it's only that...."

"I mean, really, seriously...."

"She's hurt mine really seriously before this. Did Buster get back?"

"Yeah, he was there on the verandah, waiting."

"Good. Look, I don't mean to be callous, but she came streaming out of Mrs Fern's lane without looking."

"Were you listening to the radio or anything?"

Damn him for knowing me too well.... "Yes, Marshallene was on the CBC."

[p.8]

"I wish you'd go to Dr Webber, Marjie."

"Right now I'm going to bed. There's a casserole in the oven for when Ian & Charlie come home."

I always go to bed when Barney tells me to go to Dr Webber.

I don't know that I'm not crazy, that's the problem, I mean. They all think I am & one of the signs of being crazy is denying it, isnt it? But Al Webber was at school with me & Barney & Marshallene. So what's the point of going to him?

I've spent a lot of time in bed lately. Maybe I'll spend the rest of my life there, who knows. My early ambition to be the Wyf of Bath has been thwarted by

[p.9]

Barney's persistent loyalty. The day before we got married mother said, "I'll say this for Barney, he'll stick by you," & I, who had thought he'd make a good <u>first</u> husband, went to the altar depressed.

I'm still depressed. This year I'm forty. I was always going to have an interesting colourful life....

Ma says I have no right to brood, I have everything. When she was my age....

But you know, the Depression & the war gave them something real to cope with—not the plastic dragon of prosperous boredom, but survival. Dad was killed in the second year of the war, when I was 7 and Johnny was 5. Mother leapt on her bicycle

[p.10]

and pedalled right down & got her old job back at the Collegiate. That paid better than the post office and she let two bedrooms to warworkers as well, & in her spare time she knit ditty bags and gave music lessons. She kept busy, she said, in order not to brood: she's hyperactive, my mother.

So I think I'll stay in bed now, and do the brooding she ought to have done, and I'll be all right until I hear dear Cousin Marshallene on the radio, and when the police come & get me maybe I'll use what political clout I have (I'm

[p.11]

a secret donor to the NDP) to ask them to bring in a new psychiatrist. I mean, everyone wouldn't think you were crazy to hate Marshallene Osborne, only someone like Al Webber who used to go out with her.

[p.12]

II

Before my father disappeared from the scene into the maw of
(date?) Dieppe—don't ask me the details because I don't know them, what information mother gave us at the time is so militarily unlikely that I've always suspected he met with one of those embarrassing accidents governments disguise with heroic stories—my mother supplemented his meagre soldier salary by giving music lessons and taking in boarders. Which is why I never believe people's accounts of the lyricism of childhood.

My childhood wasn't sordid. We weren't, like Marshallene's family, subject to hunger and harassment, reduced to

[p.13]

bootlegging and gambling (so it was said to make a go of it) we had a decent neat ordinary frame house, three rooms downstairs, four up, two unused forbidden balconies, a pantry with a pump & an iron sink, and a bay window in the dining room. We had a glider on the front porch, a Rochire up on blocks in the garage, and robins that shrieked half the night in the apple tree. In addition we had the enormous bounty of the railway tracks running behind the house, so you could set your watch, if you had one, by the trains. You could play house under the gone-to-seed in the backyard in the summer, and we had the kind of cellar door you could slide down if you'd been allowed to. But there was no rainbarrel. We were small town but there are limits even to that.

[p.14]

HEATING Supplies

$ $ SAVE $SV JOHNSON

[p.15]

Mother was & is a good cook, and what they call a good manager. She could balance ration coupons on the head of a pin & come up with steaming platters of what I now recognize was excellent country food: on Sundays the booming rhetoric of Dr Raeburn was followed by gelatinous skimmings of pig's feet, and servicemen (one from the East, one from the West, one from Ontario) filled the weekending boarders' oak chairs. And Johnny was old enough to take it all in & love it & collect badges. But I was a small weedy child with pale eyes & fair hair & when they were all booming away, I went upstairs & vomited.

[p.16]

I didn't do well in school—I suppose I must have had what they call a learning disability—until I was nine or so, I was always last in everything, and by the time I got over the humiliation, I began to enjoy the distinction.

Not that weakness was tolerated—she'd say "My goodness, child ... and rub olive oil in my weedy colourless hair and stuff cream down me & rub vaseline on my bony skin. But there's also a bitter satisfaction in coming last in the race. You are eventually left alone.

And I needed to be left alone.

[p.17]

You need that very badly if your mother is six feet tall & hyperactive, and your brother takes after her.

We had a healthy, outgoing, churchgoing life. Jesus hung over us, loving & watching. God saw all the little sparrows fall, especially me, who fell everyday, and blackened her mother's eye when she gave her an enema on the bathroom floor, that had Fascinating yellow & brown linoleum on it.

I watched my kids when they were little & they didn't seem to think childhood was hell & nervewrack.

But it is, you know. Adults have big teeth & strong smells & bristly chins to kiss you with as I have now. Mother was good,

[p.18]

I'm convinced of it, from her big black bun through her huge strong arms to her calves ten inches around from bicycling. She was good to us, and kind, and honest and she made sure we did things that were good for us, as she stood over the little children & clapped out $^3/_4$ time to country gardens so when they grew up they could play at parties & be popular.

She sang in the choir in her old university gown on Sundays, she marked papers after we'd gone to bed at night, she kept the house as neat as a pin. And then just as I was getting old

[p.19]

enough to get along with her, to stand equal to her, to learn from her, she adopted Marshallene Heber.

Marshallene's magnificent, everyone says she is—big, like Ma, but colourful with it—those Black Scots looks that are really Black Irish—the Maclean in her winning hand over hand over the red-haired Heber.

But when Millie Heber came around and said "Irene I'm throwing in the sponge, Joey & Lou are overseas, Byron's staying with his father, Lenoir's gone into the wrens[?] & Mona won't come with me, I can't stand it no more, in two years Marshallene'll be old enough to work for her keep,

[p.20]

she's already a big help to me.... I looked at Marshallene & I looked at the little weedy pale-eyed red-headed twins & I prayed.

Marshallene had big breasts already & her hair in rollerbangs and a snood. She wore maroon-coloured lipstick, and Maybelline. Ma called out "Marjie, make some of grandma's orangeade up for Joan & Johnny" and I knew my prayers wouldn't be answered. She wouldn't have two Johnnys in one house.

Marshallene came & stood in the kitchen doorway. She stared at me hard & I dropped the sealer the concentrated orangeade was in. I let her wipe it up.

[p.21]

Little Joan & little Johnny were sent to the Markhams in Montreal. Millie took a job as a gentleman's housekeeper in Kincardine. Byron Heber robbed a bank, which proved, as my mother said, that it wasn't always wrong to leave your husband, and Mona, who stayed home with her Dad on the farm, ran off with an Indian. Ma scrubbed Marshallene up & put her hair in pigtails. Marshallene climbed out the window at night & won $5 singing "The Bells of St Mary's" at talent night at the Imperial the-ay-ter. I thought Ma would kill her. Instead they had a talk. As a direct [continues on p.23]

[p.22]

Now—take the hate out & make it bemusement.

"If mother had understood the poetry she taught she wouldn't have kept on in the United Church."

[p.23]

result, Marshallene became a famous writer.

The meek do not inherit the earth.

Bold as brass, she was, Marshallene, and big as a house. A violation of all mother's principles, who thought the greatest sin was not to be modest and refined. But they got on like a house on fire, like sisters.

In a way, Marshallene was made for her. She had a big body & a sharp mind.

[p.24][3]

No—This didn't work
at all →

Because I would have needed a speaking voice for her & I hadn't invented it.

3 These comments on [24] are directed to the observations on [25] (regarding *Monodromos*).

[p.25]

Rescuing Monodromos
Make a new chapter.
Tell it in pieces to various people.

Bits one might put in:
"How was Rhodes?"
"Gloomily Italianate."

Method:	1st P present tense		
	Journals		
	Lists		
	Incantations		Andreas
Names:	Glafkos	Renos	Peter
	Zenon	Costas	Miltiades
	Spiros	Patrodos	Vasses
	Tassos	Georgios	Stavros

The charm of foreign environments is our superficial relation to them. We can talk about them 2-dimensionally without

[p.26]

[...]
John Rich Day
[...]

[p.27]

Objections to psychoanalysis—telling stories & paying—
self-indulgence.
Psychology as an incomplete worldview.
Truffault film—specialist can't understand some reality.
(As if novelists could!)
Making up is more fun than sorting out. Don't want to look at things psychologically—superficial reality too important—

The grey taste of Ontario—or the Navy Blue!
tacky stores in Yorkville

[p.28]

Techniques of Incarceration

—odd hours
—blame
—teasing
—powerlessness except domestically

—criticism after the action instead of help during.

—

Should have written more

Fear —esp of criticism by a loved one
—of marital quarrels
—of outright rejection
—of being cooped up
(but will coop self.)
—old—of losing children—mostly
—going into strange houses. gone

"Bear With Me"

[p.29]

John Wed Nov 5 [1974]

discussion of my attitude towards Howard's writing leads to discussion of my work—it is inwardlooking [*sic*] and unsharing
I feel at once he is talking about ivory towers [...] and that I am Rapunzel.

Lady of Shalott

What I thought of calling The West China Shore.[4]

So I am the Lady of Shallot and inside me there is a tower & inside the tower there is a box—& whoever tries to tamper with the box is tampering with me.

In that box is me & my writing.

[p.30]

I wonder if Howard isn't trying to get into the box with me & that is why I resent & fear him. Whereas before I thought he was trying to destroy the box. And if JR is trying to open the box, I have to fall in love with him—maybe the dragon who guards the treasure only lets lovers through.

Others who have been near the box—Hugh & Steve
I have gone thro' periods with both of them where I—what?—where I wanted to throw stones at them because I thought

4 This is a title later mooted for *The Glassy Sea*.

[p.31]

they thought what was in the box was not good enough.

On the other hand, with Hugh it was when he wasn't treating me as an equal. With Steve—when I was guilty as hell. But surely grounds for grievance is beside the point. If I want to get free I must find my Childe Roland & what is the treasure & why is there a dragon (or an old witch) & why I have to grovel or dominate, why I am never equal.

[p.32]

What is the difference between
Rapunzel & The Lady of Shalott?

|

Nov 14 [1974] This q[uestion] appears to be too literary—but we did talk about dragons guarding treasure & John said maybe the dragon was acting on old or incomplete orders (parallels[?] with sentry story)—better answer than my feeling there was no treasure.
[...]

[p.33]

The one useful thing that John said was that he could see me sacrificing myself again if I wasn't careful & that made me feel stronger.

—

Came home—Mother insisted on buying a Dom. Store chicken—<u>wouldn't</u> buy one at the Elizabeth—hauled me around like a kid, told me when to do things, I was nearly crazy by the time H came for supper. So drank a lot.
[...]

[p.34]

H [...] said when we married I was so shy I couldn't go into a restaurant alone & look at me now. Agrees the therapy is good & I've grown but wants me to grow back into him. I take this as pressure but know he's being fair—Still, it makes me miserable.

—

[p.35]

14/11/74 If this is my Golden Notebook I am getting into it a bit late.
Better late than never.
[DON'T re-read Lessing now.][5]

5 Square brackets appear in the original text.

This week has been one of the worst.
[...]

[p.36]

[...]
Mother + H + housing hassle = pure madness. I was NOT WELL last night. Wanted to be in John's office. Got H to rub my back.

[p.37]

[...]
I keep trying to hide from feelings. Don't want to see JR with H. But I will because I'm a good girl.

But it makes me feel they ought to get it over with & lock me up.

[p.38]

I will accept H as my <u>keeper</u>.

I feel now I want to go to an asylum. I need asylum. But of course that is not possible—the children, political resp. etc are too valuable, one doesn't leave those things behind. I won't be sent—I <u>won't</u> be driven <u>really</u> mad. (or am I now?)

I feel worse than before I went to JR.
But I was deadening it with drink then.

Or do I just want to be mad in order to escape?
[...]

[p.39]

<u>Sat</u> [...]
My instinct is to flee.
[...]
Yes, yes runaway
runaway
marily merrily
meg merrilies
[Doodles]

[p.40]

Sunday— Mother is gone
Good.

I hated having her peeing & peering in my house. Her oppressive racism. Her dislike of the puppy. Her always fussing about hair & collars. Her telling me what to eat when, how to cook the vegetables. She knows how I feel, I think & I feel sorry for that—but calling me at

Montagneses twice was really almost funny, it was as if it was a plot between her & Charlotte (but it wasn't because Charlotte is emotionally straight) to keep me from boozing it up with the neighbours.

Crumbs!
Fuss
Muss

[p.41]

I shall take every step to prevent myself doing that to my children.

At least I sent Will away. He got out of it.

Down with sentimental loyalties—filial piety. Sometimes you have to **let go**.
But how? Find a way.
DO NOT BE DESTROYED!
[Doodle]

[p.42]

Dec 11. Should have written a lot more.

John to-day—Told him about H being angry about the housekeeping Sat. He said I should have made it clear H had no right to complain. I thought I was pretty good not to burst into tears.

—

Told him about the story "Transformations"[6] —he said, it would be best to have her get herself back before she has a man. "After all, you can't tell what kind of man you want if you don't know who you are."

It reminded me of last week when he said he figured I thought I was four feet tall, except in writing; so I married someone who knew I was 4 feet

[p.43]

tall and when he started to write, I began to crack.

What else this week. We discussed the Library Board[7]—he seemed to think it would be good.
[...]

6 In this short story the protagonist Lou is struggling with depression. Published in Engel's first collection of short stories, *Inside the Easter Egg*, "Transformations" rehearses several ideas and concerns central to *Bear* (whose protagonist also is named Lou). See Verduyn, *Lifelines* 121, for more details.

7 Engel served as a member of the Toronto Library Board, 1975-77.

Booze + Antihistamine: NO!

[p.44]

12/12 [1974]
I do not think I have got this at all straight. What I am learning to do is take mature responsibility for myself & others so that I will not turn on them in the end. But H says the situation is not as bad as I think—we have had good times. I think that is true but off the point.

I wish J would go through the 4 feet tall thing again. If I think I am 4 feet tall & H knows I think I am 4 feet tall, everything is okay until I start to grow. Then he has to keep me 4 feet tall to match **him**.

–

I am still guilty about confiding in anyone.

–

[p.45]

Nor ever chaste except you
ravish me[8]—On finishing the Story of O

Now I think I see.

Public humiliation
Confession
Punishment
Dehumanization
[...]

God no it's deeper than that.

[p.46]

I want to be degraded—on one level. There's a conscious respectability that prevents my going all the way. But my instincts are in conflict with my consciousness & the third element is what H wants.

Let me get it straight now because it works in with the 4 feet tall stuff.
[...]
I am 4 feet tall except in my work.
My work starts making me feel bigger.

[p.47]

[...]
(How my mind flies away now!)
Confession. Writhing. Submission. Sulks.

---

8 The last line of "Holy Sonnet No. 14" by John Donne (1572-1631).

[...]

[p.48]

How to get out of this?

Go where your heart tells you & don't drink too much.
[...]

[p.49]

What was it taught me not to trust my own instinct & rationality.

	Mother	
First	George	—to get their love I had to abase myself,
	Howard	give up my real sexuality, my real rationality.

–

The problem is how did O & I get that way?

–

See now why John is keen on O—or do I see, quite.

–

They go on testing her to see if she'll do anything. She will. She begins by debasing herself for René & then seemingly acquiring a taste for debasement.

[p.50]

She does not debase her self with women; but is pleased to lead them to do it to themselves. So we get pain, self-sacrifice, & instruction, the female virtues [then] led to their logical conclusion—destruction of the self & of other women's selves. She accepts this annihilation probably in order to quash her destructive feelings. When René does not give her the love she wants, she accepts punishment from him because she knows she is guilty. So her feelings towards men must be hostile. She either does not get love from them, or does not get what she calls love (generosity of spirit?) She feels angry

[p.51]

& angry feelings must be punished.

–

What shall I do? How can I get rid of my albatross of guilt?

By realizing that anger is sometimes legitimate & need not be punished. By becoming a person. By taking care of myself.

–

After reading Fear of Flying:[9]
Well: exactly what I'm into & what fun. Adrian's like Rich but only a bit—

9 Erica Jong, *Fear of Flying: A Novel* (New York : Rinehart and Winston, 1973).

[p.52]

Tripping out—a good expression. I really feel happy & free tonight—as if I've understood enough to be a little liberated, as if joy were possible.

Also as if I'm hibernating at last. Alma brought me a marvellous bear. William is trying to wrangle it from me.

Ursine studies. <u>Shardik</u> has a bear-god.

I should get to the bear book now.[10]

[p.53]

[...]

Jan 6 [1975] I feel pushed, harried, haunted. Two weeks together again seem like a year. I lose the same arguments. He is good, he helps more, but he leaves me no space.

Christ he's coming downstairs. I'm tired of him because he <u>never</u> gives up—every treat becomes an imposition. I feel mean & sulky—dream all day of other men, perversely. I am on the other hand cheered by his apartment & helpful!

[p.54]

[...]

(This is not a diary it is an inner record)

[...]

[p.55]

[...]

15 Jan [1975] Add this to the typed bit.[11]

It's late & I still feel mi<u>serable</u> <u>miserable</u>. Lucia[12] tided me over for a while & then I began to feel I was Lucia (again!) and was miserable and then when they all decided they liked Lucia, then I couldn't be Lucia—got <u>out</u>

[p.56]

of the book, enjoyed it. Finished it. And came downstairs to be miserable.

What makes me miserable is that Question

DO YOU REALLY WANT A LOVER?

It **<u>scares</u>** me. Why? He said, <u>feel</u> your way through it when I said I'd think through it.

Why am I scared?

Well, I'm afraid of sex, always have been.

10 *Bear* (1976).

11 This "typed bit" was not included in the notebook.

12 A character in an early version of *Bear*.

I'm tied off—that hurts somewhere.
I'm afraid of failing to get one.
I'm afraid " " with one.
I'm in a funk, in fact, instead of a fuck.
(Howard is being very kind to me & the bitch of it is maybe I still love him, that's why P[ass?] don't want a lover. But I don't want to be the pea-soup princess any more.)

[p.57]

I have all these letters to write, why should I agonise? Maybe I can just go on, take being alive for 20 yrs.

No—no substitutes for the real thing (hold me, hold me, I'm saying inside, but to whom?)

Islands. Why? Isolation? Simplicity.

Clothes. Keerist they make me angry. I like uniforms; clothes that move on the body, [talk to John about breasts, write about breasts][13] Well even Forster couldn't connect.

Mista Kurtz, he dead.

Bridge—river—I wanted to fly out that window tonight. Fly, run, swim. Yet I won't wash my hair
(talk to John.)

[p.58]

John is <u>everything</u> to me now—yet I am impatient also to be free of him.

Christ I went in feeling healthy & superior today & came out chastened & resent it. That's off the subject.

Clothes. Lovers. If clothes get lovers will I change my clothes? They are my skin, I can't change my practical clothes.

But unwillingness to change is the big sin.
[...]

[p.59]

[...]

[p.60]

[...]

What do I feel now? If I don't want a lover, it means I am still proudly apart. But part of me always will be. What is J getting at? For a while he didn't want me to depend on a man—oh, I know—it's more taking-

13 Square brackets appear in the original text.

apart probing. The Q is not why is J being inconsistent, but how far can you go on that thought.

OK I want to be stubbornly myself, but clean, and <u>still</u> have a lover.

[p.61]

[Doodle]

If myself is not a person who has lovers, well I'll try. But decorative plumage—no.

—

Hana—remember the good things said by Hana. It's great, you're doing it, sure it hurts but I never thought you'd have the guts. Good[14]
WE ARE IN OUR PRIME.

But what if what I am saying is look at me,
I'm ugly? (Minn)

[Jan] 16th [1975] Woke at 7 knowing exactly why you couldn't feel things through by drinking—that the distortions were drink created. Why I am in bad shape; I guess because booze masks real feelings & enables one to create a sort of self-pitying hype.

[Page torn out here][15]

[p.62]

[...]
Well, yesterday was quite a trip. It was good to go with it instead of avoid it. Have I learned anything?

1) The idea of lovers hurts because I am
   1) afraid of failure
   2) afraid I really want H.
   3) afraid of not wanting sex.
   4) afraid of being a lesbian
      or a combination of these.

2) The clothing hassle has its origins in the "androgynous" side of me. Also, I do not want to pay for love in costumes, am too proud. I can <u>always</u>

---

14 This word is circled in the original text.

15 This suggests that Engel understood that destroying material is the only real guarantee of privacy. Not to destroy is to allow for readership. See Introduction.

visualize being naked & sex or wearing men's clothes—nothing in between—my usual tendency to extremes emerging extremely.

[p.63]

2 images from adolescence:

1) wearing Dad's shirts 1st time.

2) dressing up naked in silk scarves.

Androgyne by day. Women at night?
Wearing H's clothes, Dads...!

Weight: "You look pregnant"—being chased. Being fattened up.
Problem is this: I can't please others except by being ill—skinny ain't natural to me. H always said this was a rationalization. I am too proud to go around scrimping on food to get love. But being too much over weight is being sloppy.

What I feel good about is that I am returning to a state of vulnerability—I'm becoming emotionally open as I was at 13.

[p.64]

But—do I really want a lover? What does that question mean. Do I really want to open up? Do I want to share—what?
I want to get laid.
I want to be loved.
I do not want to be anyone's property again.
But that big hairy bear-man I imagine will want me as property.

–

Reading this over: I am still stubborn, I don't give in, co-operate. I am like my children, I want everything BUT ON MY OWN TERMS.
I constantly long to lie in bed or in warm water.

[p.65]

[...]
<u>Splendid</u> agonies represented here. But they all turned out to be phony—no, not phony, unnecessary in the end. No, probably necessary.

They don't seem that in retrospect.
When I read this in JR's office

[p.66]

[...]

[p.67]

"Stay away from the mailboxes, then."

"I'm worried about those 2 boys. They should be trotting along to school with bookbags on their back."

"My God—did you hear that Eddie.... She's worried about his boys. Audrey, you are incredibly naive."

"I'm naive but I'm not stupid. They come down hard on boys here. And back."

[p.69][16]

"Laddie, Aphroulla says the police are interested in the boys."

"You're going, it's not your business any more."
"I know. I just thought....
a word to the wise."
He tilts back his chair &
fiddles with the edge of the table. For a moment he is relaxed, expansive. "It's been a good year," he says, "a vintage year. You came, & solved my problems. And now you're going away."

[p.70]

"God, I hate to see you throw your life down the drain."

"No, you don't. You think you do, but you don't. My destruction is your drama."

"Is that why you wire me when you're in a fix—so you can have a witness?"

"I think so—yes. Everyone needs a witness."

"This time I think you found the price too high."

"Oh—for me, the price is always too high ... but I have to have my drama. I'm an addict—first act, Lord Fauntleroy at the

[p.68]

keyboard, second, the little bride and groom...."

"So you see your whole life as a sham production for other people, that's what makes you bitter?"

"I give it to you to see it that way. It's my farewell present."

"And if I say it's not good enough."

"It's all the present you get."

---

16 The page sequence is disrupted here in order to reconstruct the flow of the draft passage from *Monodromos* that comprises [67-72]. In writing this passage, Engel jumped around in the notebook pages.

"I'm going to miss the rest of the play, Laddie. Don't doctor the last act for me. Wherever you look, I won't be."

[p.71]

Conversation with Laddie?
Long piece
Interruption by Roger
Argument
Goodbye
We've learned so many foreign words.

——— · ——— · ——— · ——— · ———

"Aphroulla says the police are interested in the boys."
He's half drunk and I've moved a little too close to him—we are crammed around the big table—and close—I can see the pettish little lines around his mouth. I don't know how to think of him.

[p.72]

[...]

Jane Rule
write to
read

Cahier XXXI[1]

What of sinlessness? [3]

Cahier XXXI consists entirely of notes on books Engel was reading in early 1976. Their primary significance, and the purpose of reproducing a few sample pages here, is to identify some of the sources of the author's "post-Bear" novel, *The Glassy Sea*. Secondarily, the notes put 1976, the year Engel won the Governor General's Award for *Bear*, on the author's *cahier* "map." Not many notebooks emerged from the vicissitudinal mid-1970s period of Engel's life. Her visits with John Rich may explain in part why she wrote less extensively in *cahiers*, though these visits were themselves the subject of numerous entries. The psychic energy expended by her work with Rich, by the completion and public success of *Bear*, and by life's daily demands raising a family, were also factors. Even so, Engel was already onto another novel, as this *cahier* illustrates. Notes explore the "Mary versus the Martha" view of life, and a Pelagian versus an Augustinian understanding of perfection. These ideas were integral to *The Glassy Sea*. Engel was keenly interested in concepts of perfection and imperfection. Her notes were an attempt to understand how they were handled within Puritan, Christian, Protestant, even heretical frameworks. They were also preparation for the expression of her own views on the subject, in which the protagonist of *The Glassy Sea* proved helpful.

[p.1]

VI Perfectibility within [Chris]tianity

Early fathers interpreted Bible stories for practical & political reasons.
But literal interpretations of stories like that of the rich young man held out hope of perfection
→ extreme disciplines. "Counsels of perfection" laid out paths of

1 1976, "Canada Exercise Book—Cahier d'exercices" Notebook, "The Perfectibility of Man" and "M. Engel, Feb '76" written on cover; 20 pages used.

poverty, chastity & self-abnegation.
Desert anchorites followed this path as Church got more worldly. So did Pelagius, whose heresy threatened to drive landowners out of the church. Anchorites fled both money & sex (the world & the flesh.)
Ascetism not new—goes back to gen. tendencies of Jodism [?] & Essenes; Pythagoreans; Cynics; Stoics; Platonists—gen belief that way of the spirit lay through the suppression of the passions.
Restraint—Gnosticism—where body
was work of Evil One.
Anchorite & monk sought sunless perfection by renouncing the world. Any secular passion subtracted from one's love of God.

[p.2]

St Basil, after years of education, sold his goods & took up a wanderer's life C4 visiting Desert fathers who lived in "alien flesh." That flesh is alien to all ascetics is the NB point.

He decided that monasteries were superior to hermitages—more discipline, less arrogance.

John Cassion sugg[ested] monasteries as a first step e.g. Jerome's visions could first have been purged in a collectivity. Asceticism [as] rung on ladder to "purity of mind."

	Mary view	vs	Martha view
	|		|
ascetic view ⟨	contemplation of God		good works

Love of neighbour vs love of God.
In more extreme forms of Anchoritism it goes.
Human beings are to be loved only as a reflection of God's glory. A soul intent on perfection must be alone.
Anchoritism carries egocentric X[Chris]tianity to an extreme.
Monasticism gave opportunity to exercise virtues & charity.

[pp.3-10]

[Ongoing notes on various religious perspectives on human (im)perfection]

[p.11]

[...]
All mainstream X[Chris]tians have believed
only progress towards perfection
is possible.

Pelagius	Augustine
perfection by free will	perfection by Grace (?)

C)17 Perfection—by
intervention of fellow men
"civic humanists"
[accounting]

[p.12]

unbearable

[p.13]

Anson: The call of the cloister

Schedule at Littlemore

5 am	Matins & Lauds	
6:30	Breakfast	W retreat
7	Prime	Advent
7[30]	Study etc w Terce	Lent
10	Morning Prayers—Chapel	
11	Study etc Sext.	
2pm	Recreation	
3	Evng prayers—Chapel	
3[45]	Recreation	
4[30]	Study etc w None	
6	Supper	
6[30]	Recreation	
9[30]	Vespers	
10	Compline	
10[15]	Sleep	

[pp.14-18]

[Ongoing notes]

[p.19]
[...]

Deaconess:	"a woman officially charged w certain
chaperonage	functions in the church." Apostolic
welfare	trad'n
Sisterhood:	"a community of women living[2]
	a single life, in obedience
	to a fixed rule, with a

2 In *The Glassy Sea*, the protagonist Rita Heber joins a community of religious women, "The Eglantines." Later in life she helps form an alternative community of women.

	common fund, seeking to advance
vows?	the glory of God by the culture
vocations?	of their spiritual life, in closest
Superior?	union with X, and engaged in
Spiritual Superior?	Prayer or in works of mercy."
[...]	

[p.20]

[...]

Cahier XXXII[1]

Most literature is middle-class and
most personae are oneself [12].

In June 1976, with the help of proceeds from her Governor General's Award for *Bear*, Engel took her children to Prince Edward Island to spend some time by the sea and away from the city. She rented a house from a friend, Libby Oughton,[2] set up her typewriter and began two writing projects: her next novel, *The Glassy Sea*, and "Bear Summer," the typescript that constitutes *Cahier* XXXII.

As a first-page entry explains, towards the summer of 1976 Engel "had to get out of Toronto, all that worry about what reality was, what I should do with my life, whom to trust, whom to fear.... Bear Summer is for unwinding. Letting go. Living in the moment, not time past or future.... Being with my kids. Deciding. In this domestic landscape, learning how to be. Not choosing not to be." As noted earlier,[3] the 1970s were intensely productive but also frequently turbulent years for Engel. During them, she published three novels, two children's books, a collection of short stories and the short novel *Joanne*. She served as first chair of the Writers' Union of Canada and as a trustee for the Toronto Public Library, and led the lobby for Public Lending Rights for authors. These administrative and political responsibilities were in addition to those involved in raising a family and earning a living.

Though not without their rewards, the trials and triumphs of Engel's life in the 1970s took their toll. Thus even as she achieved recognition for her writing, Engel's health deteriorated and her marriage broke down. The author separated from her husband in 1975 and the couple divorced in 1977.

"Bear Summer" was an attempt at respite in what Engel herself called "a very crazy time"[4] in her life. "I came here to ... what? Unwind. Stop naming things. Suddenly I knew I was going really crazy, not connecting at all," Engel admitted [1]. As ever, writing played an important role in the effort towards mental, physical and moral equilibrium, and *Cahier* XXXII is replete with reflections

1 1976, "Bear Summer Notebook"; 26 typescript pages.

2 Author and publisher of Gynergy Press.

3 See Introduction to *Cahier* X; also Verduyn, *Lifelines* 119-24 and 143-46.

4 Interview with Carroll Klein, *Room of One's Own*.

on the nature of the art. Or rather craft, as Engel explained was her preferred conception of the activity of writing [11]. Like preceding *cahiers*, the present one contains comments on the work of other writers in addition to Engel's own. For example, in response to B.S. Johnson, she wrote: "I'm tired of fireworks, farting away about form. Want to do something transparent now.... Want to be a person in a landscape" [4]. This was the recipe for *The Glassy Sea*, the early stages of which can be traced in this *cahier*. At the time, the future Rita Heber was known as Imelda, though Engel had already determined that her protagonist would be a modern-day nun. Thus Engel's novel about a woman who has sexual relations with a bear was followed by the story of a woman who joins a convent.

Engel's "Bear Summer" *cahier* is one of the richest for reflections about writing. Whole pages consider the theory and practice of the novel and the work of other writers. Although the *cahier*'s form differs in that it consists of loose, typed pages, it performed the same function as previous notebook-style *cahiers*. Moreover, after 1976 Engel used a typewriter more often for her notebook writing. The results ranged from single sheets to dozens of typed pages. In terms of the notebooks' evolution, single sheets are challenging to place, though they often exhibit thematic or subject-oriented links. This is especially true of typed reflections on various hospitalizations Engel experienced for treatment of cancer in the first half of the 1980s, and of the increasing number of autobiographical sketches she produced during the same period. These developments still lay far ahead of Engel in the summer of 1976—"Bear Summer" as she dubbed it—when her immediate concern was to recover from "winter's craven misery" [6] and find some "paix, calme, [et] volupte"[5] [7] in life again.

[p.1]

BEAR SUMMER

The big bird is at it again, the one I have to call windhover. Up there wheeling on the wind, crying plaintively. He annoys me because I can't see him and size him; name him. He's as big as a duck up there. Floats and soars, make this whiffling sound. I want to know who he is and how he makes the sound. It's as if the wind makes it. Sad sound, too, plaintive, though he doesn't mean it.

5 This almost certainly is a reference to Charles Baudelaire's poem "L'Invitation au Voyage," *Les Fleurs du mal* (Paris: Poulet-Malassis, 1857), no doubt known to Engel through her study of French literature. The poem's refrain reads: "Là, tout n'est qu'ordre et beauté,/ Luxe, calme et volupté."

Tide's coming in. The wonky bird soars over the estuary. Must be late in the day. Watch stopped. Char's just getting up. Must be a duck. A whiffling duck.

I came here to ... what, unwind. Stop naming things. Suddenly knew I was going really crazy, not connecting at all. Had to get out of Toronto, all that worry about what reality was, what I should [d]o with my life, whom to trust, whom to fear. Couldn't figure out why I was unhappy since I had everything I wanted, more than ever in my life. Well, everything but one thing, and that one thing can't be bought. But the present seemed to be getting away from me again, so with help from my friends I got it together to shove off. To Libby's house. On the Island.

Reality is that coloured stuff out there in front of you. An actress told me that.
Bear Summer. Calling it that because Bear bought me it. Bear summer is for unwinding. Letting go. Living in the moment, not time past or future. Watching that marsh grass sway, identifying that bird. Being with my kids. Deciding. In this domestic landscape, learning how to be. Not choosing not to be.
That coloured stuff out there is green, green. Gray pink road. Red land. Silver estuary. But mostly green. With birds.
And where are my birds?

[p.2]

FOREGROUND

The goofy bird isn't there this morning and I miss him. Woke at six, came out soon after to the rising sun (already round, well-risen) sparrows in the eaves, swallows, a flight of duck, snipe. They sit on posts and cluck mournfully. In five minutes I was again irritated. Still can't get along without a hair shirt.

Thought, when I saw two swallows on a wire, what's it like to be a bird? Never wondered that before.

Also, the difference between fathering and mothering bothers me. Women's Lib to the contrary, men and women are very different. Think of that this summer.

Lots of time.

Hazan[6] says this place was a big one until the big ferry was put in at Borden in 1917. The railway came down here; then you got an ice boat across to New Brunswick: six men on either side, pulling. There was a

6 A local resident.

doctor who sold bottles of gin for the crossing. Hazan knows everything and fixes everything and lives for the return of Libby.

Kids are fascinated by Libby. Libby's house. Who's Libby? They've smoothed out amazingly in two days ... all of us have. The hysterical competitiveness is gone. They get up late and mooch off to the tide flats. Will's [...] helping Hazan get the oil stove going; also dug a great post hole for the mail box. Is cooking. Never seen him so cool. Big row over beds the first night: they took the two best rooms, leaving me a floor-mattress. They were insulted when outranked but I pointed out they wouldn't get nagged for housekeeping and usually slept on the floor at home anyway. Will sat up last night reading the shore life book, fascinated. Charlotte is writing a journal. Can't miss a night or it won't be true. I never seem to SEE them at home.

Not eight yet. HOT. Estuary changes like slow television. Hip-roofed barns across the other side, sheltered by fir trees. The wind must be awful in winter.

The marsh grass shines in the sun. No wind, today.

[p.3]

I don't want to be clever or original. Want to lope along, seeing, restoring myself.

Two crows, a red-wing, snipe, sparrow, starling, swallows, and my god the goofy bird whiffling again. Invisible so far. What is it? Up there so high. Flies like a duck, like a bee. Sound must be wings. Should go down there and spy. Hate to leave the house. Story of my life. Why I'm bushed: hate to leave, always have to.

Nearly 8. Not a sign of life in the village.

Wary of first glows. Will I be bored? When will I be bored?

Beer for breakfast. Very immoral.

John Orsmsby, the man who opened the house. Young, 21, master printer. The certainty of the young. Horror of the way he found the place: the ravages of mice. Carcases in the foam rubber mattresses, well, I must say. He worked his ass off. Must make gestures towards maintenance after this aft so he won't think it wasn't worth it.

He thinks we'll be bushed in a week but it isn't Holstein[7] and Hazan got the stove and hot water going very fast. Wants to take me to fish lobster.

This is all I felt shut off from on Marchmount: light and green and air.

Ramble, don't I? Tired of order. Processions of words.

---

7 This was a summer place the Engels had for a brief period.

Snipe on a wretched little fir in the marsh.
Bill gleaming in the sun as he calls. Bumblebee in the virginia creeper.

First cars about 8.15. Written enough.

[p.4]

Paying for being up at 6: dead tired at 4 and drinking yellow pi'son. Liquor store in Charlottetown had a sale on Pernod of all things. Slept off the breakfast beer nicely, got up, met the mailman, got word from the outside world.

[...]

Long morning. Somewhere in there I thought a lot about writing [...] reading FAR Tortuga[8] and a book of B.S. Johnson's.[9] I thought I'm too tired of fireworks, farting away about form. Want to do something transparent now. Still full of nostalgia for the kingdom but think it can be found in foreground, not psychological excavation. But not social realism either. Not any ism.

Want to be a person in a landscape. This place reminds

[p.5]

me of that Wyeth painting, Christina's world:[10] broad and windswept and green, magical in its sternness. Yet still that kind of painting fails to please me as much as other visions: Milne's, for instance, or sometimes Emily Carr's.

Why the long talks with Pat about phenomenology are good. There's something in surfaces. Because if you neglect them the world disappears. That doesn't make realism the greatest kind of art, but I think you reach the Kingdom through surfaces. If you could put into words the exact quality of light falling on the wind-blown grass all you'd be is a photographer; or perhaps if you add to the fifty shades of green in the grass the changing tide-moved estuary and the birds (afternoon birds different from morning birds, heron at low tide and the thing that is either a goof or a windhover, maybe both...) perhaps there's something there.

As my practice gets better my theory gets worse. Which is as it should be but hard on one's pretensions. Intellectual, social etc.

---

8 Peter Matthiessen, *Far Tortuga* (New York: Random House, 1975).

9 Bryan Stanley Johnson (1933-73), British novelist, author of *Albert Angelo* (1964), *Trawl* (1966), *The Unfortunates* (1969), *House Mother Normal* (1971) and *Christy Malry's Own Double-Entry* (1973).

10 *Christina's World*, (1948, tempera on panel, 32 ¼"x 47 ¾," Museum of Modern Art, New York City) is a work by American painter Andrew Wyeth (1917-), known for his portraits and austere rural landscapes.

The people I like best, like Margaret L[aurence] and Hilda Woolnough don't seem to have any pretensions at all. They just are. An enviable stage to have reached. Adele [Wiseman], too.

That snipe on the post, moaning or rejoicing is not trying to be a writer; and he doesn't go walking with a bird book. He doesn't suffer from a lust to name things. Or have hot baths, central heating, and friends. Maybe he knows in his heart that the worst thing in the world is freedom.

Except for imprisonment.

Of course the recently unmarried go on this identity search after years of defining themselves in terms of others' aims. Wouldn't it be better to do something funny?

Colour is polaroid now. Evening. Like hymns. Will go and play some on the organ. Work up the Bach.

[p.6]

Such a long, long day. Had a drink. Slept. Got up. Sunset. Was reading B S Johnson in the kitchen. Heard a strange noise which I was sure was a London crowd—the loony goony birds, two of them, soaring and whiffling, having a ball with the mosquitoes. Miles higher up than swallows. Still ducklike, still unidentifiable. Kingfishers, maybe. Perhaps Graeme will know. Or I'll call 'em Ceix & Alcyon and let them go.

Kids with John Ormsby, God knows where.

Saturday

Writing pure and simply for its own sake.

Up betimes, Mr Pepys and the birds were all playing: crows cawing after blackbirds, snipe snipping and the goofy windhovers wheeling. Found the other bird book, Libby's, and finally found that both goldeneye and pintail whistle with their wings. Suspect goldeneye as they have blunt tails. They wheel on the wind and appear to enjoy it. Wish I could. They're always way up by the sun.

Wonder sometimes when boredom will set in. [...]

Damn stove is out of commission again. Must find Hazan.

Gorgeous hot day. Feel the sun soaks all winter's craven misery out of me.

Johnson's novel is great fun. Bit too much like Charlie & the Chocolate Factory, if the poor dead sod knew it. But again, it's farting around and I hunger for something different now. How desperate all the writers are, looking for new ways of saying old things.

Green eye shade, anyone?

Got to have a go at the holes in that stove. Might be plugged. Filthy job. Courage, ma.

No luck.
Goatsbeard and yarrow and daisies and vetch.
Where will it all end.
Postman just stopped by in a red volks. Didn't need to give John my letter to take to Charlottetown. Too late now.

[p.7]

Ha. Knew it couldn't last. One of those days with not enough head space in it.

Is it because I defined the whirly bird?

(Title: Defining the whirly bird)

[...] But the truth is that unless I spend most of the morning in that fantasy I call thinking I can't get through the day at all. My gregariousness is limited to outbursts and thumps. When too many people are around I cope with it by getting drunk, or else I can't bear to be alone at all.
Christ, what a bad character: to be gregarious and solitary by turns. How confusing for the people one lives with. How writerly.

How lucky to have had some big think-spaces in the week.

Okay, unpick a few rows. What were you going to knit about Wiring ... no, writing. Place. Men and women.

Aren't I here to decide whom I want to live with where, and what I want to write?

Eliminate the first. I don't get to decide that.
Where I want to live, how, and what I want to write.
They're all tied in.

I always say I want paix, calme, volupte. Don't often get it. Nor does anyone else and in fact as a steady diet it would be boring. On the other hand paix is a necessity and there's none at the moment in Toronto. Good. You're getting on, girl.

On the other hand, a steady diet of meadowsweet? And foul winter fog?

[p.8]

What do you do about things you don't want to remember when you've said you're going to be honest?

[...]

[p.9]

Monday

A grey day, probably less chilly than it looks. I woke at about 6 and went back to sleep. Now I'm up but filled with lassitude. It strikes me I've been sleeping most of the time since about Feb. and my protests about over-activity are hypocritical. Maybe thinking IS exhausting. I feel so limp and exhausted all the time. Drink with its artificial stimulation gets me going but I jump as high as a salmon on it. What I suspect is that after the last 2 years I am kind of permanently exhausted. Anyway I can't tear around here thank God.

Finished BS Johnson's novel last night. Very funny and Beatle-ish but also tired. Polishing off your hero because you're tired of him won't do. But maybe he, like his hero, got cancer. The dead can be forgiven.

Thought about money when I first woke. T's honest stuff. I'm often blamed for liking it too much but I find it a more honest currency than emotion. As children, we were conscious of a lack of it [...]. But I think the depression must have been depressing for people like Mum and Dad because their standards were middle class and they moved such a lot which must have cost. Helen and I grew up downright allergic to sides-to-middle bed sheets and ratty towels, which were the things that allowed us to have glorious summers. Then, we were always blamed for overspending no matter how little we spent – there was some strange thinking there. When I spend ANYTHING I feel guilty now so I'd rather spend a 1000 than 100. I'm glad of some of the things I've bought, though: things that feel nice on our skin, like good sheets and sleeping bags and towels. I wish I could manage to keep nice underwear—the horror of handmedown pants is still with me—but indigo jeans in the wash have turned my whites grey and my beiges unspeakable. Surely comfort comes just after survival.

Schoolbus just came roaring down the road. Starling on the shed roof has a beard flying in the wind.

Free as a bird: nonsense It's probably hard work being a bird except in mosquito-breeding season when the meals come easy. Fancy being a young bird hungry but scared of flying.

It isn't cold outside. Just looks cold. High tide at 9 am which means little swimming. The whiffle bird is whiffling but the other birds are pretty quiet. The estuary is shining grey. Sun breaks through the clouds but to the north everything's black: storm coming from the Gulf.

[p.10]

Never forget your geography. We are on a red clay island in the Gulf of St Lawrence separated by about 10 miles of Strait of Northumberland from New Brunswick and Nova Scotia (first ferry from cape Tormentine to Borden arrives at 6.) The estuary we sit on runs north and south. The house faces east. Twenty miles North is the Gulf of St Lawrence.

The island is lacelike, indented, maybe 140 miles long and 20 to 60 wide. Much loved for potatoes and Anne of Green Gables though there are those who claim the strawberries are more important.

The climate is said to be mild but judging from the windbreaks the winter is something fierce.

Project: find an old Charlottetown paper and read the real estate ads.

Project: go back to bed.

Project: mosan Amosan.

Project: figure out how many snipe live in that swampy field. They're so noisy you think there are hundreds but are there actually more than a pair?

Project: sleep.

[p.11]

Tuesday [June] 11 or 12 [1976][11]

Another brilliant day.
If anyone gets up and disturbs me I will scream.
One lives forever in the hope of heaven but it is always severely threatened.

---

11 Here and elsewhere in the *cahier*, Engel's dates are uncertain.

Steppenwolf stimulated me last night. I can fairly well take it apart psychologically but it has the magic of Grand Meaulnes.[12] Bits about the artist and solitude contain things I want to work out too.

I have always preferred to think of myself as a craftsman rather than an artist. This is partly a safety device. It is easier to be a craftsman and at least then one is not a failed artist, i.e., a hobbyist. It also stems from my father's firm conviction that the trades are respectable, and my own tendency to keep my feet on the ground. In addition, I think back to the year in London when Romany and Johnny were crying out that I should feed them, they were artists. I, who knew a good deal more about being an artist (from Hugh MacLennan) than they did, refused a) to class myself with them and b) to say I was an artist before I was ready.

But if you told me I wasn't an artist, I was only a hack, I'd be furious. The real truth is that there is a good deal of hack in any working artist except for the odd sod who has money or needs none. People become prolific because they need to.

Am I getting off the point?
But if there's any difference between a craftsman and an artist it's a matter of aspiration. One chooses one's models at a certain point and sets sail. Hence the long silences in the twenties of any prose writer except the odd pink genius. You can try to be Virginia Woolf or Zane Grey but there's a huge gap between you and them. You set out and eventually become that elusive thing, yourself. The becoming is difficult. The art is in maintaining the craftsmanship.

The novel delights me because it is the freest form in the world. A fictional prose narrative in excess of 45,000 words. My God. It has taken me a long time to realise its freedom even to the limited extent that I do and what delights me is that [there] seems to be no coming to the bottom of it. On the other hand, I have until very recently been most interested in it in its experimental variety, believing that since there are no new things to say one must find new ways to [say] old things. This attitude I now find a bore, perhaps because I am 43 and maturing or getting over the hill, who knows which. I was very excited about the ideas about the nouveau roman

12 Alain-Fournier, *Le Grand Meaulnes* (Paris: Éditions Émile-Paul, 1913).

in France in the '60's but now I find even Butor[13] more or less unreadable, though his theory is very pure and good. I mean Niagara nothing but a bad radio script. And perhaps the nouveau roman was a necessary attempt on the part of the French to escape the roman.

I no longer think that is necessary here.

[p.12]

[June] 11 [1976] Monday evening

Cool and clear again, wind rippling the estuary. Still intrigued by the idea there might be only two snipe: their calls echo.

[...]

Cruising the bookcases: treasure. Hesse and Irving Stone, Snow and Powell.[14] Did I come to the country to be distracted and driven by Powell? Well, he's always there, and at least one falls asleep.

Awesome: a generation, maybe three's, minds formed by Penguins: Snow and Woolf and Orwell, Plomer and Murdoch etc. There's Salinger here, the Nicholson book, Gavin Maxwell, a bunch of thrillers (I thought I was the only one who ever owned "The Pit Prop Syndicate"). The house is lovely: what I'd hoped Holstein would be, roomy and shabby enough so one doesn't worry about housework, and stacked with comfy books and cushions and old postcards. It manages everything without being cute. It looks as if it artlessly grew. I could use a sieve and a potato peeler but otherwise it's a miracle. Now Hazen's got the stove going. Now Will has a bike and Char a friend and John O's brought some beer.

Gull on the inlet. The way the water scuds. The bend of the trees. Evening sun whitening gull's body. Hiproofed barns, sod[?]-sided potato barns. Church steeples every direction.

I found a little street tonight. Up past the corner if you branch right you come to about 10 houses in order. Two terra cotta, one brown, one umber, one white, one bright green, one yella. A blue, too, I think. Neat, sweet. Carving round the gables. Was there ever, however poor people are, such a domestic island.

Foreground: 104 sand dollars stretched down the railing.

---

13 See *Cahier* XVI, footnote 12 for bibliographic details.

14 Anthony Powell would be Engel's last major reading spree. See *Cahier* XLI [74] for another reference to Powell.

Weedy delphiniums and lilies. Marsh grass, angelica, road, ditch, fence, iris-marsh. Sky: mackeral [*sic*].
[...]
His wings whiffle on the downs.

Think I'll go down to the beach. At 5 it was all islanded by the incoming tide.

[p.13]

After a walk.

The mind flows so well, now and here. Not brilliantly, but there is flow, not the grasshopper activity of Toronto.

Writing, men, women: when did it occur to me that what all writers need is Norah Barnacle? The reason Murphy and I are so lyrical of each other is that neither of us is Norah and we're old enough to know it. For god's sake I don't need STIMULATING company. I hadn't bargained on getting so tired in middle age.

Reading the Hesse introduction: Milek or someone introducing Steppenwolf which Denner lectured on so unattractively I've never read it: it makes me ambitious again. To get out a BODY of work! Keep your standards high but at the same time write enough, publish enough, so that everything you do can flow.

Thinking about Mann, various others. I never thought I'd turn out such a neat writer. I suppose, if Arnold Rockman is right and you are programmed by your grandmother, I have to be neat somehow. But the epic no longer attracts me. The Magic Mountain[15] bothered me; it seemed both sentimental and lacking in economy. Much prefer Mann's novellas. They're tight.

But then haven't I spent most of my life with people who edit tape, articles and films? So how can I even understand sprawling imperfection? Yet everything that exists must be accepted and in theory Scott's as good as Jane Austen. Yet more and more, economy and simplicity are what I seek. Am I right? Or does it just happen at this age and stage?

---

15 Thomas Mann, *The Magic Mountain* (New York: Modern Library, 1927).

An aesthetic. When I was 20 I could write out an aesthetic. Not any more.
The bones are good prose and the flesh is you: that's all I know.
Oh the kid in the terrible homemade dress (or was it the jumper with RFC wings?) reciting "I'll find a way or make it!"
*So tired of trying to make it, flapping my wings endlessly.
But the energy's coming back a bit, isn't it?

[p.14]

(last night, trying to read in a room full of whizzing junebugs)

Straight realistic narrative still bores me. I don't think it gives any meaning to reality. Writing is still selective as the human mind is selective. Therefore unless one relies on simple genius (a very uncomforting word that should apply only to mathematicians) one has to take a chance on infecting one's reality with meaning. Capturing the nostalgia for the kingdom, the love of light that is art.

Does that sound like a sermon on Higher Things?

Look at this that way: the estuary and the meadows are out there. Meaningless, complete in themselves. But to each life lived near them they have a terrific relevance, visual or otherwise. For me they are a kind of 23rd psalm comfort. For others, they are a place to fish or to clam or to wander, or just home. They do exist purely and simply, not only in the mind of God, or else whenever God has a nervous breakdown they must go away. But just as it is fatal to forget that landscape is there, it is also fatal to pretend that anything can exist before a human mind without being interpreted by that consciousness. One of the ways of making fiction out of consciousness is to pretend to have another consciousness and expel that consciousness's perceptions, which I don't do much. That's doing voices. I'd rather see authors doing their own voices, not pretending to be fishermen and farmers unless they bloody well know what fishermen and farmers think. (Not pretending to be bears, either). I suppose that leads to an anthropological view of history which is dangerous and racist but it's also kind of honest. It means finally admitting that most literature is middle class and that most personae are oneself.

Well, does the reader really want the perceptions of a sophisticated city person perceiving a rural pond? Yes, if the words are painted on skilfully enough, and if ideas belong there too: i.e. Walden.

Non-fiction, though.

Fiction? The pond as the world of the snipe? The pond as part of the fishermen's life? 400 pages of pond?

I don't know. Something profound in me says Indians should write about Indians, bears about bears, farmers kids about farmers. One should not try to become anything else. Yet the masquerade has gone on for ages.

But the best masqueraders stuck to their own territory and by dealing very very well with it told us something about ours: rose above it. Flaubert, Balzac, Dickens, Eliot, Woolf even.
You cannot escape your own arrangement with society.

THE POND IS NOT MY SUBJECT.

[p.15]

The pond is my subject as it relates to me (i.e. visually). It could not become any other kind of subject for me unless it was more thoroughly part of my life.
Fiction probably arises out of a need to integrate the elements of one's life in narrative. Which is why it's so impossible to escape narrative and go into pure linguistic realms. The novel will probably always be about something more than words.

"Purism" is for the very young or the very old. Part of youth's pudeur before lived and messy reality. Older writers and artists refine and simplify and reach a second stage. Or eightieth, life being what it is.

I feel myself becoming less experimental, more classical, recognising that I'm not Sterne, not Joyce. Still don't want to be Trollope, though. Others see me as turning to fantasy, I think. Don't know if I want to go there, either. What I have to do is work out a number of theories and then give myself enough psychic space (i.e. rest) ((now there's a concatenation)) to let what I have to do occur to me.

Interestingly enough I'm beginning to wake full of energy. A week here has done me a world of good. Hell, I'm gonna get restless. But that's okay too, as long as I have thinking mornings, stop popping around my head like loose popcorn, esp on booze. Quit being hyper. Let landscape do what Valium doesn't.

I mustn't let that energy take over. I must rest and think. Then decide where I can write the next book. If not Toronto, get the courage to take off for somewhere else.[16] If Toronto, get decent help.

Hell, my mood just changed. I shot up and got out of the contemplative. Why? Sun too hot? Can't sustain. Maybe that's enough writing for now. It's so hot at 9 that even the whirlybirds have gone back to sleep.

[p.16]

[...]
Steppenwolf reminds of the Outsider.
Everything hangs together. (Skip explaining this connection: too hard)
Wonder if there's any Plato around.
Birds do have fun. Else why is that young starling airing his armpits in the breeze?

Find my mind curling around the edges of something. What?
Threw out a long letter to Peg [Atwood] and Graeme [Gibson]. Often my letters are to myself. Found some short paper for short letters. Have to get it together (i.e. all papers in one place) to pay my income tax.

Wednesday

Damp and foggy. The view reduced to further foreground. Birds lower, boats blasting the air. John up early to get the 11 am ferry. Nice fellow. Telling me about Turpin's Port Dalhousie poems. Must get.

The fir trees stand out in rows. They must be spruce or hemlock ... classic maritime Christmas card trees, in rows as for windbreaks.

Yesterday I saw a woman doctoring a dying spruce tree with a bucket of stuff. Dipping branches in. Budworm?

John Ormsby has just galumphed off down the road. What a nice young man. Hooked on printing, peddling Coach House books in the Maritimes, 21, together. Likes the kids—always something in a person's favour.

16 Engel accepted a position as Writer-in-Residence at the University of Alberta in 1977-78. She and the children moved to Edmonton for the year, staying on for a second year (1978-79) while Engel taught creative writing courses at the university.

> Sitting out on the porch. The fog is clearing but the cloud ceiling is low. Quieting effect. My friend the young starling watches from the wire. Sometimes his cry is quite sweet. I had forgotten starlings were mimics. Will he try being a typewriter?
>
> Re: leaving Toronto. In theory a great idea. If a bldg in Charlottetown were available at a great price I might try. But reading the paper remember that it's Sarnia 30 years ago. The mentality is small. The kids are used to something bigger. School is shorter, probably tougher. Talk to Fran and Ron, Vern and Marlene. Certainly you can't live in TO the way you did last year; and maybe you've run through it. But don't [forget]

[p.17]

C[harlotte]town is a small town, almost in another country (is that its appeal) and don't romanticise it. Winters are bloody awful, too.

You can't live on a farm by yourself with the kids.

Title for Story: Postmen do not pick up hitchhikers.

If Toronto were possible again, now? Much, much more silence. Good babysitter. Better rules. You can't do all the things you used to do without domestic help anymore. Lunch circuit doesn't work with the kids coming home. You have virtually no evening life except the library board. You go out of your mind with worry because where you want to be and where you're supposed to be never jibe. Therefore: good help.

But it would be so much easier down here! Hardly any phone calls, an easier town to get around and if nothing was going on for you you'd know most of the other people were in the same boat. You wouldn't sit there feeling everything goes on for the others and not for you. You hated all that superficial social life while it was going on, now you feel left out. Don't be perverse.

Goodness, a goldfinch. Forgotten their dippy flight.

Loneliness of moving, knowing no one. God, that was hard this Christmas.

Could you afford to move? Would it really lower the overhead? Don't worry too much about money: worry about increasing your cool and the quality of your life, I mean improving that. I mean, not worrying so much, stretching out, enjoying. Why do you feel less imprisoned here than there? There's nowhere to go, here. You'll get bushed.

No telephone, though, and no existential whim-whams.
Got into 2 this week, didn't you? No, those were circumstantial, dealt with easily.

Goodness, starlings raiding the sparrows' nest. No wonder he scolds.

[p.18]

8 am Thursday 24 June [1976] Hot and hazy
Ugh. I drank the wine last night. Baddish head and baddish conscience, but I found out some things about drinking.
My compulsions really are verbal: I started drinking and then wrote letters for hours. It was like the obsessive talking I do at home, esp into the telephone. But more controlled.

But booze isn't much good as a tension reliever. It knots me up. It's good for the verbosity but it doesn't do much for the psyche, I notice. Got all very Shelleyan and hectic but that's not my best key. (ah but what a splendid purgative.)

Loneliness: I love it, here. After about 2 hours of company I get very resentful. Must orchestrate the children's day so it isn't oppressive. They are getting bored with the seashore. Cripes.

One simply has to withdraw once in a while. Toronto was too much last year—all public life and no private and all the bad vibes but not any certainties in the marriage situation. Moving by myself. My God. Some friends helped but I really did it all myself. The television play was a strain. Love Jim but working under a story editor is like working in school. John [Rich] was right to drop me I think but I need close contact with someone or else [there is] absolutely no one but the typewriter.

What a year: buying the house, doing 2 books, moving, getting teeth done, the play, Willie Lawson, Felbert, library board, Arnold, the Marchmount community. Cripes. A whole picaresque novel rolled into one.[17]

---

17 The novel *Lunatic Villas* draws on these experiences.

The Marshallene idea would be a good one if Marshallene is an ex-nun called Sister Imelda. I could probably do it considering what Hugh wrote about my play: "If this is true, nobody has learned anything in the past 3,000 years."[18] I can intuit what he meant but still kind of wonder how it applies to the text. Don't dare get it out but I think it refers to the terrible cellophane wrapping of innocence I carry around, which must be more a manner than a reality. Or is it? I have to figure every experience out as if it's the world's first, whereas most people put experience in context.

Too hot.

Later. How gorgeous to be wakened by an idea rather than an alarm clock, even if the idea fades.

All the writers I know swing wildly back and forth between gregariousness and solitude. Part of the trade and not to be worried about. One must simply arrange to live so that both aspects are looked after.

Pipedream: a big old frame house near the water in C[harlotte]town. Keep it mostly as it is, live in it like an old slipper. Kids up, me down. Shabby as all hell. Put money in insulation.

[p.19]

June 25

The mail worked today. Letters from Mum and Arlene and telegram from Alma saying we got the vote in Ottawa.[19] My God. That justifies the last 3 years of tearing around, always guilty because I wasn't where the kids were. It justifies the Union's letting me have this house, too. My God, it justifies a lot of things. Maybe even the half bottle of Scotch last night. I keep wondering if it's good for the kids to see me drinking but the fact is they see what there is to see and judge for themselves. I've never been able to put them away.

How does the ribbon turner work? Mebbe with this thing?
Close it up and hope for the best. hope. hope. Yep, it worked.
Off the point.
I have often wondered about the usefulness of PLR (now called Authors'

---

18 This is a reference to Engel's manuscript play "Beat Up the Rain," written during her years in Montreal (1955-60). See letter from MacLennan dated 9 December 1959, in Verduyn, ed., *Dear Marian, Dear Hugh* 98.

19 As Engel goes on to explain, this was Writers' Union business, having to do with Public Lending Rights (PLR) for authors, a cause that Engel championed.

Compensation) but I'm sure it's a form of social justice and I know it's much needed. I can, for instance, now make a good living out of writing, but not out of my best writing, and furthermore making that good living is so tiring that it freaks me write out. Most of us need to live solitary lives most of the time, and the costs are high. The reason that the living is hard to make is beyond a doubt because this is not a book-buying culture. Even I feel slightly guilty at buying new hard-bound books. We get our new hard-bounds at the library and the reserve lists are long for new successful books. The libraries do not buy as heavily in Canadian materials as they claim, but they sure distribute what they have.

Now, if Faulkner[20] keeps his promise and we get the money we'll have the basis for various kinds of social benefits as well as the annual payment for use. Three or four hundred a year isn't much but it pays one's taxes or one's drink or one's dentist bill: better by far than nothing.

must stop this and write alma, tell her to form a collection society instanter.
[p.20]

26 June [1976]

Woke early again but cold and too lazy to write. To my horror Will got up, but he brought me coffee and I went back to sleep.

I always seem to think of good things first in the morning here. I worked out the drinking thing, now one feels freer and warmer and copes better with people but I think they gradually, for me at least, become smaller and objectified and I grow larger? They are more manageable at one stage but, as they are also objects, it is easier to insult them or be grossly sentimental with them. Eventually I guess they become Lilliputians and then crawly things. I seem to objectify in ordinary life with great difficulty—I am always afloat in involvement, in my own feeling of inferiority. Booze changes this. Unfortunately it is now changing a good deal more, as my thirst increases and my liver wears out.

Awful lecture in this from Willy Lawson this winter. Gosh, that hurt. I always felt he knew a lot but hadn't lived long enough to be tolerant. I

---

20 Liberal MP Hugh Faulkner represented the federal riding of Peterborough from 1965 to 1979. He held the portfolios of secretary of State (1972), minister of State for Science & Technology (1976) and minister of Indian Affairs & Northern Development (1977).

needed him because I was so lost and he was so helpful, but when he laid one of his puritanical numbers on it really hurt. He did, as Charlotte said, look like Jesus.
It's my diffidence that allows me to allow people in to run my life. Fortunately, it doesn't extend so far it's incurable.
I'm pretty certain when I've had enough sleep.

And sleep is such bliss here!

A real gale last night, buckets of rain, thunder, howling wind. We sat in the kitchen and, read Sinbad the Sailor. They loved it. Suddenly, we were together again, and I was useful, Charlotte read very well when my voice gave out. Rummy, stories ... it reminded me of happy times at Red Bay.[21] We felt warm and secure in that trailer at night.

But am I just avoiding the outside world. Well, why the hell not, for a while? Need to.

[p.21]

Mond[ay] no Sunday June 28 [1976]

Raining, and cold with it. In fact, a dismal day. Woke early, went back to sleep. When I woke again I made up stories about Imelda. Some of them are funny and sweet and they range over one's Toronto experience all right but would they be anything but drudgery to write? One must give Imelda some other excellent virtue besides innocence: a knowing eye, I guess.

I drank the rest of whisky yesterday; it was good, relaxing. Turned me on, removed cares. Then the kids and I read Sinbad in bed and turned in. Also made Will ground ivy tea for his stomach!

Place is a mess today.
[...]

About liberation: I'm redefining myself as most women are who have lived with men for long periods and then broken up. The pain is in deciding who you are without reference to that other person, who, having decided whom he wanted you to be, forced that image on you. I am further on with the project than I was last year but having decided that I am a writer, whether I now want to be one or not, and heterosexual and lusty does not

21 This is a memory from Engel's childhood.

do me much good as there isn't a man around and I'm too set in my ways to go out and look for one in the normal way. Also those who as writers can't live with men may be right. I think I should have my house and my kids but also some efficient method of escape from them as they dominate the scene and much as I love them, except in these kinds of holiday times they aren't enough. What I'm enjoying now is enjoying them, however.

Ha. My brain sings with Imelda. How did she meet Liquid Louie? What are the time sequences? She joined the Eglantines when she was 20, an Anglican order in London. Coming out of the Anglican manse after discussing the matter with Father Cunningham, whose head soared higher and higher as she talked, she met Asher Bowen; ten years later at Holy Trinity as the X's babysitter, she meets Asher again. He is a lawyer, son of the sheriff of her county. They married, have a son called Charles, whom she calls Chummy. When he is 5 Asher bangs him off to boarding school and runs for legislature. She helps Asher but misses the child and, firmly separated from him, sees the political scene for what it is. Begins, in the gallery of the legislature, a political reporter called Charles, a liaison with, I mean. She has also, briefly and under the influence, had an affair with Asher's manager Talkind. Talkind finds out about Charles: Asher offers [p.22] her a quiet divorce-separation naming no one if she'll just go away. Compares politics to the war saying she should have waited for him to come home. She's on the loose again. Works for a magazine, finds that other people live quite differently and breaks down quite completely when Asher introduces her to Katie, his new girl, who looks like her 20 years ago, but is of better class. Sent to Windsor for the magazine to interview a writer, she crosses and spends the night with Louie. Then heads up to the ferry house, which had been her uncle's but which Asher owns. There she runs into two hippies, Oliver and Blake, who introduce her to the joys of pot and buggery. Oliver decides to rebuild the house and over her protest does so. Is furious when she says she can't pay, nearly burns it down. Asher's secretary Anabel comes up and spends a couple of nights. Katie is pregnant and Asher will pay a good deal for a quick divorce and wants her to take Chummie, who has had a breakdown at school. She goes back to Toronto and arranges all this....

No philosophy: book must be all events and surfaces. The wisdom is in the adventures. Imelda grows by her deceptions but never loses her innocence and enthusiasm.

Monday. Crabby, I am. But oh, my goodness, why can't they play outside on a fine day like this? I'm guilty because I've been crabby, but gosh, they wrote letters all morning. Hey mum, how do you spell ... and the TLS had just come.

I try to restrict their hours so I can write too. It doesn't work. My job is to be Mrs Available and it frustrates me. I can't remember Ma as Mrs Available. She was a better manager.

Bitch bitch bit.

I read this stuff over. Like some of it. Some doesn't connect, but the transparent effect I wanted is there.

I've started Imelda. For eight pages it works. Mustn't talk about it any more.

Glorious, the sun, now. And the breeze. Perfect. I've put the table in between the house and the broken down shingled shed. Tee shirts and underpants, badly handwashed, flap on the line. On the oil stove the tea towels are cooking. Haven't boiled laundry since Europe.

TLS review talks of George Sand as dishonest. I wonder. The romantic romanticized but is it her fault? Haven't read enough of her. Perhaps men are right: they see her as maternal but unwilling to be married, a controller. Well, most of us are like that. We want to have kids, sure, but we don't want to be men's children all the time. The shrinks are right

[p.23]

that the ideal relationship involves parenting, being a child, being an equal. She hadn't had good experiences of being a child. Forgotten who her father was but her big grandmother brought her up. The male parent figures in her life were legendary heroes. The real males were weak. She set out to recreate the pattern. Michel de Bourges wasn't any kid of hers, however. Reviewer is right to talk of the hypocrisy of her romantic solutions in novels but she probably couldn't get away with more than she did. I guess I protect her because she fought a lot of my battles for me. More, anyway, than Mrs Browning.

Where shall I find my Nohant and my Musset.

Well, I've had him!

Enough of all this thinking. I've just made myself a bandanna top out of Mum's red silk scarf. Char thinks it indecent and in truth it's not pretty but wind on my skin, better than silk. Will has just peddled off in a winter pullover!

I've seen people tie bandannas around themselves better, though.

Maybe you can't write and look after kids and have a husband too. Maybe Anne's right: that's it. But you can have a fighting try because writing isn't living and living alone with kids isn't always living; so one has got to go on

trying to find ... people. Even birds come in pairs.
Splendeurs et misères … one tries hard to forget they come together.
Later. Reading Northrop Frye: fine stuff. Got my head back again and am happy, whether this is good or not.

[p.24]

30 June [1976]

How remarkably unterritorial of Libby to lend out her house. It's full of nice things too. Herbals and little arrangements of dried flowers. Rat jelly posters all over: Coach House press things. Shelves and signs and floats. Curtains of old faded country material, just as they should be.

Not in good shape today. Into the Scotch again last night, dammit. Guilt. Kids are very nice, I must say.

Why can't I content myself with the view? The wild madder is green foam in the ditches and when you look down, every blade of grass salutes.

Read a piece in the TLS about a poet called Celan I'd never heard of. He went from Heidegger to word-coining. Steiner thinks him better than Rilke. High praise. Sounds like my meat by I could never do him in German.

The weather is bad and, yes, I'm bored. Want to be active. Waiting for one of the cars on the road to be for us.
Worrying about what happened to Pat. With the air strike I'll probably never find out.

Charlotte's just left Colonel Sanders to watch over me in the doorway. Such saints we have now.
Imelda still appears, wonder if I could get some of the Writers' Union experience in there: Northern Journey, librarians, my own unwillingness to publish documents.

Must write to Gwen and Liz and Bob.

July 2 [1976]

Yesterday was vile, wet and grumpy. Ended up tantrumous. Argh. I read RIP 7, which covers a lot of Toronto at least, then started a Hornblower, for my sins. Baked all day. Children bickered. Hazen dropped by with a slurp of gin-juice. We watched a lot of tv and read a lot of Aladdin. Cooked the rest of the meat which had gone off. W. was totally uncooperative. Better day

today, surely, as it is warmer.
Where's my lovely headspace gone? Dunno. Don't care.
What's headspace anyhow? The acid vocabulary is dangerous.
I suppose I mean contemplativeness if there's such a word.

[p.25]

14 August

[...]
I don't think I need the stimulus of Toronto all that much [...]. I'm bored with my political things here because I want to get back to writing... [...]

[p.26]

[...]

Cahier XXXIII[1]

Try to explain to the storekeeper how it feels to finish a book.... Oh heck you can't explain this to anyone [30].

Following the publication of *The Glassy Sea* in 1978, Engel was contracted to write the text for a book on islands of Canada, featuring photographs by J.A. Kraulis. As part of her research, Engel travelled to various Canadian islands in the summer of 1980.[2] The bulk of *Cahier* XXXIII consists of notes she took in Newfoundland, St Pierre et Miquelon and Prince Edward Island. Some entries are little more than sketchy observations, and have not been retained, while others are near-polished prose and offer reading interest.

The new decade began with further travels. In March 1980, Engel made the long trip to Australia to speak about Canadian women's writing at a book festival and to give a series of readings. She met many writers, Australian and others, and carried out a gruelling reading schedule[3] despite health concerns. These appear in more "notes without a notebook," which Engel made on pages from notepads provided by hotels in which she stayed. While these are not in the more typical *cahier* format, like "Bear Summer" they fulfilled important aspects of the notebook function. To them, Engel confided thoughts and feelings about her experiences while in Australia, both professional (writers' festival) and personal (health concerns). Incomplete and sketchy, excerpts are included at the end of this *Cahier* XXXIII. They introduce the metaphor Engel selected for her disease, namely a crab, as in the constellation and horoscope symbol "Cancer the Crab."

Engel's travels, particularly to Newfoundland, rekindled her thoughts about moving away from Toronto. The author had always been attracted to islands. Would it be possible to live on one? True to form, she drew up a list comparing items like housing, heating, travel and entertainment costs. Her eventual conclusion was that life on an island—at least in Newfoundland—was

1 1980, large format green spiral notebook; 57 pages used.

2 Engel was accompanied by her daughter Charlotte, who was fifteen that summer.

3 17 March, Latrobe University; 18 March, Australian National University; 19 March, MacQuarrie University; 20 March, Wollongong University; 21 March, University of New England, Armidale.

not for her. "Our puritan selves flail about denying the attraction of the plastic life," she recognized. To "cure" this, one needed only to "carry water from the well for two weeks. Type with a bad ribbon on damp paper for 1 month. Talk to a few sheep" [30]. "The dream of islands," Engel decided, is "a short-term summer dream, by city guilt out of Wordsworth & grandmother's tales of how we were happier then" [29].

Reflective reasoning aside, there were practical reasons for Engel to return to Toronto, at least in the short term. She was writer-in-residence at University of Toronto for the academic year 1980-81. Engel had been writer-in-residence at the University of Alberta in 1977-78. The children had accompanied her to Edmonton, where the family stayed on for a second year (1978-79). Engel was concerned about what another move might mean for the children. Rather than take the radical step of leaving Toronto, she decided to make some modest changes to her Toronto home (described on [2] and [30]).

Meanwhile, Engel's various book projects continued apace. She was working on "The Vanishing Lakes"[4] and trying to calm her worries about its structure. An episodic structure would be fine [4]. "You have to see this novel as a sepia film," she assured herself [52]. In "The Vanishing Lakes," as in previous Engel manuscripts,[5] notebooks play a role. *Cahier* XXXIII is also concerned with characters who became part of the author's next major novel, *Lunatic Villas*, including Mrs Saxe, Harriet and Tom and their son Mick, as well as neighbour Vinnie, and finally Patsy Little ("Littlemore" in the final version).

[p.1]

Mrs Saxe

Marge reading the National Geographic

—

Vinnie: Harriet, when you've got your
martyr's crown will you
marry me?
Harriet: No, Vinnie, I won't need to.

—

Patsy Little—One's ambivalence.

---

4 "In which Tanis & Idlehorn [variously spelled as Ildelorn and Ildehorn] go up the Vanishing Lakes to seek their lost mother Iris. In the Golden City they find her & happiness of a kind, and Echina de Scandelion, the ruler, who is Belle Rivers," *Cahier* XXXV [67].

5 Barbara's notebooks in "Death Comes for the Yaya," Sarah Bastard's "notebook" and Joanne's in *Joanne: The Last Days of a Modern Marriage*.

Tom's Mick as Lothario

—

Story of Mr & Mrs Saxe & the Estates & Titles

[p.2]

House

*1 Call Hydro

2 Will's room: Wardrobe
Door
Mirror

3. Bathroom: Sink
paint
shower?

4. Char's room: bedside table
lamp
hang mirror
more desk

5. My room —bed surround
—ceiling holes
—rearrange closet.

6 Hall closet—convert to linen cupboard.

7 Hall: pictures & carpet

Living room

curtains move chesterfield throw out TV
office—bookshelves window

[p.3]

Vanishing Lakes

—abnormal people pushed to extremes by social hangups intolerable bitterness or optimism

Ellen Selkie whose deformity is operable not bitter or optimistic because operable

Clifford & Reva are stupid

Iris complex, selfish, spoiled territorial, paranoid.

Ivo—Ellen to talk to Iris to screw Clifford & Reva as workers

Master-manipulator?
A [illegible] type. Knows he will not rise. Knows Iris.

Mudd & Johnson: who, what do they want?

Kinkin Muriel
Flavia John

Eubie—keeps finding mysteries
Gunter—Muriel.

[p.4]

Structure—episodic—don't worry

1 Gunter
2 Eubie & wife
3 Gunter & Christie "There was something about a man named Mudd."

[have I enough respect for other people's
work to be good at my own?][6]

linear events: frame: 3 Search for Muriel
2 Search for Iris
IVO
ELLEN
↓ ELLEN ?
IVO present
2 Search for Iris T[ense]
3 Search for Muriel
Ellen must TAKE CONTROL.

So—make IVO a marxist
<u>MUDD</u> inherits farm

6 Square brackets appear in the original text.

Confusion when Ivo dies—IRIS can't get information from Ellen unless she is good

[p.5]

OK think of it as Shakespeare & really work it out.

It's a tragedy of 2nd generation.
The first travels hopefully.
The second is hopelessly ambivalent: John & Muriel.
[...]

[p.6]

[Names of characters]

[p.7]

Things to think over

1 Borrowed time can be extraordinarily beautiful
2 Energy is worth having

Supposing, however, there were borrowed time[s] without energy? Poverty, forget it.

USE whatever it is—grist for the mill

What can I get out of doing?
—bad public appearances
—bad boozing

What do I need? $10,000 base income
Summerplace: (island?)
(Jim?) **(who he?)**[7]
isolated house in TO ravine?
Or soundproof house? Magic place
Find out about white noise (Port Dover? Brights)
Can still do R in R job

Gentle, vague, seeming
tone

7 The words, "who he?" in darker ink, appear to have been added later.

Now: the work: Find yourself again:
Stick to Vanishing Lakes
Work it all out {
Belle Beatten
Cliffie Hobbs
Ellen Selkie

VICTOR?)
IVO Thompson
IRIS Maltby
MOUSE
JOHN
MURIEL

energy crackers

do not allow
anything to get
you off the track

Will to Y at Xmas
work out?

Gunter
Eubie
Christy
Bruce Selkie
Mudd
Johnson
McCromy
Clara Ross

[p.8]

No fools
forever

Paint this
landscape

Energy cake—Dream to make

—

nourishing hors d'oeuvres

–

Do not allow duty, disorder, despair
Don't dash around
Vegetate
Buy a sweat suit for work
Stay on main track.
[...]

Bring out—politics
ways of time—not
sordid but good
OUTGROUP, though

[p.9]

[More notes]
[...]

[p.10]

Newfoundland, July 21, 1980

Arrived at St John's—Airport Inn—got in—pretty terrible.

Sat down with phone book ... not many of the names I had listed. Phoned Cassie. She picked us up & toured us: went to Topsail Beach & Portugal Cove (not at all like Peggy's Cove) (more spread, less barren) not much sign of "real" Nfld.

Bell Island—How the rocks rear up
St John's—Signal Hill: imposing Marconi Monument

I know nothing about Nfld because it wasn't in the school books.
hotel
2x48 Char pleased w harbour—a real Japanese ship from
+ 40 meals Japan
15 phone

taxis— $15 today
$15 yday
meals—$14 (!)

How you know it's the Maritimes
—vegetation stunted
—cows by cliffs
—no mountains
—no logs in inlets (Is NFLD Shield?)
Irving oil tanks
red earth
green rocks
black cliffs—different
shingle.

[p.11]

Suddenly, in Avalon Mall [St. John's] "When I grow up I'm going to be a rich writer with a golden chauffeur."

(And yet even 10 years ago it wasn't so bad if you didn't drive.)
[...]
Cod tongues au gratin. Are they funny, Charlotte says.
Newfld is disco.
1949 it joined Canada. Did it do any good?
[...]

[p.12]

[Doodle]
Idea: The Paschal Seal

sealing & whaling = survival
greenpeace = liberal rightness
Farley
Father's practicality

Write Peggy Understanding the Hunt—it's gathering—as in blueberries.
And it's the only thing that grows

Were the old ways less savage than the new? Bardot[8] as an energy-crisis for women!
sentiment—reality
The buffalo hunt (was it also the only thing they had?) "Are we like sheep?" Are seals easier?
Are seal hunters brutish children?
How moral is the fur business
(I <u>love</u> meat & furrrr)

[p.13]

detachment from objects
(a <u>cat</u> or <u>dog</u> coat?)

What will we replace sealing with? How does that fit with Fogo resettlement[9] Is driving to a foundry better?

The last of the gatherers.
[...]

[p.14]

[...]

[p.15]

Sh[ort] Story "look like the delicate flower but be the serpent under it."[10]
If you are <u>a</u> bull?
Another one—"But Shakespeare wasn't Jewish & from Winnipeg?

"I see something—It sees me"[11]

—

K Mansfield & the Cows -
<u>**WOW!**</u>

---

8 Brigitte Bardot, a French actor who campaigned against the seal hunt.

9 Between 1954 and 1975 the provincial government of Newfoundland and Labrador and the federal government introduced three programs aimed at centralizing the population of the province. More than 300 small outport fishing communities were abandoned and 30,000 people were moved from their homes to larger urban growth centres. The community of Fogo Island debated the option of resettling but decided to stay and develop its local economy.

10 From Shakespeare's *Macbeth* Act I, Scene V, which reads "look like the inoocent flower...."

11 This is the title of a short story in Engel's first collection *Inside the Easter Egg.*

St Pierre

—always the excitement of a new island
—Fortune—the fish plant. The St Eustache
—small boat (?)
—hotel—bus—boat connection
—over a nightclub
—madame needs teeth
pincushion mouth
restaurants by reservation
French cop in képi
good grocery store
heavy trade in pure alcohol.

[p.16]

Miquelon

We leave at 7—pissing rain.
We get there at 9 – " "
The Japanese people don't go _ ∴ no jeep.
Anyway you can't see anything.

We go to the store & ask for the restaurant.
We go to the restaurant & spend our time with 2 Newfoundlanders. She speaking terrible French—and v. Irish. The man immensely likeable, from St John's, a p[ost] o[ffice] clerk—big, knows everyone.

The Island—two big knobs connected by an isthmus—big étangs, wild horses, seals.
The town—mainsquare (church, mairie P.O.) yellow RF [République Française] mailbox & Posh modern RF telephone booth.
Layout is French.
Colour of houses—bright yellow orange pink turquoise! (great in fog).
Fishing boats—goëllettes, very curved.
[Doodle]
People get clothes by catalogue from France.
Everything very cher. Cheaper in Fortune.

Restaurant I—Mrs Cox—super food
blue eyed Québécois[e]

R[estaurant]II—Mme la Soubrette—family here "always"
book of shipwreck stories
map—good

[p.17]

3 typical French
dames—<u>perfect</u> accent
the one who
is talking
"a de [la] classe"

stores— craft store I
general stores II
groceries II
bars II

The bar with the foil ceiling & the billiard table bad cognac w sweet undertaste.
beach—a soft green plant w pink & blue flowers—what?
Lots of sea urchins. Charlotte at her good work again.
School—until they're 15.
Where do they send the fish—to France?
Stuffed local crab frozen in case in store.
Vin de table in plastic jugs.
Clinic—the dentist returns 19 August.

Lovely—why? Untouched in major ways—no tarting up.
Fancy white curtains.

24 juillet The day of the motos—me black & blue

Old dames taking tea.

On prend du thé.
On a du cake.
On parle de ses affaires.

Tu as bien voulu de l'orange gazeux [*sic*]?

[p.18]

La femme parle des choses
"fines."
Ça suffit pour moi.

ps—alors
puis—alors
à demain—see ya tomorrow

point—not at all
avec son homme—w. her man

ils sont fous de leurs enfants—they are crazy abt their kids.

[p.19]

Charlotte doesn't like me to make notes or translate or BE.

Charlotte a le cafard.[12]

À 15 ans tout le monde a le cafard.

[Drawings]

Mme Mathilde a toutes ses affaires ici—elle n'a jamais d'argent ... elle fait toujours pauvre.
Une table minuscule,
La vaisselle toujours à faire...
[Doodles]

[p.20]

Gander to Carmanville [Newfoundland] $25

July 27 [1980] Tilting, Fogo island

> This is what's known as falling on your feet. I am sitting at a good old fashioned table in the Youth Hostel—the upper story of an old fish store. Right under rafters with bark on them. It's the ideal writer's room: upper story, reached by ladder-stairs (a kind of island) three windows, the one on my left showing the sun setting over Notre Dame Bay & little Fogo island. Blue bay, rosy sky dark headlands. In the foreground a square white house & three dories. Gulls tearing around the sky. The gardens fenced off with spruce pickets against free-grazing ponies and sheep. Heaven?
>
> "A boat adrift here goes straight to Tobermory in Scotland," says Mr NV Roe the island taxi driver. ($10.)

How we got here

In St John's it was pissing with rain. It cleared while we were flying to Gander—with a bunch of air cadets—all cheerfully glad to get home &

12 French for feeling blue.

narrate their adventures. We got a taxi easily for the ride to Carmanville & the ferry (this was regarded as a normal request) but arrived just in time to get drenched.

It's a big car ferry—the Hamilton Sound—& a long rough ride across—then, having failed to identify the

[p.21]

taxi, we had to ask some men for a ride. Not a bad idea, but the ones we asked had a car stuck in behind a big house trailer, which meant another 1/2 hour in the rain.

We were cold & cross by the time we got to the motel—which is not on the sea but by a bunch of lakes in the middle of the island.

(Just put the kerosene lamp on—how many years since I did that for light?) (None—because someone else always handled it).

We were cold & tired & discouraged & there was no supper being served. But I got 2 mugs of boiling water & we had instant soup & cookies & cheese & watched television & wrangled a bit—tired of each other—then about 10^{30} I went into the pub & got a double scotch & sat boldly down at a table with a couple. He was home from working in Toronto. I couldn't hear her.

The faces, half lit from the bar lights, were astonishing, round & dumpy like mine, or elegant. There were two men next to us with wire glasses & good profiles, & one of them looked like Shakespeare.

[p.22]

There must have been two or three hundred people there. The band played country-western sorts of sea-songs—the loneliness of having a husband off at sea was a theme—& it looked for a while like a Barry Fitzgerald movie. Then I got talking to the couple & Shakespeare came over & said, "I heard you talking about finding a place to stay at the sea. My mother runs the Youth Hostel in Tilting...."

So this morning I got Charlotte up early & found NV Roe who told us, as we rode across island through Barr'd Island, Joe Batt's Arm & Sandy Cove to Tilting, how they shot the last Indian just outside Joe Batts, how Cap'n Cook married a Joe Batt's girl. And then we met Mercedes, who runs the hostel & the first strangeness wore off & we landed on our feet.

All afternoon we walked with her, she & I gossiping—along the top of the cliffs—gathering bake-apples, the dog chasing sheep & horses. Harebells, buttercups & a tiny pink sort of cyclamen (there was wild rhododendron up by the lake at the motel) juniper, lichen, high bog.

Great shattered granite rocks—giant causeway things & one sheep who kept thinking the big white dog was his mum & running after him &

being disappointed: the making of a neurotic.

It was a long walk & I was tired & lightheaded from the good air. We had a tea with cheese & chicken & moose meat & rhubarb jam & were happy. And then I slept an hour.

Falling on
Your feet
In blue sky
And wet moss.

.....

Titling—whence the name? An Irish catholic village.
Barr'd Island is protestant.

Long & winding & spread out. Road newly paved. Pinkish gravel. Salmon, cod & lobster. Picketed garden allotments—turnips, potatoes, carrots.

–

Fogo is the island that refused resettlement in ___ when Premier Joey Smallwood was giving grants to communities to move "into the 20th century." One has to respect that. It wasn't cheap patriotism—it was a choice of roots over ruin. They're sometimes poor here, but they have values.

[p.24]

Travelling

Ferries—they now seem endless—motor boats, buses, taxis, friends, and on St Pierre the Moto[?] I fell off at the corner where the dead horse was. Causeways that sometimes spoil the isolation. Canadian ferries are not distinguished for comfort—though the B.C. ferries are as well kept as anyone could expect, there's something official & barren about them—but who expects gourmet delights on a two-hour trip? No, there's nothing special about them except the people on them: weathered workers, brown islanders (on the east coast with their special accents) strange tourists—placid or jolly or greedy.

But there's always a delight in being on a ship or a boat—port & starboard in the vocabulary again, the stairway a companionway, lifeboat directions even on the smaller ones. If it's only from Pender to Saturna, we are steaming away to a farther shore.

Or else flying in—away from the city—to be blanketed again in weather.

[p.25]

Weather is part of the appeal, surely. In Toronto you can hide away from it—anyway it's collective, when your basement floods, so do a thousand others—but on an island your house sticks out into the weather unprotected by streets & rows of others. Even your shelter isn't that sheltered—sometimes it's warmer out than in—and the wind howls like a wolf at the door and when the rain falls, it pelts. It's wetter than city rain & your tennis shoes catch the rain from the long grass so that summer is soakers.

Winter? I don't know, but I've been told it's all right if you can stand up in the wind & you or your neighbour owns a plough. Certainly on the west coast that's the good season—ravens croaking in the woods, fir & hemlock cloaked in the occasional blanket of wet snow. In Manitoulin they say it's all right except the phone lines blow down; in the Gulf of St Lawrence you pray for the men who are out getting seals & to hell with Greenpeace: better than unemployment, seals.

[p.26]

You don't hear of many strangers wintering on the smaller islands—oh, Farley Mowat & Michael Cook in the east, and there must be painters. Most people have the sense to come in from the cold.

I dream of it, but I couldn't do it. I'd get a cold, or the stove would go out, I'd be loco from loneliness in a week—I know myself that well; but I admire the ones who do. But without anybody? "Back & side go bare, go bare." Cold wind. Accidie. Out of paper, ribbons, ink. Freezing on the ferry. That's the real sound of the mermaids singing.

No, you'd need your own people—friends, family. Where you are half a dozen, you're OK. But not on your lone-some.

The lamp's low, now. To bed I.

[p.27]

Tosh

East coast, west coast:

~~Well, there's every difference & great lakes islands are often in between. In the east, scribbly trees, glistening ponds in the taiga & if you miss the irises, what? Work—these are working islands—only around Nova Scotia do you find grand summer houses.~~

The Cost Accounting of Romance

	Island	City
Mortgage or rent	little, unless large estate	lots.
Heat	wood, small am[oun]t oil	(oil or gas) 6-700 p[er]a[nnum]
	cost varies dep on location—PEI, NS v. expensive electricity	6-700
Taxes	low	
Services	few—street light if in village	public transport
Entertainment	nil—or in peoples homes, pub	libraries theatre movies
Medical	not always easily available, but decent	efficient perhaps over used
Shopping:	basics—good if you knit	you can't make your own typing paper [p.28]
Food	clams, mussels, fish free. Store-bought expensive. Garden necessary. Chickens or rabbits possible.	—Groceries cheaper Fish atrocious Meat expensive
Company	visiting intellectuals. Salty locals full of stories (if they can stand you.)	Sometimes none—but you are more likely to find soulmates here.

Conclusion—a shack on an island, sure; but if you run out of your own city brand of supplies & can't get off because of the weather (when it's too good, tourists pre-empt the ferry,) then you'll be slapped in the face with the knowledge of who you are. On the other hand, if your roots are really in the country, you know how to handle boats in bad weather, & your work will keep you in the winter—try it.

Points against it for M.E.: 1) The children like the city 2) Too stiff & soft for boating 3) Hate knitting. 4) Don't know how to chop wood 5) Lazy. 6) Stay home!

As a life it's better for men who enjoy physical activity. Entertainment for women—showers, quilting bees etc, inferior to male carousel probably. Better for couples.

[p.29]

Don't count on fitting in for 4-5 years.
Ordinary living more work—but less "front" (or "side"?)

In short, the dream of islands is a short-term summer dream, by city guilt out of Wordsworth & grandmother's tales of how we were happier then.

There is artist-guilt in our society as well as city guilt—those of us who make worldly entertainment are vulnerable to charges that our products are neither useful, nor moral. Some kind of austere life endured in the making of them probably compensates.

No—that's not entirely it—

The questing mind also seeks the pattern—and an island offers a knowable limited pattern of a society as well as a dream of when times were simpler. The problems occur when a man who writes novels for a living confronts a man who kills seals—a woman who paints [confronts] one who cleans & crochets. There's a meeting-ground on the basic human level, but none, perhaps (there are village Homers everywhere, though they are often the drunks) at the level where the mind plays—or gossips about the business.

[p.30]

Our puritan selves flail about denying the attraction of the plastic life. Cure for this: carry water from the well two weeks. Type with a bad ribbon on damp paper 1 month. Talk to a few sheep. Try to explain to the storekeeper how it feels to finish a book.

O heck you can't explain this to anyone.

On the other side of the account—

Sitting in Grace's kitchen

Walking along the Tilting Cliffs
Sitting in Mary's trailer
Old woods at Masset, mossy trees
Jungle trail, Galiano
Kay's cottage, St Joe's
View from this window.

Suggestions—compensations, city winter:
—frost feathers on windows.
—plastic wisteria à la Beryl
—PAINT SEASCAPES on STORM WINDOWS!
—wood stove for living room.

[p.31]

[Sketch of floor plan]

never mind if you
use some of this in
mermaid story.

Vanishing Lakes
Interview with Ellen Selkie
Regarding the Ivernian Community

Q: Miss Selkie—Dr Selkie—There are a good many confusions surrounding the formation of the Ivernian Community. Could you clear any of them up, now, for the Canadian public?

A: I'd be glad to. There's too much nonsense being talked. First of all—we were not a religious community....

Q: How do you think those rumours started?

A: Will McCrory in the valley. There's nothing to do there, so he plays let's pretend. I used to scorn that, but I've found in my life that idleness is the beginning of legend—and legend is important to society—it contains many of its great truths. Science can't bear it. So I've had to give in to Will McCrory & his stories about Ivo and the Great Religion: they're lovely, but they aren't really true.

Q How did it begin then?

A There were the five of us who came out here & Frank Church or Mudd back there who inherited the property.

[p.32]

He and Ivo used to talk a lot about the ideal community—
Q But didn't this ideal involve religion?

A Oh with Ivo you never knew—but it wasn't church religion—it wasn't theosophy for all he went through his Mme Blavatsky & Gurdjieff & Ouspensky—as I recall it he & Church—I never could make out if his name was Church or Mudd but when Ivo died I found it was Church-Mudd—talked a lot about ideal communities.

Q: And how did this one start exactly?

A: Ivo was a newspaper reporter. He was from Hamilton. His father was a railway porter. He was bright, he'd done his jr matric +2 but there was no question then of a real education. So he got jobs on papers & educated himself that way. He came to Fairlie in 1940 when I was 18.

Q: And then?

A: And then? Well—it happens everywhere. People find each other. We found WO or he found us. And Mudd & Johnson.

Q: I hadn't heard of Johnson before.

[p.33]

A: I never knew Johnson well. He was a little man and, as he wasn't conscripted, there must have been something wrong with him. Ivo was too big & Cliffie was—well, you know about him. Mudd went into the forces—that's why he gave us the land, he didn't think he'd be back. But Johnson, you could say he was a cipher. He worked in a bank & sent us exactly half his pay. That's why Ivo registered us as a religious community—how it all started—to leave Johnson something for his own old age. Because he wouldn't come out, for some reason he'd never come out, but as his wages went up he'd send more & more money. And of course after I went out & worked, I sent money too (though I ought to have sent it to my mother), so the charitable status kept our taxes down. What Johnson got out of it I don't know. He died just after Ivo & left his pittance to Iris. Ivo didn't keep letters, so we don't know now. Most likely he was a good fellow who didn't want much & wanted to share with Ivo. That's old-fashioned but you can't fault it. What good would it do psychologising that one?

Q And Mudd or Church. What about him?

[p.34]

A Frank was little like me, the size & colour of a spider—but straight. This was his uncle's place & he didn't want it. He hadn't a chick or a child. Greed only sets in when you have kids, you know. You can make one by yourself unless you're useless.
He gave the place to the community. We're waiting to hear what will happen when the rest of us die.

Q So how many of you came out?

A Belle, Cliffie, Ivo and Iris and I. The way Ivo intended it, we'd spend a year getting the place ready & then invite—well—whoever came. In fact, it took two years to build the dormitory & then after the first few, we had to make a lot of changes. So it was a while before we got off the ground.

Q What sort of changes?
A Oh—either the world had changed or we hadn't noticed how it was. People wanted more. Privacy & running water & good mattresses. We said, well it's not a hotel—but they weren't up to it. As I'm not now.

[p.35]

Maybe it depends on where you start from. A roof over my head used to be good enough for me, but I want more now.

Q What more?

A A pretty roof. Books, music, hot water. I'm as bad as the rest. I've been spoiled.

Q Tell us about the first year—before you went to the university....

A That was the tough one. John was two & Iris had just had Sallie. Belle's Bernice was a toddler & Reva was newly born. Ivo had advertised in the Atlantic Monthly & Saturday Night—and I think the Can. Farmers' Weekly. We got three Americans & two Canadians. One of the Canadians went straight home again, and the rest were all right for a while, but they didn't want to work. They liked the study sessions, but they didn't like the work. I don't blame them, looking back, they wanted a break, a holiday. On the other hand we couldn't let the harvest go to hell.

Q What kind of farming operation did you have?

A Some wheat, oats, corn, turnip & potatoes. Belle & I wanted goats but we soon enough gave up on them—eat you out

[p.36]

of house & home if you don't have fences. Either that or you play goat girl all day—we'd no time for that. The two teams of horses—they were our big investment before we got the tractor. Hens. Eventually a few sheep, cattle. It's never been a serious farming operation. Farming's either labour or machine-intensive & that means capital.

Q And on—shall I say the distaff side—?

A It's a male dream—the big stove, the big table. You don't have to actually kill anything to bake bread. We had a loom, but it was the guests who did the weaving, not Iris & Belle. They were run off their feet with the guests & the babies.

Q It sounds as if you were running a hotel—

A From the practical point of view, we were. Oh, I've worked in hotels—and what I can tell you is that we did in fact make them help with the linen—a couple chose to do without & that was their loss—& some of the food gathering—but there was a lot of work. We were all townies, we hadn't taken that into account—you couldn't just run to the store.

[p.37]

Q And the ideas?

A. That was my disillusion. Why I left for the university. Ivo got in with the ideas. The rest of us didn't.

Q And yet there were ideas. Ivernia was <u>important</u>. We used to hear about it on the CBC.

A Yes, they talked a lot about how the world should be.

Q I can't imagine you weren't there yourself.

A I was, and I wasn't. I had John & Bernice so Iris & Belle could work in the garden. It was like a flashing light—I was there & not there—one moment participating another taking a child outside ... so I never really heard the gospel of St Ivo.

Q You sound—just slightly spiteful.

A I may well be. And it will help me to be charitable about Iris. And if I am, I am tired. I will talk again tomorrow.

[p.38]

God, she thinks after he goes, I sound as mean as she was. And if that's right, she was right. He had it all. Unfair, unfair.

Though at the time—he <u>was</u> St Ivo.

But I had a way to get out—had prepared it—instinct, I guess. Iris resented it. As I did when hers came into play. (Hawaii still seems a bad end to me—except for Hawaiians. Aloha Oi & all those dreadful songs.) Yes—I wanted—what? To be there, like Ivo, like the others.

And shall I tell him about them?

No—more important to figure out if I <u>could</u> have been with them.

It was the structure of the community [that] was wrong. It put some of us in servant roles. And our inability to involve guests. On the whole.

So we weren't anything, were we?

But we were. Because in the years I wasn't there, there were times, people, when things worked—and people.

Shall I tell him about Hereward?
Ilona?
Margaret?

[p.39]

I will tell anyone anything about myself—my surfaces—look, this is the cyst on my wrist, I say, I will tell anyone stories.

But Hereward—Ilona—Margaret—they came here—they found something. Hereward is Hal now, not a famous but a prosperous, happy painter. Ilona exists & Margaret works. There were many others.

I was an unrejoicing handmaiden.

I bless Belle. She rejoiced in service.

We were castoffs & to some extent our people were castoffs. Ivo was an early psychotherapist: Oh come on to me—all ye that labour & are heavy laden. She could do that, Belle. She was simple. Salt of the earth. Oh Belle.

I love Belle & I don't know how she puts up with me.
Cliffie she misses. I don't wonder.
We've made too much of intelligence.

[pp.40-41]

[...]
[Draft of a letter never sent to Howard Engel]

[p.42]

I'm tired & irritable now & I don't want to talk to him any more. It was nice to have a drink before dinner—his vodka & our cherry wine indeed!—but irritating, irritating, so I'll just see to Belle & put these old bones to bed.

Belle, poor Belle. I said to the doctor, I won't bring her in any more & he looked, immaculate & in glasses, peeled, starched, at me as if I were a murderess & I said "Three hundred miles over those roads in the back of a pick-up truck! How would you like it?" But of course he couldn't imagine it. Doctors aren't <u>for</u> imagining things like that, so I just said I wouldn't, he could send the medicine in the post or through the doctor in Sundown. He looked more & more disapproving & dismissed me & went back & did whatever he does to Belle & eventually I was called before a supervisor, an older man, fat & square but not a bit less surgical—one longs for a hair out of place at that institute but it's their way of showing that we're the patients, not them.

"So you don't want to bring Mrs Hobbs in anymore, Mrs Selkie."

"Doctor Selkie," and I named my discipline, not that it helped.

[p.43]

Just to show, though, that one was not a nobody. He looked at me & said nothing so I spoke again to his well fed pale eyes. "She's too frail to make the trip. Surely you can see that."

"Have you nursing experience?"

"Nothing official. Only what I've learned from her."

"She'll have to come into the hospital soon."

"She wants to finish at home."

"How long have you lived there, then?"

"Nearly forty years—since '43."

"Has she children?"

"One in Vancouver, one in Calgary. They'll come. We haven't asked them yet."

"And the two of you are alone?"

"There are neighbours. And we're used to it."

"You haven't been there always."

"No—I retired two years ago. Because she needed me."

He looked at me even harder. Did he think we were Lesbians or something? Then, slowly, "You were part of that group."

"Yes—Ivo's lot."

"You're the last?"

"You can never tell who'll arrive. Ivo's boy is around sometimes. We

[p.44]

still have the dormitory & we take in whoever...."

"These days it could be dangerous."

"There's never been anyone I wasn't glad to see."

He thought a little more. To help him I said, "we have to get her into one of the farmer's panel trucks and it's too rough for her on the gravel roads. Her bedsores are bad enough."

"She should be in here. She has the insurance, doesn't she?"

"Dr Mead told me there was no hope. What's the point of having her here? At least the children can come if she's home. There's no place for them to stay here & they can't visit decently in a hospital."

"We're much better placed to alleviate her suffering."

"There must be something I can give her. Or the doctor from Sundown."

"You're regular patients of his?"

"He's new. We went to old Dr Hale."

"Who delivered the babies in those days?"

"Belle and Iris did for each other & there was an old Indian woman who could turn a breech."

"They were lucky. You're sure—there'll be no one but you this summer?"

"Not at all—there may be visitors. We had a girl from Ontario most of the winter, but she went off in the spring."

[p.45]

"The drugs I can give have to be administered by a professional."

"You couldn't stretch a point with my PhD: It's a long way for young Dr Moffat to come every day."

Suddenly he threw his pen down & pushed his chair back & said all right and I found myself subject to a lecture in pharmacy. She has ABCD & E & if you administer the wrong combination she'll be in hell. I think I know from what he said how to put her in heaven, but she's a good brave woman, Belle, she hasn't asked for that yet.

The suffering's in their eyes. It's why the doctors can't stand getting close to them I guess. Rows & rows of sad, tortured animal eyes in the beds, they see.

Oh Belle—she's good, patient, as good as Cliffie was. I won't be that good.

There, Belle, there. The young man's reading in the kitchen so I'll give you a wash & rub your sores, now. If Dorcas was here she'd know something better for them than this stuff but anything I could concoct will do more harm than good. There, Belle, lovely, there. A clean nighty. Don't worry about the wash. If there's too much for me, I'll get Edna's girl in. A spoonful of broth, something in your stomach to keep

[p.46]

the medicine comfortable. Try a little. It might go down. We had sausages & applesauce tonight. The sauce we put up last year, remember? Could you take a little now? I could put a spoonful of supper in it & it would help keep your strength up.

Belle hasn't the strength to shake her head. As if a little applesauce would help. But you give what you can.

I didn't see Ivo go, or Cliffie. I'm glad I came home for her.

I wasn't glad at the time. I didn't want to give up that trip to Finland. It seemed so bleak to come back here with the book half done & no commitment from Roberts for a research grant. But it's worked out ok. And Ivo was right—there too: you don't have to be a card-carrying Christian to realize some things are more important than getting ahead in this world.

What'll I tell him tomorrow?

Belle is ringing the little bell Irene sent her from Vancouver—a tinkling brass dinner bell shaped like a hoopskirted lady—I used to abhor that sort of thing, now I've had enough corner knocked off me I'm not sure I abhor anything.

She's low tonight, very low. The pains so bad she can't sleep. I wish she

[p.47]

could turn over. He should have seen Belle when she was young & strong as a moose. It wouldn't have helped—he'd only laugh at her as everyone else did.

Respect, that's what the community was about, Ivo said. The press has a good deal for him now he's gone. They keep wanting pictures of him. There aren't any. That's where the respect comes from.

Belle has all the signs now. I should call Irene. When she's so low I feel like giving her a little shove into yonder. There's no morality in suffering. But she doesn't want to go before Irene comes.

Oh, the look in her eyes when Irene came. "Ellen," she said, "I never dreamed I could have a beauty." Irene was clever, too. Something Iris envied. John & Sally weren't anything special & sometimes I thought Belinda was—well—wanting (Respect! I can hear Ivo saying!) But that it was Belle & Cliff had the right beauty—that didn't please Iris.

Maybe I should just tell him the truth—a bunch of misfits in the dark, that's what we were.

[p.48]

What wouldn't I give for a young man
who asked the right questions!

—

Tilting—sunset: sheep sounds, barking dogs, boat engines: men in dories jigging squid. Anchors on the shore made of 2 crossed pieces of wood & four long ribs gathered at the top, containing stones. Lobster pots handmade too. It's the nets & their weights that must cost. And the engines.

Think of it before engines. Not too bad rowing to the inshore fishery in good weather, I suppose. How far out did they go, though?
A long liner is a big boat—50 feet—goes 50 miles offshore—to the funks.

The anglican minister says "The post on Fogo Island is teaching me the virtue of patience."

1738—Settled first at Fogo
Joe Batts & Barr'd Islands next. Poole & Waterford
1874—3438 people & 18 communities
Merchants were Earle & Sons til 1967
now: 300 boats & 30 longliners
refused resettlement 1967

[p.49]

Mottos over doors—Abandon Hate All Ye
Who Enter Here—Belle's talent

Like the rabbi—ask 3 times

Bahai, CS Lewis, Communism, Therapy
but very, very early

—

Ellen—or is it my gift to reduce everything to senseless plainness, rub the gilt off. I think of my mother Annie down on her hands & knees scrubbing, I think of her thin arms & boney fingers with big bleached knuckles, or standing naked looking at her ruined body in the old bedroom mirror, shaking her head: Annie with her gift for ruin & limitation; how would she have described Versailles? "A big house with a lot of gold & mirrors."

Listen, young man, all we were was a houseful of oddballs.

[p.50]

Fogo ferry $5
Taxi to—$8
from—$8
meals, Hfax airport &
bar ($8.50)

Tilting—noticing
common wells—water carriers in frames
people who come back
1300 pound of cod
handmade anchors

—

The notebooks of IVO KOOMER

Let us withdraw from the rational in order to refresh ourselves.

Let us refresh ourselves by withdrawing from the withdrawal.

What is the source? We are as common as clay and as precious as well water. We cannot be bred. We occur. We are sometimes valued, sometimes stoned.

—

Ellen and Iris stem from the same tradition. There are things they have not been allowed to see. There are directions in which they do not allow themselves to bend. They miss the ineffable and disapprove of those who do not. The world must be as organised as a neatly printed label on a jam jar—in fact I have tried this with both of them—scrawled a word crooked on a label—it was as irritating to both of them as a grain of sand in the underclothes. It is astonishing that

Archetypes— White
Black
Big
Small
Stupid
Bright

[p.51]

they have both decided to come with me. Had they been normal, each would have succeeded admirably in the town.

Iris interests me more. There is a French word "crispé" which I cannot translate but it gives me a sense of Ellen's mind. Burnt to a crisp, perhaps.

—

The goal of being "one with the universe" is not a minor one. To achieve it you have to believe that the universe is more than numbered surfaces.

—

The children's books we were encouraged to read by the public libraries had as subjects

1) the adventures of strange adults (Caldecott etc)
2) the adventures of deprived children (Andersen, Grimm)
3) the adventures of small animals. Given a choice, we identified with the animals.

[p.52]

Ellen: I know what it is now that repels me about the young man, about all the historical questors who arrive: they are looking for magic, they're little boys who want to take the birds apart to see what makes them fly, they fail to understand that magic is in distance, displacement—telescopes and microscopes destroy it.

In fact ideas like Ivo's are common as grass, now. More and more people are feeling the need to heal themselves by living as he predicted they would want to. There's no magic in that, young man, I should say: only the profoundest kind of common sense. You can call what he did a kind of psychiatry if you want, or Theosophy, or Ivernianism—you can put any label on it you want but you won't get any further with it than the farmers did when they called us a bunch of freaks.

Belle, p.

—

You have to see this novel as a sepia film.

Three women at the Pieta of a crucified man?

[pp.53-55]

[Notes on the history of Prince Edward Island]

[p.56]

The State of Educational Publishing in Canada

This past yr yet another Canadian ed. publisher fell victim to the branch plant syndrome. With the purchase of Macmillan by Gage we have even fewer publishers able to provide school & university texts which transmit a Can. pt. of view to Can. students. The formation of Can. minds is therefore almost entirely in American hands. Oddly enough city children suffer even more than small town children who have been known to watch CBC for want of anything else.

Because education is a provincial concern exclusively Fed. policity [*sic*] has not been able to protect ed. publishing. Fifty years ago a semi-national, semi-uniform textbook system functioned accidentally because schools tended to authorize books sold in Eaton's catalogue, which tended to be the Ontario approved ones. The disestablishment of the set text has led to chaos in the publishing business and Americanization in the classroom.

A return to a strait jacket policy cannot be recommended—at the same time an effort to provide Can. materials—literary, historical, scientific—at all levels must be encouraged.

"Notes without a notebook"[13]

Australia 10/3/80

Notes without a notebook—Adele drove me to airport. 3.30 Emplaned OK 5:30 LA—long walk down <u>wet</u> aluminum staircase. Then a long wait—but so far ok. Then 12 hour flight to Auckland. When the going was rough I was <u>scared</u>—the Pacific is very big. Where do we make an emergency landing? My seatmates Uruguayan women living in Australia. No one to make bright remarks to! Just as well. But this need to talk—crickey! Arrived Auckland early a.m. I guess. Airport neat, sweet—bobbies w. shorts & white helmets sprayed plane. Had beer. Got back on. Arrived Sydney about 11. Ages waiting for luggage. leg OK but huge—<u>Barely</u> mobile.

Was <u>so</u> looking fwd to meeting Pat Yeomans. Instead kidnapped by Connie the Consulate at Canberra Oriental hotel. Ages to get room. Got in, cracked whiskey, got Pat [...] She said she'd come with a diuretic at 3.

Apparently she <u>did</u>. I kept trying to get to the door & falling asleep again. Once I got up & dressed—undressed & slept more. And everyone was <u>hunting</u> for me. But she sent me pink roses—a kind of apotheosis. We talked with Dud on the phone. Then I dined w Connie at the City Tallersale

---

Golly—REAL Sydney—tacky as hell & phoney pretenses. I insisted on dining room. Man at piano real cockney type—really good—but didn't know Rogers & Harry. Shrimp tough, food bland. Me drunk, I think.

13 MEA, Box 32 File 16.

Then—one-armed bandits. Absolutely no skill. On the poker machine I play for series not flushes. Crazy. Finally I say, enough.

Mrs Fatfoot I, who can't separate public & private—but I will persevere.

As usual. What is the cost?

Now, on to Adelaide I poured 20 oz of Glenfiddich down the toilet just now & a good thing too.

It's so much better than reality which is like a girdle.

Mrs Fat-foot speaks. [woke up at 4. Must have peed & shat 12 times—things will get better?][14] Just opened the blinds—marvellous row of tin-roofed cottages outside!

They give Sydney its dimension—without them it is Calgary.
[...]
Doctors[15] are not the heros & villains women writers say they are. Not gleaming mad scientists with razor teeth, breast cutting. Nor fathers with big wise eyes. Not even the Arrowsmiths—against everything men say they are. They are just—people. And some are sad and silent. And most of them are kind. They make me afraid. I make them afraid. With old man crab it's not, right now, a heroic struggle.

—

Man against microbe, woman against her passivity, twenty heroic views of Mt Everest. But How can I make you comfortable, the mother I never had said in my dreams.While the Mother I have said: You can't expect to be—and was right.

When I was little there were all those doctors
Haloed around the crib.
Here they are again. I am again
Small & fair (going white) and
To my surprise rather sweet and
Very sorry for myself—and—well

---

14 Square brackets appear in the original text.

15 MEA, Box 32 File 14; two pages on "Southern Cross Hotel" (Melbourne, Australia) notepad.

There they are

There is worse company.

—

Often you see me straighten
my shoulders & stare across a room.
And it is not Crab I am staring at
But Death

And I am afraid of death
Very much afraid—I am no Persephone
Who will return, I am my
numerous selves
Who will never, now, be unified.

But sometimes I see death as a lover
Very tall and male, with big soft
Nipple-less pectorals like a
kangaroo

———

It doesn't make me want to go to him.
I don't want lovers any more.
Crab's taken care of that.
I want to go on living, even at this level
petal-thin
Like a radio a person with ears
Keeps forever turned down
I don't want to dance but to
watch the flowers grow & the fecund trees

Cast their fruit & flowers and my
Big children choose their (oh, please,
lucky) fates
And the moon rise and
Don't hand me into your boat, Charon
I don't have the fare yet.
Crab, I told you not to pay him
in advance—he's not a taxi
driver, I'm not a parcel—I'm … out

Cahier XXXIV[1]

Making sentences and trying to stack them up in a book [9].

Cahier XXXIV is an amalgamation of four small files of loose pages, all notebook-style reflections with two themes in common: stages of illness and sojourns in hospital in the early 1980s.[2]

The poignant single-page entry "In the Hospital" is a recollection of an earlier sojourn in Toronto's Princess Margaret Hospital—in the maternity ward, May 1933. More hospital notes, dated 24-25 December [1980], consider the possible origins of Engel's tendencies towards romanticism—both intellectual and "emotional." Descriptions of illness dated 25 March [1981] incorporate the image of the crab that Engel used for writing about her cancer. A series of "Crab poems," a genre Engel rarely exercised, date from this period.[3] In mental combat with the crab in Engel's *cahier* entries is "pacman," a computer game character that appears to "eat" what is in its path.

Writing helped steady bouts of fear and panic that accompanied the progress of Engel's illness. "Record these feelings," the author instructed herself, 25 March [1981].[4] "Must write … Good. Shall lie down, rest and read, return to writing in an hour. Conquered it. Down, crab. I'm smug."[5] The author knew her illness was serious ("I'm not going to get out of it"[6]) but remained undaunted in her writing plans: "Do: write the children's story, the feet story, the

1 1980-81. *Cahier* XXXIV comprises MEA: Box 34 File 7 (single sheet, dot-matrix printout); Box 34 File 8 (four loose pages, handwritten); Box 34 File 9 (nine loose pages, some typed); Box 34 File 10 (two loose pages, handwritten). Notebook comprising loose handwritten and typed pages; 24 pages used.

2 Dates between square brackets are based on notebook entries.

3 See also "Crab papers March 9, 1981" MEA, Box 32 File 27. The following excerpt suggests Engel destroyed that which was not intended for other eyes, and did not destroy that which was so intended: "So why not start something unselfconscious and real, talk to the paper, put it in one of the green baskets with the poems and then one day if it seems useful get them together. Might be of use to others. If not, throw it out. Unthinkable to write without thinking of publication? What about all the stuff you throw from the middle of the night?" (MEA, Box 32 File 27)

4 MEA, Box 34 File 10 [1].

5 MEA, Box 34 File 10 [2].

6 MEA, Box 34 File 9 [1].

crab poems, the Rains novel and the Iris and Ivo one. It'll happen" (30.3.81).[7] An autobiographical statement amongst the entries sums it up pretty well: "I was always writing, writing, writing."[8]

In the Hospital[9]

I ought to like this building better than I do considering that I was born here but I have no pious natal feelings about it. Once when I was staying in College Wing I was able to look out at the Legislature—a ridiculous pink Buffalo Romanesque building that squats in a perpetual couvade on Queen's Park lawn with some kind of filial affection, because I knew my mother, who was 18 at the time, gave me to the provincial government the day after I was born; but even there, there was a lack: the provincial government was not a particularly good parent. I have no baby pictures and I don't glow at the thought of my own birth the way my ex-husband did when he said he was born in the Private Patients' Pavilion.

Certainly, it was a ward for me, though I don't know which or where, because although I have been given a wheelchair and the freedom of the hospital to prevent my coming down with a case of cabin fever, the fact is that every decade this regal agglomeration of buildings is changed and redecorated and relabelled with the names of the benefactors who donated the money for the changes so that even the staff don't know where they are half the time, and name the buildings from the streets they abut.

Gynaecology is ecstatic to have finally returned—with toney beige carpets—to the old building where the 30s Well Baby Clinic was, with its Della Robbia frieze and the owners of the big department store have erected the new skyscraper wing I now inhabit.

The rest is a maze of corridors and tunnels—some so steep that when no one (and people in wheel chairs are no one) is around, the porters race with empty stretchers.

The parts of the people hardly anyone sees have not been redecorated.

[...]

25 Dec[10]

It comes to me now that most of my French romanticism comes from mother—a sort of Enchanted April world of class & prettiness was in all

---

7 MEA, Box 34 File 9 [1].

8 MEA, Box 34 File 9 [8].

9 Ibid.

10 MEA, Box 34 File 8.

things French for her—except that which was "sordid" (i.e. had to do
w { real sex)
  grotty.
Her generation—also rivalry w. "Colinette w the Sea Blue eyes."
Add to that my <u>intellectual</u> romanticism—the effect is powerful.
Intellectual NEATNESS—that's the French thing.
[...]

30.3.81[p.1][11]

Feverish tonight and should go to bed, I suppose, but I want to write about IT because more and more it upsets people if I mention IT.

I'm upset too; 3 days on the pills and the fevers haven't gone away, the sense of being a balloon of lymph etc. Weariness: had a sandwich and a drink on the way home from work so I could stagger further.
[...]
Trying to figure out what the kids should do: pull themselves together, take responsibility; but when I say I'm sick they develop aches and pains and take to their beds. As I did, when my mother was sick. Magic thinking: if I lean on you harder, you'll have to straighten up, won't you.

No, dear. You'll have to hold yourself up. Once you learn how you'll find you like it. I do.

Do I? Mentally I lean a lot on Dr Scott [...].

Fear in a handful of dust when he isn't cheerful. When he says to remember I'm not going to get out of it. Denial must be a bugbear, lead people off on health-food kicks. I wish I could deny. Sometimes I'm phoney-cheerful. This is a deadly serious game I'm playing and it looks as if I have to play it all alone. All the other serious games are like this.

Enjoy the loneliness, must learn that. Roll with the punches.

God the idea of radiology scares me; lying passive and meek and weary and wiped somewhere half-human, for ages, it seems. Cripes.

When I pray I feel as if I'm just using God. I guess if there is a god that's what he's there for. But I can't believe in sectarian religion, that any one group is saved or chosen, and that's that. Much closer to the animistic religions,

11 MEA, Box 34 File 9.

sometimes a bit to the mystical phases of Judaism or Christianity, but then the wing veers away again and I can't believe.

Do: write the children's story, the feet story, the crab poems, the Rains novel and the Iris and Ivo one. It'll happen.

Sweating hot. Must go into another room, go to bed, strip, get cool. Shit.
[p.2]

[…]

[p.3]

2

I was brought up in a very ordinary vision of Christianity, faith existed and good works, and the promise that one would be saved by the blood of the Lamb if one kept the Commandments and accepted decency, tried to live piously. My Father's house and its many mansions was never literally described, but when I was told I was fatally ill (how melodramatic that sounds: the words were, "Well, it's cancer and not one I can cure") I discovered after probing my visionary side, dredging the depths of my imagination, that I thought Heaven was a great schoolyard and surrounded by a grey stone wall with blue glass shards stuck in it; furthermore, inside the school building were my grandmother Passmore and John Knox. And she said, "Well, Marian, you can come in and sit on that hard chair there, if you want." But she didn't welcome me.

That goes back to a grim Presbyterian vision, doesn't it? And death is Awful, is what comes after, is worse than life, which is in many respects bad enough: one colludes in evil every day, and yet if one decides to fight evil does one know what one is really fighting? (Pollution Probe is the safest charity.)

Some people seem to know what is good and what is bad; that is the advantage offered to them by philosophies which base themselves on simple rights and wrongs, Communists, Catholics, Indians, Negroes, etc being evil and the rest of us good. My view is that nothing is unequivocally evil except murderous action, and it breaks my heart not to be able to figure out which side to be on. Simple truths are a comfort: Viet Nam was bad, and so was Belsen, as history now informs us.

[p.4]

What I fear is the quisling in me: that greylag goose that will run after anything even if it is wrong. Which is why I often have to become the leader because I am afraid of myself as a follower.

I have talked to my MPP of the NDP who is/was health critic about shrinks' fees: saying I'd rather pay, thank you, but not for Dr Vernon and his clinic. Psychiatry is a different profession: you can't see your healing.

I think you are doing me much good; but the other thing that is happening, I fear, is that the cancer is moving. I'm not sure it's psychosomatic. Oh God, I'm tired of that theory but oh, fear and despair, some nights in my bed I get pacman and crab mixed up and tell the wrong one to move.

I am going to have somehow to die. My mother died bravely and I intend to do so too. But not so soon, Lord, not so soon. I shall be, as long as I can be, bloody, bold and resolute … with your help, love,

You know, I might just buy a strip of that beach for MY grandchildren to run on.

[p.5]

I woke up this morning feeling angry and frustrated at always having, so to speak, had to live someone else's life, lie on Procrustes' bed and be prevented from getting on with being me. What I would "naturally" do and what I do do are often not far apart; the pressure on me now to perform is like thumbscrews. Yet I think society probably would let me get away with quite a lot (no it wouldn't! think of all those phone calls yesterday: Do! do! do! Be a good girl now! Don't bother me. Where did you get my phone number? I have two dates for you to make speeches on) (Why did you give me that for Christmas and not this?) Anyway, it seems to me now that I should please myself more and others less; and I am tired and don't want to be pushed around any more.

[pp.6-7]

[Dream recording]

[p.8]

Marian Engel

I was born in 1933 in Toronto. My father was a highschool teacher—auto mechanics, drafting, sheet metal. Because of the way things were in the Depression, we moved a lot: from Toronto to Thunder Bay to Brantford, Galt, Sarnia, all in Ontario. Sometimes we lived in our trailer because of housing shortages. I had a sister six years older—still do, thank goodness.

I have always loved books, and when I was about eleven I started to send things to the Sunday School papers, and then to the Seventeen Magazine contests; sometimes got a prize. In those days it didn't do to mention you were Canadian. But I was—came from a family of nationalists. Father was a pilot in the first world war. Mother was the lieutenant-governor's secretary before she married. She had a typewriter.

I was good at school and not much else. I worked summers as a newspaper reporter while I was at McMaster University; went to McGill in Montreal to do an MA under Hugh MacLennan, the famous Canadian novelist. Then I taught at Montana State at Missoula for a year. Discovered I hated mountains. I became Miss Passmore the Geography at the Study School in Montreal.

In 1960 I got a Rotary Foundation Fellowship to study in France. I thought I might start a PhD but instead I worked on a television play and a novel, became bilingual, read Proust when I was in bed with jaundice in a room M.F.K. Fisher had inhabited the year before me.[12] I took up with an old McMaster friend, Howard Engel, and we went to England where we could get jobs and a marriage license. Then we went to Cyprus. I mostly worked as a translator in the credit business, but I taught a bit too and I was always writing, writing, writing.

We returned to Canada in 1963 and settled in Toronto, where I wrote a publishable book at last, "No Clouds of Glory." I also had twins, William and Charlotte. And more books, "The Honeyman Festival" in 1970. One Way Street (Monodromos) 1973. Adventure at Moon Bay Towers, 1974, Joanne, which was a radio serial, 1975, Inside the Easter Egg, 1975, Bear, which won the Governor General's Award, in 1976, The Glassy Sea, 1978, My Name is Not Odessa Yarker, 1977, Lunatic Villas (The Year of The Child) 1981 and in the same year Islands of Canada, a photographic book.

[p.9]

2

Somewhere in there I got divorced. I've also written hundreds of articles, short stories and book reviews, won the City of Toronto book prize, been a library trustee for Toronto, been Chairman of the Writers' Union of Canada and been made an Officer of the Order of Canada.

I'm tired.

I've sold my archives to McMaster University at Hamilton Ontario, my alma mater.

Canadians like my work, and it's nice to be liked. I don't sell as well in the US and UK, where Canadian is a kind of dirty word anyway; and I find that a book that does well in the UK will fail in the US. You can't win them all.

---

12 See *Cahier* II, footnote 8 for information on Fisher.

I've been writer-in-residence at a couple of universities and taught creative writing at the University of Alberta at Edmonton. I'm a stickler about grammar, which my students don't like, but I belong to that dying generation who routinely took three languages as well as English and it bothers me when students can't take their prose apart and reassemble it.

I write less than I used to because when sales are so poor there's no point in pushing yourself into martyrdom, but I still enjoy making sentences and trying to stack them up in a book.

Some day I want to write about theories of paradise.
Some day I want to write a poem. Some day I will finish the novel I am working on. Some day I will mail this....

Mar 25 [1981][13]

I shall think of this week always as batty week. Got back from Edmonton[14] Sun night very low and tired. Called Dr Scott Monday to say I felt ill, could I see him before the Apt. in April. [...] I, having told the garden designer about my innards rather than my plants, go to London to give a reading[...]. But when I get back [...] Dr Scott calls and says I am to go in on April 3 for 4 days workup before the cone biopsy which will determine whether there's to be an abdominal operation. He knows I'm feeling ill—all still in vague ways which is annoying but surely better than one shrieking big pain, but so diffuse that I complain of laziness, eat constantly thinking that might help.

There's a searing fear somewhere and I know I'm running as hard as Terry Fox.[15] I don't like to stay alone but when I'm with people I'm competitive and critical and difficult. I hide some of this, but not enough.
[...]
Get a hold of yourself, Mary Ann, be sensible. Find something scholarly to do, record these feelings [...].

Must write [...] Hah, into a practical space again. Good. Shall lie down, rest and read, return to writing in an hour. Conquered it. Down, crab. I'm smug.

---

13 MEA, Box 34 File 10.

14 See *Cahier* XXXV [53] for reference to trip to Edmonton.

15 Terry Fox (1959-81), an amputee, attempted a cross-Canada run to raise funds for cancer research. This effort caught the imagination of Canadians.

Cahier XXXV[1]

Finding a voice & a style is NB....
Can one make intelligent beauty? Surely by now! [27]

Engel appears to have used this *cahier* over a three-year period (1981-83), which causes some confusion when attempting to date entries. The opening pages of the *cahier* contain notes Engel made during a fall 1981[2] trip to Germany as a delegate of the Writers' Union of Canada at a conference about unions for artists and writers.[3] The trip was also an opportunity for a dose of cultural activity (Engel took in several art galleries and the Frankfurt Book Fair) and for a side trip to Sweden.[4] As the excerpt from [4] indicates, Engel's notes are sketchy, and not reproduced in full here. Also scaled down are notes the author took on the Establishment of Royal Principalities in Canada and on "names of former European aristocrats to be avoided" [8-10], which seem to have been intended for a story she was contemplating.

The entry "Satori," written July 13, 1982, recorded more of Engel's responses to developments in her health. What stands out once again is the vital place writing occupied throughout the author's illness. Even "1/2 hour of writing [was] enough" [11] to help get through a difficult stretch. "To write seriously again, I want that very much," Engel wrote [13]. She reviewed the manuscript "Elizabeth and the Golden City" over and over in her mind, and wondered whether her own story might not be a better one to write [12].

Even in bleak moments, Engel's critical eye remained sharp. The writer in her could step back and comment, as she did about a description of a mushroom-hunting expedition: "Some run-on sentences—development rambling, inaccurate establishment of place & time. Who is John?" [18]. She had more critical comments on her work, past and present. "How dreadful to have written [The] Glassy Sea in the housemaid's voice of Clarissa Harlowe," she exclaimed [24]. As for a play she had drafted on Pelagia—"it isn't as bad as

1 1981-83, dark green notebook; 91 pages used.23 September - 6 October 6, 1981.

3 A second delegate, Henry Beissel, represented the League of Canadian Poets.

4 6-13 October 1981. Details of Engel's itinerary are laid out in two letters dated 24 August 1981 signed by Mary Jacquist, then executive director of the Writers' Union of Canada.

Ron Hartmann said, but needs more work though I'll never do it" [25]. Engel explained:

> I've all these years been writing faster than I can think. [...] Now's the time to slow down, write Elizabeth, enjoy. Illness will hold it up, but I seem to get better sometimes. [...] I want to make something shimmering with wit & blue eyes & beauty & anger & jealousy & I think I can do it. [25-26]

"Elizabeth & the Golden City" is the subject of further entries in the *cahier* as Engel mused "how to get this book together" [39]. She also contemplated her other major writing project of the time—"The Vanishing Lakes." In her next notebook, Engel would try weaving the two narratives together. But for now they remained separate and quite different in register. In "The Vanishing Lakes," Engel experimented with the fantastic mode, the subject of more research notes[5] that she then applied to "Elizabeth and the Golden City":

> The fantasy is a search for
> the mother.
> The reality is a search for the
> father.
> The framework is a search
> for reality [71].

Engel the writer was always on the alert. During a hospital stay in April 1982, the author's roommate was an eighty-five-year-old cousin of one of Canada's early poets, Archibald Lampman. In no time, elements of the elderly woman's life, and salty snippets from Engel's conversations with her,[6] were being recorded in notes, as if they might become part of some future short story.

Cahier XXXV also records a painful period in Engel's friendship with Margaret Laurence. As if to distance or dull the hurt caused by a falling-out that occurred between Laurence and several of her friends in October 1982,[7] Engel wrote about it in French: "Crise de Margaret..." [31]. Notebook entries reveal

---

5 In the notes she compared the fantastic to literary realism [68-71].

6 "I don't know what I'm keeping that good set of dishes for" [58]; "I don't know, we've all got good sets of dishes that we never use" [59]; "Well if that's what you're having for lunch, I know why you're fat," she said to me [59]. See [56-60].

7 In his recent biography, *The Life of Margaret Laurence*, James King offers several explanations for the falling out, including Laurence's anxiety that her productivity and popularity as a writer were being outstripped by those of Margaret Atwood, then chair of the Writers' Union.

that Engel was deeply upset by the rift in the friendship. "I realize how few friends I have here & without Margaret ... Oh Margaret, Margaret I loved you, but no one is god and it is madness to believe in lies" [34]. The Engel-Laurence friendship survived the crisis, happily, and the two women resumed correspondence. Laurence wrote frequently in the latter half of 1984, the final months of Engel's life.

Other entries laced with pain in this *cahier* concern "Ruth" who figures here as a split-off "other" self incorporating negative traits. These entries, together with several about Engel's mother, were part and parcel of the author's ongoing exploration of her identity, a project that intensified in the later parts of her life.

[pp.1-2]

[Notes relating to the conference in Germany]

[p.3]

Mary Abbott Story[8]—

knives in the head
angels
When can she talk to Osborne?
Osborne[9] is last because he doesn't notice.
The gentlemen caller—has to be some kind of professional friend.

—

poetry matters }
poets don't } story
[...]

[p.4]

Social benefits[10]

pensions
health insurance
disability insurance
(dental?)

---

8 Mary Abbott is the protagonist of the short story "The Confession Tree" in *The Tattooed Woman.*

9 Osborne is Mary Abbott's husband and the last to know she has cancer.

10 This is the beginning of Engel's notes as Writers' Union delegate to the conference in Germany, October 1981.

What can we do about ACTRA's not offering these under category II?

Insurance down to $1,000
Anthology not buying.

[pp.5-9]

[More notes]

[p.10]

July 13 1982

SATORI[11]

For an hour or so today after talking to Dr T[ennen], I was in a state of perfect calm—Judy called it Satori.

It was a bit frightening (is this death?) but also very beautiful. I had no energy to waste doing things: I just stood & enjoyed the flowers.

I was not itching or hungry or hurt. I didn't want anything.

I don't like being too long with people—I'm losing interest & have no energy for them. I saw Will & he was serene. I realised that all my talk of being lazy was a denial—I really can't do much, there's no point in pushing myself as there's nothing to push. It is possible to enjoy oneself.

[p.11]

When the children make energy demands, it's different. —The highs & lows alternate very fast. Physical stuff small & annoying—electric shocks in the breasts, eye-itching then peace again—a little energy, a good creative space, $^1/_2$ hour of writing enough—Blissful sleep nightmarish dreams—no, jumble sales. small fears withdrawal—that happiness.

People mill about, I sit at the still centre—bad, good & indifferent.

[p.12]

La chair est triste & j'ai tous les livres—really. I want to write again. Endlessly turn Elizabeth in my mind—then wonder if my own story isn't better.

[...] Much to do—why bother? It's the 14 juillet[12]—should have gone to Harbourfront—but the inability to go suits me exactly.

[p.13]

To write seriously again: yes I want that very much. [...]

11 In Zen Buddhism, satori is the state of sudden, indescribable, intuitive enlightenment.

12 France's national holiday.

10 Aug

Prepare for the Golden City Now.

Collect sugar packages from restaurants; enjoy the informative decorations now; store carbohydrate for later.

—

—a night of fragmented self-accusing dreams

[p.14]

Here's something for all you kids who are going to have to write how I spent my summer holidays pretty soon.

Hilda's[13] woods aren't very many acres in extent, I suppose, and they're only partly hers—surely her husband Reshard has his name on the deed also, but he's about ideas, cedar shingles, & funny hats: Hilda's about growing & noticing things.

So when they decided to go into town to the bank, the airport & those other tedious places I'd had enough of, I stayed behind with the dogs, Luna & Scott, on the grounds that I was going into the woods to hunt chanterelles.

Hilda & I had been in the woods two days before after a rainfall and found ourselves surrounded by more varieties of fungi than I had ever seen before. We had thought we had seen delicious chanterelles but were unwilling to experiment: PEI in summer is too nice to want to die. So when her friend Viane dropped by we elicited a drawing of a chanterelle with vertical gills. It would be the colour of marshmallow peanuts in candy stores, she said.

[p.15]

When everyone had gone (including a half-naked man who'd been hitchhiking until he heard the good news, the van was going) I set out for the bush with Scott & Kaye bending low through the tunnels of old dried twigs—the lower branches of overgrown firs.

This crowded wet hillside is a perfect terrarium for the falling lichened twiglets, soft needles & leaves of spring flowers sink into a damp matrix that is dark and nourishing: every kind of fungus grows there—chrome yellow flecked white, red & pink like a bunch of floppy cigars, shiny brown, shapeless white, too. Shapely

13 Hilda Woolnough, the artist, with whom Engel stayed during a visit to PEI in 1982.

[p.16]

Amanita white, even mushrooms that pink-brown mushroom colour that looks so good on a fungus & so bad on a living room carpet. But no chanterelles. After a while I got tired of hunting & sat down on the moss—forest woman & dog stared at by Indian pipe people. I studied moss & horsetail fern & discovered a network of mushrooms the size of a pinhead & remembered the horrid story of the uni[versity] students who had died of eating the wrong magic mushrooms.

[p.17]

I just sat, after that, not frustrated in the end because I knew none of the fungus names. I sat feeling part of the primordial ooze. This was a textbook case of soil building life—establishing itself sapio-phytically on life—piling up being. It was a privilege to be part of it.

I went back to the house. John phoned, John who had wanted Hilda to make sure she looked in the stomachs of the trout when she cleaned them so he'd know what they'd eaten, what kind of flies to make next week. I wondered why I lived in Toronto.

[p.18]

In winter, they haul 4 or 5 cords of wood on toboggan into the house to keep warm. Sometimes they're snowed in for 3 weeks. Their cars give out again & again. It's no life for me.[14]

In summer, you have to flap your wings at the humming birds to get in there & weed the scarlet runner beans. It's good to go back to first principals. And we're very lucky who can.

—

Some run-on sentences—development rambling, inaccurate establishment of place & time. Who is John?

[p.19]

Aug 24

Yesterday Dr Scott told me I did not feel what I felt—in no uncertain terms. I shot back, he caved in. VERY interesting. Got a prescription—[...] Why doesn't he want me to buy my own stuff? Power I think. He's lovely, but can't bear not to be in the driver's seat.

How lovely to be free to move.

[p.20]

Been thinking about neurosis. Obviously even self destructive people act in their own best interest in their own crooked way.

---

14 Earlier, in *Cahier* XXXIII, Engel had recognized that living in Newfoundland was not an option for her either.

If you can run faster than anyone in your group, the group hates you. Therefore it is safest to cut off a foot.

If you adopt a child who is more brilliant than your child, you have to even things up somehow.

[p.21]

Mother & I got along brilliantly intellectually but emotionally we were both scared by our own needs & dependencies. She never gave up trying to make me into her own girl—I didn't fight her enough. After I was divorced she came back like a bad dream. She liked me better with one foot.

—

Hey wait—nobody did that—to me—I did it to myself by not fighting back. By trying always to be subservient even when I knew it was wrong. The lame child act. Why? I thought it would

[p.22]

make me friends, I guess. Or just not get hit.

Char—my braces are a protection.

—

Martyrdom

"Give me the crown of thorns."

[p.23]

Isaiah Berlin on the compensations of those who do not feel they belong.

revolution
identifying with the leading group & over-compensating
creating Utopias.

(about Jews but boxed in an article about being black & then moving into the Jewish intellectual world.)

Aug. 27 1982

Stronger & stronger feeling that I am standing up in a new way, standing up in a new life. Taking control—wanting suddenly an international position, a real status.

[p.24]

The bliss of things being that Mother's money[15] will allow me to do this—leave domestic bullshit & family pages behind—without denying the value

15 Mary Elizabeth Passmore had died 24 May 1982, and had left money to her daughters.

of personal relations, rise above them, write, really. Be free of gruesome "popularity," step back 2 books, breathe again.

How dreadful to have written Glassy Sea in the housemaid's voice of Clarissa Harlowe.[16]

[p.25]

I've just re-read my little play about Pelagia—it isn't as bad as Ron Hartmann said but needs more work though I'll never do it. Still, he asked for froth, got it & was wrong to complain.

I've all these years been writing faster than I can think. But I've DONE it, too: got the kids half hauled up, made a nest, financed it, really lived.

Now's the time to slow down, write Elizabeth [and the Golden City], enjoy. Illness will hold it up, but I seem to get better sometimes.

[p.26]

Models

Post-modernists are fun but how much can you write about writing & who are books for. One writes for one's peers & mine are not profs of post-modernism. Death to imitate Borges & Calvino. They are themselves, good & belong to their own sensibility.

Where do I belong? I want to make something shimmering with wit & blue eyes & beauty & anger & jealousy & I think I can do it.

[p.27]

Finding a voice & a style is NB. Mr Rochester haunts.

Elizabeth who dreams of spires….

Can one make intelligent beauty?

Surely by now!

—

Sunday

Saw H. & M. Atwood & Tiff in paper as p[aper]back writers—dreadful urge to compete!

–

2 Sept. Wed.

My blood is low again, my spirits are sinking, my footsteps in the hall repeat, "half dead, half dead." Shall I stay that way or take my pills?

---

16 Harlow is the protagonist in Samuel Richardson's, *Clarissa, or The History of a Young Lady Comprehending the Most Important Concerns of Private Life* (London: G. Goulding, 1748). Clarissa defies her tyrannical family by refusing to marry according to plan and running off with a man of whom the family disapproves.

[p.28]

Sept 29

I would so like to have a lover.

Couch in Dr T's office = bed = baby

having a baby! being a baby—one connects the two because after sex one feels like a baby.

That feeling again? Never to have it again, the thought of it makes me want to cry.

[...]

[p.29]

Move to baby theory—feel like baby, am innocent, sweet, charming, passive, pink.

My pink & blue bed.

I like innocent w sexiness.

How kinky is this—why I liked Pretty Baby.[17]

But the innocent & small <u>are</u> sexy & small things are lovable.

Must have had strong sexual feelings as a baby.

Love can do you in, baby
faster than flit.

dependency + possessiveness.

Chinchilla—a world.

[p.30]

8 Oct. [1982] Working things out

[...]

[p.31]

Elizabeth & the Golden City
A family romance

–

For all my intellectual aspirations is this a <u>serious</u> subject. Can it be?

Why not? Depends on use of detail, the effect. To be serious, avoid coyness, sentimentality.

Oct 26.

Week of dreaming.

Crise de Margaret qui nous en veut parce que Peggy l'a critiquée devant sa fille Jocelyn et a dit que l'on l'aiderait en temps de crise. Rage, orage, furie. "On a blessé ma fille." Now we are gossips & traitors & very hurt. Letters, phone calls flying.

---

17 This is a 1978 Louis Malle movie starring Brooke Shields, Keith Carradine and Susan Sarandon.

[p.32]

She is quite right that she helped me more than I did her. She'd rather die than take the lower position. The awful thing is that if she goes on drinking she will. She's written off the Union, most writer friends. Except of course Adele,[18] whose hate grows like a ball of butter, it seems.

Well, too, if Adele forms her salon, it will get the Union back to being a Union not a club.

We'll never get PLR now. Let's go for Jack [McClelland]'s[19] copyright arrangement.

[p.33]

I was hurt. Now I'm relieved. Something had to be done, Peg did it; we backed her. There's a crisis.

Oh, I hope she doesn't withdraw entirely. I hope she SEES.

It wasn't until Peggy told me drinkers were boring that I saw.

M's jealousy of P is on the surface now—Surfacing for Survival.

But oh how the storm hurt—& the words seemed to be Adele's. Which hit hardest.

[...]

Get out?

Not yet.

[p.34]

Oct 30 [1982]

Back from Montreal[20] & suddenly weeping. It was so good there & now I realize how few friends I have here & without *Margaret*. And will she savage me? Oh Margaret, Margaret I loved you, but <u>no</u> <u>one</u> is god & it is madness to believe lies.

[...]

---

18 Adele Wiseman (1928-92), author of *Crackpot* (1974), won a Governor General's Award for Fiction for her first novel, *The Sacrifice* (1956).

19 Canadian publisher whose company (McClelland & Stewart) publishes many of Canada's well-known Canadian writers.

20 Engel had been invited to give a reading at the Simone de Beauvoir Institute, Concordia University.

[p.35]

[...]

I must make new friends. Or go back to Montreal. Oh, I can't. Oh I am unhappy today as I was yesterday happy. If that is English.

Montreal: Chassidim with hats like Boyars!
Outside staircases
Simone de Beauvoir Institute

[...]

[p.36]

So this is pneumonia—
much better
when doctored!

[...]

[p.37]

Long talk w Peg abt Margaret.
She spoke to Joe.
Joe told not Marg but Adele.
Peg says the old Marg doesn't exist any more.

Adele has a new patient.

Marg's pretences are now out in the open.

She has nowhere to go.

Drinking & phoning circle—all have had treatment.

[...]

[p.38]

Fact is, I've presumed they've shared my politics—everyone is moving to the right.

[...]

[p. 39]

Do— Sort bathroom out
Get Food in
Call Lew [?]

[...]

Nov. 12

The frightful, burned face of Constance[21] a burning, (fearful?) shy dark eyes & square cornered smile, Constance who has destroyed all her childish snaps = Marian Ruth at 7, the Only Girl with the Wooden Bum.

[p.40]

[...]

Old experience somewhere, forgotten.

I want to blot it/blast it out with alcohol. I want to sleep & avoid it.

[...]

Storm coming love the violence

(kids screaming coming out of school: sirens)

Constance—her face/past burnt off. Determined not to go back. Chinchillas help me now.

Women favouring their daughters outrageously.

[p.41]

[...]

Is my untidyness a desire to be punished or a laziness or untidyness?

[...]

[p.42]

16 November

I have this day mastered the art of putting up [a] curtain track! A liberation, an epiphany.

[...]

[pp.43-44]

[Dream recording]

[p.45]

—

Article by George Steiner on Canette pointing out that as the world moves away from Freud, it goes right wing & structured & v. v.

[...]

The myth of Creation
"The morning & the evening
were the first day"

One can create only
at these quiet times.

21 A character in Engel's draft novel "Elizabeth and the Golden City."

[pp.46-47]

[...][22]

[p.48]

Sat 11 Dec

Woke with a feeling
that freedom gives fear.

Myself in a green field,
like Custer Park, alone,
not knowing which way to go.
Tendency to run to institutions—
jails
hospitals
asylums
in people who are fearful. SHELTER.

Go talk to the fox!

IRONY of getting old & established:
you stop being able to use freedom.

7 Feb 82

Alive, still
Will moved out—CAN THINK!

[p.49]

Not thinking now—receiving.

MUST go through to the other side of the looking glass.

Start at the beginning again

1) the egg

2) the roses

3) Mr Rochester MUTILATED
[...]

---

22 "Bugger off everyone," Engel wrote in a series of quick notations [46-47] about work she was doing, wanted to get done and feared not completing if house guests were on hand.

[p.50]

Feb 21 After seeing Dr Vernon

I have become an expert on fear. I should answer the phone: fear speaking.

Pacman—eat crab.

A book on fear or Paradise?

Mar 2—

After a week with Audrey[23] so happy. Odd dinner with Peggy [Atwood]—the Pythoness. After she has said the word, what can the rest of us write? Answer: You feel nothing, the answer is everything (cf Golden

[p.51]

City). But I am so much reminded of my pa's pronouncement that the very intelligent didn't see enough, were to be pitied while they judged. And she WAS tired; tonight much better.
Dr T[ennen] says convalescence is shorter if you DON'T feel deprived. I won't. I don't want my uterus.

What did I come down to write? Joy & unjoy of this week. Competition w. Peg felt strongly, fear. Love of Audrey. "Us heterosexuals," I feel. So does she.

We won't always have a lovely time but this one was a mitzvah, & I'm so glad.

[p.52]

[...]

[p.53]

[...]
A lot of the time now I feel equal to things—gotta watch my malice, though.

March 16

Timor mortis conturbat me.[24]
But Sophie had 4 kittens—fascinating black, grey, tabby, ginger—her own

---

23 Audrey Thomas, award-winning Canadian novelist, most recently author of *Coming Down From Wa* (1995).

24 "The fear of death distresses me." William Dunbar, "Lament for the Maker" (1508).

mixture sorted out. She yelled, then settled down & did a good job.
[...]
But I am physically not well—v. tired, can't sleep, crowded in the middle, sweaty etc.
Consolation prize: all new clothes for Edmonton[25]—hence no washing & ironing & why not? Lovely rose-coloured shirt & harlequin pullover for readings.

Oh dear—I've let Mother's memorial plant die. From John Fletcher.

Fred's farm[26] is beginning to look Don Millsish—but I love it.

[p.54]

[...]

March 29

Two weeks of flap—the medicos want me soon, TIMOR MORTIS gets worse & worse. I feel claustrophobic when Helen is kind, have nightmares about institutions. I am comforted by the methodical kindness of doctors who are so rational yet so low-key that I must THINK. In fact NOTHING except a lymphoma-low & a polyp could be going on.

[p.55]

I am also comforted by the purchase of a squat blue teapot—the UK—teapot I think—though delft or undecorated brown or speckled blue—but this one clings to the earth, is short & stout in the right way.

Inside myself I know I deserve the worst. Dr T[ennen] is very good about this. I dream of death & grieve for myself, he pulls me back into a sane world. I am becoming very devoted to him—which is a bit off the track. But there is a grief in me, a lack of trust, a fear, a hope, that culminate in visions of boiling oil and

[p.56]

if not heaven in a straight chair. What shall it profit a man—etc. I think I'm worldly. Migod. The unworldly are more worldly than me.

While I'm out of it, the house will be a commune—Jane, Judy, Char (GET MORE KEYS made). An experiment in negative entropy
[...]

[p.57]

[...]

---

25 See *Cahier* XXXIV [2] for reference to Engel's trip to Edmonton.

26 This is a reference to "Vanishing Lakes."

[p.58]

April 4—In hospital

It's not so bad—cool rationality is here & the doctors are there to treat the symptoms.

–

My roommate is an 85 yr old cousin of Archibald Lampman, very low but cheerful & upright. From Wyoming. A milliner with Holt Renfrew once.

–

I had a coffee when I came in and paid for it.

–

April 6 Boredom sets in
no tests today—nothing to do
Helen came w flowers & the
Globe and Mail

"The Little Milliner"

Worked Beaches, Danforth, Holt Renfrew (boss, Mrs Stinson). Cousin of A. Lampman. Fine featured, slant-eyed. Lived w. friend Katie since 1929 who lived to be 103.
[...]

"I don't know what I'm keeping that good set of dishes for."

[p.59]

"I don't know, we've all got good sets of dishes that we never use.

"Well, if that's what you're having for lunch, I know why you're fat," she said to me.

"I don't like it, up there at St John's."
"Well if you don't like it there's no use in going there!"
[...]

[p.60]

[...]

Graeme [Gibson]'s Sony walkman is <u>divine</u>—the way to handle hospitals.
[...]

[p.61]

[...]

The reality of the hospital is much less awful than the anticipation.
[...]

[p.62]

[...]
The world charged with the glory of crab?

[p.63]

The good thing is that I got my professionals separated from my friends! Doctors are doctors & lawyers are lawyers & friends are friends—& such friends!

[...]—how I've needed them & how they've responded!

Exclamation points like Queen Vic[toria]

Staff metaphors: Bone marrow like having your soul sucked out.

Cancer—fear—must be like
a rat gnawing at
you just there (the vitals).

I've been feeding that
rat.

[pp.64-67]

[Notes on thoughts in hospital]

[p.68]

[...]
May 20—TLS of May 13.

"Thoughtful remarks abound—on the meaning of treasure in adventure stories, on the voyage as 'the visiting of difference,'" on Henry James's art, "deep like that of a blind organist"?
Review of "Le Roman d'aventures" by Jean Tadie.[27]

[p.69]

p. 480 "The shocking thing abt Habegger's book[28] is not that it shows fantasy maintaining a relation w reality but, conversely, the realistic novel still deeply marked by all the failings of cheapest fantasy. It is a pity that his

---

27 Annette Lavers, "Hurrying Along," rev. of *Le Roman d'aventures* by Jean-Yves Tadié, *Times Literary Supplement* 13 May 1983: 496-97.

28 Alfred Habegger, *Gender, Fantasy, and Realism in American Literature* (New York: Columbia University Press, 1982).

fire never crosses the Atlantic to fall on George Eliot. It does fall, however, on H[enry]J[ames] & with devastating accuracy. J's fiction … is obsessed with hidden secrets because there was one their author did not know, that of the American male initiation.... In "Portrait of a Lady" he endorsed the deadly

[p.70]

female myth of self effacement...."

Then goes on to pt out that Joyce, Proust, Eliot used passive loners as heroes. "Are they not genre figures too, whose presentation is every bit as emptyingly self-flattering as that of any martyr-mother or brawny barbarian?"

—

Realism springs from the rejection of fantasy, rather than the other way round. Fantasy has as its main goal the creation & reinforcement

[p.71]

of belief structures, often (& esp. in matters of gender) with ruinous effect. Yet people indulge in it virtually all the time. The Q remains whether fantasy can ever produce anything worth while, & to this Habegger's book returns "NO" in thunder. The answer may be "yes" just the same.
Columbia Review of Gender Fantasy & Realism in A.L.
NOW—think of E & Golden City

The fantasy is a search for the mother.

The reality is a search for the father.

The framework is a search for reality.

[pp.72-77]

[...]
[Thoughts on the funeral of a Passmore family friend]

[p.78]

July 22 my friend the crab is cross-grained & cack-handed tonight. When I send the Great Crab in after him there is a crunching but one wonders how effective they are.
My legs are tired.
[...]

Aug 18

Story ideas after PEI
The Yellow House
The Unburied Treasure

[p.79]

[...] Sept 8—Period of disillusion & instability, but I am coming through, as witness a story I sketched out today about a woman spilling like a carapace (shell of cicada anyway)

Chrysallis
pea pod
milkweed pod

To emit her 4 year old self.[29]

[p.80]

What I have seen—
that my weird prejudices
go back to childhood—

[p.81]

[...]

[p.82]

The Story of Ruth

One or 2 things I know about her:
She is destructive
self destructive
passionate
throws herself at men

<u>old</u> <u>old</u> wicked (?)

She prevents me from fulfilling myself.

She is evil.

Mother did same
—I hated that side of her

[p.83]

Shall I smash Ruth?

No more than I smashed Mother—sure savage her a little, be cruel: she is.

But love her, too.

[...]

---

29 A reference to the story "In the Sun" in *The Tattooed Woman.*

[p.84]

I'm in touch with little Ruth & I've got to keep her from killing me.

[p.85]

Rose Valley PEI
16 August 1982

Dear Maggie[30]

My friends[31] who own wonderful place have gone into town & I'm alone with the dogs, cats, flowers, veg., and hummingbirds. Also an invading wasp I shut into the top of a coal-oil lamp with a book of Ja[me]s Baldwin's. So I guess I'm writing to get out of dealing with that!

I don't know why I'm thinking of you but I am—thinking also I may be going to Vancouver in Feb & might be able to afford to get down your way.

[p.86]

Poor Mother died in May & left me a surprising amount of money. I wish she'd had it herself when she was in good health.

I fought with her & I'm surprised how much I miss her—she was a tiger with me as I am with William & never stopped trying to change me.

I can hardly write by hand now!

I've been a journalist since Nov.[32] & enjoy the regular income. My health was doing OK until I got shingles May 1. I must say I hope never to organize a funeral with shingles

[p.87]

again. Eventually my blood dropped & I went back on Chemo. Zowie! I now see why people like speed.

Anyway I don't know how I am because when I'm low I'm 2 ft from the grave & when I'm up I'm fine—I guess that means I'm OK.

I've just about finished with the therapist & feel much better, but there is a kind of chemical depression with lymphoma I'll have to fight forever. The booze is OK, I was just being bad; can stop now.

Goodness, my writing is someone else's. I'll have to stop.

I'm here for another 4 days—then home to love & duty. PEI in summer is the earthly paradise. I'll be in touch about Feb. love

Marian.

[pp.88-91]

[Phone numbers and budgets]

---

30 This appears to be an unsent letter.

31 Hilda Woolnough and Reshard Gool. See also [14].

32 Engel wrote a column called "Being Here" for *The Toronto Star* for a year beginning November 1982.

Cahier XXXVI[1]

Writing
Creativity
Mothering
Giving birth
Surviving—as a writer [2]

In June 1983 Engel was an invited speaker at the conference "Women and Words," which took place 30 June - 3 July at the University of British Columbia. While the notes Engel recorded in her *cahier* during the conference are fairly sketchy,[2] an account she drafted afterwards described in some detail the activities and outcomes of the gathering as she saw them.[3] "Women and Words" involved workshops on "criticism, the media, publishing, editing, literary survival in a world still bleakly male-dominated."[4] With Joan Haggarty and Libby Scheier, Engel chaired a workshop on childbearing, child rearing and creativity, which she recounted as follows:

> I didn't know what the audience would want to hear, what I could usefully say and I really wanted to be off listening to Margaret Atwood and Phyllis Webb discussing the Muse, but the room was full and it became clear early on that the old superstition that having a child fulfilled or cancelled out your creative urges had to be slashed. No, we all said, it's supporting the child that distracts you, but responsibility feeds rather than destroys talent [...] Carol Shields brought two fair daughters who said, "It's wonderful to have a mother who's a writer." I had needed to hear that.[5]

Energized by the gathering of so many women for whom the work of words and writing seemed more important than appearances, food or popularity, Engel

1 1983, slim blue notebook; 14 pages used.
2 For this reason only a few of the more coherent passages are excerpted here.
3 MEA, Box 31 File 105.
4 Ibid. [2].
5 Ibid.

thrilled at Québec feminist writer Louky Bersianik's rallying cry: "Gynaecide est genocide!"[6] Bersianik was one of a handful of Québec women writers who attended the conference, and in whose work Engel expressed her interest. Her notes mention Nicole Brossard and Madeleine Ouellette-Michalska, and record the various goals and objectives which came out of the conference:

> Yes to a feminist dictionary.... Don't accept genocide, boycott Pay TV, get in positions of power, translate more, catch up with the Quebec feminists, demand disarmament ... remember that imagery is more effective than preaching, and that sisterly support can't do your writing for you; you do it alone; stop appropriating native women's imagery, find your own culture ... the best art is visionary and subversive.[9]

"Women and Words" was a landmark event in the development of feminist literary criticism in Canada. It articulated a genuine desire to foster active communication between women from Québec, women from Native communities, women of colour, between women right across the country. The vision of community and cooperation was strong, and must have been bittersweet for Engel, who had struggled so much on her own.

Cahier XXXVI offers few other comments on the conference itself, though a cross-reference in *Cahier* XXVII is of note. It reports Engel's discussion of "Women and Words" with a friend[7] during which she became overwhelmed by a "sudden terrible fear" that negative thoughts about her father[8] might mean she was lesbian. That Engel experienced this as a fear is a measure of the stigma that lingered for lesbians in the early 1980s, and of the importance of conferences such as "Women and Words," which helped to dismantle damaging stereotypes.

[p.1]

Criticism
Louky Bersianik—funny but couldn't hear
Ann Saddlemyer—theatre
Carolyn Hlus—gen survey
    bilingual, good

---

6 "Propagande haineuse contre la femme = génocide gynacide" [11].
7 Sara S[tambaugh], *Cahier* XXVII [17].
8 "He had too much power," *Cahier* XXVII [16].
9 MEA, Box 31 File 105.

Saddlemyer—play must be first produced. Criticism of printed text is often OK, but of performance is inadequate. Radio–BBC buys more.
But there is also a female shorthand—should we use it?
Things women are accused of: is things they ought to do, like communicate.

[p.2]

Writing
Creativity
Mothering
Giving birth
Surviving—as a writer
—as a provider
how to buy those shoes
Your history, your child, your work

<u>more</u> possible to write than
practice medicine.
early childhood → creativity
→ mothering

[p.3]

more than 700
write to funding agencies

Anna
Banana

<u>Workshops</u>

New approach to criticism
good art should be subversive
class affects writing
voice of working class, native, women of colour
writing—erotica—more space for the body
feminist presses → booksellers association formation
survival in media
personal contact —funding
become policy makers
our literature must be

restructure vocab syntax
symbolism
lesbian devel[opment].
alt[ernative] structures in a new
language
mentors, networks, support
group

[p.4]

Can[adian] feminist bookstore
network TWBS [The Women's Book Store]—85 Harbord

need of translations

pub & writers—good contracts
self-censorship & external

We covered everything

Comme<u>nts at mike</u>

1. We need to understand each other better—I will be bilingual. Need for a feminist bilingual dictionary!
2. Ruth Schiller of Can. Council—Kathy Berg
   Esther Bobak

Write your MP

3. media—journalism—lot of history, not encouraging—disillusioning

[p.5]

4 Contact w. literature in Quebec & w publishing has been good. We don't make enough noise in English Canada. Let's BOTHER people.

5 Role of corporate & technical writers
use of computers & wordprocessors
<u>Song</u> writing

6. Conference a tribute to the power of gossip—meet at Waldorf

7) Demand Spec[ial] Devel[opment] Funds for Women artists
   CFDC—% for women
   Demand all funding bodies % for women
8) Haggarty: Danger of looking for support when you should really be working on another draft.

[p.6]

We are sometimes too supportive of our own sex's work
Courageous
Subversive workshop—avoid bludgeoning with politics—lazy about imagery—moving on from
* preaching

9 Newfoundland Maison white a newfie connection as well as French—need a lot of liberation in Newf[oundland]

10 Women in academics
Tax refusal for arms[?]
(Don't collect your UIC)

11. Hearing impaired need help

12. Women of colour pleased their material dealt with not as an after thought but integral

[p.7]

Haggarty	Webb	Galloway	Meigs
Shields	Atwood	Morley	Livesay
Weinzweig	Crean	Thomas	Merril
Rule	Kostash	Batt	Brossard
Campbell		Wachtel	
Gaye Allison			

Sit in
Irene Robinson
Gloria wonderful
face
Anna
Banana

---

13 Libby Oughton of Char[lotte]town

Violence: How do women bring up sons?
workshop on humour

14 Québécoise—we are still here—thanks for the invite

15 Sexism in technical writing
What is a manhole?

[p.8]

16 a woman from Germany. Gratitude
missiles—where was Women & Peace
humour keeps us alive
commitment to Peace
(also woman from Japan here)

17 Workshop leaders should have met first.
Nothing organised for Jewish women

18 Sue Crean—
Canada Council—sit in
don't be so nice

19 Barbara Smith NWT
Native woman
more get-togethers

Resolutions

Makeda Silvera—Women of
Colour

Civil Liberties
Hiroshima & Nagasaki

[pp.9-13]

[Ongoing conference notes]

[p.14]

August
(poppies—big white ones)
lavatera
foxgloves
biennials
peonies

Cahier XXXVII[1]

There's so much writing to be done [8].

In the fall of 1983, Engel's life was complicated by the need for a hip replacement. Even with the new challenges this posed, the author pursued her writing and continued her critical reflections on the craft. Hospitalized 29 September for diagnosis, her first thought was to "get a typewriter & extra table—work a little." "I need some kind of project," she determined. "What can I write?" [10-11]. Engel decided to try merging "Elizabeth and the Golden City" and "The Vanishing Lakes." "Why not fragments?" she wondered. "Other people are brilliant at smooth flowing narrative, but I can put together bright shards" [16]. "Why is episodic/lexicographical form so much more attractive to me than flowing narrative, which people prefer to read?" she considered [31]. Her answer is worth quoting at length:

> Perhaps it's a sign of disturbance but I think rather it's that broken forms allow, like broken hearts, deeper truths to seep up—narrative flow avoids emotional points the way it is conventionally done. I am even more attracted to direct statement than I was when I was younger, and perhaps need <u>all</u> the elements to express the complexity of what I see. [32]

"I like more & more the idea of 'broken' forms allowing more psychological dimensions to come thro[ugh]," Engel made up her mind [36]. "I don't think a novel ought to be too complicated <u>to read</u> but it seems to me it can aspire to intellectual values without betraying a trust. Literature ought to exist on all levels" [36].

In an interesting aside, Engel decided she had been "snobbish about genre fiction, seen it as a room w[ith] built-in furniture—less capable of being INVENTED than 'straight' fiction but its formulas do present a rare freedom" [36-37]. The leeway she was prepared to extend to genre in general, however, did not

1 1983, "The Raspberry Notebook." Cover is a large close-up photo of raspberries; 57 pages used.

reach as far as detective novels, and her reasoning is compelling:

> In their relentless plunge towards the ending they void their own content, senselessly—they don't take themselves seriously. They divert, but they are, even when informative, well made soufflés, because they have decided to appear to ruminate & emote without going through the actual process. This is comforting for the reader—one can pretend one has shared "awful" emotions without doing it—but an empty experience, one I do not need now. [18-19]

Engel preferred the effort of Saul Bellow's *The Dean's December*, which she described as "all middle rich & good" [19]. "[It] makes me want to write a really decent book—is Eliz[abeth and the Golden City] strong enough to carry one? How do you write about a busy life?" [18].

Also on Engel's reading list at the time were investigations into the invasion of privacy by psychoanalytic criticism. The author considered findings by Edmund Wilson and Leon Edel[2] in relation to her own work—its "paranoid penultimate paragraphs" [5] which she thought stemmed from her fear of parting with her characters. She acknowledged her fear of social workers, institutionalized society, and of certain jealousies [5].

Various medical treatments Engel was undergoing seemed to affect her dream life, and *Cahier* XXXVII includes many dream recordings.[3] These in turn led to wakened introspection. "Suddenly inside myself I'm calling out for Nor again," Engel jotted [33]. This appears to be a reference to Eleanor, birth name of Engel's twin sister, and it is immediately followed by thoughts about Ruth:[4] "I cannot tell her to go away because she is part of me," Engel noted. "She is unintegrated, composed of clammy tendrils—they have to be taught to twine differently—with me instead of against me or am I being too metaphorical?" [49].[5]

The fall of 1983 was not an easy time for Engel. "I know a lot about pain now," she wrote [45], "I know a lot more than I let people know" [31]. The author expressed gratitude to her children and friends for their attentions and care.

2 Edel's works include: *The Psychological Novel*, 1900-1950 (1961); *The Modern Psychological Novel* (1964); *Literary History and Literary Criticism* (1965); *Stuff of Sleep and Dreams: Experiments in Literary Psychology* (1982). Works by Wilson include: *Axel's Castle: A Study in the Imaginative Literature of 1870-1930* (1959); *Classics and Commercials: A Literary Chronicle of the Forties* (1958); *Letters on Literature and Politics, 1912-1972*; and *O Canada: An American's Notes on Canadian Culture* (1976).

3 As before, and for the same reasons, these are not included here. There is a marked increase in dream recordings and intimate introspection from *Cahier* XXXVIII forward. Excised pages are, as before, noted with the symbol [...].

4 See Introduction, footnote 43, on the significance of the name Ruth.

5 See also [30, 33].

Thanks to them, and thanks to her writing, it was still possible to wake up, as she did on 19 October 1983, and experience the "gorgeous feeling of transcribing one's own interior" [46].

[p.1]

Chorus of Women

There go Tanis & Ildelorn
Headed for the Golden City
Who think they are looking
for their mother
Iris the unsteadfast.

The Golden City is far away
And never easy to find.

The Sea of Grass, the Slough
of Despond
The Vanishing Lakes, the Thorny
Mountains
all these must first be
traversed.
Why must they, dark and
fair
Weak & strong, young & perverse
Take up the peril of the
Quest?

[p.2]

Sore feet, a wet bed or
none
These, we tell our child
romantics
These are the perils of
the Quest.

You will not meet Bluebeard
in the Thorny hills.

Or any magic native figure.
Thirst, discomfort, pettiness:
The blisters of a minor death.

Why leave white beds,
Posters of heroes, a life of
Strawberry socials and
    peony heads
At most a sterner life of
    social service
For a useless quest?

They regard us with
    blind eyes & passion.

[p.3]

And what will you
    do when you reach
The great lyric dull
    perfection of the Golden
        City?
How will you find the
        key?

SISTERS

We shall sit in grey
at the edge of the
well
Offering stone jugs of
    water to the centurions.

At evening we shall find a
    couch
In the yellow stone house of
    Iris
Savouring the olives she
        offers us for supper
Black olives with stoney beak

[p.4]

Chorus

No one has learned anything
in the history of the world.

—

Tanis & Ildelorn walk
 on stone eggs
Preserving their innocence
On the ends of their arms
On isinglass spoons.

[p.5]

Invasion of Privacy by Psychoanalytic criticism

—Wilson & Edel

—own case—symptoms only appear in work
 paranoid penultimate paragraphs—fear of parting w characters
 fear of social workers
 institutionalised society
 certain jealousies

historical perspective—depressions, epidemics, wars

Kathleen Raine—art as compensation horrifies her.
Can you make an artist out by disturbing a child?

[p.6]

Not all artists have been disturbed children but it is safe to suppose, however, that the need for beauty surfaces with special vividness in painful lives; for imaginary friends in lonely lives (Robert Louis S[tevenson] in the land of Counterpane), for pattern in disordered lives, (excitement) it is a tribute to the human spirit that the will to create beauty, terror, pattern, joy continues even under the worst of circumstances. The rhymes & ululations with which small children comfort themselves in bed became great poems.

[p.7]

The tedium of small lives, like Jane Austen's, becomes an ordered verbal pattern as exquisite as lace; pain & madness become the vision of Turner & Van Gogh, silence the music of Beethoven.

But can a critic ever analyse these works to reveal the verity of the artist? Surely he has not enough intimate, personal information.

—— . ——

After a night of many thoughts

—the acrobatic forms of denial I have taken up include the delusion this hip[6] was psychosomatic.

[p.8]

—There is much writing to be done.
—What can I do about Char's tears but be grateful to her?

——

Now finally understanding the origins of my emotional treachery—my beating away of those I love best—the frightened, angry child inside me wanting to hit them because they cannot supply <u>her</u> cravings—formed in the incubator and never satisfied—it's too late now, as Dr Scott says. <u>Public</u> love is what one goes after in these circumstances, but it interferes w. private.

[p.9]

Vague baby memories now surfacing—a white uniform tight over a breast (maybe modern & post-op?) and a <u>very</u> hairy male body—bearish.
[...]

–

Re disease—you have
to decide how
much you can <u>bear</u>
to know.

–

There are great syllables.
MOG LOR NOR

Poe & Lost Lenore[7]

[p.10]

Mtl [Montreal] 29 Sept [1983]

I was afraid to come to this place—they gave me a private room because I can't go to Ottawa for the
[illegible]
Watching Gould & then Lyal's HOME FIRES on TV.

Everyone good to me—[...] & wanted to cry w. gratitude
Hip broken
lymphoma bad.

---

6 Deterioration in Engel's hip was part of the progression of her lymphoma.
7 From Edgar Allan Poe's "The Raven," *The Raven and Other Poems* (New York: Wiley & Putnam, 1845).

What to do?
Get a typewriter & extra table—work a little

[p.11]

30 Sept [1983] What's done can't be undone dep't—have to figure out some way to put in time. [...]

Now I need some kind of project
(Hosp[ital] very quiet in a.m. [...])
[...]
Now? What can I write?
Chorus of Women
Tanis & Ildelorn
Childhood in Windsor
Typewriter ? Foolscap pads.

[pp.12-15]

[Notes on "Elizabeth and The Golden City"]

[p.16]

Section: Lovers & Leavers

Edwina

We published her memoirs. She had not always been female & there were ways in which she would never change—she always took the head of the table, talked loudest & carved.

(Why not fragments? Other people are brilliant at smooth flowing narrative, but I can put together bright shards.)

Crabbe's beach—last stop before the Golden City.

(Instead of doing the Pilgrimage in a red & black checked pélérin you can take the Sinister Express.)

[p.17]

Sun Oct 2 [1983]

Another little pessimistic flux—but my life is in order & I can go if I must. There is in my dreams a fear of the dark, a way towards a river. & I dreamt Dr Scott told me it was glorious on the other side.

Leaving the kids would make me very sad but I know they are good people & will make out all right—Char will be happier than William but he, too, will stabilize.

What a wicked woman I am to think fleetingly "But I haven't had enough Scotch!"

[p.18]

I may get a remission.
This is a hard weekend to get through.
"The Dean's December"[8] makes me want to write a really decent book—is Eliz strong enough to carry one? How do you write about a busy life?

The Healer could be a great, funny figure.
I've got cold feet about seeing the doctors tomorrow.

—

I am tired of detective novels because in their relentless plunge towards ending they void their own content senselessly—they don't take themselves seriously. They divert, but they are, even when informative & well

[p.19]

made—soufflés, because they have decided to appear to ruminate & emote without going through the actual processes. This is comforting for the reader—one can pretend one has shared "awful" emotions without doing it—but an empty experience, one I do not need now. Whereas "The Dean's December" is all middle, rich & good.
[...]

[p.20]

Oct 4 [1983]
I feel elated at the idea of a new metal hip!

Dr Goodman says he's ordered a specially nice one—I love being childish in this way.

Hosp[itals] are more fun when I know I'm looking for daddies!
I've seen some good ones too.

Pre. op night—talked to my kids whom I looove.

11[45] Team of nurses w. flash lights interrupt nightmare—

[pp.21-27]

[Dream recordings]

---

8 Saul Bellow, *The Dean's December* (New York: Harper and Row, 1982).

[p.28]

The Linen Room—Story Title

13 Oct [1983]—happy this evening. Dr T came & congratulated me on my state of mind, was wonderful & in spite of the trailing scorpion pain in my leg I am happy. That man is restoring my dignity & sense of well being & I love him for it. So, of course, does Ruth.

—

Ideas for columns: [for "Being Here," *Toronto Star*] Synaesthesia, folk medicine, psychological biography, the loneliness of the Loch Ness Monster.

[...]

[pp.29-30]

[...]

[p.31]

[...]

Getting back to a world of good values & quietness.

Think of Ted P, Miss Lamont,[9] but if she got me to read Parkman[?] she also told me happiness

was not a value & "Children dislike Bohemia." She was right in her dry way—but sex of

course is missing. <u>Not</u> passion.

—

I know a lot more than I let people know—

—

Why is episodic/lexicographical form so much more attractive to me than flowing narrative, which people prefer to read?

[p.32]

Perhaps it's a sign of disturbance but I think rather it's that broken forms allow, like broken hearts, deeper truths to seep up—narrative flow avoids emotional points the way it is conventionally done. I am even more attracted to direct statement than I was when I was younger, and perhaps need <u>all</u> the elements to express the complexity of what I see.

—rhyme
—essay
—Greek chorus
—narrative

---

9 Kathleen Lamont, whom Engel met at The Study, the private girls' school in Montreal where she taught 1958-60.

But how hard it is to do.
"I remember being a bellied baby."
[...]

[p.33]

Suddenly inside myself I'm calling out for [Elea]Nor again.

—

Ruth slips her tendrils through the bars of a crib, hoping for the nape of a father.

—

5 pm It is taking ages to get over a nightmare about being in a medical clinic in which they treated me badly while making a fuss over me. In the end I wound up having a fistfight with [...] & lying all scrunched up on a lawn while an English woman asked where Marian Passmore was.

[p.34]

[...]
Chorus of women

There is only one life
Go from a warm bed & a big man
To a warm baby, tend it while
Your body draws on a store of
Precious affection that will
    last you through
Dry days & the scabby nights
        of age.

If you do not do this—
If instead you choose
Hot pursuit of the world &
Cold efficiency
You will get the dry days
and scabby nights
And never have had that love.

[p.35]

[...]

[p.36]

[...]

I don't think a novel ought to be too complicated to read but it seems to me it can aspire to intellectual values.

[p.37]

without betraying a trust. "Literature" ought to exist on all levels.

I've been snobbish about genre fiction, seen it as a room w built-in furniture—less capable of being INVENTED than "straight" fiction, but its formulas do present a rare freedom.

[...]

[p.38]

[...]

[p.39]

Lemon trees grow in the
Golden City

—

That year, it was if the facade of our small city began to peel and crack: I learned that people didn't like us, and we didn't like them very much.

—

I was caught between father & Frances, forced into the uncomfortable role of competent one as they complained to me about each other. I felt victorious as father bitched about Frances—responsible, the favoured one, perhaps, except that I knew he wouldn't talk so much about her if he weren't obsessed by her.

[p.40]

She began to grow coarse as Mother had said women [did] when they drank & were promiscuous. Her hair was wild & her skin clogged with makeup & she said "damn" & "shit." Older men with long jaws & crooked smiles came to the door for her—salesmen & accountants. They made father swallow his objections to Flynn who, behind his greaseball exterior, was a gentleman.

—

Those who had offered pity stopped speaking to us. I began to notice the clacking of the cups during Holy Communion. The butcher's son told me my father was a cheat when I wouldn't go out with him. I wouldn't go out with anyone.

[p.41]

[...]

[p.42]

The man across the hall plays the radio in the a.m. Unbearable.
Just finished "The Captains & the Kings"[10] almost unbearable, very beautiful. Irish ascendancy v. sad now—not responsible for fathers' sins—the sense of beauty though.

---

10 Jennifer Johnston, *The Captains and the Kings* (London: Hamish Hamilton Ltd., 1972).

Beauty & violence, Ireland, Cyprus
write about

Story about woman who breaks her hip—her old mother visits. Last of a kind (Jane & Gladys)

[pp.43-45]

[Hospital notes]

[p.46]

Birdlike, funny, British, Eliz[abeth] Jolley.[11]

Divertimento
I like more & more the idea of "broken" forms allowing more psychological dimensions to come thro.
The charm of Cyprus was the way it allowed the ancient past to show.
Should I read this detective novel?
Or have I given up shit?

19 Oct.[1983]—woke up & wrote ... gorgeous feeling of transcribing one's own interior—Tanis & Ildelorn en route to the Vanishing Lakes.

Chorus of women—advice for the old "division of labour world"

Then divide it into antiphony.

[p.47]

[...]

[p.48]

The fifties cannot have been such an awful period if they taught me such joy in music & art. There were people around always waiting to entrap children interested in art. The Sony now rubs Bach against my eardrums. This is LIVING. Different in people who know German I guess—an exoticism removed.

[...] [p.49]

Ruth—Reach

I cannot tell her to go away because she is part of me.
She is unintegrated, composed of clammy tendrils—they have to be taught to twine differently—with me instead of against me or am I being too metaphorical?

[...]

---

11 Jolley is an Australian writer, born in Britain, author of: *The Newspaper of Claremont Street* (1981), *My Father's Moon* (1989) and *The George's Wife* (1993).

[p.50]

[Dream recording]

[p.51]

[...]

Sun am

Ruthie sitting up defiantly smiling in her crib, squashing cigarettes into her gaping, greedy mouth.

—

If that was an <u>old</u> cancer in my hip I no longer have to think in terms of

[p.52]

that awful word "metastisize"(sp?) (don't even want to know how to spell it!)[12]

——

Writing it.

[...]

[p.53]

[...]

Mon wrote passage about art & escapism.
sense of a larger world than reality offers, knowledge, sheer entertainment.
As long as we are plunged in that world, we can keep at bay the horrors of mechanical &
physical plumbing, the sordidness

[p.54]

of the flesh, the lethal competition of personal relations.

Being a woman I was only partially removed from reality. Women have to learn early to deal with blood whether men wish them to hide their secrets and be ethereal or not. Childbirth later opens the body in a way one cannot pretend to escape; although the ritual shaving, enemas and episiotomy show a male eagerness to tidy the process; the fact is we are born from our mothers' guts, and the woman who tries to escape that fact has a poor time of it. In the days when "Ladies" abounded, they had servants to handle the messier aspects of domesticity, but it is my impression that few women of my mother's generation & few of mine too, have been able to avoid dealing with raw liver, uncleaned chickens, diapers, and vomit. It is not so bad

[p.55]

if you hold your nose and keep your eye on the end in sight—a good dinner, a healthy child.

---

12 The correct spelling is metastasize.

But I, like my colleagues, was shielded to a degree. Nanas did a good deal of what we call the dirty work and when it came to relationships I was protected, like a man, by having my nose stuck firmly in a book. I had a few friends—women I'd met at work on the Home & School Association—but no relationships

—

[...]

[p.56]

[...]
Re small towns, Methodism,
confession: do a number on
The Necessity of Navy Blue &
the fear of heaven
[...]
The fathering that goes on in hospitals.

—

I am half
sorry to lose this
world of blissful sleep: but the dreams have not been that good.

—

Dreams but no nightmares.
[...] [p.57]

Cahier XXXVIII[1]

Suffering grants us ... a view into Hades that makes us wise or at least thoughtful [28].

Dream recordings are the dominant feature of this *cahier*, followed by personal introspection about Eleanor and Ruth.[2] References to treasure in boxes or suitcases guarded by dragons recall earlier reflections in *Cahier* XXXI. Then, too, Engel was experiencing a period of low self-esteem. "Confidence low," the present *cahier* records [60]; "handwriting is changing again, damn it. Who am I?" [15]. By 1983, however, Engel seemed to feel that "it is safe to give 'him' the treasure. If I do, I can stop being the dragon" [35].

Inserted amongst Engel's personal introspection is her interesting reflection on narrative and its insufficiencies for her combined "Elizabeth and the Golden City/The Vanishing Lakes" manuscript. "For this book it's wrong," Engel declared, "because it leads me into tedium. So shall I decorate it w[ith] "characters" (Dickens), language (Joyce) ... how can I make it magic?" [20]. After reviewing Lawrence Durrell's effort in *The Alexandria Quartet* and Margaret Laurence's in *The Diviners*, Engel decided "one ought to go farther" [21].

Amidst the psychic upheaval of her dreams and the debilitating progress of lymphoma, writing could still work its magic for the author. "It feels good," she wrote near the end of the *cahier*.

[p.1]

Nov 4 [1983] I am happy tonight as I sometimes have been during this illness—blissed out, relaxed. Is it because I have dropped some of my obligations, don't feel I have to make too many efforts on behalf of other people? Friends are around—but I am happiest alone after a satisfactory encounter

– – –

1 1983, "The Blueberry Notebook." Cover is a large, close-up photo of blueberries; 64 pages used.

2 See [2] and [18] respectively.

> Of course I am <u>taken</u> <u>care</u> of: house in order, doctor & physio calling—why not be happy?
> Any <u>whisper</u> of obligation irritates me—but my resilience is increasing.

[...]

[p.2]

[...]
<u>Eleanor</u>? Don't want to think about her tonight. Night night.

[pp.3-4]

[Dream recording]

[p.5]

Nov 20 [1983] 2 am can't sleep, should be, considering all the scotch I've had on top (carefully) of pills—Sue Swan's "Good review special"—super!

Lying in bed thinking abt what to tell the shrink I'm closer to the core of <u>this</u> week—which is that although I <u>feel</u> very weak & terminal I'm actually much better & rather resent that because energy is causing the Pink Cloud of <u>Book</u> to evaporate & I'm getting back to personal problems—small ones—but they hark me because Book is what I want
[...]

[p.6]

I am TIRED [...] But I am NOT TIRED the way I was last week before chemo—I am not dying!... When I say I am tired I merely resent dealing w. personal relations again [...]

[p.7]

[...] I want to finish saying something [...] Still want my CLOUD.

[pp.8-9]

[Dream recording]

[p.10]

[...] Thurs [Nov] 24 [1983] Waking up thinking that I've insisted on staying in a childish fixated daughter—relationship to men—very small daughter—so that all the men I know become Daddies

[p.11]

& big authorities & when they won't stay that way I get upset. It must be that if I accept that I can be their equal it leads to sex w[hich] is dangerous.

It has led me to over-value men wait on them & be angry & disappointed. And disgusted because my adult self can't stand this. <u>Why</u> is it dangerous to stop being a baby?

[...]

[p.12]

[...]

[p.13]

[...]

Sat [26 November 1983] I wake in the night desperately afraid & full of ideas.

Sun [27 November 1983] night—can't sleep—have been reading Dr Faustus whose which's? theological premise I can't stand yet whose importance I respect (write English Marian) & at the same time finally developing Amelia—a woman with a Oatesian allure & why not & a scene where Frannie & Eliz turn on the Major when they discover the taxes on the house are unpaid.

Tiff called me Miggs – I hate that.

[p.14]

[...]

[p.15]

Nothing profound to say at all—& I thought I had. Should look for adoption papers.

Freudian slip: Where is Leo Ross' letter.
[...]
Nobody ever mentions rhythm in prose.

Handwriting is changing again, damn it. Who am I
[...]

[p.16]

[Dream Sequence]

[p.17]

[...]

Dec 1 [1983] Horrid tonight—all sore points—knee, good hip, gut—sore—throb in forehead, tiny cold—is the phlebitis worse—do I drop things because I'm sicker? Crummy thoughts.

So I pore over seed catalogues think about Amelia (have I made her too much like Ameliarian?)—also make up a small transaction w Frances & thing about newly invented Floy & her estate

[p.18]

Then there's Ruth, dancing in an old fashioned undershirt on an examining table—a shrimp for her age—wild, coy, male belly—advances to the doctor. A memory.

Brantford: the doctor w the 3 brass monkeys.

Got to finish reliving this stage & grow up before it's time to go! I must buy jack in the pulpit.[3]

Can't tell how self indulgent this lassitude is but I just gave myself a lecture & began to plan to move upstairs....

[p.19]

There's <u>mental</u> energy, thank god.
And I've always been up & down.
Nothing could be better for me than this sleeping.
[...]

[p.20]

Narrative
Ordinary hist[orical] narrative was fine for the punic wars & works for an outlandish subject like BEAR—but for this book its wrong because it leads me into tedium.

So shall I decorate it
    w. "characters" (Dickens)
            language—(Joyce)
(but of course they do much more)
    drive it deeper into inner
            consciousness, give
            it a black strain?
How can I make it magic?
One day I felt it should be a lexicon, another a faux-romance.
Certainly after Joyce & Woolf one ought to try.

[p.21]

Hitch it to philosophical concepts
    & another book as in "Vendredi"
    —can't unless that other book
    is <u>Bear</u>.

There are formal ways of making
    magic—eloquence, echo,
            elegance

3 The name of a wild flower.

and content can make it
as in The Alexandria Quartet.[4]

Class can make magic—not here?

The 3-layered way of The Diviners[5]
doesn't quite work—the
stubborn child of the
italics is a little coy.
Songs aren't integrated
But counterpoint w romance
is wonderful.

But one ought to go farther

[p.22]

[Dream recording]

[p.23]

[...]

The elements of fiction writing that's what I'm writing about, sorting out.

—

Watch[ed] Little Women[6] tonight w Char—had forgotten Jo's lover was a Professor Bear!

[...]

[p.24]

Getting on with it—

Montreal & growing up
—to be European, to be
existentialist, to be worldly, to avoid the appearance of domesticity
above all to lose one's provincialism
to be above
domesticity

Leaving: To be removed from the cosy nest of students, to move to a place
that seemed to have no intellectual climate—to live in a cold city

4 Written by Lawrence Durrell, whose work was a major literary influence for Engel.

5 Margaret Laurence, *The Diviners* (Toronto: McClelland & Stewart, 1974)

6 Film version of Louisa May Alcott's novel published in 1868.

where you had to produce legal documents to buy a bottle of wine.

The process of being educated seemed to involve divesting oneself of home, hearth, family.

[pp.25-26]

[Dream recording]

[p.27]

[...]

Dec 16 [1983] Women who want to be beaten must have somewhere developed the idea (at 2, three?) that
sexual intercourse is a beating?
What grownups do, but painful & dangerous … in order to grow up they choose beating.
What this has to do with lack of self esteem (& jack and the pulpit) I don't know.
Well I know about the plant.

cf articles in New Yorker on origins of Oedipus complex

My dislike of this concept—I want now to <u>respect</u> the elders.

[p.28]

Sat night—Maybe I didn't feel good enough to turn into a woman at 12 or 13 but the cruelty of sexism is to lock all women into the domestic world regardless of their ability.

The revolution had to come when they stopped being able to get servants to make up for their lacks. Of course the first woman to be able to read her marriage contract began to crack the mould.

Suffering grants us—look this up—a view into Hades that makes us wise or at least thoughtful—look this up—wound & bow explanation.

Domesticity takes tremendous manual ability—as does farming. When <u>everyone</u> has to do this, many fail. Women shut away from variety of possibilities come enraged.

[p.29]

18 Dec [1983] The promise of the new land is always healthy children. Riches, too, but the first is the main context—and we are all bigger than our ancestors though not as longlived.

Getting on for 1984 the mood is apocalyptic—fires, bombs, accidents. We must be convinced the Orwell vision is the end. Dying people ought not to write about the future. They think badly of it.

Hades passage in Greek book—copy. Have a bath; it'll warm you up. Who's talking? Me to me, Sara, not someone outside. I'm Iris, too.

[pp.30-31]

[Dream recording]

[p.32]

Dec 20 [1983] from The Gods of Greece
Arianna Stassinopoulos & R Beny[7]

Hades

Hades teaches the need to "practice death" daily—evaluate the lesser in our lives in terms of the greater. Hades is Pluto.... Symbol the cornucopia(?).

Also a physical realm—cave entrance to Hades on Styx.

H[ades] invests the darkness in our lives—depressions, anxieties, upheaval, grief—with power of illumination & renewal.
Instances of what is hidden rising from below....
Renewal through spiritual death—a richer & more conscious life.

[p.33]

What we are in the process of becoming is infinitely greater than what we are. Life becomes relieved of having to be a vast defensive arrangement against psychic realities! [...]

[p.34]

Oh, how I have been surrounded by flowers—& desired & needed it.

———

ask about seephoning

———

7 Arianna Stassinopoulos and Roloff Beny, *The Gods of Greece* (Toronto: McClelland & Stewart, 1983).

Nannie in a circle of trees,
which are as men walking.
Who is the magic boy?
Nannie is cold.
Nannie is hungry.
The trees protect Nannie, but
    they never come near.
She wants them to come near.
One day a tree will come near.
It will be scary.
Nannie is small & trees are big.
The trees protect Nannie from
    the ladies
And the other children.

[p.35]

<u>Wed</u> The right present is the treasure.

——

It is safe to give him the treasure
If I do, I can stop being the dragon.

——

[p.36]

[Dream recording]

[p.37]

22 Dec [1983] New post solstice resolutions.

1. The dragon to give up her treasure to the man.

2. Nannie must take the hand of the Magic Boy and go beyond the circle of the Protectors (men as trees rooted) towards the outside world.

Then she must leave the Magic Boy because he belongs in the magic wood.

Dec 26 [1983] Reading <u>Mecca</u>—if I survive this torture I will be strong, strong, strong.

[pp.38-39]

[Dream recording]

[p.40]

Dec 28 [1983] Decided to take a grip on physio situation
[...]

Rage gives energy!

Probably for psycho-sociological reasons it is acceptable for an artist to be mad & for a man to be a cripple—but crippled woman isn't on the cards.

[pp.41-46]

[Dream recording]

[p.47]

15 Jan [1984]—On hearing the word "Sarassin" & thinking Saracen: it is the writers who are capable of making the gross changes in human thought in the collectives, as psychiatrists do in personal relations. Scott & the current crisis in the Middle East would be a thesis—Scott romanticised Arabs as Saracens.

—

[...]

[pp.48-59]

[Dream recording]

[p.60]

Sat—writing again & it feels good
confidence low, though

Tylenol: 12 a day
12)150 = 12.5 days
3
When did I get it? Last Sat?

[...]

[pp.61-64]

[Dream recording]

[loose page]

<u>MARIAN ENGEL</u>[8]

Born in 1933 in Toronto, Marian Engel (nee Passmore) grew up in Galt, Hamilton and Sarnia. She was educated at McMaster and McGill universities. She received a Rotary Foundation Fellowship in 1960 to study French literature in Aix-en-Provence and lived in Europe for some years—experience reflected in most of her writing, especially <u>One Way Street</u>, which is set in Cyprus, "one of those regions a prey to passionate dissatisfaction, like Ireland." By contrast, the heroines of this and her other early novels feel themselves outsiders in a "rigid" Canadian world

8 As noted earlier, towards the end of her life, Engel sketched various short self-portraits, such as this one. See *Cahier* XXXIV [8-9].

and fulminate, like Sarah Porlock in her first novel, against "the long colonial sleep." Sarah is the most embittered of her heroines, the one most constricted by sex and society; a disenchanted teacher of literature, she complains.... "We keep ourselves isolated from—the passion of making literature—from the passion of discovery.... I want to get into a world where creation--creation of anything—is a fact, where ideas are important, where people are tough on you and where if you turn out something good nobody, but nobody, will say it's 'cute.'" One finds an echo of this in Mrs. Engel's statement, during an interview published in 1973, that "People don't understand fiction in this country ... people are really, I find, very keen not to believe that there is such a thing as imaginative creation"—but she also observed that "people are recognizing that writers will help them with their identity crisis." The acclaim given her novella, Bear, will doubtless have reinforced this latter view, though it is first and foremost an "imaginative creation." The Glassy Sea, her most recent novel, won the Canadian Authors' Association Silver Medal for fiction in 1979.

Novels: No Clouds of Glory, Toronto, Longman, 1968; republished as
Sarah Bastard's Notebook, Paperjacks, 1974.
The Honeyman Festival, Toronto: Anansi, 1970.
Monodromos, Anansi, 1973: republished as One Way Street, Paperjacks, 1974.
Joanne, Paperjacks, 1975.
Bear, McClelland & Stewart, 1976.
The Glassy Sea, McClelland & Stewart, 1978.

Short Stories: Inside the Easter Egg, Anansi, 1975.

Interview: in Ed. Graeme Gibson, Eleven Canadian Novelists, Anansi, 1973, pp. 89-114.

[loose page]

SAILORS ENCAMPMENT CEMETERY[9]

1. Red Granite marker, older limestone base VICTORIA RAINS 1841 1909
Owen R Rains 1830 1927 Separated by cross. Same name other side RAINS

9 This is part of Engel's research on William Kingdom Rains (The Major) and St Joseph's Island.

II small uniform 1 to r Owen T Rains 1857 1967
Mother Father Nora
Clara Robinson 1870 1962 Linda Richardson 1975 1958
The named ones are separate markers.

III Our dear Mother Mary Ann Haller 1947

John M Haller 1885—1963

Brukhart, Frank 1879 1936 Ruby 1887-1967

IV Frances Melvina wife of Arthur M Rains 1st stone marked

died Dec 23 1919 aged 66 years 8 months

RAINS & IHS Markers in this plot
Arthur M Rains d. June 191928 [*sic*] aged 87 years 3 mos.
In mem of Arthur Clarence Rastima Rains d Stept[*sic*] 5
1884 aged 1 year and 10 mos.

V Frances Rains b June 21 1811 d Dec 24 1892 Aged 81 years

Alice G dau of Wm and Frances Rains d July 28 1902 aged 63 yers

Mary Alma McLeod belov. dau. of John and Linda McLeod

b April 28 1874 d August 21 1882 aged 3 yrs 3 mos.

Linda A. Hursley infant daughter of Gord and Alma Hursley

b July 3 1886 d Sept 7 1886 aged 2 mo 4 days

Constance K Rains d August 30 1910, aged 65 years

Cahier XXXIX[1]

You can't have everything—but once you are a belonger you leave something else out—commitment always means loss, curtailment of possibility & I never can face that. [19]

Cahier XXXIX, spanning the months between February and September 1984, has two main ingredients: sixteen pages of recorded dreams (Engel called them hallucinations), in which a great number of individuals from Canada's literary and cultural scene make their appearance; and outlines for the novel Engel was working on (the combined "Elizabeth and the Golden City/The Vanishing Lakes"). The *cahier* also records Engel's pleasure at the thought of possibilities offered by another spring.

[pp.1-15]

[Dream recordings]

[p.16]

Wed 22 Feb [1984]
[...] After these & many other hallucinations caused by calcium poisoning etc—home hell. Well, sort of. Involvement of spine not good. Fancy a tumour on the sciatic nerve?

[p.17]

Still, ought to be able to hobble on for a little bit. Have a spring perhaps?

What interests me is the indescribable appearance of that little psychosis: "I'm sorry I'm filthy & bad tempered." So you have to find someone who [illegible] you that way.

[p.18]

"Day is dying in the west"[2]—JB
Mays The Major said
—

1 1984 (February-September), "The Orange Notebook"; Engel has jotted her height and weight on the cover; 28 pages used.

2 Hymn composed by William F. Sherwin (1826-88) in 1877.

Lost in mine own alchemy
I ought perhaps to be an old (as Elizabeth is now) scholar man, a creature of dust & parchment ... but heigh, ho, I never was born to be an old man—it's over the hedge with you
Arthur, canter the next corner & get along there to duty & see about [illegible] & get it
down straight.

Aug.
15.
1951. up [illegible] like
the good old man himself.

[p.19]

March 4 (?) [1984] Sunday

Great cheer after visiting Joe.

March 8 [1984]—Char to Miami—visit from Howard—cheer, regret, sentiment then the thought "I don't want a [Christ]ian burial—I want to go where I belong, to the crossroads w. a stake through my heart."

You can't have everything—but once you are a belonger, you leave something else out—commitment always means loss, curtailment of possibility & I never can face that.

"Thank you Theratron II"

[p.20]

[...]

[p.21]

[...]

—March 12 [1984] I am spoiled w. a new housecoat, an odd geranium, a baby's breath terrarium, tulips
& Iris, a muffin, strawberries, soap I LOVE IT & them: Iris (!) Aasta, D. L. Stein. A <u>new</u> kimono cheers me up—renewal is important—I felt like a birthday child.

[...]

[p.22]

[...]

17 March [1984]. Yesterday Dr Scott said he thought people just got cancer if it was their karma—which is probably as true as anything gets—I tend to believe in the fates & the norms, myself. But it's depressing when I face what a pickle I'm in. The radiation is doing its job but I won't be the same person again & that's that. I'm resigned, not enraged, but very sad.

Thank God the estate making is done.

[p.23]

[Dr] Tennen came Thursday & it was a pure delight to see him.

Now in September [1984] condition is improving—after 2 ops, 2 lots radiation, 2 calcium attacks I can still stagger—but THINK better & want to talk about novel—from the plethora of pages I could unearth

2 generations or 4

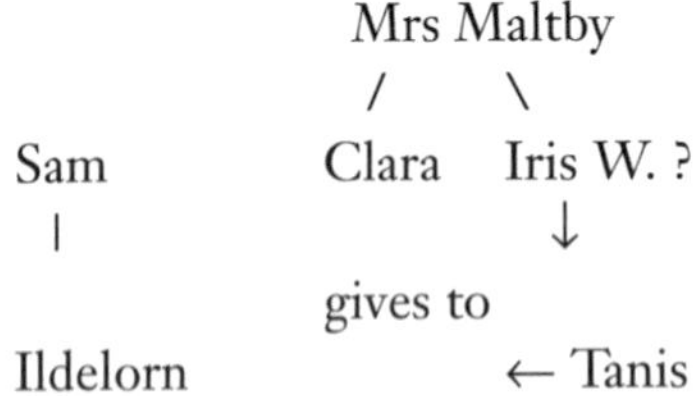

[p.24]

Begin w death of Clara.
Gunter living at house w
Tanis & Ildelorn & Sam.
Girls find Reva & go to
hunt for Iris.
Meanwhile IRIS, IVO (John)
Reva Clifford (Bernice etc
Ellen Leeser
have gone west to
Fugitive Lakes.
Farmed w difficulty.
Ellen Lee becomes leader.
Reva is ousted.
Iris & Ivo move on.
McCrory is guardian of the valley.

Tanis & Ildelorn compete for
John or McCrory.
Tanis paints—is prisoner.

[p.25]

And these were the generations.
(SAM) (the Major?)
Cora, Clara, Tanis, Constance
(IVO) (the Major?)
Iris Ildelorn Agnes
Belle Revars, Reva ↘ Beva?
(Clifford)
Annie Lever, Ellen Lever—Schine de Scandelion

The Fugitive Lakes—shedding its
sociological dress & detail

Schine de Scandelion who was
crooked & cruel

[pp.26-28]

[Inventory of household items; sketch of property in Wilmot Valley, PEI]

Cahier XL[1]

Looking in mirrors ... saying goodbye to myselves [2].

With the help of an inheritance from her mother, Mary Elizabeth Passmore,[2] Engel was able to realize a number of wishes in her later years, including a garden from which she derived much pleasure. Though she called upon the skills of professional gardeners, the author had a hand in the garden's design. This *cahier* contains a sketch of her plan, complete with desired location for various plants. Lists of flower names here might be compared with those found in earlier notebooks.

It is almost certain, from the match of the lined paper and the opened staples at its centre, that this is the *cahier* in which Engel wrote her last short story, "The Steam Wheelchair." The story pages were removed and eventually archived separately.[3] Elsewhere *Cahier* XL records Engel's trip to Paris with Charlotte and William at Christmas 1984. Relevant excerpts have been inserted into the next *cahier*,[4] Engel's last, written during the final months of 1984 and early 1985.

[p.1]

Call Sheridan nurseries
about paving w. unilock stones
digging up back, putting in trellis.

[Map of garden] crab apple?
mountain ash?
Russia olive?
Forsythia?

1 1983, 1984-85, baby blue notebook "from Vera," "Garden Book & Paris Book —anyway, pleasure," written on the cover; 18 pages used.

2 Mrs Passmore had died 24 May (Engel's birthday) 1982.

3 In MEA, Box 33 File 54.

4 Three loose pages pertaining to Engel's trip to Paris, catalogued in MEA, Box 34 File 16, have also been inserted into the next *cahier* (XLI).

Call Sheridan nurseries
about paving w. unilock stones_
digging up back, putting in trellis

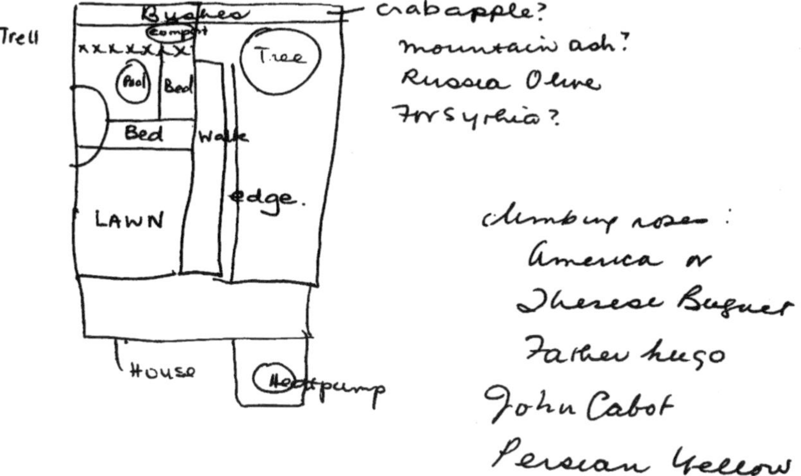

for Fence: SilverLace -
Honeysuckle

Between Fence + Trellis: Raspberries.

Page 1

climbing roses
America or
Thérese Bugnet
Father Hugo
John Cabot
Persian Yellow

for Fence: Silver Lace-
Honey suckle

Between Fence & Trellis: Raspberries.

[pp.2-14]

[Notes on trip to Paris and dream recordings]

[p.15]

[...]
Jan. 22 Found this yesterday while hunting wheelchair story [...][5]

[p.16]

Actually it sounds good. I wake with a sense of beatitude. Malin stands before me holding out a cup of early morning tea. "Nadia's off," he says. "We thought we'd go on a picnic—after of course your doctor's appointment."

He said that in such a way that I thought of cool Finnish lakes birch trees & cold champagne. "Shall I open your shutters?"

"Not yet—thanks" The cicadas were sawing already. I thought of cicada skins."

—

Which is somehow superbly pretentious—very amusing to do first thing.

Brown walls, yellow mums—Oblong picture frame along the bookcase.

[p.17]

[...]
Important to note down visitors because I have these moments of feeling abandoned. [...] I'm OK—
just scared of being a captive.

[p.18]

[Names of friends]

---

5 "The Steam Wheelchair," a short story which, as suggested in the introduction (*Cahier XL*), Engel must have removed at some point, for the story pages are separately catalogued in MEA, Box 33 File 54.

Cahier XLI[1]

January 12, 1985
I've had a very great deal. A <u>very</u> strange life when you consider how many identities I have had & how my work has been such a struggle for identity. [70]

While Engel often wrote in more than one notebook at a time—the account of her trip to Paris at Christmas 1984 being yet another case in point—this *cahier* contains her final entries. The progress and treatment of her cancer are understandably prominent topics in the *cahier*. But vying for space were the author's plans for, and ever evolving perspectives on, writing and life, with a powerful "autobiographical note" opening the *cahier*.

Amongst her writing projects, Engel was compiling a selection of short stories for her posthumous collection *The Tattooed Woman*. *Cahier* XLI records her deliberations over which stories to include [13]. Elsewhere, the *cahier* presents more draft passages of what Engel now referred to as "The Vanishing/Fugitive Lakes." She remained keen about "Elizabeth and the Golden City." On an outing to a bookstore with her son William, 8 September 1984, she purchased *Vanessa Bell*,[2] confiding to her notebook a subsequent exclamatory "wow for Golden City. Feeling brilliant" [45].

Engel's reflections on writing included an acknowledgement of the influence Lawrence Durrell had exerted on her work,[3] and thoughts about Anthony Trollope, Anthony Powell and Georg Lukacs. Trollope had finally shown her the "limits of realism," she decided [36], while Powell's twelve-volume *A Dance to the Music of Time* had been a massively overwhelming reading experience for her, the end of which she was glad to see.[4] She begged to differ with Lukacs on his ideas about the novel as bourgeois epic beyond which artists have a duty

1 1984 (July) – 1985 (January), dark blue notebook; 79 pages used.

2 Frances Spalding, *Vanessa Bell* (New Haven: Ticknor & Fields, 1983).

3 Engel seemed to believe that this was "becoming a shameful confession" [19].

4 "Monday January 21—hardly know who I am after a massive 12-volume Anthony Powell session. I don't care about symphonic form, it doesn't really add up—Proustian but not great—too many dangly modifiers, sensationalism; glad it's over" [74].

to move.[5] Engel was not prepared to reject experimentalism in conformity with socialist realism.

In matters of health, it was very significant to Engel to learn that her illness had originated some ten years earlier,[6] in the mid-1970s, a time of highs and lows in her life. "Ten years—So my weight problem wasn't a weight problem and my drinking problem wasn't a drinking problem—all those years," she mused [20]. But in characteristic manner, Engel did not let herself off the hook: "No, part of it was real—or I would have known" [20].

Even though she was fully aware that her time was limited,[7] Engel maintained a firm focus on writing. "Now how can we handle this new series of hurdles," she asked when health care procedures grew more complicated; "turn the book into them I guess," she proposed by way of answer [24]. "I can acknowledge that I'm going to die," Engel stated frankly in another entry, "but everything inside me says Oh God, not yet! Write end of Ildelorn (think out tonight)" [25]. Time and again, her writing was reason enough for Engel to stay the course of illness. "NOT <u>this week</u> my spirit says. Recasting the books in my mind" [29]. "Inside myself I say NOT YET. [...] Get a typist" [30-31]. On 30 August 1984, Engel was "Thinking about novel again. Form is <u>bad</u>. Immense detail wrong. [...] Discontinuity is best for me with this kind of material. So I may break through" [35]. Even in highly emotional moments, such as that recorded in the following excerpt, Engel's sharp-eyed writer-self remained alert to possibilities for her work-in-progress:

> In the midst of death I think only of life—have I loved carelessly? Painfully, trying to hop ship & lyricize licking the windowpanes[8]—because I could not get in (use that for Elizabeth in Montreal) I shortened it for rhythm. [40]

As late as 12 January 1985 Engel urged "The book CAN be finished I think. But do I try too hard? No [...] Finish book I'm sure I can" [69].

---

5 See Georg Lukacs, *History and Class Consciousness*, 1923 (English translation 1971) and *The Theory of the Novel*, 1920 (English translation 1971). In *The Historical Novel*, 1936-37, Lukacs analyzed the growth of historical awareness among novelists, and in *The Meaning of Contemporary Realism*, 1958 (English translation 1969), he argued that the artist had a duty to do more than mirror the despair and futility of the bourgeoisie.

6 Engel first mentions this in an entry dated 20 July 1984 (XLI [15]).

7 "Home care—going on what is basically a terminal plan I guess" [22].

8 Literal English translation for the French "le lèche-vitrines"—window shopping.

Marian Engel died 16 February 1985. Only months earlier, on 19 August 1984, the author had taken down a quotation from Carlos Fuentes, in the *New York Times Book Review* section:[9]

> You start by writing so as to live, and you end up by writing so as not to die. Sometimes I feel I have to hurry up or I won't be able to say what I want to say ... that is what Scheherazade did. That is how fiction began.... [34]

That, too, is how this volume of Marian Engel's notebooks ends. The last words are hers.

[p.1]

July 5 1984

Vera [Frenkel] as always rescues
me with notebooks in hospitals

head vacant
[...]

[p.2]

July 9 [1984]

Much better. Now I shall try to write an autobiographical note.

I tell at parties how I am an adopted person with a lost twin & this is true. But let's get the 2 families straight.

1. I was born May 24, 1933, in Toronto, a second twin. My name was Ruth. Eleanor came first.

2. Our mother was 18, just out of Central Commerce. Her mother, a widow, was a cost acct for Eaton's. Times were bad. They lived on Walmer Rd.

3. They gave us to the Children's Aid.

4. I was sickly, E. aggressive.

---

9 Nicholas Shrady, "Carlos Fuentes: Life and Language," *New York Times Review* (19 August 1984): 1, 26-27. This article is an interview with the Mexican writer Fuentes, whose first novel *Where the Air Is Clear* (1958) is widely considered to mark the beginning of the "boom" of contemporary Latin-American literature.

[p.3]

After several changes of home & hospitalizations I was adopted by Fred & Mary Passmore in P[or]t Arthur in 1935-7? (at about 3)—then it got made legal.

They had already a daughter Helen (b. 1927) They changed my name to Marian.

I do not remember Eleanor but still suffer from a burning rivalry with her. Helen & I have had these years to work it out—love, hate, competition—everything—but she is not the sister spectre in my work, the twin, the "other."

I was nearly 50 years old before I realized that this was a dreadful story—neither of us with anything but each other—the dark rivalry instead of love—the emptiness &

[p.4]

loneliness & hate & I'll get you & I got adopted first, you hurt me I'll hurt you—I've never looked her up.

[...]

They found her a home on a farm a year after me. She married young. I envied her that for years.

The Passmores didn't like to talk about adoption. It must have

[p.5]

been hard. God. Mother & I fought like Will & me. And then her background—her mother dying when she was born. "Why wasn't Maude better to me? she'd ask. You'd think a 10 year old girl..." We now know that Maude felt robbed. Surely—Mother, looking for a mother—instinct, spread it down. Too young Maude must have hated the baby—Tom & Vernon, who tortured her, too—She took their mother away.

She couldn't bear the thought of children being abandoned—so she took me. But I was sure she was going to go off & find another one—blind, maybe, or with curly hair. Father suited me—there was an absoluteness there—but of course it's easy for $^{1}/_{2}$ h[ou]r a day! He had that steadiness that comes from being loved, though.

[p.6]

[...] Mother's bro[ther]s Welles & Bill had it, too, the secure elder children who remembered their mother.

How hard lives are! How hard Mother & I were on each other at the end. How this affected Helen is another problem. But when she confessed that she had thrown me down hills in the stroller I finally loved her more—because she had shown her reality not just her pseudo mother piety which I saw through at 3, I am not nice to other women in terms of power &[...] so I try to control myself esp. when I think

[p.7]

I'm off being good. A bad sign. Do only children know about nature in tooth & claw? I think they're probably a little tender—they don't get to try out their death wishes as early. [...] Anyway, those of us who have had siblings have more interesting pushes & shoves. At least you realize you have to push (unless you're Baby.) [...]

[p.8]

July 9ish [1984]
Last Friday night—a fly on the wall at TGH would have heard Gwen MacEwen, Judy Merril & M Engel discussing with MUCH mirth who they'd have been if not novelists—Judith Grossmann couldn't make herself even contemplate going away to live in a dorm w. other women—there was therefore only CCNY for her—it wasn't real—she married to spite her ma, who wanted her to be a writer—but not that kind. Gwen knew "real" life was outside the campus—and besides, who else had finished high school. Poetry burned in the cafés—she waltzed after leaving the archaeologist she had meant to be behind. She could write in Arabic by the time she was 24.

I was the bourgeois little prize bitten one—though Judith

[p.9]

would have done it my way from a small town—me & my hot pants & wild ambition—the ever-bitten other—wanting it all—getting a lot of it too—Becky Sharp,[10] a bit—but not really wanting the social part: a hang up for husbands & ungenerous of me too, come to think of it.

But we do choose to a degree—how do I convince Char of that?

We all chose to be writers & therefore NOT traditional women. We also tried to get it both ways at other points—with husbands, children, cafés – etc. Didn't get it all—got in all our odd ways, now more, now less. Threw away some good rind—not perhaps knowing it was.

—

Who is my sister now. Bright Hel[en], Dark Eleanor? We are all grey—

10 This 1935 drama, directed by Rouben Mamoulian, involves a sharp-witted mercenary attempting to climb the ladder of social success at any cost.

[pp.10-12]

Marsupial Approaching[11]

[...]

[p.13]

A brilliant mix & it is bullshit to romanticise the pre-adoptive situation—so please don't. Steady, therapeutic givers—give. & I must have been difficult.

There is no existential truth here—no, I mean—romance or truth—illness is worth fighting but not worth thinking about.

—

Stories for Penguin[12]

1 Bernard Orge
2 Mme ~~Eglantine~~ Hortensia
3 Vanishing Lakes
4 Under the Hill
5 In the Sun
6 Tattooed Woman
7 Anita's Dance
8 Blue Glass & Flowers?
9 Feet
10

[p.14]

Write: Ildelorn & the Blue Tower
Withdrawal
Quiet
Eventual journey to blue hills.

Oh thine eternal bride of quietness.

The stones are
loud on the beach

The melancholy [illegible] withdrawing roar is getting near. There is sometimes a glitter. Who gave you your imagery?
[...]

11 What follows is a word-play sequence probing Engel's pre-adoptive years (ages 0-3).

12 These were for the collection *The Tattooed Woman*.

[p.15]

July 20 [1984]—After a wild 4 days of mad depression I am beginning to be able to read & focus again. Still obsessed by the disease but getting the picture straight a bit—there IS more treatment available but I am very frail & can have none right now. It was comforting to know it's 10 years I've had the disease, not 6 or 7—I feel less a wimp. Interesting too—that was when the inability absolutely to hold liquor began.

[...]

Ten years is respectable.

[p.16]

[...]

When time stopped my white count was. 5. Monday I am promised chemo. How much can it do?... How weak I am. I am only beginning to know. Yet I'm glad struggled through.

[p.17]

Famous last words

I've had a really good run
for my money.
[...]

Sun July 20 [1984][13]—the experience that's left no residue in my life is the [Toronto Public] library board.

[p.18]

Pain is what of course makes it possible to die. Viz The Women of Trachis[14]

Sometimes I don't think the best of me has been allowed out—too many complexes or not enough forms? I didn't often Seize the Day. The younger child's passivity. Playing dumb in order to be liked. Taking 2nd place because its RIGHT. Well—that's what I was—#2 child.

[...] We get the position we choose—but it has taken me all my life to realize this.

—

Funny—one ought to have last wishes & desires—I want
the house to be ok, I want, I mean, the

[p.19]

family in it not to disintegrate. But other than that—ivory, apes & peacocks? The odd cherry is OK—morning coffee.

---

13 Either the date (20 July) or the day (Sunday) is incorrectly noted here.

14 A play by Sophocles.

(2 books I bought for the titles & NEVER remember the titles of—IVORY APES & PEACOCKS SECONDARY WORLDS)[15]

[...] book influences—Durrell is becoming a shameful confession!

Thinking about 10 years ago—my weariness, the bad effect of booze. And it was cancer—but there were no concrete symptoms so I simply blamed myself. I would have.

[...]

[p.20]

Ten years—So my weight problem wasn't a weight problem and my drinking problem wasn't a drinking problem—all those years.

No, part of it was real—or I would have known. But weight. How everyone nagged & how I felt I needed the ballast. And how right I was.

But we'd all have had to be different people to avoid this. [...]

Tues a.m. Woke in the night
painfree—like a miracle—
clarity of mind came
and charity, all the
virtues.

[p.21]

I must forgive myself my odd self—accusing mental states, my fits of passivity (the minute the pain flees I accuse myself of being lazy) and not compare my pain to other peoples'. I know what made Terry Fox run[16] but I don't have to run so I will do what work I can & want to. Continue to enjoy friends [...]

Pain causes my ego to slip gear & my sense of reality to stray when it goes—the relief?—if one is not too dopey. Chemothe<u>ra</u>py hurray. The worst part was the cold cap, which unbalanced me.

Now for Trollope.[17]

[p.22]

Home care—going on what is basically a terminal plan I guess—but it's a set of safeguards. [...]

---

15 James Huneker, *Ivory Apes and Peacocks* (New York: Scribner, 1932); W.H. Auden, *Secondary Worlds*; the T.S. Eliot Memorial Lectures Delivered at Eliot College in the University of Kent at Canterbury (London: Faber and Faber, 1968).

16 For more information see *Cahier* XXXIV, footnote 15.

17 Anthony Trollope (1815-82), prolific writer known for his "Barsetshire" series and the "Palliser" novels.

[p.23]
Wheat bran—get. Busts, losses, recessions elicit darkening hypotheses like—Mr Lukacs' conviction that we are approaching the close of the Modern Age.... He also feels that we must develop a firmer grasp of the doctrine of Original Sin & abandon our religion of progress.... At the risk of appearing in my great-grandmother's mental clothes, however, I must confess that it seems to me that since the fall of the Roman Empire... which was a slave empire... the story of the west <u>has</u> been progress....

—

So one has to continue to believe that on the <u>whole</u>, life is progress—but there are accidents—like this, like the Dark Ages.

Power is the thing to think about.

[p.24]
Now how can we handle this new series of hurdles—turn the book into them I guess.

——

New beginning—Events, like pharmaceuticals, have minor as well as major side effects. The death of president Kennedy, for instance, in addition to its general effect on history, has added immensely to the quality of funerals—the brave figure of his wife J[acqueline] Onassis now being the model for all widows who can still stand up right & weigh under 300 lbs.

[p.25]
I can acknowledge that I'm going to die, but everything inside me says Oh God, not yet!

—

Write end of Ildelorn (think out tonight). Then Major—death sequence.[18] Then Zeitgeist thing. Then try to screw it together!

-

Zeitgeist—you can't avoid it. It names your children & forms your politics E[lizabeth] and F[rances] [in "Elizabeth and the Golden City"] were formed by sexual-release period—then came women's liberation AND Canadian nationalism.

---

18 The sequence is a two-page draft passage archived in MEA, Box 34 File 18, in which Elizabeth, who is hospitalized, describes her thoughts:

"Now everything—medals, prizes, excuses for past neglect—is sliding into my lap & I am a<u>fraid</u>.

I must be dying."

Excerpted and included at the end of *Cahier* XLI [3].

Everything led to Eliz taking a grip on things—She didn't quite make it but nevertheless.

[p.26]

Regime home
early—get up
milk & sandwiches
(HAM, egg, cheese)
Write
back to bed w juice

———

Anti Americanism is facile

——

[...]
Don't be any more dependent than you have to.

Isn't Char just as scared?

[p.27]

If it's happening Will is right to stick around—maybe if it isn't he's wrong.
Bad case of terminal nerves

Can feel people advancing & withdrawing—[...]

–

I'm freaking other people out—I have to be careful.

[illegible]—typewriter ribbons. Stamps.

Don't forget Dr Scott's basic elegance.

You <u>can</u> make the novel "Sex & Death" & make it funny & good.

[p.28]

Friday—life a constant process of taking control [...]

—

In the hospital tears <u>work</u>—they do something for you if you are a suck. They feel needed. Though you must still be responsible.

At home—never. [...]

[p.29]

Sat
Dammit my lungs are filling up w. yellow muck. Pneumonia is the old man's friend. Or is it cat or comforter. The way I've smoked! Why shouldn't I pay. Get Vera to get antihistamine and remember nurse comes tomorrow.

NOT this week my spirit says. Recasting the books in the mind—
[...]

–

Thurs
forced to deal w reality by all these people around. Will's cough is AWFUL.

[p.30]

Wed Aug 1? [1984]
I know perfectly well I'm losing the fight—they've drummed that into ME—but to mention it to me is now to appropriate it—it is My death. That's what's wrong with Kubler Ross' theology I think—to become a spirit guide is to be a thief of a singular experience.

Inside myself I say NOT YET.

Then too, they encourage me to hope—because they don't know what will happen. How long. It's a schizoid situation—hope & reality always in conflict. Fight. Don't fight—I hate the dying day the way the light wobbles & falters, the air conditioning begins to freeze me.

[p.31]

Maybe one wants death to be secret & proud.

Get a typist.

Life-enhancing things are best—commissions & phone calls from Ginger & Weaver.[19]

The thought of leaving makes me cry. Of not being independent is much worse—that's a box. So I do a lot of pretending.

"Give yourself permission"—from Vera, heard first, useful.

"Bull-shit" just as useful—life phases—protection from the Puritan in me.

Death is still unthinkable most days—but with me now, lay advice not much good, as in wheelchairs—people imagining they are a solution when they're a hangup—need a wheeler.

[p.32]

My God the possibilities for victimization. No wonder the old grow angry & difficult. [...]

I think I should just try to be happy. Period.

Aug. 6. [1984] 2^{30}a.m. not well, finished [The] Last Chronicle of Barset[20]

---

19 Virginia Barber at Penguin Books and Robert Weaver at CBC.

20 *The Last Chronicle of Barset* (1867) by Anthony Trollope. This is the last novel in the "Barsetshire" series.

—pain in lungs—Otherwise happy—God, giving one's responsibilities away helps—[...]

I keep thinking of my tendency to get myself bullied as a twin—reflex—I hunt for her all the time.

[p.33]

[...]
The Swings—a twin story—do it.

Why Tanis? Tanit?[21]
Eliz liked the name Tanis.

Numb fingers. From cream? Peace, though—good. Make lists

[p.34]

Wheelchair—I don't want to be pushed around—worked that out with dear Gwen.

—

Aug 16 [1984]—tremendous feeling of being rich & fruitful. Fridge full of peaches & mushrooms, making chutney.

—

Aug 19 [1984]—"You start by writing so as to live and you end up writing so as not to die—Sometimes I feel I have to hurry up or I won't be able to say what I want to say... that is what Scheherazade did. That is how fiction began..."

Carlos Fuentes
NYT BR 19 Aug
84

[p.35]

[...]

30 Aug. [1984]

Thinking about novel again. Form is bad. Immense detail wrong.
JT [Dr Tennen]—talking about unconventional arrangements being best—in my head I remember this. Think suddenly—of course—discontinuity is best for me with this kind of material. So I may break through.

[p.36]

[...]

---

21 Tanis/Tanit was a Phoenician goddess. Engel may have encountered the story of Tanis while living in Cyprus.

Different form could get rid of set-piece "characters" like Lalice—a joy to invent—Trollope did them better. Perhaps he has finally shown me the limits of realism.[22]

[p.37]

McCrory takes both girls
Eliz is banished to town
Guarded by John
(Ildelorn) Ellen Lee suffers sex jealousy
John is gay
Eliz gets out of dependency—anger Allen & Major
No France
No publishing
No sophistication
Ellen Lee—death & lies
John Cruikshank
Ivo & Iris?[23]
Ivo a communist

[p.38]

[...]
Presents from Paris[24]
—music tapes
—material
—wallpaper/Plant permit

Nov. 22 [1984]—what was all that? Re the hypnotist the relief the seduction of giving over control to a pair of blue eyes[25]

[p.39]

under controlled circumstance

I've always liked losing control, being, at least temporarily, a leaner. No wonder I can't stand up but experience has taught me that its safer to be a leader than a follower (Hitler's influence on my generation? Church demagogues?)

I long to lean—give over. Every time it's a disaster. Other people aren't safe. [...] Did I learn this from Mother? She was an orphan too.

22 Earlier *cahiers* record Engel's longstanding interest in literary realism.

23 A chart of characters follows.

24 Engel is thinking ahead to her trip to Paris and to gifts to bring home. The notebooks she was working in at the time include several lists of gift ideas for various friends.

25 See [56] (bottom) to [57].

Salt tears, salt snot—unmemorable, don't, Marian.
[…]

[p.40]

Leaving the house I think only of
coming back to it.

In the midst of death I think only of life—have I loved carelessly? Painfully, trying to hop ship & lyricise

licking the windowpanes—because I could not get in (use that for Elizabeth in Montreal)
I shortened it for rhythm.

Put out garbage, walker, cat.
[...]

[pp.41-44]

Our Things[26]

[...]

[p.45]

Sept 9 [1984]. This week Char started Vic[toria College, University of Toronto] & Will Geo[rge] Brown College.
Will & I went in a taxi to Book City & I bought pb books
Life of Vanessa Bell—wow for Golden City. Feeling brilliant.
[...]

[p.46]

Garden is Keatsian w the verbena all over.
[...]

[p.47]

[Dream recording]

[p.48]

[...]

Structure of novel
Fugitive Lakes
First Person
Deaths
Education
Literary exchange
Publishing
[illegible] & Cherrystones

---

26 Engel created an inventory of belongings and individuals to whom they might be left.

[p.49]

Marriage
Illness
money prospects
3 or 4 short stories
[...]
28 Sept [1984]—High energy have a bad leg & bad cold. Trying to go through work. Pain hurts.

[p.50]

Dec 1 [1984]—After dreary weekend making phone calls—everyone NICE. I feel it will be a good week [...]

—

Dec 2 [1984]

The Murder of Maugher[27]

Now I was given to mourning & moaning, proceeding by wail & complaint thro' tantrum to change & I knew this was wrong—it irritated others, who kept their woes to themselves. When, however, I became conscious that I was in a poor position, & that

[p.51]

I could change this eventually, if I worked out a way, a sort of leaven worked through my spirit giving rise to a gaseous state of irritation and the rest was inevitable.

When, therefore, my moaning caused it finally to occur to me that I was unnecessarily unhappy in Toronto—or perhaps common sense simply stepped in & showed me that it was possible for most people to be happy there & I ought either to leave or to try—I began to endeavour to work out the cause of my grief, & I settled on Alexander Maugher.

[p.52]

Now I could as easily have pinned my plight on E. Lennox, who had a martyred streak, or A. Silliher, a foolish dictator. F. Silliher, though I tried to be loyal to her, had her oppressive side as well—rivalry tended to encourage her to squash my initiatives as it always had—or Walker Barber, the personnel officer, who had, while pretending to encourage me at the Bank, cut me off from any enjoyable acquaintance with fellow workers. Even Reikyn, I suppose, could be blamed for something, even little Alan, who had been born without imitation but I wouldn't blame

27 A draft passage of "The Vanishing/The Fugitive Lakes."

him, he was too soft & lovely.

But who, 9 or 10 times out of 10, makes a woman unhappiest?

[p.53]

Her mother? Mine was dead. No satisfaction in blaming a dead woman & anyway, husbands now were being made to take the brunt. I realised bitterly & vengefully that Alexander Maugher was who had been standing between me & happiness & I resolved, whether or not he was beautiful as a butterfly & brave as a queen, to avenge myself on his straight nose & crisp curls, blue eyes, absence & manly bearing.

[p.54]

The whiskery bastard, I said, to walk into my life & destroy it.
Walk out again & take what was left. I'll get him.

Because it was when I had married the Merchant of Semen that everything had gone wrong, hadn't it?

It was he who had cut off my friendship with both Lalice and the Dean of Women; who had separated me from the possibility of a scholarship to graduate school—and involved me in this ridiculous situation at the Bank—married women being still segregated to a degree from wise virgins.

It was he who was hindering me from operating as a translator as well—for surely only someone who was <u>a</u> <u>person</u> <u>in</u> <u>her</u> <u>own</u> <u>right</u> could get close enough to

[p.55]

an author to become his English voice—spouses have to be relegated to corners before this can happen—and in our family we were not in the habit of relegating spouses to corners or even
ditches.

He was a bad man, I thought, to come & go like that & spoil my life.

[p.56]

<u>Method</u> The Poisoned Pearl
(an Onion)

Fencing lessons

Men are the cause of all the trouble
(slash)
husbands
sex
<u>You</u> A Maugher

(where is your mother to drink for
you the poisoned pearl?)

An Onion—or the Poisoned Pearl
A History of Marriage
good interlude

---

11 Dec [1984] Fascinating time chez
Dr Banach the hypnotist
(Get a better pen!)

[p.57]

On instructions to "float" experienced a kind of spiritual massage—saw colours as he indicated I might try—but mostly allowed the words to wash over me—comfort—new sensation—new experience—float—

inside a seashell. Fluorescent colours w black floating, comfort—was able to suppress cynicism, criticism (he is pretty good but not John Donne[28]) felt oddly as if I'd been at a good sermon. Not sure if I can turn it on myself but this is a painful evening—up too long with Clay D—Nice time though—I am floating a little.

Wide awake though, again.

[p.58]

Trying to divide real worry from self-pity. Anyone else's concern enhances my own—yet I have to say, "I can't do that—" in order to save myself. And the weather is damp for bones. Or are things going badly again. I am so scared of having a calcium attack that I'm afraid I'll bring one on.

Distraction necessary.

Almost ready for Tanis & Ildelorn section.

Tiff Elspeth's essay IS reductionist.[29]

(Sudden realization of desire to be cruel to certain nice, hopeful young male writers years ago—Why? Not cruel, but I

---

28 Engel, the literary critic and writer, surfaces here.

29 Elspeth Cameron, "The Inner Wars of Timothy Findley," *Saturday Night* 100 (January 1985): 24-33. Cameron presents a lengthy biographical portrait of Findley, widely known as the author of *The Wars* (1977) and a friend of Engel's.

[p.59]

didn't want to read their books, fulfil their hopes, be mother.)
Perhaps simply too busy—perhaps fear of rivalry—no, there's a "nice" doglike hope that brings out the worst in ME—it's the part of me that Dennis Lee is disappointed in. He always wants me to take more interest in new writers. I am resistant to others' taste—or maybe his is too United Church—the sin in sincere. Why this tack?
[...]

[p.60]

Roe[30] was tall & thin with a nose like a needle; beside him Mr Norman looked short & stout; though there was not much more than an inch between them, the contrast in fleshiness was as acute as the contrast in mind. For though it was Norman who, a year younger, had been able to finish his education & study accountancy, it was Roe who was educated. He had learned a great deal around Mr Allen's potbellied stove and read enormously from lists provided by the eclectic group, half sect half cell, that met with the herbalist, and although there were patches in his exposition that seemed almost crazy with ideas, just as there are writers & critics who were clearly not products

[p.61]

of Northrop Frye, so Roe's mind was unstamped by the Whigginess of the Ontario Education System and free to range in unrecommended pastures. His periods as Rosicrucian, communist, Buddhist had left him not cranky, but diverse in his sympathies.

—

Jamaica—Maxine & safety pins wilder than any W[est] Indian. I had seen & I realized suddenly that those I knew were university people or nurses, more British than the British, desperate to be something other than the piccaninnies prejudice could describe them as; but Maxine lacked pretensions—there was no servant in her & little lady; she had a

[p.62]

fierce quality of her own from the tatted hair to the pink heels slopping over the cheap high heeled sandals and that quality said "Get out of here girl, he's my man." I looked at her and saw razors.

The villas public room was bare but clean in a climate where white wood work must have been an effort. She brought me a glass of punch on a silver tray in a sparkling glass set it before me on a polished table without servility. Curled up in a curiously shiny Windsor chair and sat silently cunning, staring at me. I saw no reason, historically why she should like

---

30 More excerpts from "The Vanishing/Fugitive Lakes."

white women, but wanted her to like me, wanted some warmth from my father's woman.

[p.63]

There wasn't going to be any. Why should there be?

"I sent money," he muttered. "You never wrote."

"He didn't tell us. We thought you'd just disappeared."

"Bloody Arthur. Still, it's over." His shoulders, always, I thought, the most expressive part of a man—whereas it is the neck, the heft of a head, where we locate emotion in a woman, sagged again.

"You get out," Maxine said. "He old. He tired."

I wanted to ask a million more things, but his eyes agreed with her.

"Anyway, we made out all right." Scanlon's wording. His own.

"I'm glad."

"Should Nannie come?"

[p.64]

Maxine looked blazes at me.

"If she will."

"There are all these cheap charters."

"God knows, we need them. Tell her to spend." He had no animation left & his breath was short as he stood up. I gave him a limp sort of hug. He turned his cheek to my kiss "Good-bye."

"He not glad you came," Maxine said fiercely at the door.

"Speak for yourself," I hissed at her, thinking, two can play. I saw him dead, the villa empty, the Windsor chair in a shack somewhere. All there was for her. Who said I was nice?

My driver was waiting impatiently, took us breakneck down the hairpin hill. "Home before dark, these drivers are bad, man," he

[p.65]

said. I sat in the front not wanting to play Mrs British. Then wondered if he thought I was issuing an invitation. Then if I wanted one. But he was a wry ordinary man, middle-aged, well-spoken, courteous, of the old school. He told me he was a widower, lived in a distant town, was proud of his new bus, but was otherwise quietly silent. It was my own thoughts that were loaded with need.

I didn't so much think about Father as ooze backwards up the road to him—as if we were leaving a lymphatic snail trail behind us—a silver emotional thread that would gleam on the gravel road until dawn's dew erased it.

[pp.66-67][31]

23 Dec. [1984]

The drugs have given me a Chinese face,
a frog's chin, a moustache, whiskers.
I look at myself & say, "someone
else"—all I can say.

Before I go I want to crutch around my
house looking in mirrors & saying goodbye
to myselves.

Paris, Dec 24/5 [32] [1984]

After a farewell [...] at the airport [...] long OK flight over night landing OK & wheelchair person took us to carousel. The wheelchair failed to show up. He took us to arrivals hall & Air Canada etc. & we waited until after noon (from 8 a.m.) until a clerk discovered that Air Canada had not put it aboard, so Air France did, & the Air France terminal was 5 km. Char lost her temper & bitched while Will & I were patient. People & dog-watching! Finally went to Roissy with him, got chair & he drove us to hotel. Will bathed, went over to explore, goofed on money, overtipped, enjoyed himself. C & I slept. Called Sharon Rainy. Rooms in attic, blue toile de j. in wallpaper, sous les toits, up 1 escalier from left, hard. Very crippled. Out for sup—found BAD grill place in Rue de l'Harpe! Then rows of lovely ones in de la Huchette. Home. Sharon & Richard take W & C to mass at N[otre] D[ame] de P[aris] while I lie inundated by the sound of bells, feeling one thinks better in Paris? Does one?

[p.2] 25/12/84 [33] Xmas morning in Paris—the rich ringing of real bells—a two-note ring—CHRÍST BÓRN. Victory.

Well, there were railway bells, too. Last night—ND de Paris—enveloping. Worth the trip. The day was not great. Wheelchair & 1 temper lost.

---

31 Inserted here is an excerpt from *Cahier* XL (MEA, Box 34 File 15) [2]. Page numbers of excerpted material appear at the left margin.

32 Excerpt from MEA, Box 34 File 16 [1]. Inserted pages numbered on left.

33 Excerpt from MEA, Box 34 File 15 [2-15].

[p.3] Wednesday—Xmas day—lovely breakfast together—W & C escape to adventure, I feeling ill & scared, sleep. Jane phones. Lunch at nearby Italian place. Kids patriotically walk me to ND de P but it's cold & I am heavy. Long aft naps. Will continues to sleep. Char & I dine late in Rue de l'Harpe, a not bad French place as opposed to the ghastly grill last night. I have sole, wine, duck pâté. We buy a greek sandwich for Will. He's worried when we get back at 11—shoe on other foot. I get stuck in bath. We are all keeping notebooks & losing our negative streak. Helen phoned when I was bathing (she just phoned again—I said we were serene—true)

Right hip bad

[...]

[p.4: Sketch of the week's itinerary including places to visit and items to purchase]

[p.5] Wed—Pizzeria 210F—3 of us—good Xmas marrons! Coquilles St Jacques [...] Hip better back worse—but I walk better.
Supper—Coupole—too much to eat—but fun I think. Taxi: 25f each way. No wheelchair today.

[p.6] [...] Are we having a good time? I think so—and behaving well. We love breakfast. Today St Germain des Pres.

—

Sudden tears for the shame of the past when the harder I tried to be honest, intelligent, balanced, straight forward, a good mother, the worse I failed & fell.

[p.7] Surely that was partly the disease. Or perhaps that virtue in a vacuum is impossible? It's as if I was a sort of toy which didn't balance if left perfectly upright—it was all right if it had a lean to it. Someone ought to have told me, I say in despair, that it was all right not to be perfect. I am ashamed but also annoyed because what I remember is trying very hard and getting no joy in return. For years things were bleak & awful & unendurable without pills or drink & I felt it was WRONG to live like that but found no solution. JT [Dr. J. Tennen] let me out of the cage partly—the examination of

[p.8] the early, hurt past was an immense benefit. But also, of course, medical treatment has made a difference. I have dropped some of my overstriving personality & am more content—but being able physically to relax is just as important—I am happy now in a way I've never been before & off the rack. The possible contents me. I take immense pride in the kids' virtues & don't put up with their vices. I am more annoyed though with people who are discontented as I was previously. I want to say, "But you can walk."

Powell is better than I thought.

[p.9] Get out & shop a bit today. I think. Orangerie? Telephone.

—

My memories of mother are physical—boney fingers, white [quite lovely] body watching herself age & saying she wasn't doing badly. Hands pushing me away—I advanced & hurt her. Wanting me to tweeze her, being afraid to. Terrible sackcloth nighties, exercises on the floor [illegible]. "Wash my back." Was this phys[ical] repulsion the underside of a kind of lesbianism? Perhaps more a real fear of her aggression—she hugged as hard as she pushed & kissed with terrible smacks & controlling inconsistency. What a complex woman. Perverse. Want to hit her still.

[p.10] Love her. Though. Never got away [...]

[pp.11-12] [Dream recording.]

[p.13] Sat a.m. [28 Dec 1984] Jane & Charlotte have just waltzed out into the brilliant sunlight—the walls of Paris are the same mellow gray & yellow & the sky blue—people on the tower of N.D de Paris—gargoyles protruding in silhouette & I can see them from here—superb!
Will, looking divine in his black jacket, has gone to Beaubourg. We will go to Place des Vosges for lunch. I <u>long</u> to shop.

Dinner last night at Pactole (?)—Breton nouvelle cuisine—barely cooked, <u>beautiful</u> sauces. (Vinegar & ginger on sliced raw smoked fish.) Pont l'Evesque cheese! For a moment I could even <u>taste</u> the difference.

[p.14] Imported cheeses don't ripen. What was the other cheese?

Cloud in left thigh—in another week it will be intolerable—but in another week one will be home.

And I have switched thinking tracks & <u>am</u> much happier—"clear"— no barrier between me & reality that I feel. Too much preoccupation w self & illness but how can one help that.
[...]

[p.15] But my good leg is kicking up which leads to thoughts
of games and candles—when is living not living etc. I want to
go home. Will talk to Adrienne.

Char should go to Douanier Rousseau with Frank & Barbara.[34] I should finish book.

(She did) I went home on the Wed [1 January 1985] Very happy.

[p.68][35]

Jan 9 [1985] Returning from hospital after a week
[...]
Jan 12 [1985]—Woke realising that this really is a very difficult time for us all. I am trying to put a book

[p.69]

together while barely able to move. [...] And I am becoming a burden. Though it is not quite time to give up. I don't know what to do—keep plugging, I guess. The book CAN be finished I think. But do I try too hard? No [...]

[p.70]

12 Jan [1985] still

> Why not cry? Giving up
> your real life is the biggest
> thing you do.

I wonder if anyone will think it strange not to turn down this street any more.

Is this all? I've had a very great deal. A very strange life when you consider how many identities I have had—how my work has been such a struggle for identity.
[...]
Finish book. I'm sure I can.

[p.71]

I think I should just let myself be exhausted for a bit instead of desperately reaching out.

---

34 Frank and Barbara Hermann, family friends.

35 This page marks the end of excerpts from MEA, Box 34 File 15 and the return to *Cahier* XLI.

Helen phones & gives me courage to start going through ms. can't find part I want but outline is good, now. Mind back. Panic & fear strike when I find radio broken—too many radios have broken. Loneliness. Fight it. You can do it, Marian. Or shall I just collapse?

How often in my early life I felt this cold wind without knowing what it was. But I had Mother to protect me.

[p.72]

Well most lives just trail off.

I don't have to go out into the terrible winter weather

Though I miss weather
[...]

[p.73]

Monday—ordinary flu—an awkward moment though before I realized I'd been drinking cranberry juice.

Yesterday [...] Danaë[36] became extremely interesting on the subject of the way art takes up time—you get started & it's time to clean brushes. Writing is not that hard, but I find my life falls apart—the plans other people have for it—when I get going again.[...]

Darn it all, I was writing & now I can't get back the mood.

[...]

Montreal[37] —keep plugging

[p.74]

Monday Jan 21 [1985][38]—hardly know who I am after a massive 12-volume Anthony Powell session. I don't care about symphonic form, it doesn't really add up—Proustian but not great—too many dangly modifiers, sensationalism, glad it's over.

[p.75]

[...] Jan 30 [1985] finally had chemo—What a relief![39]

---

36 The artist Danaë Chambers was Engel's friend.

37 This is a section in "Elizabeth and the Golden City."

38 The next day, 22 January 1985, Engel made entries in another notebook, *Cahier* XL, as indicated by the following excerpt [15]:
Jan — 22 [1985] — Found this [*Cahier* XL]
yesterday while hunting wheelchair
story—[...]

39 This is the final dated entry. Engel used the last few pages of the *cahier* [76-79] to list items and individuals to whom she wished to leave them.

Elizabeth[40]

Friday night is the only night it is necessary to sit up & worry, so, having read the Major's notebook I'll set to work on my own. I want to make sure that this nurse is all right before I lie down & sleep beside an unguarded intravenous stand. Friday is the odd night in the nursing shift of three days on, three days off. It's then that you get the strange nurses: odd accents or shapes or colours, an odd rag that used to pass for a uniform & what hospital am I in tonight. They're from some odd agency, the sweepings of the steppes, the kind of women who looked normal 25 years ago in their clumpy worn shoes but who now in Toronto The Trendy, are Martians. They are often kind—more willing to offer back rubs & other small (large) services than the trim graduates of the even cycles, but two weeks ago one of them (who was unimpeachably anglo-saxon so I can't be accused of racism) tried to restart an empty intravenous & fill my veins with air. I stayed awake all night

[p.2] hunched like a caged monkey against my bed rails & got so sleepy I burned a cigarette hole in my sheet (which I trimmed with my scissors so it would look like a tear, but it didn't) and told the desk nurse when she came in to water my flowers at 4 in the morning, and she hasn't been back. But Friday nights are clearly dangerous and I shall stay up another hour to make sure Nurse Kay (brown cardigan, yellow nylon pantsuit, honest West Indian accent) knows how to manage: you can't be too careful.

Flowers from: Amelia (fourth time: reproach while thanking)
Norbert Platt—why?
Lucia
Anna Plunkett – thank
Ag—send birthday cheque

I don't trust all this kindness.
It feels terminal.

40 At the time of her death, 16 February 1985, Engel was still working on "Elizabeth and the Golden City," of which this passage is an excerpt (MEA, Box 34 File 18). It is included here for its link to Engel's life which she lived from beginning to end *as a writer*.

Shaggy Dolittle is looking after the house. Nancy Birch hasn't billed me for doing my taxes. I am a person to whom presents have always been suspicious—what do you want from me that you should give me things? Now everything—medals, prizes, excuses for past neglect—is sliding into my lap & I am <u>afraid</u>.

[p.3] I must be dying.
[...]

APPENDIX 1

Cahier archive locations

Cahier I	Box 34 File 1
Cahier II	Box 6 File 1
Cahier III	Box 6 File 2
Cahier IV	Box 6 File 3
Cahier V	Box 6 File 4
Cahier VI	Box 6 File 5
Cahier VII	Box 6 File 7
Cahier VIII	Box 6 File 6
Cahier IX	Box 6 File 8
Cahier X	Box 6 File 9
Cahier XI	Box 6 File 10
Cahier XII	Box 6 File 11
Cahier XIII	Box 6 File 14
Cahier XIV	Box 6 File 12
Cahier XV	Box 6 File 13
Cahier XVI	Box 6 File 15
Cahier XVII	Box 6 File 27
Cahier XVIII	Box 34 File 2
Cahier XIX	Box 6 File 16
Cahier XX	Box 6 File 17
Cahier XXI	Box 6 File 18
Cahier XXII	Box 6 File 19
Cahier XXIII	Box 6 File 20
Cahier XXIV	Box 6 File 21
Cahier XXV	Box 6 File 22
Cahier XXVI	Box 6 File 24
Cahier XXVII	Box 34 File 3

Cahier XXVIII	Box 34 File 4
Cahier XXIX	Box 33 File 85
Cahier XXX	Box 6 File 28
Cahier XXXI	Box 14 File 16
Cahier XXXII	Box 14 File 15
Cahier XXXIII	Box 34 File 6
Cahier XXXIV	Box 34 Files 7, 8, 9, 10.
Cahier XXXV	Box 34 File 11
Cahier XXXVI	Box 34 File 5
Cahier XXXVII	Box 34 File 12
Cahier XXXVIII	Box 34 File 13
Cahier XXXIX	Box 34 File 14
Cahier XL	Box 34 File 15
Cahier XLI	Box 34 Files 15, 16, 17, 18.

WORKS CITED

Abley, Mark. "Dire Things: An Interview with Margaret Atwood." *Poetry Canada Review* 15,2: 1, 3, 28-29.

Benstock, Shari, ed. *The Private Self: Theory and Practice of Women's Autobiographical Writings*. Chapel Hill: University of North Carolina Press, 1988.

Blanchot, Maurice. *Le livre à venir*. Paris: Gallimard, 1959.

Blodgett, Harriet. *Centuries of Female Days: Englishwomen's Private Diaries*. New Brunswick, NJ: Rutgers University Press, 1988.

Bloom, Lynn Z. "'I Write for Myself and Strangers': Private Diaries as Public Documents." In Bunkers and Huff, eds. *Inscribing the Daily: Critical Essays on Women's Diaries*. Amherst: University of Massachusetts Press, 1996. 23-37.

Braham, Jeanne. "A Lens of Empathy." In Bunkers and Huff, eds. *Inscribing the Daily: Critical Essays on Women's Diaries*. Amherst: University of Massachusetts Press, 1996. 56-71.

Bunkers, Suzanne L. and Cynthia A. Huff, eds. *Inscribing the Daily: Critical Essays on Women's Diaries*. Amherst: University of Massachusetts Press, 1996.

Buss, Helen, ed. "Writing and Reading Autobiographically: Introduction to *Prairie Fire's* 'Life Writing' Issue." 16,3 (Autumn 1995): 5-15.

Culley, Margo, ed. *A Day at a Time: The Diary Literature of American Women from 1764 to the Present*. New York: Feminist Pat CUNY, 1985.

———, ed. *American Women's Autobiography: Fea(s)ts of Memory*. Madison: University of Wisconsin Press, 1992.

della Casa, Jennifer Gillard. "The Author as Activist: Marian Engel and the Writers' Union of Canada." MA thesis. Trent University, 1996.

Fothergill, Robert A. *Private Chronicles: A Study of English Diaries*. London: Oxford University Press, 1974.

Garay, Kathleen E. *The Marian Engel Archive. Library Research News* 8,2 (Fall 1984). Hamilton: McMaster University, 1984.

———. *The Marian Engel Archive, Second Accession, Finding Guide*. Hamilton: McMaster University, 1994.

Godwin, Gail. "A Diarist on Diarists." *Antaeus* 60-61 (Autumn 1988): 9-15.

Hamsten, Elizabeth. *"Read This Only To Yourself": The Private Writings of Midwestern Women, 1880-1910*. Bloomington: Indiana University Press, 1982.

Heilbrun, Carolyn G. *Writing a Woman's Life*. New York: Norton, 1988.

Hogan, Rebecca. "Engendered Autobiographies: The Diary as a Feminine Form." *Prose Studies: Special Issue on Autobiography and Question of Gender* 14,5 (September 1991): 95- 107.

Huff, Cynthia A. "Textual Boundaries: Space in Nineteenth-Century Women's Manuscript Diaries." In Bunkers and Huff, eds. *Inscribing the Daily: Critical Essays on Women's Diaries*. Amherst: University of Massachusetts Press, 1996. 123-138.

Hutchman, Laurence. "An Interview with Louis Dudek." *The River Review* 1 (1995): 63-78.

Jelinek, Estelle, ed. *Women's Autobiography: Essays in Criticism*. Bloomington: Indiana University Press, 1980.

———. *The Tradition of Women's Autobiography: From Antiquity to the Present*. Boston: Twayne, 1986.

Kadar, Marlene, ed. *Essays in Life Writing*. Toronto: Robarts Centre for Canadian Studies, York University, 1989.

———, ed. *Essays on Life Writing: From Genre to Critical Practice*. Toronto: University of Toronto Press, 1992.

King, James. *The Life of Margaret Laurence*. Toronto: Knopf, 1997.

Klein, Carroll. "A Conversation with Marian Engel." *Room of One's Own* 9,2 (June 1984): 5-30.

Lejeune, Philippe. *On Autobiography*. Ed. Paul John Eakin. Trans. Katherine Leary. Minneapolis: University of Minnesota Press, 1989.

———. *Le Moi des Demoiselles: Enquête sur le Journal de Jeune Fille*. Paris: Editions du Seuil, 1993.

Lensink, Judy Nolte. "Expanding the Boundaries of Criticism: The Diary as Female Autobiography." *Women's Studies* 14 (1987): 39-53.

Mairs, Nancy. *Remembering the Bone House*. New York: Harper & Row, 1989.

Marcus, Jane. "Invincible Mediocrity: The Private Selves of Public Women." In Benstock, *The Private Self: Theory and Practice of Women's Autobiographical Writings*. Chapel Hill: University of North Carolina Press, 1988. 114-146.

Middlebrook, Diane Wood. "Telling Secrets." In Rhiel and Suchoff, *The Seductions of Biography*. New York and London: Routledge, 1996. 123-130.

Miller, Nancy K. *Getting Personal: Feminist Occasions and Other Autobiographical Acts*. New York and London: Routledge, 1991.

Neuman, Shirley, ed. *Autobiography and Questions of Gender*. London: Frank Cass, 1991.

Olney, James, ed. *Studies in Autobiography*. New York: Oxford University Press, 1988.

Podnieks, Elizabeth. "(Life-)writing a Modernist Text: The Literary Diaries of Elizabeth Smart, Antonia White and Anaïs Nin." PhD thesis. University of Toronto, 1995.

Rhiel, Mary and David Suchoff, eds. *The Seductions of Biography*. New York and London: Routledge, 1996.

Rosenwald, Lawrence. *Emerson and The Art of the Diary*. New York: Oxford University Press, 1988.

Simons, Judy. *Diaries and Journals of Literary Women from Fanny Burney to Virginia Woolf*. Iowa City: University of Iowa Press, 1990.

Smith, Sidonie. *A Poetics of Women's Autobiography: Marginality and the Fictions of Self-Representation*. Bloomington: Indiana University Press, 1987.

Verduyn, Christl. *Lifelines: Marian Engel's Writings*. Montreal: McGill-Queen's University Press, 1995.

———, ed. *Dear Marian, Dear Hugh: The MacLennan-Engel Correspondence*. Ottawa: University of Ottawa Press, 1995.

Webb, Phyllis. "Read the poems, read the poems. All right?" In Williamson, ed. *Sounding Differences: Conversations with Seventeen Canadian Women Writers*. Toronto: University of Toronto Press, 1993. 321-339.

Welter, Barbara. "The Cult of True Womanhood: 1820-1860." *American Quarterly* 18 (1966): 151-174.

Williamson, Janice, ed. *Sounding Differences: Conversations with Seventeen Canadian Women Writers*. Toronto: University of Toronto Press, 1993.

what I should to is intersperse little case-histories.

---

something enigmatic which one approaches sideways, grasps here + there, by means of researches that have nothing to do with what lit. is _essentially_, but which seeks to neutralise + reduce, or rather descend, with an elusive movement, into a level where only impartial neutrality ~~speaks~~.

Non-literature.

Those are the contradictions. Only the work matters – but the work is what takes us to the point of pure inspiration

The book is the important thing: away from genres, rubrics, prose, poetry, novel, eye-witness account ~~[illegible]~~ refusing to be categorised As if it were the 'essence' of literature.

But the essence of lit is to escape definition as essential which wld stabilise it. Art is always becoming. To be an artist is to be unsure that there is such a thing as art. Every book looks passionately for a non-book. Every book decides for itself what lit is. Every writer answers the question what is LIT